The Importance of Being Rational

The Importance of Being Rational systematically defends a novel reasons-based account of rationality. The book's central thesis is that what it is for one to be rational is to correctly respond to the normative reasons one possesses. Errol Lord defends novel views about what it is to possess reasons and what it is to correctly respond to reasons. He shows that these views not only help to support the book's main thesis, they also help to resolve several important problems that are independent of rationality. The account of possession provides novel contributions to debates about what determines what we ought to do, and the account of correctly responding to reasons provides novel contributions to debates about causal theories of reacting for reasons.

After defending views about possession and correctly responding, Lord shows that the account of rationality can solve two difficult problems about rationality. The first is the New Evil Demon problem. The book argues that the account has the resources to show that internal duplicates necessarily have the same rational status. The second problem concerns the deontic significance of rationality. Recently it has been doubted whether we ought to be rational. The ultimate conclusion of the book is that the requirements of rationality are the requirements that we ultimately ought to comply with. If this is right, then rationality is of fundamental importance to our deliberative lives.

Errol Lord is Associate Professor of Philosophy at the University of Pennsylvania. He works in ethical theory, epistemology, the philosophy of action, and aesthetics. He has published papers in *Mind, Philosophy and Phenomenological Research, Oxford Studies in Metaethics,* and *British Journal of Aesthetics,* among other places. He co-edited *Weighing Reasons* (OUP, 2016) with Barry Maguire.

T0355466

The Importance of Being Rational

Errol Lord

OXFORD
UNIVERSITY PRESS

OXFORD
UNIVERSITY PRESS

Great Clarendon Street, Oxford, OX2 6DP,
United Kingdom

Oxford University Press is a department of the University of Oxford.
It furthers the University's objective of excellence in research, scholarship,
and education by publishing worldwide. Oxford is a registered trade mark of
Oxford University Press in the UK and in certain other countries

Published in the United States of America by Oxford University Press
198 Madison Avenue, New York, NY 10016, United States of America

British Library Cataloguing in Publication Data
Data available

Library of Congress Cataloging in Publication Data
Data available

ISBN 978-0-19-881509-9 (Hbk.)

ISBN 978-0-19-288203-5 (Pbk.)

To Anne

Yet the thing is not altogether desperate; for we have some arguments to guide us . . .

(Newton, 1953, p. 24)

Preface

This book is the culmination of a project that has spanned the last ten years. The project started when I was an undergraduate at Arizona State. I had the privilege of attending Doug Portmore's seminar on reasons and value. It was for that class that I first wrote about the connection between reasons and rationality. During the same semester I attended Doug's class, I also attended Stew Cohen's seminar on Williamson's *Knowledge and its Limits*. Although I did not write about reasons or rationality for Stew, his seminar had a profound effect on my philosophical trajectory. I thank both Doug and Stew for their teaching, their kindness, and their support. I also thank Bach Ho and Shyam Nair for their intellectual companionship during my ASU days.

After ASU, I entered the PhD program at the University of Nebraska-Lincoln. My plan was to work on normative ethics. This changed about a month into my first semester. I gave my first talk as a graduate student at the in-house talk series for graduate students. UN-L has a great tradition of inviting all first year faculty to these talks. I was lucky enough to have Dave Sobel and Jan Dowell at my talk. I gave the paper I had written for Doug the previous spring. I had actually wanted to talk about contractualism, but didn't have anything I was happy enough with. I'm glad I didn't because the discussion of my paper that day was exhilarating enough to cause a serious obsession with the connection between reasons and rationality. I have to thank Dave especially for pushing me just hard enough to very badly want to solve the obvious problems. I was so worked up that I was madly writing notes on the back of scrap paper on my bus ride home. Dave was quite surprised when I pulled out these same pieces of paper that night at a department party. I continued to work on these issues for much of my time at UN-L, eventually writing an MA thesis on the topic. I was helped by many at UN-L. I owe a very large debt to Mark van Roojen, who was my main advisor. Without Mark, I would have never been admitted to Princeton. Without that I am confident that this book would not exist. I also thank Al Casullo, Jan Dowell, Cullen Gatten, John Gibbons, Reina Hayaki, Cliff Hill, Tim Loughlin, Jennifer McKitrick, Joe Mendola, Dave Sobel, Steve Swartzer, and Adam Thompson.

After Nebraska I was fortunate enough to come to Princeton. When I began the PhD program at Princeton I planned to write on the broader topic of whether reasons are the fundamental constituents of the normative. My thinking on that topic continually led me back to the central ideas of this book. This convinced me to write a dissertation defending a reasons based account of rationality. That dissertation is this book's immediate predecessor.

Princeton was an ideal place for me to develop intellectually. I look back on that time in the way that Tim Riggins looks back on high school. It was an ideal philosophical environment for me. I have many to thank. First and foremost, I thank my official advisors, Tom Kelly and Michael Smith, and my unofficial advisor, Gideon Rosen. All three were truly fantastic to work with. They all provided invaluable feedback on countless occasions, both about my work and about life. They were great colleagues and are great friends. I'm honored to know them.

The book has undergone a tremendous amount of revision since its days as a dissertation. Chapters 4 and 6 did not exist in the dissertation and the views defended in them transform the account (I think for the better). It was a slog bringing them into existence. This endeavor was greatly helped by my time as a visiting researcher at the University of Oxford in spring 2015. I visited the New Insights and Directions for Religious Epistemology project. I thank John Hawthorne—the project's director—for the support. I also thank Billy Dunaway, Rachel Dunaway, and Julia Staffel for their time and support when I was in Oxford.

By far the biggest incentive for finishing the book was provided by a graduate seminar at Penn in the spring 2016 semester. I thank the students of that seminar—Ben Baker, Grace Boey, Chetan Cetty, Sam Fulhart, and Max Lewis—for their help and patience. Daniel Whiting read the manuscript and sent comments on all of the chapters as the seminar progressed. This was incredibly generous of him. His comments were very helpful and led to many changes.

Work on the final revisions of the book was greatly helped along by the excellent comments provided by OUP's readers Alex Gregory and Eric Wiland. I thank them for taking the time to engage with the book so thoroughly. Shyam Nair and Kurt Sylvan also provided extremely helpful comments in the final weeks of revisions.

Thanks next to John Broome, Mark Schroeder, and Timothy Williamson. Their work serves as a touchstone for the kind of work I hope to do and for the best versions of all sorts of views about all sorts of things. I end up disagreeing with all of them, but the book is undoubtedly better because these three are the three that are most often in the back of my mind. I thank Mark in particular for also being a mentor and friend even though he had no obligation to do so. In my fourth year out of graduate school I am just now realizing how enormously generous Mark was to support me and my work when I was at Nebraska. I will be forever grateful for this help.

Many audiences have helped to make the book better. I discussed ideas from the book at the 2008 UT Austin Graduate Conference, the 12th Annual Oxford Graduate Conference, the Cologne Summer School in Philosophy, the CRNAP Networkshop at the L'Institut Jean Nicod, the Northern Institute of Philosophy at the University of Aberdeen, Franklin & Marshall College, Vassar College, the University of Edinburgh, the University at Buffalo (SUNY), the University of California-Santa Barbara, the University of Pennsylvania, the Georgetown Conference on Reasons and Reasoning, the Rocky Mountain Ethics Congress, the Wisconsin Metaethics Workshop, the University of Reading, Birkbeck, University of London, the University of Geneva, Dartmouth, the Leipzig Conference on Reasoning, and many times at both the University of Nebraska and Princeton. I thank members of the audiences at all of these places. I especially thank Neil Sinhababu for formally commenting in Austin, John Broome for formally commenting in Oxford, Jens Ziska for formally commenting in Paris, and Andrew Huddleston for formally commenting in Princeton.

In addition to those already mentioned, I thank Ashley Atkins, Ralf Bader, Derek Baker, Sam Baker, Nick Beckstead, Bob Beddor, Selim Berker, John Brunero, Tim Campbell, Dave Chalmers, Richard Yetter Chappell, Ryan Cook, Aaron Cotnoir, Anthony Cross, Simon Cullen, Jordan Delange, Sinan Dogramaci, Billy Dunaway, Julien Dutant, David Enoch, Steve Finlay, Daniel Fogal, Samuel Freeman, Nate Gadd, Ken Gemes, Josh Gillon, Javier Gonzalez de Prado Salas, Dan Greco, Mark Harris, Bennett Helm, Jennifer Hornsby, Jonathan Jenkins Ichikawa, Frank Jackson, Karen Jones, Rishi Joshi, Benjamin Kiesewetter, Boris Kment, Raffi Krut-Landau, Barry Lam, Max Lewis, Alida Liberman, Kathryn Lindeman, Eden Lin, Susanne Mantel, Corey Maley, Jimmy Martin, Brennan McDavid, Aidan McGlynn, Tristram McPherson, Angela Mendelovici, Carla Merino-Rajme, Lisa Miracchi, Andreas Müller, Shyam Nair, Ram Neta, Cory Nichols, Thomas Noah, David Nowakowski, Rachel Parsons, Lewis Powell, Kristin Primus, Joe Rachiele, Mike Ridge, Jacob Ross, Susanna Siegel, Vanessa Schouten, Andrew Sepielli, Nate Sharadin, Derek Shiller, Sam Shpall, Dan Singer, Holly Smith, Justin Snedegar, Ernie Sosa, Jack Spencer, Daniel Star, Noel Swanson, Pekka Väyrynen, Gerard Vong, Ralph Wedgwood, Michael Weisberg, Daniel Wodak, Jack Woods, Alex Worsnip, and Helen Yetter Chappell.

A version of chapter 2 was published as 'The Coherent and the Rational,' *Analytic Philosophy* (2014) 55(2), 151–175. A version of chapter 8 is forthcoming in *Mind* (doi: 10.1093/mind/fzw023). A version of chapter 7 has been commissioned for *The New Evil Demon: New Essays on Knowledge, Justification, and Rationality*, which is under contract with Oxford University Press. I thank Oxford University Press and Wiley for permission to reuse the material.

Thanks to Daniel Star for the cover photograph. The room at the top of the stairs will always have a special place in my heart.

Seven friends deserve extra thanks. All have provided help that goes well beyond what I deserve. They have enriched my life and my work. I hope to know them for the rest of my life. They are Barry Maguire, Shyam Nair, Whitney Schwab, David Plunkett, Kurt Sylvan, Jonathan Way, and, most especially, Andrew Huddleston.

Last but not least, I thank my family. I thank my parents and my parents-in-law. I thank my kids for being a constant source of wonder and fun. And I thank my wonderful wife Anne. It is with all my heart that I dedicate this book to you.

EL

Princeton
July 2017

Contents

Part III. Correctly Responding to Reasons

Part IV. Two Problems Solved

PART I

Initial Motivations

PART 1

Introduction

1

Introduction

Reasons Responsiveness, the Reasons Program, and Knowledge-First

We devote a good portion of our lives striving to figure out what it makes sense to do, believe, intend, desire, and hope for given our often limited information and abilities. In other words, a good portion of our lives consists in striving to be rational. This book seeks to understand what exactly we are striving for. In it, I explicate and defend a general and unified account of rationality. By the end, I hope to show that we are not mistaken for devoting so much of our lives to being rational. Rationality, in my view, is of fundamental *deontic* importance—i.e., in my view, rationality plays a fundamental role in determining how we ought to react to the world.

The thesis of the book is that what it is to be rational is to correctly respond to possessed objective normative reasons. I will call this view of rationality *Reasons Responsiveness*. I will do three things in this introductory chapter. First, I will briefly explicate what I take this claim to involve. Second, I will explain some background motivations for pursuing the project as I do. Third, I will explain the book's plan.

1.1 An Ideological Primer

1.1.1 Rationality, what

Rationality is talked about in many different ways, both in everyday life and by theorists of various stripes. One consequence of this is that there are many different concepts of rationality. These concepts pick out different properties. Before the book really gets going, I must say something about some of the core features of the property I am interested in (and thus something about which concept I am employing).

The property I am interested in is the property that has been at the heart of certain debates in metaethics and epistemology. As we'll see in chapter 2, the debates in metaethics have focused on the relationship between rationality and a certain kind of coherence. The guiding assumption of much of the metaethical literature is that the type of rationality at stake is the type that explains why one is irrational when one is incoherent. While I give an unorthodox explanation of this data, I still hold that the type of rationality I am theorizing about is the type that explains the irrationality of incoherence.

This is not the most fundamental feature of the kind of rationality I am interested in. Instead, the most fundamental feature is its connection to certain sorts of praise and criticism.[1] When one is rational in the relevant way, one is worthy of a certain kind of praise. And when one is irrational in the relevant way, one is open to a particular kind of criticism. When one is incoherent one is open to this sort of criticism. This is why it was natural to focus on incoherence, although as I'll argue in chapter 2, the focus on incoherence has led some to make some overgeneralizations about the nature of rationality.

What kind of praise and criticism is at stake? (Parfit, 2011, p. 33) nicely brings out the point:

When we call some act 'rational', using this word in its ordinary, non-technical sense, we express the kind of praise or approval that we can also express with words like 'sensible', 'reasonable', 'intelligent', and 'smart'. We use the word 'irrational' to express the kind of criticism we express with words like 'senseless', 'stupid', 'idiotic' and 'crazy'. To express weaker criticisms of this kind, we can use the phrase 'less than fully rational.'

(Kiesewetter, 2017, p. 39) makes similar remarks, albeit more tentatively (despite the tentativeness, he clearly endorses this picture):

Ordinary attributions of irrationality are commonly understood as criticism. Moreover, the criticism involved seems to be personal criticism: when agents get called irrational, they do not merely understand this to mean that they fell short of some evaluative standard; they feel personally criticized for their responses.

The sort of credit or blame one is open to when one is rational or irrational is thus a very personal evaluation. To react rationally is to show good sense; to react in a fully irrational way is to be stupid or crazy. One can react in a less than fully rational way without being crazy, but one will always be less than reasonable or sensible when one reacts in ways that fall short of full rationality.

Given the connection between rationality and these sorts of evaluation, most in metaethics and epistemology have thought that rationality is tightly connected to one's *perspective*. This view has manifested itself in metaethics via the thought that rationality is tied to coherence.[2] Some in epistemology have taken this tack. However, the most popular expression of this idea in epistemology has come from those who think that rationality is tied to a proper response to the *evidence*.[3]

---

[1] Cf. Kiesewetter, 2017, ch. 2.

[2] The main proponent of this view is John Broome (much of the work culminated in Broome (2013)). Other proponents are Kolodny (2005), Schroeder (2009b), Brunero (2010), Way (2010a).

[3] The number of prominent proponents of evidentialism is massive. Feldman & Conee (1985) brought the term 'evidentialism' to the fore. Williamson (2000) provides a popular view that is very different from Conee and Feldman's.

The literature in metaethics and the literature in epistemology have thus largely diverged from each other about which parts of one's perspective matter when it comes to rationality. Metaethicists have focused on certain combinations of reactions whereas epistemologists have focused on individual reactions. As we'll see, on this issue I agree with the epistemologists. The proper focus is on reasons for particular reactions.

That said, there is an important similarity between nearly all views about rationality in metaethics and a prominent group of views about rationality in epistemology. The common feature is the assumption that rationality solely depends on *internal* features of the agent.[4,5] According to this internalist tradition, the perspective that is relevant to rationality is the purely internal perspective. In both metaethics and epistemology internalism has been trenchantly attacked in the last twenty-plus years. One general theme of many of these attacks is that rationality is not *important* if it is merely internal. In epistemology this theme is exemplified by those who complain that internalist notions of rationality lead to skeptical worries when they are necessary conditions for *knowledge*.[6] In metaethics this theme is exemplified by those who argue that requirements that demand coherence are not *deontically significant*—i.e., it is not the case that we always ought to comply with such requirements.[7]

A common reaction to these worries is to move to a view of rationality that places little emphasis on the perspective of the agent. As one might expect, by doing this one easily loses any connection to the sort of praise and blame that Parfit refers to. This has led many to think that non-perspectival externalist views are not even candidate views of rationality since they fail to explain essential features of the sort of rationality in question.

The view defended in this book is a kind of perspectival externalism. As we'll see, I think rationality is essentially perspectival. However, the perspective that is relevant is not purely internal. The perspective that is relevant depends on facts that are outside of one's head. To put it colloquially, the reactions that are rational are determined by the information that one has, including information about the world outside of one's head. The resulting view of rationality maintains the connection with praise and blame and, I claim, is of great importance.

---

[4] In epistemology, see BonJour (1980), Feldman & Conee (1985), Fumerton (1995), Pollock & Cruz (1999), Wedgwood (2002, 2017). In metaethics, see Kolodny (2005), Wedgwood (2007, 2017), Schroeder (2009b), Broome (2013).

[5] There are many different notions of 'internal' floating around in the literature. The least partisan notion is spelled out in terms of supervenience. Thus, many often define internalism as the view that justification supervenes on some sort of internal states. I prefer cashing things out in terms of dependence because supervenience could be true even if it were the case that what is rational is determined by external facts. In fact, in chapter 7, I will argue that my view is precisely like this. See Ichikawa (2018) for related discussion.

[6] See, for example, Williamson (2000).   [7] See, for example, Kolodny (2005).

1.1.2 Reasons Responsiveness as a real definition

The next point to make is that I see Reasons Responsiveness as providing a *real definition* of *the property* of being rational.[8] Thus, according to Reasons Responsiveness, the essence of the property of being rational is that the bearer of this property is correctly responding to the objective normative reasons that are possessed.

Real definition, it should be said, is a metaphysical matter. I am thus not providing a theory about the semantics of our talk about rationality, nor am I providing an account of the *concept* of rationality. I am providing a theory about the nature of the thing that our concept *refers* to. While it is plausible that the nature of our concept places some constraints on theories about the metaphysics of the referent of our concept (rationality, e.g., couldn't turn out to be composed out of footballs), when one provides a real definition, one is not providing an analysis of our concept.

Many different things can be rational—people, actions, intentions, beliefs, fears, joys, preferences, credences. Reasons Responsiveness provides a real definition of the property that all of those things have when they are rational. Thus, Reasons Responsiveness predicts that people, actions, intentions, beliefs, fears, joys, preferences, and credences (among other things) are rational when they correctly respond to possessed objective normative reasons.

It's not immediately clear whether the rationality of agents is more fundamental than the rationality of reactions or *vice versa*. According to the Agent First view, particular reactions of an agent—actions, intentions, beliefs, desires, etc.—are rational in virtue of the fact that the agent rationally reacts in those ways. According to the Reaction First view, agents are rational in virtue of the fact that their reactions are rational. I'm inclined to accept the Reaction First view. Agents correctly respond to reasons when their reactions are correct responses to the reasons they possess for those reactions. Thus, what is fundamental are the reactions and the possessed reasons for them. The rationality of people falls out of the rationality of their reactions.[9] Although I am inclined towards this view, I will not defend it here. Either view sits well with Reasons Responsiveness.

I should contrast Reasons Responsiveness with other views that hold that there are reasons to be rational. According to a type of view that has received an enormous amount of attention from John Broome and Niko Kolodny, there are reasons to be rational.[10] However, on this view, what is rational is not determined by reasons. Instead, rationality is determined by facts about coherence.[11]

---

[8] For substantive views of real definition, see Wedgwood (2007), Rosen (2015).

[9] This is not to deny that there is a *capacity* that can be aptly called rationality. People might have that capacity independently of the rationality of their particular reactions. But having the capacity is not sufficient for having the property of being rational, as I understand it. In order to have that property, one's reactions must be rational.

[10] This view is discussed most prominently in Kolodny (2005, 2007a,b) and Broome (2005a,b, 2007c, 2008a).

[11] Chapters 2 and 8 will discuss these views extensively.

According to the type of view discussed by Kolodny and Broome, we can discover what the requirements of rationality are independently from whether there are reasons to be rational. Once we do this, we can then ask if there are any reasons to comply with the coherence requirements. Broome focuses most of his energy thinking about whether the fact that rationality requires ϕ-ing is itself a reason to ϕ. Kolodny (and Broome to some extent) explores different possibilities. However, both discussions assume that the requirements of rationality are a function of something other than reasons.

Reasons Responsiveness is significantly different from the view that Broome and Kolodny discuss. I have no interest in defending the view they discuss. I am not, that is, interested in whether we have reasons to comply with coherence requirements.[12] I am instead interested in whether the requirements of rationality are themselves determined by reasons. This is what Reasons Responsiveness predicts. We will return to the relationships between Reasons Responsiveness and coherence requirements in chapters 2 and 8.

1.1.3 Objective normative reasons, what

Now let me briefly introduce the basic ideology of Reasons Responsiveness. I'll start with *objective normative reasons*. Objective normative reasons are facts that count in favor of various reactions.[13] Usually they are facts about the world (as opposed to facts about one's mental states). Some examples: The fact that I promised to give this chapter to someone tomorrow is a reason for me to write this introduction as soon as possible. The fact that it is going to rain in the city I'm traveling to next week is a reason for me to intend to bring an umbrella. The fact that you yawned is a reason to believe you didn't get enough sleep last night. The fact that you would be better off if you got a job is a reason for you to desire to get a job.

One project I do *not* take up in this book is the project of figuring out *what it takes* for some fact to be an objective normative reason.[14] I am taking it for granted that there are objective normative reasons. That said, I do think there are some earmarks of normative reasons that we can use as heuristics for determining whether some fact is a normative reason. Not all of these earmarks are completely theory-neutral, but I think that nearly all going theories of normative reasons embrace some of them.

---

[12] It is important to note that this is not equivalent to the claim that we always have reasons to be in a coherent state. In chapter 2, I will argue that whenever we are incoherent, we are doing something we possess decisive reasons not to do. But this isn't to immediately say that we have reasons to comply with the coherence requirements. This is just to say that we have reasons to do something that guarantees that we are coherent. In order to have reasons to comply with coherence requirements, we need to have reasons to be coherent that are over and above our reasons to have particular attitudes. This is spelled out more fully in chapter 8, §8.2.2.

[13] There are many ways in which this gloss is unsatisfactory. One is the famous wrong kind of reasons problem (see D'Arms & Jacobson (2000), Rabinowicz & Rønnow-Rasmussen (2004), Schroeder (2010), Lord & Sylvan (MS)). Another that arises in the epistemic case is exactly which probabilifying relation must hold—e.g., whether it must be objective or if it can be subjective. See Sylvan (2016) for more on this.

[14] For my initial forays into this inquiry, see Lord & Sylvan (MS) and Lord (MSb).

One earmark is that objective normative reasons are the types of things that explain whether an attitude or action has strict normative statuses like justification, rightness, or correctness.[15] If some fact f can explain why some action ϕ is justified, right, or correct, then (it is very likely that) f is a normative reason to ϕ.

Another earmark is being able to justifiably ϕ *for f*. When one ϕs for f, f is the consideration that moves one to ϕ. If one can justifiably ϕ with f as one's reason for ϕ-ing, then it is very likely that f is a normative reason to ϕ.[16]

A third earmark is the possibility that the relevance of f is mitigated by some other facts. Objective normative reasons can be *defeated* by other considerations. The reason to write this introduction isn't as weighty when I have multiple chapters that also need to be written than when it is the last thing I have to write. The fact that I have multiple chapters to write weakens the reason to write this introduction. Thus, if it seems like the relevance of f to ϕ-ing can be attenuated (or intensified) by adding or subtracting facts, it is very likely that f is a normative reason.

At various points in the book, I will use these earmarks to help determine whether some fact is a normative reason. In some cases, I will use the earmarks to argue that facts that many take to not be objective normative reasons really are objective normative reasons. I thus think there are more normative reasons than many moral philosophers. It will be important for the plausibility of my view about rationality that there are more reasons than is traditionally thought. So the views in the book do depend on taking some stands on issues having to do with what it takes to be a normative reason. All of my arguments for my extensional claims will rely on the earmarks. Since (at least some subset of) the earmarks seem to me to be absolutely central to the notion of a normative reason, I am moved by my arguments. It's important for me to confess at the outset though that I will not be directly engaging with systematic theories of what it takes for some fact to be an objective normative reason. There are only so many battles I can fight.

1.1.4 Possessed normative reasons, what

There are a lot of normative reasons out there. Many of them I don't know anything about. The ones I don't know anything about are reasons for me to act, believe, intend, and desire, but they aren't reasons to act, believe, intend, and desire that I *possess*.[17]

---

[15] Not everyone thinks that all of these statuses are explained by reasons—e.g., McHugh & Way (FC) and Maguire (FC). Nevertheless, even these authors think that *some* strict statuses are explained by normative reasons (for Way and McHugh, I take it, deontic strict statuses fit the bill; for Maguire it will be strict statuses for actions).

[16] There is a large debate about whether being able to ϕ for f is *necessary* for f to be a reason to ϕ (see, e.g., Setiya (2007b), Manne (2014), Markovits (2014)). I needn't take a stand about this issue in order to use this as an earmark, for everyone thinks that we can react for most reasons even if there are some exceptions.

[17] Kiesewetter (2017, 2018) argues that there is no distinction here by arguing that the only reasons there are reasons that are within one's perspective (this view is also held by Gibbons (2010, 2013) and is flirted with by Dancy (2000). Most of what Dancy says is weaker than Kiesewetter's view and is, I think, more naturally accounted for by the view I defend in chapter 8 and in Lord (2015)). All of the facts that recommend that are outside of one's perspective are merely *potential* reasons on his account. His main motivation for adopting this view is to defend a view like Reasons Responsiveness, especially in light of the counterexamples discussed in chapter 2. I see little reason to go in for Kiesewetter's

In order to possess a reason, I need to stand in some special epistemic relation to the fact that constitutes that reason. For example, I possess the reason to intend to take my umbrella next week because the weather report informed me that it is going to rain in the city I am traveling to. Similarly, I possess the reason to believe you didn't get enough sleep because I saw you yawn.

As we will see in chapters 2 and 4, standing in the privileged epistemic relation to some fact that is a reason is not sufficient for possession. One can stand in the epistemic relation but fail to possess the fact as the reason it is if one doesn't 'see' the normative relevance of the fact. Chapter 4 will provide a view of what it takes to 'see' the relevance.

I think that the only reasons relevant to rationality are the possessed reasons. This is because it is implausible that reasons completely outside of your ken can affect what it is rational for you to do. If I have no clue that you just yawned, the fact that you yawned doesn't have any effect on which stance it is rational for me to take on the question of how much sleep you got last night. On the other hand, if the fact that you yawned is within my ken, it does seem to bear on which stance I should take on that question.

In chapters 3 and 4, I will defend a novel view of possession.

1.1.5 Correctly responding to possessed normative reasons, what

Suppose the fact that you yawned is a strong enough reason to make it rational to believe you didn't get enough sleep last night. And suppose further that I both possess that reason and believe that you didn't get enough sleep last night. Is this sufficient for my token belief to be rational? In a word: No.

The reason why this is not sufficient for my belief to be rational is that it is possible for all of that to be true even though I don't *correctly respond* to the reason provided by the fact that you yawned. In the simplest kind of case, this is because there is no connection at all between my belief and that reason. Suppose I believe that you didn't get enough sleep because it's Tuesday and I believe (without good reason) that you never get enough sleep on Monday nights.

This case highlights the common distinction between *ex post* and *ex ante* rationality.[18,19] When a reaction is *ex ante* rational for an agent *A*, *A* is in a position to react rationally. The fact that you yawned, when it is possessed as a reason to believe you didn't get enough sleep last night, makes it the case that it is *ex ante* rational for me to believe you didn't get enough sleep last night (absent defeaters). However, it being

more extreme view, especially given the many theoretical roles unpossessed reasons can play—e.g., in giving accounts of *correctness* (cf. Schroeder (2015c), Lord (2018a)), *advice* (cf. Lord (2015)), and value (cf. Ewing (1959), Scanlon (1998)), among many other things. Further, as I will show in chapter 2 (cf. Lord (2014a)), one doesn't need to adopt Kiesewetter's extreme view in order to defend an account like Reasons Responsiveness.

[18] Epistemologists usually mark this distinction by appealing to propositional and doxastic rationality. I do not use those terms because they do not fit well with all reactions that can be rational—e.g., it makes little sense to speak of an action being doxastically rational. The original idea was introduced by Goldman (1979) using the *ex ante* / *ex post* language. See Wedgwood (2013) for further discussion about the terminology.

[19] As a follow-up to note 18, it should be pointed out that not everyone thinks that the propositional/doxastic distinction lines up perfectly with the *ex ante* / *ex post* distinction. For one detractor, see Ichikawa & Jarvis (2013).

ex ante rational to believe you didn't get enough sleep last night does not guarantee that I have a token belief that is rational. For one, I might not believe you didn't get enough sleep (hence the name *ex ante*). Further, I might have a belief that is not formed in the right way to count as rational. When this happens, I am *ex ante* rational but not *ex post* rational. On my view, in order for a token reaction to be *ex post* rational, one has to respond *for* the reasons that make the reaction *ex ante* rational. This is what I think it is to correctly respond to the reasons you possess.

Thus, on my view, a token ϕ-ing is *ex post* rational when (i) one possesses normative reasons to ϕ that are sufficiently weighty, and (ii) one ϕ-s for those reasons.

In chapter 5, I will defend a view of what it takes to ϕ for normative reasons. In chapter 6, I will defend a view about what it takes to react for motivating reasons. As we will see, I think these are different in kind. I thus end up defending a disjunctivist view about reacting for reasons.

1.1.6 The requirements of rationality

Reasons Responsiveness provides a real definition of the property of rationality. It does not provide a real definition of *rational requirement* or *rational permission*. It does direct us towards views about requirements and permissions, though. Rational requirements and permissions will be connected to correct responses to the possessed reasons. Rational Permission and Rational Requirement are plausible claims (although not real definitions) about permissions and requirements in terms of correct responses:[20]

> **Permission-Correctness Link:** A reaction R of an agent A is rationally permitted just in case R is a correct response to A's possessed reasons for and against R.

> **Requirement-Uniquely Correct Link:** A reaction R of an agent A is rationally required just in case R is the only correct response to A's possessed reasons for and against R.

While I think that Permission-Correctness Link and Requirement-Uniquely Correct Link are true, I also think we can say more. This is because we can say more about when a reaction is a correct response and more about when a reaction is the only correct response. We can do this by appealing to *possessed sufficient reasons* and *possessed decisive reasons*.[21]

When a set of reasons S for a reaction R is sufficient, S is just as weighty as the weight of the sets of reasons to react in ways other than R. When S is decisive, S is weightier than the weight of the sets of reasons to react in ways other than R. I think we can give a real definition of rational permission in terms of sufficiency and a real definition

---

[20] As we saw in the last subsection, one can have the correct response even though one does not correctly respond. This is important to remember when interpreting Permission-Correctness Link and Requirement-Uniquely Correct Link.

[21] For more on these notions, see Schroeder (2015d), Lord & Maguire (2016), and especially Lord (2018a).

of rational requirement in terms of decisiveness. This gives us Rational Permission and Rational Requirement:

Rational Permission: What it is for a reaction R of agent A to be rationally permitted is for the reasons A possesses for R to be sufficient.

Rational Requirement: What it is for a reaction R of agent A to be rationally required is for the reasons A possesses for R to be decisive.

A prediction of Rational Permission is that you are only rationally permitted to do things that you possess reasons for that are just as weighty as the reasons you possess to do anything else. A prediction of Rational Requirement is that you are only rationally required to do things that you possess reasons for that are weightier than the reasons you possess to do anything else. I think these are plausible predictions. If you possess reasons to ϕ that are weightier than the reasons you possess to ψ, ψ-ing is not rational. If the set of reasons you possess to ϕ are weightier than the reasons you possess for any other reaction, then you are not rational if you do not ϕ.

We can extract from Rational Requirement the following requirement schemata:

Action Schema: If the set of reasons S that A possesses to ϕ is decisive, then A is rationally required to ϕ.

Belief Schema: If the set of reasons S that A possesses to believe p is decisive, then A is rationally required to believe p.

Intention Schema: If the set of reasons S that A possesses to intend to ϕ is decisive, then A is rationally required to intend to ϕ.

As it is with normative reasons, I will not be defending analyses of sufficiency and decisiveness. I have defended the views I just explained elsewhere (as have others).[22] I will assume that reasons can weigh up in such a way that the reactions they favor are permitted or required. As far as background assumptions in philosophy go, this seems like a dialectically solid one. I am happy for the main conclusions of the book to be conditional on there being sufficient and decisive objective normative reasons.[23]

Further, I do not think that the most interesting action lies in whether there are sufficient or decisive objective normative reasons. The most interesting action lies in whether we can connect these things to one's perspective in the way that rationality is connected to one's perspective. For this reason, I will be centrally concerned in the book about what it takes to possess reasons and correctly respond to reasons.

---

[22] See Lord (2018a), Schroeder (2015c,d). For a similar view, see Horty (2012). For more general discussion, see Lord & Maguire (2016).

[23] As we will see later, sufficiency and decisiveness are relative in important ways. As I will argue in chapter 7, the relevant weighings for rationality are the weighings of possessed reasons against each other. The results of these weighings will often diverge from the results of the weighings of all of the reasons against each other. So, to be more precise, I think the main results are conditional on there being sufficient and decisive possessed objective normative reasons.

It is here that I will connect objective normative reasons to particular people in particular situations.

With this primer on the ideology in hand, let me turn to some background motivations for the project.

1.2 The Reasons Program and Knowledge-First

1.2.1 The Reasons Program

One of the big ideas in metanormative theory in the last twenty-five years is the idea that normative reasons are fundamental in some sense. While there are various ways to understand this thought, the version that excites me the most holds that reasons are *metaphysically fundamental*. Once again, there are many ways of understanding what this amounts to. As I think of it, reasons are metaphysically fundamental because they are the fundamental *normative* entities. To use a physical analogy, they are the building blocks of normativity. *How* (if at all) they build up normativity is an interesting and undertheorized question. Sticking with my preferred ideology, I am interested in defending the claim that reasons are normatively fundamental because we can provide real definitions of all of the complex normative properties in terms of normative reasons. I will call this view *Reasons Fundamentalism*. Reasons Fundamentalism is the main tenet of what I call The Reasons Program.

For the sake of clarity, it must be said that Reasons Fundamentalism *does not* entail that reasons are *primitive*. That is, it does not entail that reasons are fundamental *tout court*. It just says that reasons are normatively fundamental. It might be that we can provide a real definition of reasons in terms of something that is not normative.[24]

Reasons Fundamentalism is an extremely ambitious claim. It commits one to many different controversial claims all across normative philosophy. It commits you, for example, to defending reasons based accounts of evaluative properties like goodness, badness, betterness, worseness, good for, bad for, deontic properties like rightness, wrongness, ought, required, permitted, rational, correct and hypological properties like blameworthiness, praiseworthiness, virtue, and vice.[25] It also commits you to ruling out any other normatively fundamental entities. Defending Reasons Fundamentalism is thus a monumental task. Hence its philosophical interest.

One method—a method that is admittedly slow—of defending Reasons Fundamentalism is by defending real definitions of particular normative phenomena in terms of normative reasons. As you may have guessed, I see this book contributing

---

[24] For versions of this project, see Schroeder (2007), Lord & Sylvan (MS).

[25] I've carried out some of this work elsewhere. For a partial defense of a reasons based account of evaluative properties, see Lord & Sylvan (MS). For a reasons based account of moral rightness/wrongness, see Lord (2016a). For a reasons based account of ought, see Lord (2015, 2017b) (see also chapter 8). For a reasons based account of correctness, see Lord (2018a). For a reasons based account of praiseworthiness, see Lord (2017a).

to a pursuit of this method. One motivation for the book, then, is to show that we can do some impressive theoretical work by analyzing rationality in terms of reasons.

Given that rationality seems like a normative property, reasons fundamentalists need to be interested in it. This is motivation enough for someone like me to have an interest in the correct theory of rationality. In fact, though, there are much more interesting reasons for fundamentalists to be interested in rationality. This is because much of the literature in the last twenty years about rationality has been about how rationality comes apart from normative reasons.[26] Most of the most prominent theorists about rationality in the last twenty years have thought that there was a gap between what rationality requires and what the reasons require.

If this is right, then the fundamentalist is faced with an uncomfortable dilemma. The dilemma hinges on whether she holds that rationality is normative. If she thinks that it is, then Reasons Fundamentalism is false. Rationality is normative but cannot be understood in terms of normative reasons. This is the dilemma's first horn. One obvious way out of this is to deny that rationality is normative. But that is a very surprising claim. Indeed, many will think that it is a Moorean truth that rationality is normative. At the very least, few neutral observers will be willing to give up the claim that rationality is normative just to hold onto Reasons Fundamentalism. This is the second horn of the dilemma.[27]

The debate about rationality, then, is a debate that is particularly hostile for the fundamentalist. Given this, I think it is a good place to locally test the plausibility of fundamentalism. That is what I will do here. As we'll see, I think that theorizing about rationality in terms of reasons is a fruitful enterprise. This will in turn provide some support for Reasons Fundamentalism. For the most part, I will not engage with arguments against fundamentalism per se. Instead, I will focus on arguments that threaten my views about rationality. Many of these are also arguments against fundamentalism insofar as they threaten a reasons first account rationality.

---

[26] There are two main camps that think that reasons and rationality come apart. The first camp thinks this because they think that rationality merely requires coherence. Since you can be coherent and not do what the reasons require, people in this camp conclude that what rationality requires comes apart from what the reasons require. This camp is led by John Broome (see especially Broome (1999)). I defend my view against this camp in chapters 2 and 8 (as we'll see, things have gotten more complicated since 1999). The second camp thinks objective reasons and rationality come apart because they think that what rationality requires is determined by *apparent or subjective* reasons, which are determined by one's beliefs. Since one can have false beliefs, what apparent reasons require and what the objective reasons require can come apart. Thus, theorists in this camp infer that rationality and reasons come apart. The founder of this camp is Parfit (1997). I defend my view against this camp in chapters 3, 4, and 7.

[27] Although rarely discussed explicitly, this seems to be the horn that most fundamentalists embrace. This is explicit with Parfit (see Parfit (2011)). Scanlon also seems to take this tack (see Scanlon (2007)). Although not a card carrying fundamentalist, Niko Kolodny also takes this tack in Kolodny (2005, 2007a).

1.2.2 Knowledge-first

While metaethicists have been interested in the Reasons Program, epistemologists have become interested in their own debate about fundamentality.[28] This debate is about the relative fundamentality of *knowledge*. This epistemological debate has been about whether we should understand knowledge in terms of notions like rationality or justification or whether we should instead understand notions like justification and rationality in terms of knowledge.[29] Those who take the latter route have come to be known as proponents of knowledge-first epistemology. Just like it is with Reasons Fundamentalism, there are many ways of understanding this program. I will again have a metaphysical understanding. More specifically, I will understand the knowledge-first program as claiming that we can provide real definitions of properties like justification and rationality in terms of knowledge.[30]

This book will also defend a knowledge-first view of rationality. This is because, as we'll see in chapter 3, I will argue that the best way to understand the epistemic condition on possessing a normative reason is in terms of knowledge. Specifically, I will argue that in order to possess a reason, one must be in a position to know the fact that constitutes that reason. Since I analyze rationality in terms of possession, and possession (partly) in terms of knowledge, I end up analyzing rationality partly in terms of knowledge. This is enough to make me a proponent of knowledge-first epistemology. I see the fruits of this book as strong reasons in favor of such an approach.

It is also worth noting that not only do I think that knowledge-*that* is more fundamental than rationality, I also think that knowledge-*how* is more fundamental than rationality. This is because I analyze both possession and correctly responding to reasons in terms of knowledge-how. Indeed, the real definition of possession that I will defend in chapter 4 defines possession directly in terms of knowledge-how. According to that view, what it is to possess a reason r to ϕ is to be in a position to manifest knowledge about how to use r to ϕ.[31] In chapter 5, I will argue further that what it is to correctly respond to a reason r to ϕ is to *manifest* one's knowledge

---

[28] This was sparked mostly by Williamson (2000)'s claims that evidence is knowledge and that we should analyze justification in terms of evidence.

[29] As far as I know, no one has suggested that knowledge is epistemically fundamental in the way that reasons fundamentalists suggest that reasons are fundamental. Rather, the debate in epistemology has been about the relative fundamentality of knowledge and rationality/justification. Thus, I am not embracing the claim that knowledge is fundamental *tout court*. It might be that it is analyzable. That project obviously has a bearing on the Reasons Program. If knowledge is normative, then the Reasons Program demands that it be analyzed in terms of reasons (see Schroeder (2015b,c), Lord (2018a)). This will be difficult if my knowledge-first version of Reasons Responsiveness is true since one of the most popular analysans of knowledge is rationality/justification. This still does not rule out analyzability since knowledge might be non-normative (see Sylvan (FC)). I am undecided on these issues.

[30] Cf. Ichikawa & Jenkins (2017).

[31] You might wonder where knowledge-that went. I argue that knowing the fact that constitutes r is a necessary condition of being in a position to manifest the relevant know-how.

about how to use r to ϕ. Thus, not only does the book defend a knowledge-first view that has had much of the spotlight recently, it also defends a relatively neglected knowledge-first view.

As it is with fundamentalism, I will largely not directly engage with arguments against the knowledge-first program per se. Instead, I will focus on arguments against my particular views about rationality. Many of these arguments—especially those in chapters 3 and 7—are arguments against the knowledge-first program. I think my views win the day. While there might be more general reasons against the knowledge-first program, I will argue that a particular implementation of the program does well on the ground, as it were.

1.3 The Plan

Here is the plan. The book is broken up into four parts. The first part provides initial motivations for Reasons Responsiveness. Part I is made up of this chapter and the next. Chapter 2 will situate and defend Reasons Responsiveness in the debate about rationality in metaethics. As I said above, this debate has been dominated by the thought that rationality is constitutively tied to coherence. It has become popular to believe that rationality merely requires coherence. This is pretheoretically unintuitive, for it seems very plausible that some actions and attitudes are sometimes rationally required. Reasons Responsiveness predicts this. The chapter will have two goals. The first is to show that Reasons Responsiveness can withstand the scrutiny of some prominent arguments by John Broome for the conclusion that rationality does not consist in correctly responding to reasons. The second goal is to show that Reasons Responsiveness can explain the most important data motivating the coherentist view, which is that, at least usually, one is irrational when one is incoherent. Reasons Responsiveness can thus explain the data motivating its metaethical rivals while avoiding some unintuitive predictions.

Part II is about possessing reasons. It is made up of chapters 3 and 4. Chapter 3 is about the issue that has occupied nearly all of the literature's attention. This is the question of which epistemic relation is needed for possession. I will lay out three roles that possession is supposed to play. I will then argue by elimination that the best theory holds that in order to possess r, one must be in a position to know r. Chapter 4 is about an issue that has almost been completely neglected by the literature. Nearly all have thought that meeting the epistemic condition on possession was both necessary *and* sufficient for possession. I argue first that this is false (we will also see why this is false in chapter 2). The epistemic condition is merely necessary. One also has to meet what I call the practical condition. In order to meet the practical condition, one must be sensitive to the way in which the fact is a reason. I will argue that the practical condition is being in a position to manifest knowledge about how to use the fact as a reason. I will argue, finally, that rather than thinking possession is a conjunctive relation, we should think that being in a position to know r is a background condition on being in a position to manifest knowledge about how to use r. This gives us the view that what it is for an agent A to possess a reason r to ϕ is for A to be in a position to manifest knowledge about how to use r to ϕ.

Part III is about responding to reasons. It is made up of chapters 5 and 6. In chapter 5, I defend my view of correctly responding to normative reasons. This view is tightly connected to my view of possession. I argue that what it is to correctly respond to normative reasons is to manifest one's knowledge about how to use r as a normative reason. As I understand it, this is a causal account of reacting for normative reasons. Causal accounts have infamous issues with *deviant causal chains*. The main argument I give for my view is that my view can solve these problems with deviant causal chains. This is because, when one manifests one's know-how, dispositions that are directly sensitive to normative facts are manifesting. Thus, the competences involved in the relevant know-how make one directly sensitive to the normative facts. This is what is needed to avoid deviant causal chains.

An interesting consequence of this view about reacting for normative reasons is that it seems to leave out a closely related phenomenon, which is reacting for *motivating reasons*. It's clear that sometimes we react for reasons that aren't normative reasons, either because we are misinformed or because we have the wrong normative views. My view of reacting for normative reasons cannot be extended to explain these cases. This doesn't sit well with most work on the relationship between these cases, which holds that we must understand them both in terms of the same relation. This dialectic is the context for chapter 6, where I argue that we should be *disjunctivists* about reacting for reasons in the sense that we should think that there are two different reacting for reasons relations. There is the reacting for normative reasons relation and the reacting for motivating reasons relation. In chapter 6, I sketch a new view of reacting for motivating reasons and show how it is connected to my account of acting for normative reasons.

With the main ideology of my view in hand, Part IV is about two important problems in the debate about rationality. It is made up of chapters 7 and 8. Chapter 7 is about the New Evil Demon problem for externalist views of rationality. Externalist views hold that the rational status of our attitudes and actions doesn't supervene on our non-factive internal states—i.e., on the states that we can be in even if the content is false. Externalist theories are plagued by the New Evil Demon problem. In order to see the problem, reflect on the following two characters. Sam inhabits the actual world. She thus sees lots of sights, hears lots of sounds, and learns lots of things via inference. Now consider Pam. She is Sam's non-factive internal state duplicate—i.e., Sam and Pam have all the same non-factive internal states. The catch is that Pam is radically deceived by an evil demon. None of her beliefs about the external world are true. Many have the strong intuition that Sam is rational just in case Pam is. It is hard to see how the externalist can capture this thought since the externalist thinks that Sam and Pam have much different rationalizers (since they are in much different positions with respect to the external factors relevant to rationality).

I am an externalist. This is because I think that the reasons you possess are facts that you are in a position to know. Thus, on my view, Sam has many more reasons than Pam since she's in a position to know many more facts about the external world. So I have the New Evil Demon problem. I argue that my view can solve the problem. That is, I argue that on my view Sam is rational just in case Pam is. This is so despite the fact that they don't possess the same reasons.

I also argue that there is another problem, the New New Evil Demon problem, that is even worse than the New Evil Demon problem. The New New Evil Demon problem is anchored in the thought that even if Pam always possesses sufficiently strong reasons, it is implausible that she always correctly responds to those reasons. Thus, it is implausible that her token attitudes and actions are rational. I argue that my view about reacting for a normative reason gives us the resources to solve this problem. Thus, I think that my view can solve both Evil Demon problems.

The final chapter is about the deontic importance of rationality. Despite a long history of thinking that rationality has a tight connection with what we ought to do, it has recently become popular to think that it is not the case that we ought to be rational. The final chapter takes up this challenge. I argue that my view can vindicate the claim that we ought to be rational. Indeed, I argue that what we ought to do *just is* what we are rationally required to do. Thus, rationality has ultimate deontic significance.

I argue for this by arguing that what we ought to do is a function of the normative reasons we possess. The anchor of the argument is that in order for some reason to obligate, it has to be potentially action guiding in a certain sense—it has to potentially be the reason for which one acts. The rub is that a reason can be potentially action guiding in this sense only if we possess the reason. At the end of the day, I argue, both our full stop obligations and the requirements of rationality are a function of the reasons we possess. That is, our full stop obligations just are what rationality requires of us.

I thus end up thinking that rationality is centrally important to the task of figuring out how to live. The importance of being rational is that by being rational we are living up to the standards we are obliged to live up to.

2

The Coherent and the Rational

2.1 Introduction

Sometimes you are rational only when you have particular beliefs, intentions, desires, or perform particular actions. To give some examples, given that the evidence overwhelmingly supports believing that the earth is older than 300 years (and I'm considering whether it is), it would be irrational for me to not believe that the earth is older than 300 years. Similarly, given my (rational) intention to provide for my children's basic needs and my (required) belief that in order for me to provide for them I must make money, it seems like I would not be rational if I didn't intend to make money. Finally, given that I (rationally) desire to eat my supper by 6 and I know that in order to do that I have to go home in 7 minutes, it seems like I would not be rational if I didn't go home in 7 minutes. It's clear: Sometimes rationality requires me to have particular attitudes and perform particular actions.[1]

Or maybe not. As it happens, the most popular view of rationality in the literature on practical reason denies that rationality ever requires one to have particular attitudes or perform particular actions.[2,3] At least pretheoretically, this is extremely

---

[1] Let me say up front that I am *not* stipulating that I would be *coherent* if I were to fail to believe the earth is 300 years old, if I failed to intend to make money, or if I failed to get home in 7 minutes. Worsnip (2016, 2015b,a) interpreted my presentation of these cases in Lord (2014a) as stipulating that I would be coherent yet irrational if I failed to do any of those things. I wasn't intending that interpretation of these cases then and I am not now. It might be that Worsnip is right that I would be incoherent if I failed to do any of the things I just claimed I'm required to do. All I want to do right now is pump intuitions about there being requirements to react in particular ways. I will return to some of Worsnip's criticisms of my views below.

[2] Indeed, on the view of the most famous defender of these views, John Broome, actions cannot be rational or irrational at all. He holds that only attitudes can be rational and irrational. See, for example, Broome (2013, ch. 1).

[3] Worsnip (2015a) develops a contextualist semantics for 'rationality requires' that delivers the result that rationality does sometimes require particular attitudes even though Broomian wide-scope requirements are the fundamental requirements of rationality. On his view, for example, the following sentence will come out true in most contexts: 'If you believe that you ought to ϕ, then you are rationally required to intend to ϕ.' This will come out true on Worsnip's view because the antecedent of the conditional *restricts* the worlds that we evaluate a la Kratzer (2012) such that the only worlds relevant are worlds where you believe you ought to ϕ. Worsnip further holds that the standards for evaluation we use are given by the wide-scope requirements. Given this set up, intending to ϕ will be rationally required given that you believe that you ought to ϕ just in case in all the worlds where you comply with the wide-scope requirements, you intend to ϕ. This result will follow just so long as rationality requires that [you intend to ϕ if you believe you ought to ϕ]. Hence that conditional comes out true. This is clever, but it is not fully satisfactory. This is because this sentence also comes out true: 'If you are not going to intend to ϕ, then rationality requires you to not to believe you ought to ϕ.' In many cases this is a bad result. Suppose all of the evidence suggests that you

surprising. Despite this, there are few explicit defenses of the view that rationality sometimes requires particular attitudes and the performance of particular actions.[4] This chapter will offer a defense of such a view in the context of the literature on practical reason.

I will start by explicating some of the main contours of the debate over rationality in the literature on practical reason. We'll begin this explication by getting clear on just what people are trying to explain when they're offering theories of rationality.[5] I will then give an initial explication of Reasons Responsiveness. The first main aim of the chapter will be to rebut a prominent challenge to Reasons Responsiveness. This challenge is, I conjecture, the main reason why the view receives little support in the literature on practical reason. I think this is unwarranted given the relative ease of meeting the challenge. The second main aim will be to explain how my view captures the motivations of coherentists. Meeting both aims will provide strong initial motivation for Reasons Responsiveness.

2.2 The Debate as it Currently Stands

The starting point for the current debate in the literature on practical reason is the claim that you are irrational if you are incoherent in certain ways. The paradigm is means-end incoherence. You are means-end incoherent when you intend to ϕ, believe that in order to ϕ you must intend to ψ, but fail to intend to ψ. Other examples include akrasia—believing that you ought to ϕ but failing to intend to ϕ—and having inconsistent intentions. For the most part, the whole debate about rationality is about what best explains why you are irrational when you are incoherent in these ways.

Given this motivation, the debate has focused on *conditional requirements*. This is because the incoherence data is about which *combinations of attitudes* are irrational. For example, not having the intention to ψ when one intends to ϕ and believes that in order to ϕ one must intend to ψ seems to be a paradigmatically irrational combination. Conditional requirements are tailor made to explain why it's bad for certain combinations of facts to obtain. This is because they require things only given some other facts. Given these thoughts, we might be tempted to endorse something like Means-End N:

Means-End N: If you intend to ϕ and believe that in order to ϕ you must intend to ψ, then you are rationally required to intend to ψ.

ought to ϕ. Given this, it's plausible that rationality requires that you believe you ought to ϕ. It doesn't seem like you can get out of this obligation simply by not intending to ϕ!

[4] This is true for different reasons in the metaethics literature than it is in the epistemology literature. It's true in the metaethics literature because most think that the view is false. It's true in the epistemology literature because most people think it's obviously true—at least since the death of a particularly naïve form of coherentism.

[5] As I say above, the context will be the literature on practical reason. That said, a good bit of the chapter is about epistemology. This is in line with the literature on practical reason since the default view is that the practical and epistemic will be treated in similar ways (see, e.g., Kolodny (2007b), Schroeder (2008), Broome (2013)).

Means-End N explains why you are irrational when you are means-end incoherent. For every time you are means-end incoherent, you will lack an intention that rationality requires you to have—viz., the intention to ψ. This is because 'rationally required' only scopes over the consequent of the conditional. For this reason Means-End N is a *narrow-scope* requirement (hence the 'N' in the name). Notice also that, according to those who endorse Means-End N, rationality sometimes requires you to have particular intentions. So far, so good.

Despite its ability to account for the incoherence data, most ethicists think that Means-End N is obviously false. This is because, they have thought, it gives rise to objectionable bootstrapping.[6] The basic thought behind the worry is that it's implausible to think that you are required to intend to ψ, *for any* ψ, simply in virtue of having some other intentions and beliefs. For example, it's implausible that you are required to intend to become the King of France simply in virtue of the fact that you intend to be a European monarch and you believe that in order to become a European monarch you have to be the King of France. After all, it seems like it would be more rational for you to resolve the incoherence by giving up your intention to become a European monarch than to form the intention to become the King of France. Giving up your end certainly seems *permitted* by rationality. Means-End N seems to rule this out.

This problem is even worse if you think rationality is deontically significant in some sense—i.e., bears on what you ought to do.[7] There is a spectrum of ways that rationality could be deontically significant. On one extreme, necessarily you ought to do what rationality requires of you. Means-End N seems hopeless if you think rationality is deontically significant in this sense. It is uncontroversial that it is not the case that you ought to intend to be the King of France simply because you intend to be a European monarch and believe that you must be the King of France in order to be a European monarch. On the other end of the spectrum of deontic significance lies the view that there is always a reason for you to do what rationality requires. It doesn't follow from this view that you ought to always do what rationality requires. Often the reason you have to be rational will be outweighed by stronger reasons. This still seems implausible to most.[8] That is, it still seems implausible that you can bootstrap into existence a reason to intend to be King of France simply by intending to be a European monarch and believing that you must be the King of France in order to be a European monarch.

These objections have led nearly everyone to reject narrow-scope requirements like Means-End N. This has not led them to reject the incoherence data we started out with, though. For the most part, the literature hasn't doubted that the primary concern for

---

[6] See, for example, Bratman (1987), Broome (1999), Brunero (2010).

[7] In §8.2 of chapter 8, I will go through the arguments briefly explicated here in more detail.

[8] Schroeder (2004, 2005b) argued that this isn't in fact implausible. He later gave that up (see especially Schroeder (2009b)). Smith (2016) argues that intentions always do provide reasons.

a theory of rationality is to account for the incoherence data. Since the (purported) problem with Means-End N is that it forbids too much, philosophers have thought that the fix is to propose requirements that *merely* ban incoherence. They have thought, that is, that instead of 'rationality requires' taking narrow-scope over the consequent of the conditional, it instead takes wide-scope over the whole conditional. So, the thought goes, we should replace Means-End N with Means-End W:

Means-End W: You are rationally required to [intend to ψ if you intend to ϕ and believe that in order to ϕ you must intend to ψ].

Means-End W doesn't give rise to any objectionable bootstrapping. This is because you comply with it when you drop your intention to be a European monarch. Nevertheless, Means-End W provides an explanation for why you are always irrational when you are means-end incoherent. You are irrational when you are means-end incoherent because you violate Means-End W when you are means-end incoherent—i.e., a conditional you are rationally required to make true is false.

A striking feature of Means-End W is that it doesn't ever require you to have any particular attitudes. You comply with it as long as you are coherent. This is the feature that allows the view to avoid bootstrapping. You comply with Means-End W, and are thus instrumentally rational, when you drop your intention to be a European monarch and/or drop your belief that in order to be a European monarch you must be the King of France.

This is, at least in a rough way, the direction the debate about practical rationality has taken in the last twenty years. The focus has been on how to explain the irrationality of the incoherent states, and people have been driven to the wide-scope view by these types of considerations. Moreover, if you focus solely on the irrationality of the incoherent states, it seems like the same type of arguments in favor of wide-scoping will crop up in each case. This leads to the acceptance of whole-hog wide-scoping, or something near enough. This has come to fruition especially in the work of John Broome. Broome is, as far as I can tell, a whole-hog wide-scoper (although see note 11 below).

However, avoiding the bootstrapping objections in this way comes with distinctive costs.[9] Most importantly for my purposes, whole hog coherentism makes bad predictions about other cases. To take the case from the opening lines of the chapter, it doesn't seem right to say dropping my intention to provide for my children's basic needs is on a par when it comes to instrumental rationality with my forming the intention to make money.[10] Coherence doesn't always seem to be *sufficient* for

---

[9] Cf. Kiesewetter (2017, ch. 6).

[10] Wide-scopers might try to temper this bad result a bit by arguing that, at least sometimes, I won't be able to give up some of the antecedent attitudes. They could then follow Greenspan (1975) and hold that if you ought (ϕ or ψ) and you can't ϕ, then you ought ψ (for further discussion of this principle, see Setiya (2007a), Schroeder (2009b)). The pure coherence result would thus not follow in cases where you can't give up one of the antecedent attitudes. Indeed, the wide-scope requirements would collapse

rationality.[11] Even if it is a fact (and it is) that I'm irrational when I'm means-end incoherent, it's not right to say that I'm instrumentally rational so long as I'm coherent. And this point seems to apply *mutatis mutandis* for all of rationality.[12]

This seems like a classic case of philosophical impasse. Both views capture some of the data while making some bad predictions. On the one hand, the narrow-scoper captures the idea that coherence isn't always sufficient for rationality, but (purportedly) predicts that it's always irrational to drop ends once we have them. On the other hand, the wide-scoper captures the idea that it's (sometimes) rational to drop ends, but predicts that it's always rational to drop ends.

Perhaps the debate between the wide- and narrow-scoper is at an impasse. I don't think that this entails, however, that there is an impasse over the debate over *rationality*. I think there is a third, better, kind of view about rationality. This is Reasons Responsiveness.

It turns out that there hasn't been much discussion of views that understand rationality in terms of objective reasons, at least in the literature on practical reason. This is reflected by the fact that most of the debate has been about the wide- and narrow-scope requirements. There has been *some* critical discussion of the idea, most notably Broome (2007a, 2013). Broome argues that what's rational is not determined by reasons. My defense of Reasons Responsiveness, then, will start by defending the view against Broome's criticisms. By the end, we'll have a more fleshed out version of

into the narrow-scope ones if it was never possible to give up the antecedent attitudes. Because of this, nearly everyone since Greenspan has thought that this is a *objection* to wide-scoping. But in our context it helps with the pure coherentism charge (of course, it only helps insofar as you think the narrow-scope requirements are plausible). Thanks to Michael Smith for raising this possibility.

[11] As it happens, even Broome agrees that coherence isn't always sufficient for a particular token attitude to be rational. This is because he thinks there are some negative 'basing' requirements. These requirements forbid having or dropping attitudes for particular reasons. The paradigm example is dropping your belief that you ought to ϕ *because* you realize you aren't going to ϕ, anyway. This seems irrational. Broome explains this by appealing to the basing principles. The basing principles never require you to have particular attitudes, though. They only forbid you from having or dropping particular attitudes for particular reasons. Thus, on Broome's view, it's always permissible to drop your belief that you ought to ϕ, just so long as you don't do it for particular reasons (cf. Way (2011) for a similar view). See Lord (2014b) for critical discussion of the work Broome (and Way) tries to do with these basing requirements.

[12] A possible response to the cases I gave at the beginning of the paper is that by dropping (for example) my intention to provide for children's basic needs, I am making it the case that I am incoherent in other ways—e.g., I might believe that I ought to provide for their basic needs (cf. Worsnip (2015b)). Given normal background conditions, this is plausible. Thus, the wide-scoper does have some explanation of why I am irrational if I drop my intention to provide for my children's basic needs in this case. However, this doesn't spoil the point; it just pushes the issue back. This is because the (whole hog) wide-scoper is committed to thinking that, as far as the enkratic requirement goes, it would be just as rational for me to drop my belief that I ought to provide for my children's basic needs as it is to form the intention to provide for their basic needs. That doesn't seem right. Now, of course, the wide-scoper could insist that if I dropped that belief, I would fall into yet another incoherent state. But then we can run the same argument with respect to that one. This cannot go on forever. Thus, I think that the only way that the wide-scoper could show that one will always end up incoherent in these chains of attitude revisions would be to insist that there is some attitude A that one *necessarily* has that *necessarily* conflicts with at least one attitude or lack of attitude in these chains. This is an extremely strong claim that I am very skeptical of. Thus, even though this reply puts off the issue for a while, I don't think it succeeds fully.

Reasons Responsiveness. I will then explicate a strategy for accounting for the data that motivates the wide-scope and narrow-scope views. This strategy will be overly simplistic in a crucial way. That will require complications that are introduced in §2.5.

2.3 Broome's Challenge

Broome (2007a, 2013) wants to know if rationality consists in correctly responding to reasons. He argues that it doesn't via counterexample.

Broome is interested in showing that Equivalence is false:

Equivalence: Necessarily, you are rational if and only if you correctly respond to reasons.

Equivalence is weaker than Reasons Responsiveness. It merely says that correctly responding to reasons is a necessary and sufficient condition for being rational. Reasons Responsiveness entails this, but it also makes a claim about what it is to be rational. Since I hold Reasons Responsiveness, I also hold Equivalence.

Broome argues against Equivalence by arguing against the necessity claim—i.e., the claim that if you are rational, then you correctly respond to reasons. Here's one case from Broome (2007a).[13] Suppose Lois goes to her local seafood restaurant. She orders her favorite dish. Unbeknownst to her, the fish contains salmonella. The fact that the fish contains salmonella is, let's stipulate, a decisive reason not to eat the fish. However, it seems like Lois is rational to eat the fish given her ignorance of the salmonella. This case, then, seems like a case where someone is rational even though they don't do the thing that the reasons decisively support.

Broome does not consider the distinction between the reasons that are possessed and the reasons there are. This is a mistake, for once we pay heed to this distinction, it's clear that this version of Lois's case does not pose a problem to Reasons Responsiveness. Lois's case is a problem for views that accept Action All:

Action All: If the set S of all the objective normative reasons decisively supports ϕ-ing, then rationality requires you to ϕ.

Lois's case is certainly a counterexample to Action All. It's very implausible—and Lois's cases bring this out nicely—that you're always irrational when you fail to do things that all the reasons support.[14] This is because it's obvious that (at least sometimes) when you are ignorant of some reason r to ϕ, r does not affect the rational status of ϕ-ing.

---

[13] In Broome (2013) he doesn't give a specific case, but merely the schema for the type of case he provides in the earlier paper.

[14] This, like all claims of interest to philosophers, is controversial. Some, like Gibbons (2010), Kiesewetter (2018, 2017), hold that only facts within your perspective can be normative reasons. I think this is to throw the baby out with the bath water. Facts outside of our perspective can have the hallmark features of normative reasons. We can explain their added powers once they are in our perspective by appealing to the distinction between normative reasons there are and the normative reasons one possesses. See n. 17 of chapter 1 for more.

Lois's case, however, is simply not a counterexample to Reasons Responsiveness. Recall from chapter 1 that Action Schema is a plausible requirement given Reasons Responsiveness:

Action Schema: If the set of reasons S that A possesses to ϕ is decisive, then A is rationally required to ϕ.

In order for Lois to possess the fact that the fish contains salmonella as a reason to not intend to eat the fish, she has to have epistemic access to the fact that the fish contains salmonella. But Lois does not have epistemic access to the fact that the fish contains salmonella. Indeed, it's crucial to the case that Lois is ignorant of the salmonella. Given her ignorance, she doesn't possess the reason provided by the fact that there is salmonella in the fish. Since she doesn't possess that reason, it doesn't bear on whether she's rational. Moreover, given the other things she knows, it seems rational to eat. So this case does not cause trouble for Reasons Responsiveness.

Broome doesn't just rely on this version of the case. He also presents a second, more challenging, version of the case. In this version of the case, Lois does know that the fish contains salmonella. However, in Broome's telling, Lois rationally does not believe that that fact constitutes a reason to not intend to eat the fish. While he does not fill out the story, we can imagine that Lois has been told by a reliable source that salmonella is one of the many kinds of bacteria found in food that is harmless to humans.

This second version of Lois's case is much more troubling for Reasons Responsiveness. This is because the fact that the fish contains salmonella *is* in Lois's epistemic ken in this case, and that fact constitutes a weighty reason not to intend to eat the fish. But it still doesn't seem that it is irrational for her to intend to eat.

I think what cases like this really show is that meeting the epistemic condition on possession is *insufficient* for possessing some fact as a reason. To see this, notice that while the fact that the fish contains salmonella is in Lois's epistemic ken, it doesn't seem to be available to her *as a reason to not intend to eat the fish.*[15] Given the way that she is, it would be bizarre for her to refrain from intending to eat on the basis of the fact that the fish contains salmonella. At best she would be acting like a hypochondriac. At worst she would just be unintelligible. In any case, it doesn't seem like she can rationally refrain from intending to eat on the basis of the salmonella.

For these reasons, I don't think we should see this version of Lois's case as a counterexample to Reasons Responsiveness. Rather, I think we should see it as a counterexample to a particular view about possession. According to this view, meeting

---

[15] It does seem available to her *as a reason* for some reactions. For example, it is available to her as a reason to believe that at least one person eating at that restaurant has salmonella in their dinner. This reinforces the point that facts constitute reasons for particular reactions and one fact can constitute a reason for many different reactions. We can possess a single fact as a reason for some reactions and not others that it is a reason for. This can have surprisingly wide reaching consequences. For discussion of a consequence for the epistemology of aesthetics and morality, see Lord (2016b) and Lord (2018c).

the epistemic condition on possession is both necessary *and sufficient* for possessing a reason. This case shows that this view is false.[16]

What fills the gap in this case is what I call *the practical condition* on possession. The basic idea behind the practical condition is that in order to possess some fact *as a reason to* ϕ, one must be in a position to respond to that fact as a reason to ϕ. I'll call this principle Possession Enables Rational Routing. What is wrong with Lois in this second case, then, is that she fails to meet the practical condition. This is because she is not in a position to respond to the fact that fish contains salmonella as a reason to refrain from intending to eat.[17]

This response to the case isn't fully satisfying without a concrete and plausible view of the practical condition. While chapter 4 is dedicated to defending such a view, it's worth going through part of the dialectic here.

At first pass, you might think that you meet the practical condition just in case you believe p is a reason. This is the view that Broome seems most sympathetic to in Broome (2007a).[18] It also seems to be the view that T.M. Scanlon endorses in Scanlon (1998, 2007). I don't think believing p is a reason is necessary for meeting the practical condition, however. I think this would underdetermine the extension. We'll stick to the easy cases. It seems like creatures that lack enough of the concept of a reason to have beliefs about reasons can still meet the practical condition. My 4 year old son, for example, is in a position to use the fact that he won't get his dessert unless he eats his dinner as a reason to eat his dinner. But I don't think he believes that that is a reason to eat his dinner. Similarly, my dog is in a position to use the fact that the food is stored under the sink as a reason to pace incessantly around the sink until she's fed, but she doesn't believe that that fact is a reason to pace.

So what are the less conceptually sophisticated members of my family doing in these cases when they use those facts as reasons? They are, I think, manifesting certain dispositions—some of which are the same kinds of dispositions one has when one believes that p is a reason. The most salient disposition in these cases is the disposition to (competently) use p as a premise in reasoning. My dog is disposed to move from the judgment that the food is kept under the sink to the act (or intention to act) of incessantly pacing by the sink. Similarly, my son is disposed to use the claim that in order to get dessert he must eat his dinner as a premise in a piece of reasoning that culminates in him eating his dinner (or intending to eat his dinner).

---

[16] As it happens, nearly everyone who has theorized about possession makes this assumption. For several examples, see the first page of chapter 4.

[17] In earlier work (Lord (2014a, 2013)) I cashed out the practical condition in terms of treating things as reasons. I no longer hold that view and aim to replace it with the account defended in chapter 4. In chapter 5, I appeal to something like treating in my account of reacting for motivating reasons. See n. 35 in chapter 6.

[18] There he says that the reason why the fact that there is salmonella doesn't affect the rationality of eating is because Lois doesn't believe that the salmonella constitutes a reason not to eat. In a different context (namely, Broome (2014)) he argues that believing p is a reason to ϕ is not necessary for treating p as a reason to ϕ, for reasons similar to the ones articulated below.

Perhaps an example involving theoretical reasoning will crystallize the point. Imagine I believe it's 2 pm on Tuesday and I believe that if it's 2 pm on Tuesday, then I should be writing. If I'm rational, I will be in a position to use the contents of those beliefs as reasons for thinking I should be writing. Most importantly, this means that I am disposed to form the belief that I should be writing when I believe the other propositions. It seems like an overintellectualization to say that I don't treat those premise beliefs as reasons unless I believe they are reasons. It seems like I am doing all that needs to be done to meet the practical condition by being disposed to use them in reasoning in certain ways.

While I think it is right that being in a position to manifest certain dispositions is sufficient for meeting the practical condition, it is important to be clear about which dispositions are involved. Not any old disposition to use the content of my antecedent beliefs (that it's 2 pm on Tuesday and the content of my belief that if it is 2 pm on Tuesday, I should be writing) as a reason to believe that I should be writing count. For example, I might be so disposed because I'm disposed to believe that I should be writing on the basis of any claim whatsoever. In that case, while I am disposed to use the contents of the antecedent beliefs as reasons, I am not disposed to use them as *the reasons that they are*.

These cases show us that the practical condition requires that one be disposed to use facts that constitute reasons as the reasons that they are. In the natural rendering of the modus ponens case, I am so disposed because I am disposed to conclude that I should be writing via modus ponens. When we are disposed to use facts that constitute reasons as the reasons they are, we *know how* to use those facts as reasons. Thus, the practical condition requires that we know how to use facts that constitute reasons as the reasons they are. Further, since one can have this know-how but not be in a position to manifest it (e.g., one might be ignorant of the fact that constitutes the reason), the practical condition requires that one be in a position to manifest the relevant know-how.

I can now provide a fuller explanation of what's going wrong in the second version of Lois's case. Lois does not meet the practical condition on possession because she is not in a position to manifest knowledge about how to use the fact that the fish contains salmonella as the reason that it is to refrain from intending to eat. Indeed, it's plausible that she simply does not know how to use the particular fact as the reason that it is. She does not have this know-how because of her false beliefs about salmonella.[19] Of course, she has the capacity to gain this know-how. If she were to learn that salmonella

---

[19] There is a case to be made that she does have the relevant know-how given all of the closely related know-how that she has (e.g., we can imagine that she knows how to use the fact that there is e. coli in the fish as a reason to refrain from intending to eat). Even if this is right—and I think it's not clear if it's right—my point is not spoiled. That is because even if you think that she has the relevant know-how, it is uncontroversial that she is not in a position to manifest it given her false beliefs about salmonella. That is the crucial point for my explanation of Lois in this case. Thanks to Max Lewis for pushing me to clarify this.

does cause humans to become sick, she would very likely gain this know-how. But then it would be plausible that she possessed that fact as a reason for refraining. It would also seem rationally required for her to refrain from eating. This is exactly what our more fleshed out version of Reasons Responsiveness predicts.

This feels like progress. While Broome's cases aren't counterexamples to Reasons Responsiveness, reflection upon them has helped us flesh out some of the required details. With this view in hand, let's return to the initial motivations of the debate between the wide- and narrow-scoper.

2.4 What about Coherence?

As we've seen, the debate between the wide- and narrow-scoper is anchored in the claim that incoherence is irrational. I think that it is a datum that you are irrational when you are incoherent in certain ways under certain conditions. I have yet to say how Reasons Responsiveness accounts for this. I have said, of course, that I reject certain views that do capture this. In particular, I reject views that hold that being coherent is both necessary *and sufficient* for being rational. I do think that in the vast majority of cases one must be coherent in order to be rational. As we will see in the next section, I don't think coherence is metaphysically necessary for rationality. There are important exception cases. I will argue in the next section that it is a virtue of my account that they explain these cases. In this section, though, I am going to assume that there are no exception cases. This is to make it easier to state the strategy and defend it. Once I get the strategy on the table, I will complicate things by discussing the exceptions.

The general idea is that whenever one is incoherent, one is failing to correctly respond to the reasons one possesses. My strategy for showing that this is true is to show that in paradigm instances of (irrational) incoherence, one is always violating one of the requirements that are determined by possessed reasons. To put it the other way, in all paradigm instances of (irrational) incoherence, the reasons one possesses requires one to do something that would make one coherent.[20] One dialectally unfortunate aspect of this strategy is that a complete implementation of it would take a lot of time and space. I will not attempt to completely implement it. Instead, I will go through five particular cases. While the first case is one of the easier ones to account for using this strategy, the other four are some of the hardest cases for the strategy. My hope is that by showing that there is good reason to think that the strategy works for these harder cases, I will provide good evidence that the strategy can be generalized.

---

[20] Kiesewetter (2017, chs. 9–10) adopts the same strategy. His view fails to fully account for the hardest cases, however. His arguments against some of my particular claims will be discussed below.

2.4.1 Closure

Let's begin with the easier case in order to get a feel for the strategy.[21] Suppose that you believe p, believe if p then q, but fail to believe q.[22] You are closure incoherent, and, very plausibly, irrational. Why are you irrational? Recall Belief Schema:

Belief Schema: If the set of reasons you possess decisively supports p, then you are rationally required to believe that p.[23]

If you combine this with the very plausible Closure Transmission

Closure Transmission: If the reasons you possess decisively support p and the reasons you possess decisively support if p then q, then the reasons you possess decisively support q.

then we can explain why you are always irrational when you are closure incoherent.[24] I think you are irrational because Reasons-Coherence, Closure is true:

Reasons-Coherence, Closure: If you are closure incoherent, then you are not correctly responding to all of the reasons you possess.

Reasons-Coherence, Closure is true because it will either be true that you possess decisive reason to believe p, decisive reason to believe if p then q and thus by Closure Transmission possess decisive reason to believe q, or you won't. If you do possess decisive reason to believe p, decisive reason to believe if p then q, then you'll possess decisive reason to believe q, and thus you are irrational when closure incoherent because you don't believe q. If you lack decisive reason to believe p or lack decisive reason to believe if p then q, then you will be irrational when closure incoherent because you hold one of those beliefs and you are rationally required not to. Either way, you will be irrational when closure incoherent.

---

[21] For discussion of an even easier case—viz., the case of believing p and believing $\neg p$—see Kolodny (2007a).

[22] And suppose that you are considering q, q is a matter of importance for you, etc.

[23] This is not the most general requirement applying to doxastic stances towards propositions. It will get us all we want for belief regarding p. This is because it will explain why you are required to believe p when you possess decisive reason for p and why you are required to believe $\neg p$ when you possess decisive reasons for $\neg p$. However, this leaves out withholding. A more general principle says something like: For any stance S towards p, if you possess decisive reasons to take S towards p, then you are rationally required to take S towards p.

[24] Kiesewetter (2017, ch. 9) actually denies Closure Transmission. He does this because he thinks it is possible for there to be cases where the probability for p and if p, then q is barely high enough for the reasons to believe to be decisive even though the probability of $(p \wedge p \rightarrow q)$ is not high enough for the reasons to believe the conjunction to be sufficient. I think that Kiesewetter's (merely assumed) probabilistic view about the weights is overly simplistic, although I do think there are transmission failures in the neighborhood that will be discussed below. If one is convinced that there are cases of the sort Kiesewetter attempts to refer to, then see his discussion for a more complicated explanation of a weaker version of Reasons-Coherence, Closure.

2.4.2 Narrowly inconsistent intentions

Let's look now at the case of inconsistent intentions. This is, surprisingly, the most difficult case. Suppose that you intend to ϕ and intend to $\neg\phi$. You have what I will call narrowly inconsistent intentions and are, plausibly, irrational. In order to vindicate my strategy, I have to show that whenever you are like this, you are failing to correctly respond to the reasons you possess. It is easy to show this in many cases.

Recall Intention Schema:

Intention Schema: If the reasons you possess decisively support intending to ϕ, then you are rationally required to intend to ϕ.

Now suppose you have decisive reason to intend to ϕ. In all cases like this, we can use Inconsistent Transmission-Narrow

Inconsistent Transmission-Narrow: If the reasons you possess decisively support intending to ϕ, then the reasons you possess decisively support not intending to $\neg\phi$.

to explain why you are irrational when you have narrowly inconsistent intentions. If you possess decisive reason to intend to ϕ, then by Inconsistent Transmission-Narrow you possess decisive reason not to intend to $\neg\phi$. By Intention Schema you are rationally required to not intend to $\neg\phi$. Thus, if you have narrowly inconsistent intentions when you have decisive reason to have one of the intentions, you will be irrational for having the other intention.

This would be all that I need if for any ϕ and $\neg\phi$, one either possesses decisive reasons to intend to ϕ or decisive reasons to intend to $\neg\phi$. As many have pointed out, though, this claim is false.[25] This is because there are cases where one possesses *merely* sufficient reasons to intend to ϕ and merely sufficient reasons to intend to $\neg\phi$. So, for example, at least before I started revising, I possessed merely sufficient reasons to intend to revise this chapter and I possessed merely sufficient reasons to intend to not revise this chapter.

Now imagine that I intend to revise this chapter and intend to not revise this chapter. I am irrationally incoherent. However, it doesn't look like I can not use Inconsistent Transmission-Narrow to explain why. This is because Inconsistent Transmission-Narrow is a principle about *decisive reasons*. It doesn't seem like I possess any decisive reasons in this case. Thus, I need another explanation of this case.

Some have thought that intending to ϕ itself provides a reason to ϕ.[26] One might think this can help here. This is because, you might think, the extra reason provided by the fact that I intend to revise makes the reasons I possess to intend

---

[25] The analogous claim for belief is very plausibly true. This is the claim that for any p, one either possesses decisive reasons to believe p or decisive reasons to not believe p. For related discussion, see Kolodny (2007a), Way (2013).

[26] For example, Schroeder (2009b), Smith (2016).

to revise decisive. We could then use Inconsistent Transmission-Narrow to explain why I'm then rationally required not to intend to not revise. Let's call this explanation Intentions Provide Reasons.

There are two serious problems with Intentions Provide Reasons. First, it's not clear that it can actually explain what needs to be explained, for notice that I *also* intend to not revise. That intention provides me with a reason to intend not to revise. Thus, it looks like we can use the same story to generate the conclusion that I possess decisive reason not to intend to write. But then it looks like we are committed to thinking that I both possess decisive reasons to intend to revise and possess decisive reasons not to intend to revise (and likewise for intending not to revise). Thus, it looks like this story makes these cases into *rational dilemmas*. No matter what I intend I will be irrational. That's not right.

This objection moves too quickly. This is because one could reply that once I form one of the intentions (suppose it's the intention to revise), I no longer have sufficient reasons to intend to not revise. This is because it follows from our analyses of decisiveness and sufficiency in chapter 1 that if I possess decisive reasons to intend to ϕ, I do not possess sufficient reasons to intend to $\neg\phi$. Thus, this reply continues, once I form the intention to revise, the reason my later intention provides to intend to not revise cannot make the reasons to intend to not revise decisive. So the dilemma doesn't arise.

While this is true as far as it goes, it doesn't go far enough. For it crucially relies on my forming one intention before forming the other. But it's possible for me to form both intentions at once. The above reply isn't available in that case. It seems like the reasons in favor of each intention will once again be equally weighty. So either one lacks decisive reason for each and thus we don't have an explanation of the irrationality or one has decisive reason for both and we have the dilemma.

Even if this problem could be avoided, there is another damning problem. In some cases I have merely sufficient reasons for an intention even after I form that intention. It might be that even after I form the intention to revise, the reasons I possess to intend to revise are merely sufficient. This follows from the fact that sometimes it's permissible for me to change my mind about revising. I might start revising and realize that I'd rather not revise. In many cases it will be permissible for me to then drop my intention to revise.

It's important to be precise about what the revision data is. It is *not* intuitive that after I form the intention to revise, I am permitted to form the intention to not revise. So my reasons to revise are not sufficient because I also possess sufficient reasons to intend to not revise. What *is* intuitive is that in some cases where I already have the intention to revise, I have merely sufficient reasons to have the intention to revise and merely sufficient reasons to *not* have the intention to revise. That is to say, the alternative to having the intention to revise I possess sufficient reasons for is not having the intention to revise; I do not possess sufficient reasons for having the intention to not revise.

This is a problem for the view under consideration because it holds that the additional reason provided by the fact that I intend to revise makes the reasons I possess to intend to revise decisive. If it did do that, though, then I wouldn't be permitted to not have the intention to revise—when the reasons to intend to revise are decisive, I lack sufficient reasons for all of the alternatives. Sometimes I do have sufficient reasons to not have the intention to revise, though. So this can't be the right explanation.

What I need, it seems, is for the weight of the reasons for (at least) one of the intentions to change in light of the fact that one holds the other. Intentions Provide Reasons attempts to give me this, but it doesn't seem to do it in the right way. Fortunately, there are at least two ways for some fact f to affect the weight of reasons in favor of ϕ-ing. One way is for f to provide a reason to ϕ or provide a reason against ϕ-ing. Thus, providing additional reasons for the end is one way in which an intention to ϕ might increase the weight of one's reasons to pursue the necessary means (via some transmission of weight principle). However, it is not the only way. For another way f can affect the weight of reasons in favor of ϕ-ing is by *intensifying* or *attenuating* the weight of the *other* reasons there are for ϕ-ing. For example, the fact that you just took a pill that makes some red walls appear blue isn't itself a reason to disbelieve that the wall that seems to you blue is blue. Instead, it just weakens or attenuates the weight of the reason provided by the appearance. Similarly, the fact that today is the last day to see a special exhibition at the local art gallery doesn't provide a further reason to go to the gallery. It *intensifies* the weight of the other reasons I have to go see the special exhibition.[27]

This offers me a life line in these cases. For it might be that even though Intentions Provides Reasons is not right, facts about intentions attenuate or intensify some of the reasons. As it happens, I think this is what happens. In particular, I think that the fact that I intend to revise attenuates my reasons to intend not to revise to the point of being insufficient. If those reasons are insufficient, then the reasons not to intend to not revise are decisive. Thus, I am irrational in these cases because I intend to not revise. Let's call this view Intentions Attenuate.

Intentions Attenuate does not have the problems that Intentions Provide Reasons has. First, it cannot give rise to dilemmas. This is because, on this view, intentions do not make the reasons for either intention decisive. So one cannot bootstrap into a dilemma by forming both of the intentions.

Despite this, one might object that Intentions Attenuate gives rise to a form of reverse bootstrapping. This is because when one has both intentions, facts about each intention will attenuate the reasons for the other intention. Further, goes the objector, my story commits me to thinking that the attenuation will make each set of reasons

---

[27] For more on attenuators/intensifiers (also known as modifiers), see Dancy (2004a), Schroeder (2011a, 2012), Lord (2016a), Bader (2016), Lord & Maguire (2016).

insufficient. Thus, when one has both intentions, one has decisive reasons to revise both of them.

Notice, first, that there is no sense in which this is a dilemma. Even if my view predicted this, one could easily become fully rational by dropping each intention. I'll consider whether this is a bad prediction in a moment. Before that, notice that this objection is too quick for the same reason that the first pass of the dilemma objection to Intentions Provide Reasons was too quick. This double attenuation won't occur when one forms one of the intentions temporally prior to the other. In those cases, once one forms the first intention, one loses sufficient reasons for the other. Thus, one will be irrational for forming the second intention. Given this, it's implausible that the attenuation of the one's reasons for the first intention would make one's reasons for the first intention insufficient.

There is no denying that it's *possible* that one forms both intentions at the same time, though. In these rare cases, I think that my view predicts that once the intentions are formed, one has decisive reasons to drop both of them. This prediction is initially strange (although not devastating like the predictions of Intentions Provide Reasons), but I think it can be vindicated by thinking about things from the deliberative perspective. If one were in one of these cases, I don't think either option would seem privileged from the deliberative perspective. Yet, given normal background conditions, it would be clear that one is in a bad situation. Given these facts, I think the most sensible option is to drop both intentions and start over.[28] My view predicts this. So I don't think that the double attenuation prediction sinks Intentions Attenuate.

So it looks like Intentions Attenuate doesn't have the first problem of Intentions Provide Reasons—the bootstrapping problem. It also doesn't have the second problem. This is because it doesn't predict that once I form the intention to revise, my reasons to intend to revise are decisive. Rather, it predicts that my reasons to *not* intend to not revise are decisive. This fact does not guarantee that my reasons to intend to revise are decisive. And, in the relevant cases, it is not plausible that they are. This is because, in the relevant cases, my reasons to intend to revise are merely sufficient and my reasons to not intend to revise are merely sufficient.

A natural question to ask at this point is what the reasons to not intend to revise are. After all, paradigmatic reasons to not intend to ϕ are reasons to intend $\neg\phi$. Further, one might think that whether the reasons to not intend to ϕ are sufficient depends on whether the reasons to intend $\neg\phi$ are sufficient. If this were true, my explanation would be ruined. This is because I am claiming that in the cases where dropping my intention to revise is permitted, I possess sufficient reasons to not intend to revise even though my reasons to intend not to revise are insufficient. The right answer to this question is that the reasons to not intend to revise are provided by the same facts that are reasons to intend not to revise. They are facts that count in favor of doing the other things that are worth doing.

---

[28] Of course, once you start over, you can re-form one of the intentions.

To make it concrete, let's just consider one option—replying to emails—and one reason for that option—the fact that I need to write the emails by tomorrow. The fact that I need to write the emails by tomorrow is both a reason to intend not to revise and a reason to not intend to revise. My view predicts that, in this case, *once I intend to revise*, the fact that I need to write the emails by tomorrow provides a sufficient reason to not intend to revise but does not provide a sufficient reason to intend not to revise. That is, it is permissible to not intend to revise but it is not permissible to intend to not revise. Of course, once I drop my intention to revise, the fact that I need to write the emails tomorrow goes back to providing a sufficient reason to intend not to revise.

I grant that this is complicated, but it seems just as complicated as the data. It seems to me that this is *precisely* what the data suggests. Once I intend to revise, I am not permitted to form the intention to not revise. However, I am permitted to drop the intention to revise. Further, the reason why is that there are other worthwhile options. If I decide to drop my intention to revise, then all of the options are back on the table. I can then permissibly decide to intend not to revise. Intentions Attenuate predicts all of this. I see this as an impressive virtue.

Further, the general phenomenon here is not theoretically problematic. Single facts often constitute reasons for multiple reactions. The fact that the burger is high in fat is a reason for me to desire to eat the burger, a reason for me to intend to eat the burger, a reason for me to *not* desire to eat the burger, a reason for me to *not* intend to eat the burger, a reason to desire *not* to eat the burger, and a reason to intend to *not* eat the burger. Sometimes some of those reasons are sufficient and others are not. The reason to desire to eat the burger might be sufficient but not the reason to intend to eat the burger, for example.

The upshot here is that Intentions Attenuate seems to explain a particularly complicated data set. Further, it retains the natural thought that forming an intention makes a difference in cases of mere permissibility. I think this is all evidence in favor of Intentions Attenuate.

Still, one might still wonder whether there are more direct reasons to believe Intentions Attenuate. I think that more direct reasons to believe Intentions Attenuate are provided by intuitions about deliberation. In order to appreciate these intuitions, it's helpful to fill in more of a theory about what modifiers (i.e., intensifiers and attenuators) *are*. On the most worked out view of modifiers, modifiers are themselves reasons.[29] They are reasons to place more (intensifiers) or less (attenuators) weight in deliberation on the reasons that are modified. Let's call this the Higher-Order View of modifiers.

This theory of modifiers allows us to test our intuitions about the role that facts about intentions should play. Intentions Attenuate, together with this theory of

---

[29] See Schroeder (2012), Horty (2012).

modifiers, predicts that the fact that I intend to revise is itself a reason to place less weight on the reasons to intend not to revise. This is an intuitive prediction, I think. After all, it seems like the fact that I intend to revise should play *some* role in deliberation. But it is not particularly plausible that I should take it as a reason to revise. After all, if I did that, then it's not clear why I would often think it's permissible to drop my intention to revise. Rather, it seems to bear on deliberation by forcing the considerations in favor of intending not to revise out, as it were. This is some evidence in favor of Intentions Attenuate.

One might worry that despite the preceding virtues, Intentions Attenuate fails for a flat-footed reason.[30] Imagine a humdrum case of wrongdoing: Adrian the advisor doesn't show up to a meeting with his advisee because he becomes engulfed in video games. It doesn't seem like Adrian's wrong is less wrong simply because he intends to do something other than what he ought to do—viz., play video games. But it looks like Intentions Attenuate predicts this. After all, Adrian's intention to play video games attenuates his reason to meet his advisee. His reasons to meet the advisee are thus less weighty than they would be in virtue of his intending.

I am fine accepting the prediction, but I don't think we should take the prediction as too damning. One reason why is that, as Mark Schroeder has shown, our intuitions about negative reason existentials are systematically unreliable.[31] Given the Higher-Order view of modifiers, our intuitions about Adrian just are intuitions about negative reason existentials. The question is whether the fact that Adrian intends to play video games is a reason for Adrian to place less weight on his reasons to meet his advisee. Intuitions to the contrary are intuitions that that fact is not a reason. We shouldn't put much weight on such intuitions.

Now, of course, this would be a problem if the fact that Adrian intends to play video games makes it the case that he ought not meet his advisee. I don't think this is likely to happen, though, at least in all cases where the reasons in favor of playing video games are much weaker than the reasons to meet the advisee. I don't have a knockdown argument for this, but I also don't think that Intentions Attenuate on its own makes these sorts of cases particularly likely.

Now I am in a position to explain Reasons-Coherence, Narrowly Inconsistent Intentions:

Reasons-Coherence, Narrowly Inconsistent Intentions: If you have narrowly inconsistent intentions, then you are not correctly responding to all the reasons you possess.

There are four kinds of cases. In the first kind of case, one starts off with decisive reasons for one of the intentions. In these cases, one is irrational when one has inconsistent intentions because she always had decisive reasons not to have one of

---

[30] I thank a referee for raising this objection.   [31] See especially Schroeder (2007).

the intentions. This follows from Intention Schema and Inconsistent Transmission-Narrow. In the second kind of case, one has decisive reason to not have either intention. In this kind of case, one is irrational when one has inconsistent intentions because one is required by rationality to not have either intention.

In the third kind of case, one starts off with merely sufficient reasons for each intention. Further, one forms one intention prior to the other (let's say the intention to ϕ comes first). In this case, one is irrational because one possesses decisive reasons not to have the intention to $\neg\phi$. This is because the fact that one intends to ϕ attenuates the reasons to intend to $\neg\phi$ to the point of being insufficient. In the final and rarest kind of case, one starts off possessing merely sufficient reasons for each intention. Further, one forms both intentions at the same time. In this case, one is irrational because one possesses decisive reasons to not have either intention. This is because the fact that one intends to ϕ attenuates one's reasons to intend to $\neg\phi$ to the point of being insufficient and the fact that one intends to $\neg\phi$ attenuates one's reasons to intend to ϕ to the point of being insufficient. Thus, in these cases, one is rationally required to drop both intentions.

2.4.3 Broadly inconsistent intentions

The last subsection focused on intentions that are narrowly inconsistent. The intentions were narrowly inconsistent because they were intentions to perform an act and its negation. These are not all of the cases of inconsistent intentions though. There is a wider class of cases that involve an intention to ϕ, an intention to ψ, and a belief that one cannot both ϕ and ψ. These are broadly inconsistent intentions. In paradigm cases of broadly inconsistent intentions, one seems irrationally incoherent.

My view can easily explain many of the cases.[32] Suppose I possess decisive reason to intend to go to the office tomorrow and I possess decisive reason to believe that I cannot go to the office tomorrow if I go to New York tomorrow. Suppose further that I intend to go to the office tomorrow, intend to go to New York tomorrow, and believe that I cannot go to the office tomorrow if I go to New York tomorrow. We can use Inconsistent Transmission-Broad

Inconsistent Transmission-Broad: If the reasons you possess decisively support intending to ϕ and the reasons you possess decisively support believing that you cannot ϕ and ψ, then the reasons you possess decisively support not intending to ψ.

to explain why I am irrational. I am irrational because I have an intention—the intention to go to New York—that rationality requires me not to have.

---

[32] In the main text I will not discuss cases where you lack sufficient reason for the belief. In those cases you will be irrational for having the belief. I should also note that when one's belief is false yet rational, my view predicts that one possesses decisive reason to (at least) not have one of the intentions.

Similarly, we can explain why I am irrational if I lack decisive reason to intend to go to the office or lack decisive reason to believe that I cannot go to the office and go to New York. In those cases I will be irrational for having those attitudes.

Once again, the picture is complicated by cases of mere permissibility. Fortunately, I think the basics of the story about narrowly inconsistent intentions apply here as well. Suppose that right now I possess sufficient reason to go to law school next year, sufficient reason to go to medical school next year, and decisive reason to believe that I cannot both go to law school and medical school next year. Suppose I believe that I cannot do both, intend to go to law school, and intend to go to medical school. I am irrationally incoherent. It's not clear which attitude I possess decisive reasons not to have.[33]

Suppose I decided to go to law school first. In that case, the fact that I intend to go to law school attenuates the reasons I possess to go to medical school to the point that they are insufficient. I am thus irrational for forming the intention to go to medical school. Of course, this doesn't necessarily mean that I lack sufficient reason to drop the intention to go to law school. I might, in which case it is permissible for me to revise (and *mutatis mutandis* if I formed the intention to go to medical school first).

If I formed the two intentions at exactly the same time, then facts about each intention will attenuate the reasons for the other to the point where I have decisive reason to drop both. For the reasons outlined in the last subsection, I do not find this to be an unacceptable prediction.

All of this amounts to an explanation of Reasons-Coherence, Broadly Inconsistent Intentions:

Reasons-Coherence, Broadly Inconsistent Intentions: If you have broadly inconsistent intentions, then you are not correctly responding to all the reasons you possess.

It's worth pointing out that the same intuitions I marshaled in favor of Intentions Attenuate in the last subsection apply to broadly inconsistent intentions too. The Higher-Order View of modifiers and Intentions Attenuate predict that the fact that I intend to go to law school is a reason to place less weight in deliberation on the reasons to go to medical school. I think this is a plausible prediction. The fact that I intend to go to law school should play some role in my deliberation. It doesn't seem like it should play the role of a reason to go to law school. Instead, it seems to rule out the reasons to go to medical school. This is some evidence for Intentions Attenuate.

2.4.4 Means-end incoherence

With inconsistent intentions on the table, we can move onto means-end incoherence. Similarly to inconsistent intentions, one kind of case is easy for me to explain.

---

[33] I could repeat the dialectic between Intentions Provide Reasons and Intentions Attenuate here, but I won't.

Suppose you possess decisive reasons to intend to ϕ, possess decisive reasons to believe that in order to ϕ you must intend to ψ, but fail to intend to ψ.[34] If we combine Intention Schema with the very plausible Means-End Transmission

Means-End Transmission: If the reasons you possess decisively support intending to ϕ and the reasons you possess decisively support believing that in order to ϕ you must intend to ψ, then the reasons you possess decisively support intending to ψ.

then we can explain why you are irrational. It follows from Means-End Transmission and the fact that you possess decisive reason to intend to ϕ and decisive reason to believe that in order to ϕ you must intend to ψ that you possess decisive reason to intend to ψ. Thus, if you are means-end incoherent, it follows from Intention Schema that you are irrational because you lack an intention—the intention to ψ—that rationality requires you to have.

We can provide similar explanations when you possess decisive reasons not to intend to ϕ or possess decisive reasons not to believe that in order to ϕ you must intend to ψ. In those cases, you will be irrational when means-end incoherent because you have an intention or belief that rationality requires you not to have.

Things become more complicated in cases of mere permissibility. To use the earlier example, right now it's permissible for me to revise this chapter and it's permissible for me to send some emails. Imagine I decide to revise and I know that in order to revise I must intend to open my word processor, but I don't intend to open my word processor. I'm irrational. It doesn't look like I can use either of the above explanations. It's not true that I possess decisive reason not to have the end or not to have the means-end belief. So those aren't the attitudes that are irrational. But it also seems like I don't possess decisive reasons to have the end, and hence it doesn't seem like Means-End Transmission can help explain why I'm required to take the means.[35] So it is puzzling how it is that I am going wrong when I am means-end incoherent.

An analogous puzzle arises for views about what all the reasons require (as opposed to what the reasons one possesses require). That puzzle has been discussed at great length in that context.[36] The puzzle of mere permissibility has proven hard to solve.

---

[34] And your plans to ϕ are relevant to current planning, and you have access to your intention to ϕ and your means end-belief, et cetera.

[35] Some think that a similar puzzle arises in the case of belief. It should be noted that although it's uncontroversial that there are cases of mere permissibility when it comes to practical matters, it's very controversial whether there are cases of mere permissibility in the epistemic case. Many explicitly reject that such cases are possible. See, for example, Feldman (2003, 2007), White (2005), Kolodny (2007a). Some defenders of the claim that there are cases of epistemic mere permissibility include Harman (1986), Rosen (2001), Kelly (2010), Ballantyne & Coffman (2011), Schroeder (2012). Although I think it's plausible that there are cases of mere permissibility in the epistemic case, the details would take us too far afield here. I don't think it makes a difference to my explanation of Reasons-Coherence, Closure.

[36] See, for example, Broome (2001), Scanlon (2004), Brunero (2007), Kolodny (2007a, 2018), Schroeder (2009b), Way (2010a, 2011).

There are several different candidate solutions. Fully getting into the details of these views would take us too far afield. However, I will sketch and motivate my preferred solution to the puzzle in the context of that literature.

It is again helpful to contrast my view with a version of Intentions Provide Reasons.[37] If my intention to revise the chapter provides a reason with at least *some* weight, then there's a chance we can explain why I'm irrational for not intending to open my word processor. This is because, it seems, in cases of mere permissibility, we just need a little more weight in favor of the end one actually intends to pursue to make the reasons in favor of that end decisive. The thought is that the reason provided by one's intention can provide this extra bit of weight. And once one has decisive reason to pursue the end, we can use a principle like Means-End Transmission to explain why you are required to take the means.

There are several problems with this explanation. I will mention the two problems that I think are most damning (the first problem is developed nicely in Way (2013)). It is important that the reasons provided by one's intentions are usually quite light weight. This is needed to avoid the bootstrapping worry. However—and this is the first problem—if they are light weight, then it is implausible that they will be able to explain all cases of mere permissibility, for it's not true that all cases are cases where the reasons there are for the various permissible ends are *roughly equal* in weight.

In some cases the merely permissible options are incommensurable. I might have the choice to take a job as a philosopher or to take a job as a lawyer. It might be that both are permissible, but not because the reasons there are for each option are commensurable and of roughly equal weight. The reasons there are for each option might be sufficiently weighty to make it permissible to pursue that job even though we can't directly compare the weights of the reasons. Moreover, in cases in incommensurability it is well known that adding a light weight reason in favor of one side doesn't necessarily give one decisive reasons to act in that way.[38] To see this, imagine that the law firm, in an effort to recruit me, offers me a $500 signing bonus. This gives me an extra reason to become a lawyer, but it doesn't seem to make the reasons in favor of becoming a lawyer decisive.[39] Thus, establishing that there is a light weight reason provided by one's intention to be a lawyer isn't sufficient for establishing that one has decisive reasons to become a lawyer. Without this, the Intentions Provide Reasons theorist cannot explain all the cases.

The second problem for this explanation mirrors the revision problem we saw above.[40] In some cases it is permissible to revise one's intention. On Monday I might form the intention to be a lawyer. After a good night's sleep I might change

---

[37] Schroeder (2009b) tentatively defends a solution to the mere permissibility problem by appealing to Intentions Provide Reasons. I think that Way (2013) raises additional worries to the ones I'll focus on here, some of which I think are damning (cf. Kiesewetter (2017, ch. 10)).

[38] Cf. Chang (1997).

[39] See Hare (2009, 2010) for arguments that these reasons are decisive.

[40] This objection is pushed in Broome (2001) and Brunero (2007).

my mind—i.e., I might drop my intention to become a lawyer. In many cases this seems perfectly reasonable. It doesn't seem like Intentions Provide Reasons can accommodate this. For once I form the intention to become a lawyer, I have decisive reasons to have that intention. But if I have decisive reasons to have that intention, I do not have sufficient reasons to drop that intention. It thus follows that I am not permitted to revise. This is the wrong result.

Despite the fact that Intentions Provide Reasons is implausible, it is very plausible that choosing one of the ends makes a difference to which means you should pursue. Before you make a decision there are no particular means you ought to pursue. After you make a decision there are. One might think we need to abandon this idea if we abandon Intentions Provide Reasons.

Fortunately, modifiers can help us here too. Even though it's implausible that intentions affect the weight of our reasons to take necessary means by providing reasons to pursue the end, it is quite plausible that they affect the weight of our reasons to take the means by modifying the weight of those reasons. More specifically, it is quite plausible that our intentions *intensify* the weight of the reasons we already have to take the means. Moreover, I claim, when ψ-ing is necessary for ϕ-ing and one has sufficient reason to ϕ, the fact that one intends to ϕ intensifies one's reasons to ψ to the point of being decisive. I'll argue for each claim in turn.

The argument I will provide here for Intentions Intensify will be anchored in the fact that Intentions Intensify avoids the main problems with Intentions Provide Reasons. Given the antecedent plausibility of the claim that our intentions make some difference to what we should do (at least in these cases), this will be a serious virtue of the view.

First things first, there is no threat of bootstrapping. In a case where there are no reasons to pursue the end, there won't be any reasons to pursue the means (because of the end). Thus, intending the end won't intensify the reasons to take the means because there won't be any reasons to take the means.[41] One might worry that one can bootstrap into sufficient or decisive reasons to take the means in cases where one lacks sufficient reasons to pursue the end. That is, it might be that the fact that you intend intensifies your reasons to take the means to a point where they are sufficient or decisive even though you lack sufficient reasons to pursue the end.

I don't think this is possible. If your reasons for pursuing the end are insufficient, then they will be defeated by some reasons. Those reasons will also defeat your reasons to take the means, even if the fact that you intend to pursue the end intensifies your reasons to take the means. Since there are defeaters of your reasons to pursue the end, the intensification will not be enough to make your reasons to take the means sufficient. Why is this? The intuitive idea is that the defeaters of the end trump the

---

[41] It's also plausible that intending the end won't intensify other reasons to take the means. The fact that ψ-ing is necessary for ϕ-ing doesn't seem to be a good candidate for explaining why reasons to ψ that are completely independent of ϕ-ing are intensified.

intensification. If the end is impermissible, the fact that the means are necessary can't intensify the reasons to take the means enough to make the reasons sufficient.

Of course, you might have other reasons (or there might be other intensifiers) that make your reasons to take the means sufficient or decisive. But as long as your reasons to pursue the end are insufficient, the fact that you intend the end won't intensify your reasons to take the means enough.

Intentions Intensify avoids bootstrapping but also avoids the problem with incommensurability. The problem there, recall, was with the claim that the reason provided by the intention made one's reasons to pursue the *end* decisive. In cases of incommensurability, adding a light weight reason to one side doesn't always make the reasons in favor of that side decisive. According to Intentions Intensify, one's intentions don't affect the reasons in favor of pursuing the end. They affect the reasons to take the means. Moreover, they do this not because they add a light weight reason, but by intensifying.[42]

Finally, Intentions Intensify can also explain the revision data. This is because it avoids commitment to the claim that once you intend to pursue the end, you have decisive reason to pursue the end. Intentions Intensify avoids this problem because it holds that one's intention affects the weight of one's reasons to take the means. One's intention does nothing to the weight of the reasons to pursue the end. Thus, it might be permitted to drop one's intention after one forms it, although it is not permitted to keep one's intention but fail to take the means.

While this isn't a complete defense of Intentions Intensify, it is a good start. Showing Intentions Intensify isn't enough to fully solve the problem of mere permissibility. In order to fully solve the problem, I have to explain why this intensification always makes the reasons to ψ decisive. It is once again helpful to break down the problem into different kinds of cases. Before we start, it is important to keep in mind that I hold a *comparative* view about sufficiency and decisiveness. In order to ruin my strategy, there need to be cases of mere permissibility where one intends one of the ends but one has equally weighty reason to do something other than take the means to that end. Given this, we need to focus on the reasons for doing other things. There are two different genera of cases. On the one hand, we have cases where one gains no new reasons throughout the process. On the other hand, we have cases where one does gain new reasons after one intends one of the ends.

Let's start with the first genus. In the first kind of case in this genus, one believes that one cannot take the means to both ends. My options are to write emails or revise. And suppose that the relevant means are opening one's browser at t and opening one's word processor at t. Now suppose that I intend to revise and I believe that I cannot both open my browser at t and open my word processor at t.

---

[42] As a referee points out, there is a version of Intentions Provide Reasons that maintains that intentions just provide reasons for the means. This version does avoid some of the problems (e.g., the revision problem) but it doesn't solve all of the problems (e.g., the problems about how the weighing works).

Notice that if it is not possible to take the necessary means to both ends, it is not possible to execute both of the ends. This means that the ends in these cases are broadly inconsistent. My view from the last subsection thus predicts that the fact that I intend to revise attenuates the reasons to intend to write emails to the point of being insufficient. If this is true, though, then the reasons to take the means to writing emails are also insufficient. For they were sufficient prior to my decision only because the reasons for writing emails were sufficient. Thus, the reasons for intending to open my web browser are not sufficient in this case. If they aren't sufficient, then it follows that my reasons to open the word processor are decisive.[43]

In the second kind of case in this genus, one does not believe that the means are incompatible. So, for example, suppose I have merely sufficient reason to watch the game and merely sufficient reason to drink the beer. A necessary means to watching the game is to turn on the TV. A necessary means to drinking the beer is picking up the bottle. I can do both of these things. Now suppose I intend to watch the game but I do not intend to drink the beer. What we want is that I now possess decisive reason to turn on the TV. But it's not clear why this is the case even if my intention intensifies the weight of the reason to turn on the TV. This is because it's still plausible that I have sufficient reason to pick up the bottle. But if I have sufficient reason to do that, it seems I do not have decisive reason to turn on the TV.

The problem with this objection is that it misdescribes the relevant facts. The reasons I possess to turn on the TV are decisive when they are weightier than the set of reasons for *the alternatives*. But picking up the bottle is not an alternative in the relevant sense. The alternatives in the relevant sense are the things I could be doing *instead of turning on the TV*. Since I can pick up the bottle and turn on the TV, picking up the bottle is not something I could do in lieu of turning on the TV. So having sufficient reason to pick up the bottle is no barrier to having decisive reason to intend to turn on the TV.

Of course, there are ways of picking up the bottle that are alternatives to turning on the TV. For example, I could pick up the bottle with both hands or I could pick up the bottle in such a way that the remote is flung across the room. These possibilities do not pose a problem because they make the case into a case where the necessary means are incompatible with the end I've chosen. In other words, they make the cases into cases of broadly inconsistent intentions. So the earlier explanation applies.

Now let's turn to the second genus.[44] In these cases, my reasons change over time. There are four kinds of case, two of which raise interesting issues.[45] In the first kind

---

[43] Kiesewetter (2017, §10.3.2) claims that cases like this sink my entire explanation of the instrumental case. He doesn't consider whether an explanation of broadly inconsistent intentions can help, though. I think it is clear that these cases do not sink the explanation.

[44] I am going to assume that all of the cases we are about to consider are cases where one cannot pursue the necessary means of each end.

[45] I won't consider cases where you lose or gain reasons for the instrumental belief. Those cases aren't very interesting. Gaining reasons for the belief won't change the fact that you have decisive reasons to have

of uninteresting case, you gain reasons to intend the end you in fact intend. These are uninteresting cases because in these cases the case for taking the means to that end (and the case against the other end and means) is only made stronger. Similarly, in a second kind of uninteresting case, you gain additional reasons to intend the means to your intended end. Again, in these cases the reasons to take the means to the intended end are simply stronger, which is no threat to my strategy.

The other two kinds are more interesting. In the third kind of case, you gain new reasons to intend the end you happen not to intend. One might think that these additional reasons make the reasons to take that end sufficient, which would in turn make the reasons to take the means sufficient. If the reasons to take the means to the unintended end were sufficient, then the reasons to take the means to the intended end couldn't be decisive.

I admit that there will be cases where additional reasons for the unintended end make a difference. But it can't be this difference exactly. Suppose I intend to revise but gain a new weighty reason to email. Suppose that I learn that I must reply to an important email within 20 minutes and it will take me at least 15 minutes to write the email. In this case my reasons to intend to revise are defeated. So I am irrational if I keep my intention to revise. What I am required to do is drop that intention and form the intention to email.

In this case it is obvious that the reasons to intend to revise are defeated. There will be cases where it's not so obvious. Suppose that I have two hours in which I must write a 15 minute email. Must I drop the intention to revise? Probably not, but then I don't think it's plausible that one's reasons to intend to write the email are sufficient, given that I retain the intention to revise. After all, I am permissibly pursuing an end that is incompatible with writing the email right now. This isn't a *proof* that the reasons to intend to write the email cannot be made sufficient while the reasons to intend to revise are also sufficient, but I think it's the best that can be done.

In the fourth kind of case, one gains new reasons to take the means to the unintended end. These needn't be reasons for the unintended end. For example, I might find out that an important email just arrived in my inbox. This is not a reason to intend to write emails, but it is a reason to open my web browser. One might think in cases like this I gain sufficient reasons to take the unintended means. If I do, I cannot have decisive reasons to take the intended means.

Again, I do think that sometimes gaining these kinds of reasons makes a difference. When it does, though, the reasons to have the intended end and the means to that end are defeated. If the new email is sufficiently important, I should drop my intention to revise and form the intention to read the email (which will require me to form the intention to open the browser). When the new email is not important enough to force

the belief. If you gain reasons not to have the belief or lose reasons to have the belief, you might cease decisive reason to have the belief. But then you will be irrational for having the belief.

me to stop revising, I lack sufficient reasons to open the web browser. After all, I cannot do that and do the thing I am permissibly intending to do.

It seems, then, that all of the kinds of cases can be handled by my view. Since these are all of the kinds of cases that can arise, I think that the intensification will be decisive. Now my arguments here obviously rest on intuitions about the cases. I don't see any other way of proceeding. Principles have to run out somewhere. I think that I have stated the most interesting principles in the neighborhood and I think that the intuitions about cases help confirm the principles.

As it was with Intentions Attenuate, I think that intuitions about the role that facts about intentions should play in deliberation provide evidence in favor of Intentions Intensify. The Higher-Order View of modifiers and Intentions Intensify predict that the fact that I intend to revise is a reason for me to place more weight on the reasons in favor of opening my word processor than on the reasons in favor of opening my browser. This is an intuitive prediction. After all, the fact that I intend to revise should play some role in deliberation. Further, I think that it should play a *positive* role in deliberation—it should play a role in explaining why the positive case for taking the means to revising win the day.[46] When I intend to revise, the reasons in favor of opening the word processor seem more important than my reasons to open the web browser. This is because, I claim, the fact that I intend is a reason to place more weight on the reasons to open the word processor. This is further reason to believe Intentions Intensify.

Before completing the explanation of why one is irrational when means-end incoherent, it is worth pausing to consider an objection to my view raised by Kiesewetter (2017). Kiesewetter claims that my view 'cannot be sensible' on the grounds that it (allegedly) predicts that in cases of mere permissibility it is permissible to [drop the end and intend the means]. To use our concrete case, Kiesewetter's claim is that my view predicts that it is permissible to [drop the intention to revise and intend to open the word processor]. Unless there are independent reasons to intend to open the word processor, Kiesewetter does not think this combination is reasonable. Kiesewetter's argument relies on the following transmission principle (which he fails to argue for): If you have decisive reasons to ϕ and sufficient reasons to ψ, then you have sufficient reasons to [ϕ and ψ].

Although initially plausible, I think we should be dubious of Kiesewetter's transmission principle. To warm up to the point, notice that my view gives an attractive explanation of why it is unreasonable to [drop the intention to revise and form the intention to open the word processor]. It is because the sufficiency of the reasons to

---

[46] This is why I think facts about intentions intensify in the means-end case and attenuate in the consistent intentions case. One could, of course, hold that the fact that I intend to revise attenuates the reasons to take means to the unintended end. That view could generate the result that I have decisive reasons to open the word processor. It would be fine if that view were true, but it doesn't mesh well with my intuition that the fact that I intend to revise plays a positive role in explaining why the reasons to open the word processor are decisive.

form the latter intention depends on one not dropping the intention to revise. Once we appreciate this dependence, it is easy to construct cases where it appears that the decisiveness of some reasons depends on not reacting in some way that is permitted. Here are two such cases (the first one happens to be actual).

It is plausible that given that I live in the U.S., I have decisive reasons to save for my children's college education. This does not mean, though, that I have decisive reason not to move away from the U.S. Indeed, I think I have sufficient reason to move to, say, Germany. So I have decisive reason to save and sufficient reason to move to Germany. It does not follow that I have sufficient reason to [move to Germany and save]. Indeed, given the cost of university in Germany, I do not think I would have sufficient reason to save were I to move to Germany.[47]

Now for the second case. Suppose that I am training for a marathon and have a minor injury. This injury requires that I take a pill one day this week. On the day that I take the pill I mustn't run. Given my training regimen, on the days where I do not take the pill I ought to run. Now suppose it is Monday. I haven't taken the pill nor have I made a decision about whether to take it that day. I have sufficient reason to take it and sufficient reason not to. Suppose that, as a matter of fact, I will not take it that day. It's plausible that I ought to run, then. Still, the fact that I will not take it doesn't entail that I lack sufficient reason to take it. So I have decisive reason to run and sufficient reason to take the pill. It does not follow that I have sufficient reason to [take the pill and run]. On the contrary, by stipulation I have decisive reason not to [take the pill and run].

Although much more could be said, I will conclude the discussion of this objection by noting that in many dialectical contexts cases of mere permissibility would themselves provide plausible examples in tension with Kiesewetter's principle. Again, it seems to me that the data itself suggests that these are cases where one has decisive reasons to take the means but only sufficient reasons to take the end. The fact that my view is able to explain this is a virtue of the view even if it means that we must reject Kiesewetter's principle.[48]

---

[47] One might worry that this example fails because of considerations to do with time. In particular, one might think that I don't have decisive reasons to save enough for college now and sufficient reasons to move now. Instead, one might think that I have decisive reasons to save a certain amount (short of enough for college) now and sufficient reasons to move later. This is different than having decisive reasons to save and sufficient reasons to move at the same time. It could of course be this way, but it needn't be. Take next Tuesday. As a matter of fact, I will be a resident of the US next Tuesday, which happens to be the first day of the month which we can suppose is the day I need to save. Given those facts, I will have decisive reasons to save next Tuesday. But I don't think this means that I will lack sufficient reasons to move to Germany next Tuesday. Still, I won't have sufficient reason to save and move to Germany next Tuesday.

[48] This is far from the final word. Two issues are worth flagging here. As Shyam Nair has pointed out to me, it looks like giving up Kiesewetter's principle will force us to give up the principle that if one possesses decisive reason to ϕ and possesses decisive reasons to ψ, then one possesses decisive reasons to [$\phi \land \psi$]. Many will balk at this, although I note that it looks like we could modify the cases above to get a case that looks like a counterexample (just imagine I have decisive reason to move to Germany or decisive reason to take the pill today). Still, I realize that this is at the very least a dialectical cost.

To summarize my explanation: When you are means-end incoherent, I think you are irrational because Reasons-Coherence, Means-End is true:

Reasons-Coherence, Means-End: If you are means-end incoherent, then you are not correctly responding to all the reasons you possess.

There are three kinds of case. In the first, you possess decisive reason to intend to ϕ and decisive reason to believe that in order to intend to ϕ, you must intend to ψ. In these cases you are irrational because you lack an intention—the intention to ψ—that rationality requires you to have. In the second kind of case, you possess decisive reason not to intend to ϕ and/or you possess decisive reason not to believe that in order to ϕ you must intend to ψ. In these cases you are irrational when means-end incoherent for having the antecedent attitudes.

In the third kind of case, you start out possessing merely sufficient reason to intend to ϕ (and you have decisive reason to believe that in order to ϕ you must intend to ψ). When means-end incoherent in these cases, you are irrational because rationality requires you to intend to ψ. It does this because the fact that you intend to ϕ intensifies the weight of your reasons to ψ to the point of being decisive. You might continue to have merely sufficient reasons to intend to ϕ because the reasons you have to not intend to ϕ might be sufficient.

2.4.5 Akrasia

So far we've looked at one case involving just beliefs (closure), one case involving just intentions (narrowly inconsistent intentions), and two cases involving both beliefs and intentions (broadly inconsistent intentions and means-end incoherence). I'll end by discussing a third case involving beliefs and intentions: Akrasia.

Suppose I believe that I ought to ϕ but fail to intend to ϕ. I am irrationally incoherent. Since there are only two attitudes in this case, there are only two ways in which I could fail to correctly respond to the reasons I possess. I could be irrational because I lack sufficient reason to believe that I ought to ϕ. In that case, I am irrational when akratic because I have a belief that rationality requires me not to have.

Suppose I have sufficient reason to believe that I ought to ϕ. Given this assumption, if my strategy is going to succeed, it must also be the case that I have decisive reason to intend to ϕ. In other words, Enkratic Transmission-First Pass needs to be true in order for my strategy to succeed:[49]

The second issue worth flagging is that it looks like the cases I have given turn on actualism about obligation being true, which, as applied to my cases, holds whether I have decisive reason to save depends on whether I decide to stay in the U.S. and whether I have decisive reason to run depends on whether I decide to take the pill. In other work Kiesewetter argues against actualism in order to defend a different transmission principle (Kiesewetter (2015)). In order to fully vindicate my response here, I would need to engage with that work. I note, though, that my cases are interestingly different from the cases that Kiesewetter focuses on because my cases do not involve the agent doing something they ought not do.

[49] There is some recent discussion and defense of the thought that rational beliefs about what one ought to do are infallible (see Littlejohn (2012), Way & Whiting (2016), Kiesewetter (2016, 2017)). I am

Enkratic Transmission-First Pass: If you possess sufficient reason to believe that you ought to ϕ, then you possess decisive reason to intend to ϕ.

If Enkratic Transmission-First Pass isn't true, then there could be cases where I rationally believe that I ought to ϕ but rationally fail to intend to ϕ. For if Enkratic Transmission-First Pass isn't true, then there are cases where I possess sufficient reason for my belief that I ought to ϕ and either (i) possess merely sufficient reason to intend to ϕ (and thus permissibly not intend to ϕ) or (ii) possess decisive reasons not to intend to ϕ (and thus permissibly not intend to ϕ).

Enkratic Transmission-First Pass has some intuitive plausibility. As Way & Whiting (2016) point out, the following transition seems to be an indefeasible pattern of correct reasoning: RATIONAL BELIEF THAT I OUGHT TO ϕ $\Rightarrow$ INTENTION TO ϕ.[50] This pattern is correct because of the relationship between what you ought to do and facts about what you are required to intend to do. It is indefeasible because one cannot add any facts that would render the transition incorrect *assuming* one's belief that one ought to ϕ remains rational. The rationality of one's belief is of course defeasible. But if the rationality of one's belief is defeated, then making the transition is no longer correct because the input to the pattern is no longer present.

Still, one might be worried about Enkratic Transmission-First Pass for at least two reasons. First, notice that unlike all of the other transmission principles I've articulated so far, Enkratic Transmission-First Pass seems to transmit *sufficient* reasons to *decisive* reasons. This is unusual and one might worry that we can never get decisive reasons from sufficient reasons.

This would be a worry if there were cases of mere permissibility when it comes to beliefs. If I have merely sufficient reasons to believe that I ought to ϕ, then I could permissibly fail to believe that I ought to ϕ. And if I permissibly failed to believe that I ought to ϕ, then it is unclear why I would still have decisive reason to intend to ϕ.

There are two replies to this worry open to me. First, I can insist, not without plausibility, that there aren't cases of mere permissibility when it comes to beliefs. One cannot have merely sufficient reasons to believe p and merely sufficient reasons to take some other doxastic stand towards p. This is very plausible when we compare believing p and disbelieving p. It is hard to imagine a case where one could have merely

---

sympathetic to the arguments given in those papers. Nevertheless, it's important to point out that my strategy does not commit me to thinking that rational beliefs about what one ought to do are infallible. My strategy just commits me to the claim that one possesses decisive reasons to intend to ϕ when one rationally believes that one ought to ϕ. On many views of obligation, one can possess decisive reasons to intend to ϕ even if one ought not ϕ. In chapter 8, I will argue against those views and defend the view that what you ought to do is determined by the possessed reasons (cf. Lord (2015); Kiesewetter (2017) defends a similar view). Thus, if you combine the arguments in chapter 8 with the arguments in this section, you get an argument that rational beliefs about what you ought to do are infallible.

[50] The small cap forumulations refer to attitude *types*. '$\Rightarrow$' refers to a basing transition (this needn't be inferential).

sufficient reasons for believing both *p* and disbelieving *p*. The evidence is never that permissive.[51]

A harder case arises when the options are between believing/disbelieving *p* and withholding about *p*. It is more plausible that there are cases where you possess merely sufficient reasons to believe/disbelieve *p* and merely sufficient reasons to withhold about whether *p*. For example, I possess decisive reasons to believe that I am writing right now. In virtue of this, I also possess reasons to believe that I am writing right now or I am Elvis. One might think that when it comes to the disjunction, I have merely sufficient reasons to believe and merely sufficient reasons to withhold. This is bolstered by the fact that, at least before thinking of the example, I did not believe the disjunction and I seemed rational.

While it was true that I was rational before I thought of the case even though I didn't believe the disjunction, this doesn't show that I possessed sufficient reasons to withhold from believing the disjunction. Withholding is a doxastic *stance*.[52] When one withholds about *p*, one takes a stand when it comes to *p*. Before I thought of the example, I didn't rationally withhold from believing the disjunction. Instead, I just had no doxastic stance at all with respect to that proposition. Having no attitude whatsoever is not the kind of thing that there are reasons for.[53,54] It is not a reaction of mine. It is a lack of reaction on my part. Once we take this into account, this doesn't seem to provide us with a good example of epistemic mere permissibility.[55] For it does seem irrational to *withhold* belief in the disjunction. Once I consider the disjunction, I am rationally required to believe it.

Still, one might think that there are cases where withholding and believing are both permitted because it is not transparent that the evidence decisively supports one of them. Whether this is the case is a matter of great controversy. I cannot solve this controversy here. My view is this: I doubt that these cases can arise because I think that the fact that the evidence is not transparent is itself a reason to withhold. Thus,

---

[51] Again, for defenses of this thought, see Feldman (2003, 2007), White (2005), Kolodny (2007a). For detractors, see Harman (1986), Rosen (2001), Kelly (2010), Ballantyne & Coffman (2011), Schroeder (2012).

[52] See Friedman (2013, 2015) for defenses of this sort of view of withholding.

[53] Of course, one might have reasons *to make it the case* that one has no attitude at all towards a proposition. But these will always be reasons to have some reaction or other.

[54] While I think the claim in the text (about reasons-*for*) is uncontroversial, the lesson I am drawing from it is a bit controversial. This is because some think that there are reasons-against having attitudes that themselves can make it the case that we are required to lack an attitude. In fact, Schroeder (2012)'s account of reasons to withhold crucially relies on reasons-against playing this role (cf. Snedegar (FC)). For pushback on this idea, see Lord (MSb).

[55] To be clear, I am *not* claiming that it is *impermissible* for one to have no attitude. However, it doesn't follow from that that I have a permission with <TAKE NO ATTTITUDE TOWARDS <I AM WRITING RIGHT NOW OR I AM ELVIS> as its content (I will use '<CONTENT>' to pick out contents that are individuated as potential objects of thought). Compare this with my being alive. I am doing nothing impermissible by being alive (we can suppose). It doesn't necessarily follow from this that I have a permission that has as its content <BE ALIVE>. (Compare with Broome (2007b)'s notion of a source sense of requirement.) Thanks to a referee for making this salient.

I think that when one gets into one of these situations, one gains an extra reason to withhold that tips the scales in favor of withholding. This doesn't mean, of course, that one cannot have a relatively high credence in p. It just means that one cannot rationally go all the way to believing p.

For these reasons, I think that Epistemic Sufficient-Decisive Transmission is true:

Epistemic Sufficient-Decisive Transmission: If you possess sufficient reasons to take doxastic stance D towards p, then you possess decisive reasons to take doxastic stance D towards p.

If Epistemic Sufficient-Decisive Transmission is true, then in all of the cases where one rationally believes that one ought to ϕ, one possess decisive reasons to believe that one ought to ϕ. Thus, the relevant transmission principle needn't transmit sufficient reasons to decisive reasons. In every case where the antecedent of Enkratic Transmission-First Pass is true, one will possess decisive reasons to believe that one ought to ϕ. Thus, if Epistemic Sufficient-Decisive Transmission and Enkratic Transmission-First Pass are true, Enkratic Transmission is true:

Enkratic Transmission: If you possess decisive reasons to believe that you ought to ϕ, then you possess decisive reasons to intend to ϕ.

Enkratic Transmission does not transmit sufficient reasons to decisive reasons.

Even if Epistemic Sufficient-Decisive Transmission isn't true, cases of epistemic mere permissibility needn't sink my strategy. This is because I already have a way of dealing with mere permissibility. While it is right that it is hard to see why one would possess decisive reasons to intend to ϕ if one permissibly fails to believe that one ought to ϕ, it is not that hard to see why one would possess decisive reasons to intend to ϕ when one permissibly believes one ought to ϕ. If Epistemic Sufficient-Decisive Transmission is false, then I would instead think that the fact that one believes one ought to ϕ intensifies one's reasons to intend to ϕ to the point of being decisive. This would explain why it is never rational to be akratic but also why nothing is necessarily amiss if one permissibly fails to believe one ought to ϕ and also fails to intend to ϕ.

I'm sure some will be very skeptical of the claim that facts about what I believe can play this intensifying role. I am skeptical myself. But I think that this skepticism is driven mostly by a skepticism about cases of epistemic mere permissibility. Unlike intentions, it doesn't seem plausible that there are cases where we can permissibly go either way when it comes to beliefs about what we ought to do. This is why it seems implausible that we can change the weight of our reasons to intend by deciding to believe something about what ought to be done.

The second worry one might have about Enkratic Transmission is about potential counterexamples. To see a recipe for potential counterexamples, it helps to first think of paradigm cases of coming to have a rational belief about what one ought to do. In paradigm cases of coming to have a rational belief about what one ought to do, one's belief is sensitive to the weight of the possessed reasons in favor of the various options. Suppose my options are between continuing to work all evening and going home for supper. Suppose I promised to be home for supper and I have no impending deadlines. Given that I know all of this, the reasons I possess decisively support going home. When I come to rationally form the belief that I ought to go home, my belief is sensitive to facts about deadlines and facts about what I promised.

These are the paradigm cases. There are some cases that are not paradigmatic. These cases might be counterexamples to Enkratic Transmission. To take one case, imagine that a reliable friend just told me that I ought to go home for supper, but didn't tell me anything about why. One might think that this testimony provides decisive reason to believe I ought to go home even though it doesn't provide decisive reason to intend to go home. The reason why it doesn't provide decisive reason to intend to go home is that it is not the sort of thing to be a reason for intention.[56] With this case in hand, we can see what the recipe is for creating potential counterexamples: Find cases where one has some evidence that one ought to ϕ that is provided by a source that is only indirectly related to features of ϕ-ing.

The problem with this recipe, I think, is that it has too narrow a conception of normative reasons. The fact that a reliable friend told me that I ought to go home for supper *is* a normative reason for me to intend to go home for supper. In fact, given the stipulations of the case, I think it is a decisive reason for me to intend to go home for supper. We can see that this is plausible by using the earmarks I sketched in chapter 1. First, the fact that a reliable friend said I ought to go home for supper counts in favor of intending to go home for supper. I will certainly treat that fact as counting in favor of going home in deliberation. It's not as if I will think: Well that does support thinking that I ought to go home, but it doesn't speak to whether intending to go home is the thing to do whatsoever. I would be confused in having this thought.

Second, it seems like I can rationally intend to go home *for* this reason. After weighing up the considerations, I can decide to intend to go home for supper in light of the testimony. This is strong evidence that the fact about testimony is a reason to intend.

Finally, it seems like the normative power of the fact about testimony can be defeated. If another reliable friend comes along to tell me that I ought to continue working, I have much weaker reason to intend to go home for supper than before. Similarly, if the second reliable friend tells me that the first testifier is in fact not my friend, but my friend's twin brother who happens to be a compulsive liar, I will have much less reason to intend to go home for supper.[57] This pattern of defeasibility is just the pattern that normative reasons exhibit. This is strong reason to think that the fact about testimony is a normative reason.

---

[56] See, for example, Broome (2008b), McNaughton & Rawling (2011), McKeever & Ridge (2012). My discussion here mirrors my discussion in Lord (2014a, 2017b, 2010). For a similar reply, see Kiesewetter (2017).

[57] To riff on Lehrer & Paxson (1969).

Thus, I don't think that these cases are counterexamples to Enkratic Transmission. While the reasons in these cases are not paradigmatic reasons for intention, they are reasons for intention nonetheless. Further, it remains plausible that if they are sufficiently strong to rationalize a belief that one ought to ϕ, they decisively favor intending to ϕ.

When one is akratic, then, one is irrational because Reasons-Coherence, Akratic is true:

Reasons-Coherence, Akratic: If you are akratic, then you are not correctly responding to all the reasons you possess.

You will either possess sufficient reasons to believe you ought to ϕ or you won't. If you don't, then you possess decisive reasons not to believe you ought to ϕ. In that case, you are irrational when akratic because you have a belief that rationality requires you not to have. Suppose you do possess sufficient reasons to believe that you ought to ϕ. First, it follows from Epistemic Sufficient-Decisive Transmission that you possess decisive reasons to believe that you ought to ϕ. It then follows from Enkratic Transmission that you possess decisive reasons to intend to ϕ. Thus, when you are akratic in these cases, you are irrational because you lack an intention rationality requires you to have.

In this section, I have argued that at least when it comes to five paradigm instances of incoherence, it is plausible that whenever you are incoherent in these ways, you are failing to correctly respond to the reasons you possess. Given that four of these cases pose *prima facie* problems for my general strategy for accounting for irrational incoherence, I think that the preceding stories provide strong reason to think that the strategy can be fully generalized. If it can, then Reasons Responsiveness can explain why one is irrational when one is incoherent.

As I said at the top, I have proceeded under the assumption that whenever one is incoherent in these ways, one is irrational. I think this assumption is false. In the next section, I will discuss two important ways in which one can be rational even though one is incoherent. My account can explain why this is. I take this to be a virtue and not a bug.

2.5 Practical Condition Failures, High-Order Defeat, and Rational Incoherence

This section is about two different threats to the explanatory strategy just deployed. Both threats involve cases with characters who are incoherent yet correctly respond to their possessed reasons. There are two different ways to look at these threats. On the one hand, one could see them as trouble for Reasons Responsiveness.[58] One will see things this way if one holds onto the view that one is always irrational

---

[58] Cf. Worsnip (2018).

when incoherent. On the other hand, one can see these cases as casting doubt on the claim that one is always irrational when incoherent. Seen in this light, the cases are not threats to Reasons Responsiveness. In fact, when seen in this light it is a virtue of Reasons Responsiveness that it can explain what is going wrong in cases of rational incoherence. Unsurprisingly, I will argue that we should see the threats in the second way.

2.5.1 Practical condition failures

The explanatory strategy defended in the last section made liberal use of transmission principles like Closure Transmission:

Closure Transmission: If the reasons you possess decisively support p and the reasons you possess decisively support if p then q, then the reasons you possess decisively support q.

Closure Transmission has two features worth highlighting right now. First, Closure Transmission is about *possessed* reasons. Second, it not only says that *some* reason to believe q transmits from reasons to believe p and reasons to believe if p, then q, it says that *decisive* reasons to believe q transmit from decisive reasons to hold the antecedent attitudes.

The explanation for the first feature is obvious in this context. The transmission principles relevant to this discussion are transmission principles involving possessed reasons. However, this feature complicates things. I conjecture that most readers find Closure Transmission intuitively plausible. For at least some of those readers, this intuition is bound up with an intuition that Closure Transmission All is plausible:

Closure Transmission All: If there are decisive reasons to believe p and decisive reasons to believe if p then q, then there are decisive reasons to believe q.

Since Closure Transmission All is about all the reasons, it could be true for some p and some q even though no one possesses the reasons for p and if p, then q. Not so for Closure Transmission. Thus, in order for Closure Transmission to be true, the correct account of possession must support it. Purely epistemic conceptions of possession plausibly can do this just so long as Closure Transmission All is true. Suppose $[r, t]$ are decisive reasons to believe p and if p, then q. By Closure Transmission All it follows that $[r, t]$ are decisive reasons to believe q. Purely epistemic views of possession maintain that in order to possess $[r, t]$, one just needs to stand in some epistemic relation to $[r, t]$. Suppose for simplicity that the epistemic condition is knowledge. Since $[r, t]$ are decisive reasons to believe p, if p, then q, and thus q, anyone who knows $[r, t]$ will possess decisive reasons to believe p, if p, then q, and q.

As we saw above (we will see this more comprehensively in ch. 4), purely epistemic views of possession are implausible. They must be supplemented with a practical condition. Once we do that, though, the prospects for principles like Closure Transmission become dicier. This is because the practical condition looks to open the door to cases where one knows $[r, t]$ yet doesn't *possess* decisive reasons *to believe q* because one is not in a position to manifest knowledge about how to use $[r, t]$ (or p, if p, then q) as reasons to believe q.[59] I will call cases of this type cases of practical condition failures. If these sorts of cases exist, then you can have a case where one is closure incoherent yet correctly responds to all of the possessed reasons.

Are these cases possible? To start towards an answer, it will be helpful to see that a certain batch of examples that one might think fit the bill do not in fact fit the bill. Suppose that some complicated mathematical claim M entails another complicated mathematical claim N. And suppose that $[r, t]$ (i) entail M and if M, then N and (ii) I am conceptually sophisticated enough to believe $[r, t]$. Finally, suppose I know $[r, t]$. One might think that were I to believe M, if M then N yet fail to believe N I would be closure incoherent yet correctly responding to all of my possessed reasons. This is because, given how complicated M and if M, N are, I do not know how to use them (or $[r, t]$) as reasons to believe N.

Thinking of this sketch of a case reveals a crucial underdescription. For as I've described it, I haven't specified whether I am conceptually sophisticated enough to believe M and N. If I am not, then the example is spoiled in two ways. First, I am unable to believe M, if M, then N yet fail to believe N. More interestingly, I cannot possess reasons to believe M or if M, then N—a necessary condition for something being a reason to believe p for A is that A can believe p. To simplify discussion below, let's call this the Limiting Case.

With the Limiting Case in hand, let's turn to a general strategy for blocking these cases. I've started with closure for a reason. Namely, there are popular views about what it takes to possess the concept IF . . . THEN that provide materials for resisting the possibility of these cases. According to these inferentialist accounts, in order to possess the concept IF . . . THEN I need to be able to infer the consequents from antecedents.[60] One way of spelling this idea out more is to say that in order to possess the concept IF . . . THEN I must know how to infer consequents from antecedents.[61,62]

Now consider any particular case that is supposed to be a case of practical condition failure: Rohan believes p, if p, then q but fails to believe q. If the inferentialist idea is correct, then in order for Rohan to token the belief if p, then q, he has to know

---

[59] I've put the point in terms of my substantive account of the practical condition. One can substitue alternative views if one wants.

[60] See Peacocke (1993), Hale & Wright (2000), Boghossian (2003) for defense. See Williamson (2003), Horwich (2005), Schechter & Enoch (2006), Besson (2009) for objections.

[61] As far as I know no one appeals to know-how. Usually inferentialists appeal to dispositions to infer.

[62] There are two importantly different tasks inferentialism has been asked to perform in the literature. One is a task only having to do with what it takes to possess certain concepts. Another has to do with the justification of certain rules of inference. Many (e.g., Boghossian (2003)) are interested in providing an account of why we are justified in using certain rules of inference on the grounds that being disposed to use those rules is consitutive of concept possession. I am *not* trying to use inferentialism for this purpose. I am only interested in it as a view about concept possession. Thus, I don't think that my use is open to the sort of overgeneralization worries that dominate so much of the literature (see Schechter & Enoch (2006) for a nice summary).

how to infer q from p. This, though, is very close to the practical condition. Thus, if inferentialism is correct, there is some hope that you must meet the practical condition when it comes to p and if p, then q in order to even believe if p, then q.

It must be said that knowing how to infer q from p is not the know-how required by my practical condition. The know-how required is knowing how to use p as the reason it is to believe q. There are ways of knowing how to infer q from p that don't amount to knowing how to use p as the reason it is to believe q. For example, one might know how to infer q from p when p makes q statistically likely. As that example shows, however, other ways of having the relevant know-how will all be ways that intuitively don't count when it comes to possessing the concept IF . . . THEN. The know-how involved in possessing IF . . . THEN is tied up with the way in which p provides a reason for q when q is entailed by q. Because of this, I think it is plausible that the know-how involved in possessing the concept IF . . . THEN is the know-how involved in meeting the practical condition.

This, I think, gets us the result that if you meet the epistemic condition when it comes to p and if p, then q (this is an important qualification), then you possess p and if p, then q as a reason to believe q. Given Closure Transmission All, it is plausible that if you meet the epistemic condition when it comes to p and if p, then q, then you possess decisive reason to believe q.

This is not enough to vindicate Closure Transmission unless it turns out that every time one possesses decisive reason to believe p and decisive reason to believe if p, then q, one possesses p and if p, then q as reasons to believe q. But this is false. Cases where one possesses decisive misleading evidence for p or if p, then q are counterexamples. In these cases, one will possess some reasons $[r, t]$ to believe p and if p, then q but fail to possess p or if p, then q. Still, one might know how to infer q from p in these cases and thus meet the inferentialist constraint. If one fails to know how to infer q from $[r, t]$, then one might end up with a practical condition failure.

The crucial claim at this point is Double Closure Transmission:

Double Closure Transmission: If you possess $[r, t]$ as decisive reasons to believe p and decisive reasons to believe if p, then q, you possess $[r, t]$ as decisive reason to believe q.

It is far from clear that inferentialism about IF . . . THEN is going to secure Double Closure Transmission. At this point a concrete case is needed. Unfortunately, it is not entirely clear how to construct the best case. This is because of the lesson we learned from the Limiting Case. It is hard to construct concrete cases because it is unclear how to specify conditions under which one fails to meet the practical condition even though one is conceptually sophisticated enough to have the beliefs involved in closure incoherence.

Here is a stab at a case. Suppose that Sarina learns via testimony that if the amount of nitrates and phosphates is high enough in the lake near her house, then there will be a harmful algal bloom (HAB). She is not entirely sure what nitrates, phosphates, and harmful algal blooms are, but she is competent enough to have thoughts about them. Suppose further that she comes to possess decisive reason to believe that the amount of nitrates and phosphates is high enough—she reads that the amount is N (an amount she learned is high enough) in a report written by her town's environmental review board.

If this is a case of practical condition failure, it needs to be that Sarina is not in a position to manifest knowledge about how to use the fact that the expert said that if the levels are high enough then there will be a HAB and the fact that the amount is N as the reasons they are to believe that there will be a HAB. This would secure that she does not possess those facts as reasons to believe there will be a HAB. It also needs to be, though, that Sarina is in a position to manifest knowledge about how to use the fact that the expert said that if levels are high enough there will be a HAB as the reason it is to believe the conditional and be in a position to manifest knowledge about how to use the fact that the amount is N as a reason to believe that the levels are high enough. This would secure that she does possess decisive reasons to have the antecedent beliefs. This would be a bizarre psychology to have, especially if inferentialism is true. If inferentialism is true and she has the conditional belief, we know she knows how to make the inference. So her failure would have to lie elsewhere. But if she does possess the reasons to believe the premises, it's not clear where the failure will lie.

This is obviously no proof that it is impossible for Sarina to have the relevant bizarre psychology. Let's suppose she does and this is a case of practical condition failure. The next question is whether she is irrational for being closure incoherent. It is not so obvious. After all, she possesses decisive reasons for the antecedent beliefs. It doesn't look like she should give those up. But as she is right now she cannot competently form the belief that there will be a HAB. So it's unclear why she would be compelled to form the belief that there will be a HAB.[63] If that's right, though, then it's not obvious why we should think she is rationally compelled to become coherent. None of the ways for her to do that seem permitted—or, at the very least, staying incoherent seems permitted.[64]

The upshot of this discussion of closure is twofold. First, I think that it brings out just how bizarre one would have to be to land oneself in a closure case of practical condition failure. This is obvious if some sort of inferentialist view is correct. Even if it is not, I still think a psychology capable of a practical condition failure when it comes to closure is bizarre. Still, I don't want to deny that such a psychology is possible even if inferentialism is true. Once we attend to such a psychology—and

---

[63] While I think this is very plausible, it has become controversial largely because of Lasonen-Aarnio (2010). See also Pryor (FC).

[64] This argument assumes that there aren't rational dilemmas (*pace* Christensen (2007, 2010, 2013)). I am willing to countenance the possibility of dilemmas, but I think much more would need to be said in favor of the closure coherence requirement to persuade me that this case is such a case.

this is the second upshot—it is not at all clear that it is irrational in virtue of being closure incoherent. If that is right, then such cases are not clearly a threat to Reasons Responsiveness. For all that has been shown, Reasons Responsiveness can show that whenever one is incoherent *in an irrational way*, one is failing to correctly respond to the possessed reasons.

Of course, this discussion has only been about closure. There are four other incoherent combinations discussed above and many others not discussed at all in this chapter. One might worry that one or both of the upshots about closure fails to apply to those cases.

I cannot hope to even partially defend an extension of the upshots. Still, there is considerable authority I can appeal to when it comes to whether inferentialism or something like it extends to the other cases. Ralph Wedgwood has argued that in order to be conceptually competent with the deliberative sense of 'ought,' one must be disposed to intend to ϕ whenever one believes one deliberatively ought to ϕ.[65] Again, this is very close to the practical condition. If it is right, then it is plausible that whenever one meets the epistemic condition for the reason provided by the fact that one ought to ϕ, one possesses the fact that one ought to ϕ as a reason to ϕ.[66]

Matters are slightly different when it comes to the cases involving intentions. Rather than defend inferentialist theses about the *content* of the relevant states, I think the best route is to defend broadly inferentialist views about what it takes to *have the relevant intentions*. Again, there is considerable authority to appeal to. Michael Bratman has argued that in order to have the intention to ϕ, one must be disposed to take believed necessary means to ϕ-ing.[67] A natural extension of this view—an extension that helps with the case of inconsistent intentions—is that in order to intend to ϕ, one must be disposed not to intend to $\neg\phi$. Again, these claims aren't the exact claims I need in order to show that the practical condition is met, but they are very close. If they obtained it would be plausible that practical condition failures when it comes to these combinations are bizarre.

It is harder to make a case for the second upshot without paying close attention to particular cases. I won't do that here. I will leave this as a lacuna. My strong suspicion, though, is that such attention will reveal that it is not obvious that practical condition failures are irrational when it comes to the other combinations.[68]

2.5.2 Higher-order defeat

Practical condition failures threaten the claim that possessed reasons for the antecedent reactions transmit to possessed reasons for the consequent reactions.

---

[65] See Wedgwood (2001, 2006a, 2007). See Paakkunainen (2014) for further discussion.

[66] A similar dialectic as the dialectic about Double Closure Transmission will play out here. My basic response is the same.

[67] See Bratman (2013) especially.

[68] Thanks to Daniel Whiting for making it clear to me that I must add this subsection. I apologize for not doing full justice to the issues here.

Another batch of cases threaten the claim that *decisive* reasons the antecedent reactions transmit to *decisive* reasons for the consequent reactions. For reasons that will become clear in a moment, I will call these higher-order defeat cases. Unlike practical condition failures, for any particular incoherent combination, it is very easy to come up with concrete cases of higher-order defeat. Here are three that have received a tremendous amount of discussion:

Preface Paradox

Rebecca has just finished her first book. She possesses sufficient reasons to believe each individual claim in the book. However, she also knows that given her fallibility, it is quite likely that there is at least one mistake. So she fails to believe the conjunction of all of the claims in the book.[69]

Misleading Testimony

Miss Marple is a detective who is famously good at assessing evidence. Miss Marple is investigating a murder that took place at the mansion on the hill, and she takes her great niece Mabel along with her. Miss Marple and Mabel set about the mansion collecting clues. Unfortunately, in their initial sweep of the house, nothing that they learn offers any kind of significant support to any particular hypothesis about who committed the crime. As part of her training of Mabel as her apprentice, after they have finished examining a crime scene, Miss Marple always tells Mabel what her own assessment of what the evidence supports. On this occasion, Miss Marple makes an uncharacteristic error, and declares to Mabel, the clues lying around the house that you have seen up to this point support believing that the vicar did it. ((Worsnip, 2018, p. 22), inspired by Coates (2012), Horowitz (2014))

Incompetence Pills

Sally has just performed an ordinary piece of everyday reasoning. She has inferred that the Frosty Mug is still open from the claims that Southfork is open and if Southfork is open, then the Frosty Mug is open. However, moments after making this inference, her trustworthy doctor friend arrives to tell her that she has been slipped a pill that makes her incompetent at performing even the simplest bits of ordinary reasoning. She thus drops her belief that the Frosty Mug is open (while retaining the other two beliefs).[70]

---

[69] Cf. Makinson (1965). In Makinson's formulation, the character disbelieves the conjunction. I have only stipulated that Rebecca fails to believe the conjunction. If you think it matters that she disbelieves it, then you can add that detail.

[70] It is important for my purposes that the evidence provided by the doctor is misleading—i.e., that Sally has not actually taken the incompetence pill. If she did take the incompetence pill, then it is plausible that she doesn't meet the practical condition and thus doesn't possess sufficient reasons to believe the Frosty Mug is open. Cases like Incompetence Pill are discussed in many places (and usually the interest is in cases where the higher-order evidence is misleading). See, for example, Schoenfield (FC), Elga (MS).

All of these cases put pressure on transmission principles like the ones I appealed to in the last section. Rebecca's case puts pressure on the claim that if you possess decisive reasons to believe $p, q \ldots n$, then you possess decisive reasons to believe $(p \wedge q \ldots \wedge n)$. Mabel's case puts pressure on the claim that if you possess decisive reasons to believe that you possess sufficient reason to believe p, then you possess sufficient reason to believe p. And Sally's case puts pressure on Closure Transmission.

The cases exert this pressure because it looks like higher-order facts provide reasons that defeat the transmission of the weight of the first-order reasons. In Preface Paradox, the fact that Rebecca is fallible (plus the fact that the book contains a lot of claims) provides a reason for Rebecca to not believe the conjunction. In Misleading Testimony, the fact that Marple said that the evidence supports believing the vicar did it provides Mabel a reason to believe that the evidence supports believing the vicar did it. In Incompetence Pills, the fact that Sally took the incompetent pill provides a reason not to believe that the Frosty Mug is open.

If the higher-order reasons do defeat the first-order reasons in this way, then we can get cases where one is incoherent even though one correctly responds to all of the possessed reasons. Rebecca is correctly responding to her reasons to believe the individual claims by believing them. She is also correctly responding to her reasons in not believing the conjunction. So we have a case where Rebecca correctly responds to the possessed reasons even though she believes all of the conjuncts without believing the conjunction. Mabel correctly responds to all of her possessed reasons by believing that the evidence supports believing the vicar did it and correctly responds to her possessed reasons by not believing the vicar did it. Finally, Sally correctly responds to her reasons by believing that Southfork is open and if Southfork is open, then the Frosty Mug is open and also correctly responds to her reasons by dropping her belief that the Frosty Mug is open.

My reply to cases of higher-order defeat is similar to my reply of practical condition failure. First, I think that it is harder to get oneself into some of these cases than many in the literature seem to think. That said, it seems to me that these cases are possible. When they do occur, however, I do not think it is plausible that the characters are irrational.

Let's start with the cases that I think are hard to get oneself into. These are cases like Misleading Testimony. Misleading Testimony belongs to a genre of cases that have received a huge amount of attention recently.[71] These are cases where there is a mismatch between the strength of one's evidence for p and the strength of one's evidence that one's evidence sufficiently supports p. Misleading Testimony is a case where the strength of Mabel's evidence that the first-order evidence sufficiently supports p is misleading. As a matter of fact, the first-order evidence on its own does not sufficiently probabilify the claim that the vicar did it to justify believing that he did

---

[71] See Coates (2012), Horowitz (2014), Greco (2014), Worsnip (2018), Titelbaum (2015), Lasonen-Aarnio (FCa), Pryor (FC).

it. Nevertheless, Marple's testimony is very good albeit misleading evidence that the first-order evidence does sufficiently probabilify. There are also cases where the first-order evidence (ostensibly) sufficiently supports p even though there is also sufficient reason to not believe that the evidence sufficiently supports p.

A pervasive assumption in the literature about these cases is that whether or not one possesses sufficient *reasons* for belief just depends on how probable the content is given the evidence.[72] An underexplored reaction to these cases is to doubt this assumption. This is my reaction to the cases.

I grant that it is easy to come up with cases where the probability that p given the evidence for and against p is high even though the probability that the evidence sufficiently supports p is low. Similarly, I grant that it is easy to come up with cases where the probability that the evidence sufficiently supports p is high even though the evidence does not make p very likely. But this does not mean it is easy to come up with cases where one possesses sufficient reasons to be epistemically akratic—i.e., for there to be a mismatch between your higher-order beliefs about the evidence and your belief about the first-order question.

Let's start with the cases where the probability that p given the evidence is high even though the probability that the evidence sufficiently supports p is low. The facts that make the probability that the evidence sufficiently supports p low are themselves reasons to withhold belief about p. Further, if those reasons are strong enough to justify believing that the evidence doesn't sufficiently support believing p, they are strong enough to decisively support withholding judgment about whether p.

My opponents will likely complain that this is not plausible given that the evidence in fact makes p highly probable. If that's the case, then why can't one believe p? In a moment I will sketch a view that makes sense of why withholding is required even if the evidence makes p highly probable. Before I do that, though, notice the similarity between this response and a response a whole-hog objectivist might give to someone who thinks we are sometimes required to believe falsehoods because of misleading evidence. The whole-hog objectivist thinks we should only believe the truth.[73] Most reject this on the grounds that when misleading evidence is strong enough, we ought to believe falsehoods.[74] The objectivist might retort by pointing out that in these cases the truth is on the side of disbelief. If p is false, then why can't one believe $\neg p$? This, it seems to me, is analogous to my opponent responding by pointing out that the evidence makes p probable.

Still, one might think the difference between me and those who deny objectivism is that the deniers of objectivism have a natural story about why we should deviate from the truth. I have yet to provide an equally compelling story about why we should

---

[72] To be fair to participants in the literature, many are explicitly interested in the relationship between coherence norms like the Enkratic requirement and evidentialism (e.g., Worsnip (2018), Lasonen-Aarnio (FCa)). So the debate about what it is rational to do is somewhat beside the point in those discussions.

[73] See Unger (1975), Sutton (2007), Littlejohn (2012).

[74] Or, at the very least, it is permissible to believe falsehoods.

withhold despite the fact that the evidence makes p very likely. Here is one such story. According to Jane Friedman (2013, 2015), to withhold belief about whether p is to have an interrogative attitude towards whether p—e.g., wonder about p, be curious about p, or deliberate about p. When you take one of the other stances—belief or disbelief—you settle whether p. Not so with withholding. When you withhold, you commit to being unsettled by adopting an interrogative attitude.

If this is right, then reasons to withhold are reasons to adopt interrogative attitudes.[75] The considerations that provide such reasons will be of many different kinds. One source of such reasons, I claim, is higher-order evidence. Further, if such evidence is sufficiently strong to justify believing that the evidence doesn't sufficiently support p, then it provides decisive reason to withhold about p. To see how plausible this is, think of things from the deliberative perspective. The higher-order evidence certainly seems highly germane to the question of whether to believe p. I grant that it won't always sufficiently lower the probability that p, but it might demand that one form an interrogative attitude about whether p. In other words, it might demand that one keep the question of whether p open in deliberation. I think that is what it does in the cases that have been of interest in the literature on epistemic akrasia.

While this is obviously far from a complete vindication, it does provide a rationale for thinking that sometimes we ought to withhold despite the fact that the first-order evidence makes p probable. Higher-order evidence seems to bear on whether we should leave the question of whether p open. Further, when it is strong enough to demand that we believe that the first-order evidence doesn't make p probable, it is plausible that we should leave the question of whether p open. To do this is to withhold, according to Friedman's plausible view about withholding.

This leaves the other batch of akrasia cases. These are cases like Misleading Testimony where the first-order evidence does not sufficiently support believing p but one receives misleading higher order evidence that sufficiently supports believing that the first-order evidence sufficiently supports believing p. In these cases withholding is not as obviously relevant as in the first sort of cases (which is why some, like Worsnip (2018), focus on such cases). It still might be relevant, though. This is because the first-order evidence might provide decisive reason to withhold about the question about what to believe about what the evidence supports. Consider a version of Mabel's case where she and Marple thoroughly examine every surface of the house and discuss the evidential force of each bit. By the end Mabel is convinced that the house offers up nearly no evidence at all about who did it. To her shock Marple says that the evidence in the house clearly supports believing the vicar did it. In this version of the case, it does not seem implausible to me that Mabel should withhold on the higher-order question because the first-order evidence provides decisive reasons to do so.

---

[75] See Friedman (2015). For reasons I spell out in Lord (MSb) I don't think this is exactly right, but it is near enough for current purposes.

On the other hand, the case might proceed like this.[76] It might be that they go through the house in silence. Mabel notices several things that seem clearly relevant but they point in competing directions. Further, she is not quite sure which directions all of them point. Does the placement of the decanter support thinking the butler did it or the valet? She's not sure. As a matter of fact, the first-order evidence is a wash, but this is not clear to Mabel. Marple then asserts that the evidence clearly supports thinking the vicar did it. In this version of the case, it seems to me that Mabel has decisive reason to believe the vicar did it.

Worsnip (2018) grants that the higher-order evidence could require Mabel to believe the vicar did it, but argues that this is not guaranteed. He does this by arguing that the higher-order evidence will, at least sometimes, be stronger evidence for the higher-order question than it is for the first-order question. Given this, he thinks there must be some case where the higher-order evidence is strong enough to justify believing the higher-order claim but not strong enough to justify believing the first-order claim.

I am willing to grant that the higher-order evidence might raise the probability of the higher-order claim more than it raises the probability of the lower-order claim.[77] This doesn't necessarily settle the relevant question, though. It might be that the probability of the higher-order claim is higher than the probability of the lower-order claim and yet there is still not a mismatch in which epistemic reactions Mabel has sufficient *reason* to have. When it comes to the sufficiency of Mabel's reasons, I don't think it is plausible there can be a mismatch between the higher-order question and the lower-order one. A full defense of this must be saved for another day.

So much for the cases that I am skeptical about. The other two forms of cases are more likely to occur. Cases like Preface Paradox can arise. However, when they do I do not think it is plausible that one is irrational for being incoherent. The reasons one possesses for each conjunct are sufficient and withstand reexamination (we can assume). So it doesn't look like one is required to give up any individual belief. But facts about one's own fallibility give one strong reason to withhold about the conjunction. Given this, it doesn't look like believing the conjunction is permitted. But then it is very unclear why one would think that one is rationally required to be coherent.

Again, this assumes that there are not tragic rational dilemmas. While I am willing to consider this possibility, much more would need to be said about the relevant coherence requirement to make me believe this is one such case.

Similar things can be said about cases like Incompetence Pills. We can assume that the possessed reasons for the antecedent attitudes are decisive and withstand

[76] For what it is worth, this is how I understood Worsnip's presentation of the case when I first thought about it.

[77] It should be said that Worsnip does not explicilty argue that the relevant gap in support arises because of a difference in probabilifying. However, he does appeal to claims about likelihood. It seems to me like he is implicitly relying on what I want to deny. It also should be noted again that Worsnip is arguing that there is a conflict between coherence and the evidence so it might be that his target is not my sort of view.

reexamination (and, of course, that the pill is known not to target the method one used to acquire them). But the fact about the pill gives one decisive reason to withhold judgment about the conclusion. So it doesn't look like one is permitted to be coherent. So one is rational in being incoherent.

While this section has left many interesting questions open and has not provided a full defense, I hope that it has shown that there are plausible things to be said in favor of Reasons Responsiveness. Not only are there resources to exploit to limit the number of cases of conflict between possessed reasons and coherence, when those resources are tapped there is still something plausible to be said in favor of rational incoherence.

2.6 The Myth of the Coherent

The explanation offered above of why one is always irrational when incoherent (and why one is always coherent when rational), is very similar to things that have been said by Joseph Raz and Niko Kolodny (see, e.g., Raz (2005b), Kolodny (2005, 2008a,b)). Both Raz and Kolodny are skeptical about coherence requirements of rationality—requirements that directly require coherence. Despite the similarities between my view and theirs, I think there is a very important dissimilarity that should be explicitly pointed out. I'll explain this after briefly spelling out Raz and Kolodny's views.

Both Raz and Kolodny are skeptics about coherence requirements of rationality. However, they see the appeal of the coherence requirements, and thus a big part of their debunking strategy is an explanation of why we are tempted to think that there are coherence requirements. Their explanation holds that we are tempted by coherence requirements because it is true that, whenever we comply with all the requirements of reason, we are coherent, and that whenever we are incoherent, we don't comply with the requirements of reason. Thus, the coherence facts fall out of more basic requirements of reason. Since all we wanted to account for were the coherence facts, there is no reason to posit requirements that directly require coherence.

This is obviously very similar to my view. However, it must be stressed that for Raz and Kolodny, the requirements of reason are completely independent of *rationality*. The requirements of reason, on their view, are determined by *all of the reasons*. They assume that these requirements are the ones that determine what we ought to do and believe. They think that rationality is about coherence. They thus become skeptics about rationality by being skeptics about coherence.

A skeptic about rationality I am not. Indeed, one main aim of this chapter is to show that Reasons Responsiveness can plausibly account for the data important to recent discussions of rationality without incurring the most damning problems for rival accounts. A big part of my approach is a rejection of the type of coherentism advocated by wide-scopers. In this way I am like Raz and Kolodny. Moreover, like Raz and Kolodny, I think that there are more basic requirements that explain the coherence facts. Finally, like Raz and Kolodny, I think that these more basic requirements are a function of normative reasons. However, and this is the rub, unlike Raz and Kolodny, I think that these more basic requirements *just are* the rational requirements. Raz and Kolodny's mistake is that they have too narrow a conception of what the options are. We can embrace their skepticism about coherence requirements without embracing skepticism about rationality.

Finally, it is worth pointing out that the explanation given in the last section *doesn't* immediately entail that the wide-scope requirements are false. In fact, if we hold a certain kind of deontic logic (standard deontic logic happens to be a member of this kind), then it turns out that requirements like Action Schema will *entail* the wide-scope requirements. Let me quickly explain.

The relevant principle holds that if you are required to ϕ and ϕ entails ψ, then you are required to ψ—call this Inheritance. If Inheritance is true, then the requirements appealed to in the previous section will entail the wide-scope requirements.[78] To see this, just note that in all the worlds where one complies with all the requirements appealed to above, the conditionals that the wide-scope requirements scope over are true. This fact, together with Inheritance, entails the wide-scope requirements—i.e., entails we are required to make those conditionals true. This shows two things. First, Raz and Kolodny must reject Inheritance in order for their hostility to the truth of wide-scope requirements to make any sense at all.[79] Second, and more importantly, my explanation of the fact that if you are rational, then you are coherent isn't hostile to the truth of the wide-scope requirements. Indeed, it might be positively friendly to the truth of the wide-scope requirements.

If I were to embrace Inheritance and thus embrace the thought that requirements like Intention Schema entail the wide-scope requirements, then I can answer a popular objection to myth views. This objection starts by asking us to imagine someone that is incoherent—means-end incoherent, say. Suppose it is our monarch loving fool (who intends to become a European monarch and believes that in order to become a European monarch he must become King of France). The thought behind the objection is that he is making not one but two rational mistakes. He is irrational for having that end and having that means-end belief, but he is *also* irrational for being incoherent. If he were to form the intention to become the King of France, he would be rectifying one of his rational mistakes. He'd be more rational than he was before. This doesn't seem compatible with myth views because they seem to predict that his only rational mistakes are having the end and the means-end belief.

---

[78] Just to be clear, I'm not endorsing Inheritance. It leads to lots of problems. I mention it here because I think it is important to notice that the so-called myth view requires supplementation if it is going to help explain why the wide-scope requirements are false. For a fuller discussion, see Broome (2007b, 2013), Lord (2018b).

[79] I draw out this point more in §8.2 in chapter 8 and especially in Lord (2018b).

However, as we've seen, myth views aren't incompatible with the truth of wide-scope requirements. In fact, the requirements that myth theorists hold dear to their hearts might actually entail the wide-scope requirements. If they do, then the intuition that drives the objection can be captured. It's true that our poor fool makes three mistakes and it's true that he is more rational after he forms the intention. However, the myth theorists adds, he is still irrational for having the end and the means-end belief. So even if he can comply with *a* requirement of rationality by forming the intention, he isn't complying with all of the requirements.[80]

2.7 Back to the Beginning

Recall what the debate between the wide- and narrow-scoper is about. In the first place, it is about what the best explanation is of why you are irrational when you are incoherent. That is to say, it is about what the best explanation is of the fact that it is necessary to be coherent in order to be rational.

Narrow-scopers think that being coherent is necessary, but not sufficient. However, as the wide-scopers are keen to point out, the narrow-scope view seems to deny sufficiency in an implausible way. It doesn't seem like you are always rationally required to intend to ψ when you intend to ϕ and believe that in order to ϕ you must ψ. Sometimes you are rationally required to give up one of the antecedent attitudes instead.

Wide-scope requirements are compatible with saying that sometimes you should give up the antecedent attitudes. The wide-scope view—the view that holds that all the requirements are wide-scope—holds that the narrow-scope view is implausible because, in fact, being coherent is both necessary and *sufficient* for being rational. The failures of the narrow-scope view directly motivate the claim that being coherent is both necessary and sufficient for being rational.

This itself is implausible for a variety of reasons. Most fundamentally, it's implausible because it seems obvious that sometimes rationality requires us to hold particular attitudes or perform particular actions. Without some alternative account of why being coherent is insufficient, perhaps we should throw up our hands, be wide-scopers, and call it a day.

---

[80] As a referee pointed out to me, appealing to Inheritance to reply to this objection might be to throw the baby out with the bath water. For if Inheritance is true, then anytime anyone does anything, one will do something they ought to do. If Inheritance is true, then any requirement entails an infinite amount of other requirements. While this is true, if the view defended in this chapter is true, then there is something that distinguishes the wide-scope requirements. Namely, they pair up in an interesting way to the way that reasons transmit. This distinguishes them from the infinite amount of pure spandrels. Further, given plausible views about what constitutes *good reasoning* (see Broome (2013), McHugh & Way (2016)), the patterns of transmission the wide-scope requirements track will be the patterns one must instantiate in order to be a minimally good reasoner. Thus, those who are incoherent are bad reasoners. This doesn't vindicate the deontic significance of the wide-scope requirements, but it helps explain the fascination with them.

This is no longer our epistemic position. For I've offered another account of why being coherent is insufficient. It's because what's rational is determined by the reasons you possess, and the reasons you possess sometimes require you to hold particular attitudes or perform particular actions. Moreover, my view lacks the problems that the traditional narrow-scope view has. My view not only is compatible with the claim that sometimes you are rationally required to give up the antecedent attitudes, it can give a principled explanation of what needs to obtain for this to be the case.

My view can also explain the initial data, which is that being coherent is necessary for being rational. This is because it's plausible that when you are incoherent you are not correctly responding to some of the reasons you possess. I think this provides strong initial motivation for Reasons Responsiveness. It shows that Reasons Responsiveness is a view that should be taken seriously. Whether it is the view we should accept at the end of the day will depend on whether we can develop the ideology it deploys in a way that bears theoretical fruit. The rest of the book will aim to show that we can do just that. We will start with what it takes to possess normative reasons.

PART II

Possessing Reasons

Summary of Part I and Introduction to Part II

Part I provided initial motivations for Reasons Responsiveness—the claim that what it is to be rational is to correctly respond to the possessed normative reasons. Chapter 1 laid out the main motivations for the book and introduced the main moving parts. Chapter 2 was primarily situated in the metaethical literature about rationality. It motivated Reasons Responsiveness by showing that it can handle the data that motivates rival coherentist views. I argued that Reasons Responsiveness makes plausible predictions about when one is irrationally incoherent (and when one is rationally incoherent) without incurring the vices of coherentist views.

In Part II, I turn to defending my view of possession. I will do this over the course of two chapters. In chapter 3, I will defend a view about the epistemic condition on possession. I will do this via process of elimination. I will consider several different divisions between views in the literature. I will argue for one side of each division. The conclusion is that the epistemic condition is being in a position to know. Chapter 4 begins by arguing that meeting the epistemic condition is not always sufficient for possession. This is because we sometimes meet the epistemic condition but fail to appreciate the normative significance of the relevant fact. In order to fill this gap, we must meet what I call the practical condition on possession. I argue that the practical condition is being in a position to manifest knowledge about how to use the reason as the reason it is. In the end my view of possession is that what it is to possess a reason r to ϕ is to be in a position to manifest knowledge about how to use r as the reason it is to ϕ.

3

What it is to Possess a Reason
The Epistemic Condition

3.1 Introduction

As we saw in the first half of chapter 2, it is important to pay heed to the distinction between the reasons there are and the reasons that are possessed. There are many reasons for each of us to react in a variety of ways that fall outside of our ken. All of the following facts, for example, are reasons for me regardless of whether I am aware of them: the fact that the baby is crying is a reason to believe she is hungry, the fact that Arzak is in Spain is a reason to intend to go to Spain, and the fact that the light is green is a reason to drive through the light. That said, some of the reasons there are can play certain explanatory roles in virtue of the fact that they are possessed. For example, I might possess a reason for believing the baby is hungry because I *hear* her crying, I might possess a reason for intending to go to Spain because Anthony Bourdain *informed me* that Arzak is in Spain, and I might possess a reason to go through the light because I *see* that the light is green.[1] I must have some type of access to the facts that are the reasons that I possess, even though I don't need to have access to facts that are merely reasons for me to believe, intend, and do things in order for those facts to be reasons.[2]

As we also saw in chapter 2, it's plausible that only the reasons you possess bear on the rationality, justification, or reasonableness of your actions and attitudes. If r is a reason to ϕ that you don't possess, r can't contribute to the rationality of ϕ-ing. If I have no access to the fact that the baby is crying but I believe she is hungry, my belief is not made rational, if it's rational at all, by the fact that the baby is crying. Conversely, it's plausible that if I possess some reason, r to ϕ, then r affects the rationality of ϕ-ing. The reasons you possess seem to be *difference makers* when it comes to what it's rational for you to believe, intend, and do.

---

[1] The fact that all of the epistemic relations I cite here entail that I know the facts in question is no accident. As we'll see, everyone agrees that I meet the epistemic condition on possessing reasons when I know the reason. It's very controversial whether knowing the reason is also necessary.

[2] As I pointed out in some notes in chapter 2, this is somewhat controversial. See Gibbons (2010, 2013), Kiesewetter (2017, 2018) for dissent.

Even if we take it for granted that only the reasons we possess contribute to the determination of which reactions are rational, it is still an open question what it is to possess a reason. In chapters 4 and 5, I will offer an answer to this question. In the end, I will argue that what it is to possess a reason r to ϕ is to be in a position to manifest knowledge about how to use r as a reason to ϕ.

I will split the discussion up into two chapters. This chapter is about the *epistemic condition* on possession. It's universally recognized in the literature that in order to possess r, one must stand in some privileged epistemic position with respect to r. There is, as one might expect, tremendous controversy about which epistemic relation is the privileged one. In this chapter, I will argue that the relevant epistemic condition is *being in a position to know*.

In chapter 4 I will expand on the argument from chapter 2 that meeting the epistemic condition isn't enough. In addition to being in one's epistemic ken, reasons that are possessed need to be within one's *practical* grasp. What this comes to is also a matter of controversy. I will argue that for a reason to ϕ to be in one's practical grasp is for one to be in a position to manifest knowledge about how to use that reason to ϕ. I will argue further that being in a position to know the fact that provides the reason is a *background condition* on being in a position to manifest the relevant know-how.[3] Thus, in the end I will argue that what it is to possess a reason r to ϕ is to be in a position to manifest knowledge about how to use r to ϕ.

I will not start by directly arguing for this view. Instead, I will split the discussion into two parts. In this first part, I will focus solely on the epistemic condition. In the first part of chapter 4, I will focus on the practical condition. I will then argue directly for my view. I proceed in this less direct way because it is the easiest way to engage with existing discussion. Further, by proceeding in this way, it will be easier to provide independent arguments for different parts of my view. This will make it clear that each part receives support independently of the other parts.

In order to focus discussion, it's important to be clear about what theories of possession have to account for. This is the only way to assess the virtues and vices of the various theories. It's plausible that there are at least two tight connections between the reasons you possess and the reactions that are rational. On the one hand, it's plausible that if some reason r to ϕ contributes to the rationality of ϕ-ing, then you possess r. If a reaction of mine is irrational because I don't take into account some reason, then I better have some access to that reason. And, on the other hand, it's plausible that if I possess r to ϕ, then r makes a difference to the rational merits of ϕ-ing. Of course, this doesn't mean that possessing r always *changes* the rational status of ϕ-ing. It's just

---

[3] To be clear, being in a position to know is a background condition on being in a position to *manifest* the know-how. I am not claiming that one must be in a position to know the relevant facts to *have* the relevant know-how.

that it has an effect on the rational merits—i.e., the merits of ϕ-ing from the point of view of rationality—of ϕ-ing.[4] I propose we accept this as a working hypothesis.[5]

Working Hypothesis: You possess reason r to ϕ iff r affects the rational merits of ϕ-ing.

Working Hypothesis provides two ways to test the plausibility of views of possession. First, it's a major strike against a theory if it's possible to satisfy the conditions that the theory proposes for possessing r to ϕ even though, intuitively, r doesn't affect the rational merits of ϕ-ing. Second, it's a major strike against a theory if it's possible for r to intuitively affect the rational merits of ϕ-ing even if you don't satisfy the conditions the theory proposes for possessing a reason. These will be the main tests we will use to evaluate theories.

The plan for this chapter is this. In §3.2, I will introduce a taxonomy for the various views about the epistemic condition. There will be three different divisions between the views. In §3–5, I will argue against my opponents' views by arguing for one side of each division. In the end, only one view will be left—viz., that you possess r only if you are in a position to know r.

3.2 A Taxonomy

Many views about the epistemic condition have been defended. I will present the views by explicating three key divisions that separate the various views. Each view takes a stand on each division.

High Bar v. Low Bar

The first division is between High Bar and Low Bar views of the epistemic condition.[6] High Bar views hold that in order to possess a reason, you have to stand in some positive epistemic relation with the reason. Two popular High Bar views hold, respectively, that you possess r only if you know r and you possess r only if you rationally believe r. The High Bars are knowledge and rationality. To make reference

---

[4] It does this, I think, by contributing to the weight of the set of possessed reasons to ϕ.

[5] I am serious when I say that this is just a working hypothesis. I thus do not mean to trivialize the debate that was the focus of chapter 2. As I see the dialectic, chapter 2 significantly raises the probability of Working Hypothesis, which is to say that it significantly raises the probability that possessed reasons are constitutively tied to rationality. Still, I don't mean Working Hypothesis to conceptually rule out that Broome et al are correct about the nature of rationality.

Further, I don't mean to trivialize debates about whether there is really more than one perspectival notion. Sylvan (2016, MSb), for example, suggests that there are apparent reasons and possessed objective reasons. Sylvan argues that rationality is a function of apparent reasons and justification is a function of possessed objective reasons. He thus denies Working Hypothesis (although he accepts a nearby claim about justification). Since I think rationality and justification come to the same thing, I agree with Sylvan about justification but disagree about rationality. I won't adjudicate this here, but will note that Sylvan could agree with everything said below as applied to justification instead of rationality.

[6] This terminology comes from Schroeder (2011b), but the debate goes back to at least Feldman (1988).

easier, I will call the first view P→K and the second view P→RB.[7] Other possible high bar views will be introduced below. For now it's only important to know what it is to be a high bar view.

Low Bar views, on the other hand, place a low bar on the epistemic condition. They don't hold that you have to necessarily stand in some positive epistemic relation to r in order to meet the epistemic condition for possessing r. The most obvious low bar view holds that you possess r only if you believe r. For reasons that Schroeder (2008, 2011b) makes vivid, the best low bar view seems to be that you possess r only if you have a presentational state with r as its content.[8] Presentational states are states that represent their contents as being true. Schroeder holds that not only are beliefs presentational states, but perceptual states are as well. We'll call these low bar views P→B and P→Pres, respectively.

Holding v. Non-Holding

A second division has to do with whether the epistemic relation essentially involves having some mental state with the consideration that is the reason as the content. Theorists who are committed to Holding views think that the epistemic relation essentially involves having some mental state with the reason as the content. All of the views we've looked at so far, both High Bar and Low Bar, are holding views.

There are possible non-holding views, though. Consider the familiar distinction between *ex post* and *ex ante* rationality. You are *ex ante* rational to believe that p just in case p is supported by sufficient justifiers. However, this isn't enough to have an *ex post* rational belief that p. In order to have an *ex post* rational belief, there must be an appropriate connection between your belief and the justifiers of the belief. The important point here is that p can be *ex ante* rational for you to believe even if you don't believe it.[9] So one possible (high bar) non-holding view is that you possess r only if r is *ex ante* rational for you to believe—P→EAR.

There is an analogous distinction to be made with knowledge. Just as you can have *ex ante* rationalization for p without *ex post* rationalization for p, you can be in a position to know p without knowing p.[10] This opens up the door to another non-holding view. Namely the view that holds that you possess r only if you are in a position to know r—P→PTK.

---

[7] In general, I'll use 'P→x' to refer to views that hold that you possess r only if you stand in the x relation to r. Those in the literature tend to use '=' instead of '→.' This is because they have apparently thought that standing in the epistemic relation is both necessary and sufficient for possessing a reason. As we saw in chapter 2, there are compelling reasons to think this is false. Hence my use of '→.'

[8] I won't discuss Schroeder's reasons in depth. My arguments will work against any low bar view (e.g., the view that the relation is just belief).

[9] Consider this trivial example. I am *ex ante* rational in believing that I'm typing right now. *A fortiori*, I am *ex ante* rational in believing that I'm typing right now or I'm Elvis. At least before I thought of the example, I didn't believe the disjunction even though I was *ex ante* rational in believing it.

[10] The example in n. 9 can equally well illustrate this distinction.

Factive v. Non-Factive

The final division in our taxonomy is between factive views and non-factive views. Factive views hold that the epistemic relation you must bear to a reason is factive. An epistemic relation is factive just in case you can only stand in that relation to p when p is true. Non-factive views hold that you can stand in the epistemic relation necessary for possession to propositions that are false.

So far, only P→K and P→PTK are factive views (given the widely held assumption that one can have false rational beliefs). P→B, P→Pres, P→RB, and P→EAR are all non-factive views. However, you can still think rationality is as high as the bar goes even though one can only possess truths as reasons. For you could hold that the epistemic relation is rational true belief, or *ex ante* rationalization in a truth—P→TRB and P→TEAR.[11]

The following table represents our taxonomy.

Table 3.1. Epistemic Condition Taxonomy

View	High Bar v. Low Bar	Holding v. Non-Holding	Factive v. Non-Factive
P→B	Low Bar	Holding	Non-Factive
P→Pres	Low Bar	Holding	Non-Factive
P→RB	High Bar	Holding	Non-Factive
P→EAR	High Bar	Non-Holding	Non-Factive
P→TRB	High Bar	Holding	Factive
P→TEAR	High Bar	Non-Holding	Factive
P→K	High Bar	Holding	Factive
P→PTK	High Bar	Non-Holding	Factive

I will argue that the correct view has to be a High Bar, Non-Holding, Factive account by arguing first against Holding views, then against Low Bar views, and then against Non-Factive views. Since there are two High Bar, Non-Holding, Factive views—P→TEAR and P→PTK—I will end by arguing for P→PTK over P→TEAR.

3.3 Against Holding Views

Holding views of the epistemic condition all share a commitment to the view that the epistemic relation involves being in a mental state that has the reason as its content. I think that Holding views are too restrictive. Consider the following case.[12]

---

[11] Another route, one that avoids some of the objections I'll press below, is to hold that justification itself is factive. This is argued for by Unger (1975), Sutton (2007), Littlejohn (2009, 2012).

[12] For similar cases, see Neta (2008)'s counterexample to P→K and the main cases in Gibbons (2006, 2013).

Out of the Ordinary

Each morning I casually peruse a magazine while I eat my breakfast. I am doing this on Monday morning. As I'm doing this, my wife tells me that she has an unusual schedule that day. Given her unusual schedule, I need to pick up my son from school (this is something she almost always does because we have agreed that that is one of her daily tasks). She speaks clearly when she tells me these facts, and she is a mere 10 feet from me. However, I am engrossed just enough in the *Newsweek* I'm reading to not process the information. Given the fact that picking up my son is not one of my usual tasks, I believe that I don't need to pick him up that day. My son doesn't get picked up on time.

Let's focus on the rationality of my belief that I don't need to pick up my son that day immediately after my wife tells me this information. Intuitively, this belief is not rational. After all, my wife just told me some very pertinent information that decisively supports thinking I need to pick him up. Further, it seems like my wife can *criticize me* for continuing to believe that I don't have to pick up my son given that she just provided me with that pertinent information. This criticism seems to be a rational criticism. She could—and likely would—point out that I am being idiotically careless. She thus could aptly point out that I am being irrational given my perspective. The information she provided me is staring me straight in the face (calling me straight in the ear?).

However, I don't have a mental state that has <MY WIFE CAN'T PICK HIM UP> as its content.[13] Thus, according to Holding views, I don't possess that reason. By Working Hypothesis, then, that reason shouldn't affect the rational merits of my belief that I don't need to pick him up. Moreover, it seems that all the other reasons I possess sufficiently support the proposition that I don't need to pick him up. Holding views seem to entail, then, that my belief that my schedule is not unusual is rational. My wife would disagree.

A defender of the Holding accounts might reply to these intuitions by agreeing that there is *some* rational failure here but insist that the real source of my failure at the breakfast table is that I possess decisive reasons to listen to my wife. Thus, what is irrational about my breakfast table routine is that I fail to listen to her, not that I continue to believe that she will pick my son up. Since it's plausible that I do know some things that provide me with strong reasons to listen to my wife, this reply certainly muddies the waters in a way that's helpful to Holding views. That said, I don't think that this response is adequate.

The reason why I think this response fails is that it will not be able to cover the full range of cases. First, consider a variant on the original case. Suppose that I have strong reason to believe that my wife will be speaking to her sister on the phone for

---

[13] Throughout the book I will use '<CONTENT>' to pick out contents that are individuated as potential objects of thought (it would be fine by me to think of these as Fregean propositions).

the next 20 minutes. While she is on the phone she remembers that she needs to tell me that she can't pick up my son that day. So she comes into the room and says just what she says in the original case. In this version of the case, I submit, I don't have the strong reasons I normally have to listen to everything my wife says. After all, she's on the phone and I have some reading I want to do. Nevertheless, I submit, it's irrational for me to believe that she will be picking up my son later that day at the moment after she says what she says. She provided that information in a clear way and I was just not paying enough attention. At least at the beginning of her assertion directed at me, it was reasonable to not listen to the content. But this doesn't get me off the hook for what was said. She could still criticize me for continuing to believe that I don't have to pick up my son. If this is right, then the defense of Holding accounts fails to fully generalize. It's not true that all cases of the relevant type are cases where one fails to respond to known reasons to generally pay attention.

To further bolster this conclusion, think of cases where you get unexpected information from strangers. Suppose Sam is at a pub and needs to go to the bathroom.[14] The door is locked when she gets to the bathroom. A fellow patron says to her—again, in a clear voice from a reasonable distance—that the toilet has been acting strange lately and that it's wise not to use it. While she hears the fellow patron's voice, she is thinking about something else just enough not to register the information. The door opens, she goes in, and an unpleasant time is had. Was it rational for Sam to believe that the toilet was okay when she walked into the bathroom? I submit that it was not. Her fellow bar goer gave her all the information she needed to rethink her plan. If a group of Sam's friends saw this scene (and heard what the patron said), they would not think Sam was totally off the hook when she comes out of the bathroom in distress. They could rightfully point out that the stranger told her not to go in there. For this reason she should have known better. Therefore, she was irrational (or at least less than fully rational).

However, it's not plausible that Sam possessed strong reasons to generally listen to everything that was said by her fellow bar goers. Suppose that on the way to the bar another bar goer said something to her about their pet hamster. Was she irrational in not listening to that? No. So, again, I think that the reply on behalf of the Holding account does not generalize enough. The best explanation of why Sam is irrational is that she came to possess the reason to believe that the toilet was not working even though she didn't have a presentational attitude with that as its content.

Non-holding views can easily account for why Sam and I are not rational. It's because I possess the reasons provided by my wife's testimony and Sam possesses the reason provided by the stranger's testimony. P→EAR (and P→TEAR) holds that I possess those reasons because those propositions are *ex ante* rational for me. P→PTK holds that I possess those reasons because I'm in a position to know them.

---

[14] This riffs on a case from Gibbons (2013).

On non-holding views, inattentiveness does not get one off the hook for taking into account reasons that one has what we'll call *broad access* to. For now I won't analyze what broad access comes to. We've seen two proposals—viz., being *ex ante* rational and being in a position to know. What's important right now is that there is good evidence that the reasons you merely have broad access to affect the rational status of your beliefs (and other attitudes and actions). Non-holding views can account for this, holding views cannot.

3.4 Against Low Bar Views

I have not given you enough information yet to evaluate the plausibility of low bar views. For I have not given you a low bar analysis of what the necessary and sufficient conditions are for something to be a reason you possess. It's certainly false that all the contents of all your beliefs or presentational states are reasons you possess for everything whatsoever. That is to say, I've told you the epistemic condition that must be met, but I haven't told you what condition must be met to make the content a possessed reason.

While there hasn't been a tremendous amount of discussion on this score, it's clear what the intuitive idea is that low bar theorists are attracted to.[15] The basic idea is that the content p of one of your presentational states is a reason to ϕ only if p is an objective reason to ϕ if p is true.[16] Given Working Hypothesis, low bar views thus hold that the contents of all of your presentational attitudes that are objective reasons if true affect the rationality of your reactions.

This prediction seems obviously false.[17] Let's just think about the epistemic case. Suppose r is a reason to believe p. Plausibly, what it means for r to affect the rationality of believing p, in this case, is for r to put you in a better evidential position with respect to p when you possess r. But it's incredibly plausible—indeed, some call it a truism[18]—that you aren't put in a better evidential position with respect to p when you *irrationally* believe r. So if Working Hypothesis is true, then low bar accounts are in trouble. Since Working Hypothesis is intuitively plausible, low bar accounts are in trouble from the beginning. Moreover, I think that Working Hypothesis can be bolstered by thinking about the relationship between the objective weight of reasons—i.e., the weight reasons have when weighed against all of the

---

[15] See Schroeder (2007, 2009b), Way (2009, 2010a, 2012), Parfit (2011), Vogelstein (2012).

[16] There is disagreement about whether the analysis should be in terms of counterfactuals or some other type of conditional. All extant views, with the exception of Vogelstein's, at least sometimes cash things out in terms of counterfactuals. I strongly suspect that counterfactual analyses are false for general reasons. In personal communication Schroeder has expressed serious doubts about whether a counterfactual analysis can work.

[17] Neta (2008) presents counterexamples to many low bar views that exploit this weakness.

[18] For example, Feldman (1988), Schroeder (2011b).

reasons—and the subjective weight of reasons—i.e., the weight reasons have when weighed against all of the reasons that are possessed.[19]

The intuitive idea driving the argument is something like this: Reasons for belief are the types of things that rationalize beliefs. The point of coming to possess reasons to believe is to come to be in a better position with respect to what you're rational in believing. Minimally, gaining p is to come to be in a better position with respect to p itself. This is an essential role that possessed reasons play.

Here's the argument:

(1) If p is an objectively sufficient reason to believe p and you possess p, then you possess a subjectively sufficient reason to believe p.

(2) If p, then p is an objectively sufficient reason to believe p.

(3) If p, then if you possess p, then you possess a subjectively sufficient reason to believe p.

(4) If you possess a subjectively sufficient reason to believe p, then you are *ex ante* rational in believing p.

(C) If p, then if you possess p, then you are *ex ante* rational in believing p.

If this argument is sound, then low bar views are false. For suppose p. Suppose you believe p, but p is not *ex ante* rational for you. The low bar accounts hold that you possess p. But it follows from the contraposition of the conclusion of the above argument that if you are not *ex ante* rational in believing p when p is the case, then you don't possess p.

Recall the basic idea behind the argument is that an essential role that possessed reasons play is putting one in a better position with respect to what it's rational to believe. The argument extends and precisifies this basic idea. It does this by making claims about the connection between the subjective weight of certain reasons that are possessed and the objective weight of those reasons. The objective weight of some reason r is just the weight it has when weighed against all the reasons. Few reasons always have sufficient objective weight. But a special class of reasons for belief do. Namely, all of the truths. For any true proposition p, p is an objectively sufficient reason to believe p. This is not to say that there aren't objective reasons to not believe truths. It is to say, though, that the objective reasons to believe falsehoods are always objectively insufficient. This seems correct. If you were omniscient, you would only possess sufficient reason to believe the truths. You would never possess sufficient reason to believe something false, even though you would possess lots of reasons to believe false things (and to withhold belief in true things).

So when p is true, p will be an objectively sufficient reason to believe p. If this is right, then it seems very plausible that if you were to come to possess p, you would

---

[19] The word 'weight' does not figure in any of the premises of the argument below. Recall from chapter 1 that sufficiency is a central notion in my account of weight.

gain a sufficient reason to believe p. It's hard to see what good comes from gaining p as a reason if you can't even be rational in believing p!

You might not be convinced by this because you might be suspicious of the claim that p is a sufficient reason to believe p—i.e., you might doubt (2). After all, you can never become rational in believing p by *inferring* p from p. But why not if p is a sufficient reason to believe p? The answer is that in order for the output of a pattern of inference to be rational via the inference, one must be rational in believing the inputs. But if you are already rational in believing p, then certainly no new justification will be *transmitted* via the inference. And if you're not already rational in believing p, then justification won't be transmitted via inference because there is no justification to transmit in the first place. But this very plausible story is compatible with p being sufficient reason to believe p. It just shows that you can't get a rational belief that p via an inference from p.[20]

You still might not be satisfied with this. For suppose p, suppose you possess p and suppose the argument above is sound. Thus, it follows that p is *ex ante* rational for you. What are your sufficient reasons for believing p? Suppose the answer to this is simply p. If this is right, then it's very plausible that you can come to believe p because of p. This follows from the plausible principle that if the members of some set of reasons you possess S sufficiently support p, then you can come to believe p because of the members of S. If this is right, then in this type of case it must be that you can believe p because of p. Some find this to be implausible.

This is an interesting challenge that I can't fully deal with here without further resources that would take us too far afield. I talk about these issues extensively in chapter 7 using resources defended in chapters 5 and 6. I'll say a few words here about how I think we should meet this challenge and how this relates to the current dialectic. I think the answer is that you can base your belief that p on p, even though you can't do this via inference. Such basing is always uninferential.[21] In the paradigm case, you come to believe p because of p when you see p. Roughly, you base your belief on p not because you infer p from p, but because you come into perceptual contact with the fact that p, which stands in the right causal relationship with your belief to become the basis of the belief. If this is right, then you can base your belief that p on p, even though this is never inferential.[22]

---

[20] For similar remarks, see Sylvan (2016, p. 366).

[21] Uninferential here just means not-inferential. You might not like this terminology (I don't). I use this terminology in order to avoid confusions that inevitably arise when you use the more common non-inferential. Chapter 7 discusses this more.

[22] I think there is uninferential basing even in cases where you don't come into the kind of contact with the fact that p that you do when you see p. To give the most extreme case, I think you can believe p on the basis of p even when your belief was formed inferentially. This is because I think that what it is to base a belief that p on some reason r is for r to sustain the belief. What it is for r to sustain A's belief that p is for A to be disposed to drop the belief if A loses r. I think you can be disposed to drop your belief that p if you lose the reason constituted by p. And when you are, you base your belief that p on p (at least partially).

So, roughly, this is how I see the terrain. p is a sufficient reason to believe p. You can never be *ex post* rational in believing p *because* you infer p from p. This isn't particularly problematic because we have a principled explanation for why not. If you are going to be rational in believing p because you infer it from something, you'll have to be rational in believing the things you infer it from.[23] But you can still form a rational belief that p because of p. This happens in cases of uninferential belief forming processes like perception. As I see it, the main burden of the current challenge is to motivate (i) that p is a sufficient objective reason to believe p (when p) and (ii) that when you possess p you can sometimes base a belief that p on p. I believe I have met this burden.

The final comment I'll make about this challenge is about our dialectical situation. I think that low bar theorists only really gain an advantage over high bar views if they agree with the essentials of the view about basing I just briefly sketched. The best low bar view, P→Pres, gains an advantage over high bar views precisely because it holds that you possess p whenever you perceive p. And this allows a straightforward explanation of why it is that you possess the same reasons for belief in both the case of veridical perception and the case of non-veridical perception.[24] But this works only if you think that you can come to have a rational belief that p by basing a belief that p on p in some of those cases. Moreover, it's very implausible that you can gain justification by basing a belief that p on p by inferring p from p. So my opponent will have to toe the same line I just tried to toe.[25]

(3)—if p, then if you possess p, then you possess subjectively sufficient reason to believe p—follows from (1) and (2). (4)—the claim that if you possess sufficient reason to believe p, then you are *ex ante* rational in believing p—follows from my analysis of rational permission in chapter 1. Since I think (1) and (2) are quite plausible, I think the conclusion is quite plausible as well.

As it happens, the main defender of the low bar views, Mark Schroeder, explicitly recognizes that he has to deny Working Hypothesis (see Schroeder (2011b)). So my defense is incomplete without considering what he has to say about it. I don't think anything he says should give us much pause.

Before I start, I should be clear about what Schroeder hopes to achieve and what I hope to achieve. Schroeder is interested in *simply making room* for low bar accounts by casting doubt on what he sees to be the best two routes to high bar views. I think

---

I think this is actually a virtue of the view, for it allows one to explain certain otherwise troubling cases of memorial knowledge.

[23] As I say in n. 22, it might be that *once* you justifiably infer p from some other propositions you're rational in believing, you are then in a position to uninferentially base that belief on p.

[24] Of course, it's not clear at all if this is that much of a virtue, or even if it's a virtue at all. Williamson (2000, ch. 8) argues that it's a bug that leads to skepticism. I agree even though I also think it's a virtue in some ways. But certainly it's been popular to think it's a virtue since at least 1983 when Cohen & Lehrer (1983) appeared. This is the main topic of chapter 7.

[25] This is exactly how the low bar story goes in Schroeder (2011b).

that he achieved in that aim. So I am not attacking the main thesis he was advancing. Rather, I want to consider whether the considerations he adduces in favor of the Low Bar view (even if they were just in defense of making room for the view) are strong enough to justify seriously doubting Working Hypothesis. I don't think they are. This might not spoil his point in Schroeder (2011b), but it certainly bears on the larger debate between us.

His case is broken up into two parts. In the first part he considers an indirect argument for a high bar account. The argument is indirect because it runs through an auxiliary premise—viz., that positing a high bar is the best way to explain why one is not put in a better evidential position with respect to the consequences of p when one irrationally believes p. He resists this claim by arguing for an explanation of the fact that you aren't in a better evidential position with respect to p's consequences when you irrationally believe p that is compatible with low bar views. The second part of his case involves a direct argument for a high bar view. It's direct because it appeals directly to intuitions about whether certain characters possess reasons. He argues that such intuitions are unreliable. With this précis in mind, let's turn to more of the details of each part.

The Indirect Argument

Schroeder, following Feldman (1988), thinks that it's a truism that when you're *ex ante* irrational in believing p, you aren't in a better evidential position with respect to the consequences of p in virtue of believing p. Feldman at least flirts with the thought that you can get from this and something like Working Hypothesis to some high bar view. Schroeder's target isn't exactly the inference to a High Bar view from something like Working Hypothesis and our truism. Rather, Schroeder is concerned with showing that positing a high bar isn't needed to *explain* the truism. Schroeder's strategy is to explain the truism in a way that's compatible with low bar views. By doing this, he shows that low bar views are compatible with the truism, and thus we shouldn't think accounting for the truism weds us to high bar views.[26]

Schroeder's explanation is that whenever you irrationally believe p, p is guaranteed to be *completely* and *generally* defeated. The defeat will be general because it will be irrational to treat p as a reason for anything (even though it will still be a reason you possess for lots of things). The defeat will be complete because p will have no weight whatsoever (even though it will still be a reason). If this is right, then our truism is explained—when you believe p irrationally, you won't be in a better evidential position with respect to p's consequences. This explanation is compatible with low bar views because it's compatible with you possessing p when you irrationally believe p. It's just that despite the fact that you possess p, it will be irrational to give p any weight whatsoever when it comes to anything, including the question of whether p. Thus,

---

[26] Schroeder's arguments, then, directly confront Neta (2008)'s arguments against low bar views (although Neta's paper is not explicitly discussed).

Schroeder denies that if you possess a reason r to ϕ, r affects the rational merits of ϕ-ing, which is the left-to-right direction of Working Hypothesis.

I'm not that interested in explaining the truism. In fact, I suspect Schroeder's explanation is correct. But it also doesn't speak against Working Hypothesis at all. This is because, in giving his explanation, Schroeder doesn't have to make any claims about the relationship between the reasons you possess and your evidential position. So while his explanation is compatible with low bar views, it is also compatible with high bar views.

While it's obviously necessary for low bar theorists to offer some explanation of the truism that's compatible with their view, it is very, very far from being a sufficient defense of their view. Working Hypothesis still seems like an incredibly plausible hypothesis about the connection between the reasons you possess and rationality. It's hard to see at this point why we should sever the connection between possessing p to believe q and p affecting the rationality of believing q.

Think of it this way: The claim that whenever you irrationally believe p, p will be completely and generally defeated doesn't speak to the relationship between irrational beliefs and possession. It is compatible with this explanation of the truism that you do in fact possess p when you believe it irrationally. But mere compatibility is not good reason to sever possession from a high bar. At best Schroeder's argument shows that a reason to wed possession with a high bar does not obtain.

The Direct Argument

Schroeder anticipates this, and thus tries to argue that we shouldn't trust our intuitions about the relationship between possession and a high bar. In particular, he thinks we shouldn't trust our intuitions about negative existential reason claims. He thinks we shouldn't trust our intuitions about these claims because they are unreliable.

His favorite illustrative example of this is Lehrer & Paxson (1969)'s Tom Grabit case. In that case, you see someone who looks just like Tom Grabit steal a library book. The fact that you saw this is a reason to believe Tom stole the book. However, Tom happens to have a twin brother, Tim, who is a kleptomaniac. This fact is, intuitively, a defeater of the first reason. The orthodox opinion about this case is that the fact that Tom has a kleptomaniac for a brother makes the fact that you saw someone that looks just like Tom steal a book no reason at all to believe Tom stole the book.[27] Schroeder rightfully points out this is a mistake. For imagine that Tom and Tim have another identical sibling, Tam, who is also a kleptomaniac. In that case, it seems you have even less

---

[27] This opinion is seen as orthodox, I think, because of the tremendous influence of Pollock & Cruz (1999)'s discussion of *undercutting defeat*. They define undercutting defeaters as defeaters that make it the case that the original reason is not a reason at all once defeated. The Tom Grabit example is supposed to be a paradigm of this kind of defeat.

reason to think Tom stole the book. So you must have some reason in the case where it's just Tom and Tim.[28]

Once again, I agree with Schroeder. I think we should be wary of our negative existential intuitions about reasons in particular cases. We are quite likely to get it wrong for roughly the reasons Schroeder elucidates. However, I think that at least in the larger dialectic Schroeder is misapplying these lessons here.

The rub is this: The current debate doesn't turn on the intuitions Schroeder shows are problematic. Our task is *not* to evaluate whether there is a reason in some particular case. We *already know* that Schroeder's low bar view predicts there will be some cases where you will possess p as a reason to believe q even though p has *no weight whatsoever*. This itself is implausible.[29] We needn't worry about our unreliability at picking which cases are cases of this type. This is what our unreliable negative existential intuitions are trying to track. They're trying to track when it is that something has no weight whatsoever. We aren't very good at this, as the Grabit examples show. Let Schroeder pick the cases, then. We can ask whether, in those cases, you possess p to believe q even though p has no weight whatsoever. It doesn't seem like you do. It seems like, if we have any grip on possessing reasons at all, you can possess p only if it affects the rationality of believing p's consequences.[30]

For these reasons I am not moved to abandon a high bar view because of what Schroeder says. He doesn't attack Working Hypothesis. He merely argues for an explanation of the truism that is compatible with denying Working Hypothesis and argues that our intuitions about when there aren't reasons are unreliable when applied to particular cases. I agree with the main claims of both parts of Schroeder's argument. The catch is that they're neither here nor there.[31]

---

[28] Schroeder also offers an debunking explanation of why we are unreliable. I don't go into that here because I agree with it and it's irrelevant to the point I want to make.

[29] It is also worth noting that it seems like this commits Schroeder to denying standard conditional probabilistic accounts of evidence. This is because, for Schroeder, reasons for belief are always evidence. But if we can possess a reason r to believe p that has no weight whatsoever, then it's implausible that the conditional probability of p given r will be greater than the probability of p on its own. After all, if it were greater, then it would be plausible that the reason would have some weight. Thanks to Tom Kelly for pushing me to mention this.

[30] Here's another way to put the point for those who are familiar with the details of Schroeder's paper. He tries to show that if you don't argue for a high bar view with an indirect argument through the truism (which he shows won't work because his explanation of the truism is compatible with low bar accounts), then the only way to argue for it is through appeal to negative reason existential intuitions. This conditional is false. The Working Hypothesis gives us an independent way to test the theories. Moreover, its plausibility doesn't rest on negative reason existential intuitions. Negative reason existential intuitions are thus neither here nor there.

[31] It must be noted that Schroeder makes explicit in Schroeder (2008, 2011b) that his main motivation for going low bar is to account for some vexed data in the epistemology of perception. Specifically, he holds that low bar views can give the most elegant explanation of why both the deceived and the non-deceived have rational perceptual beliefs. I agree that his low bar view provides a nice explanation. Importantly for our purposes here, Schroeder at least implicitly recognizes the intuitive power of Working Hypothesis because he sees it as a major obstacle for providing his explanation. Despite the elegance of his view about the epistemology of perception, I am unmoved by what he actually says with respect to Working

3.5 Against Non-Factive Views

Non-factive views hold that one can stand in the epistemic relation with propositions that are false. Non-factive views fail because they cannot account for the fact that if you possess some reason r to ϕ, then you can ϕ because of r.

Let me be clear that we are interested in a particular kind of explanation. There are many true explanations of any particular reaction. The type of explanation I am interested in here is what I call a *normative achievement* explanation. The best way to cotton onto this type of explanation is by example. I believe the heat is on in my office. It's also warm in my office and cold outside. There is a tight relationship between my belief that the heat is on and these other facts. I believe the heat is on in my office *because* it's warm in my office and cold outside. This explanation is true partly because I correctly inferred that the heat is on in my office from the claims that it's warm in my office and cold outside. This is why my inferred belief constitutes a kind of *rational achievement*. To put it another way, this is why my belief is *rationally creditworthy*.

To take another example, I intend to exercise three times a week. It's also true that exercising three times a week is very good for my health. There is a tight relationship between my intending and the fact about my health. Indeed, I intend to exercise three times a week *because* it is very good for my health. This is why my intention is a rational achievement. In other words, this is why my intention is rationally creditworthy.

When a reaction of mine can be explained via a normative achievement explanation, I react *for* normative reasons that I possess. And when I react for normative reasons that I possess, my reaction is sensitive to the reasons I possess *qua* the normative reasons that they are. This is why reactions that are done for reasons that I possess are rational achievements and are rationally creditworthy. It is because it is an achievement to react to possessed reasons as the normative reasons that they are.

Right now I will rely on an intuitive understanding of this type of explanation. Some of the features will become more clear as we go. In chapters 5 and 6, I will defend an analysis of what it is to react for a possessed reason.

Here is an argument for why non-factive views cannot account for the tight connection between possessing a reason r to ϕ and being able to ϕ because of r:

The Argument from Reacting for Reasons

(1)   If you possess reason r to ϕ, then you can ϕ because of r.
(2)   If you can ϕ because of r, then r.
C.   Thus, if you possess reason r to ϕ, then r.

(1) is intuitively plausible. It is also widely accepted. This is because it is widely accepted that one can *react for* possessed reasons.[32] When one does this, one reacts

Hypothesis. I won't go into the issues in epistemology of perception because it would take us too far afield. Much of chapter 7 is about this issue.

[32] See, for example, Neta (2008), Schroeder (2011b), Comesaña & McGrath (2014).

because of the possessed reasons. For now I will take (1) for granted; two subsections from now I will consider a challenge to (1).

I'll break the following discussion up into two subsections. In the first subsection, I will defend (2). As we will see, my strategy for defending (2) involves positing two different ways one can react for a reason. In the second subsection, I will use this distinction to defend (1).

3.5.1 For (2)

(2) maintains that when a reaction of yours is a rational achievement in virtue of the fact that you reacted because of a particular reason r, r is true. A very general reason for thinking this is true is that in general 'x because y' statements are factive. That is to say, in general 'x because y' can be true only if y (and x for that matter).

A more specific reason to believe (2) is that particular normative achievement explanations seem factive. Consider some cases:

Normal Colloquium

Today there is a department colloquium. It is at the usual time for such events, 4:00 pm. I notice that it is 3:55, and is thus time to walk over to the building where the colloquium is taking place. On my way I see my friend Dan. He asks me why I'm going to Robertson Hall. I tell him it's because colloquium starts at 4:00.

Unusual Colloquium

Today there is a department colloquium. This talk, however, is not at the usual time. It is at 4:30. I am unaware of this fact (despite receiving numerous emails that said so). I believe it is at the usual time. So at 3:55 I start walking towards Robertson Hall. I see Dan, who asks me why I'm going to Robertson. I tell him it's because colloquium is at 4:00.

My explanation of why I'm going to Robertson Hall makes sense in Normal Colloquium, but is puzzling in Unusual Colloquium. Suppose Dan reads his emails more carefully than I do, and he calls me out in Unusual Colloquium. He says, 'No. Colloquium is not at 4:00 today. It's at 4:30.' It would be odd, I think, for me not to retract my claim after Dan says this. It would be odd, that is, for me to reply like this: 'Really. Well I guess I can go back to my office. Still, I was going to Robertson because colloquium is at 4:00.' Instead, it would be much more natural for me to retract my earlier claim and say 'Well, I thought colloquium was at 4:00. Thanks for setting me straight.'

As it happens, many disagree with my diagnosis of what's going on in Unusual Colloquium.[33] These philosophers think that it would be very odd for me to decide

---

[33] There has been extensive discussion of these issues. Much of it is inspired by Dancy (2000). See, for example, Dancy (2004b), Millar (2004), Hornsby (2007), Mele (2007), Lord (2008), Miller (2008), Littlejohn (2012), Comesaña & McGrath (2014), Fantl (2015). The best discussion I know

that the reason why I walked to Robertson isn't that the colloquium is at 4:00 even after I find out that the colloquium isn't at 4:00.

The issue is vexed. Those who deny (2)—let's call them non-factualists—do not deny that I would retract once Dan corrected me in Unusual Colloquium. But they think there is an independent explanation of this compatible with non-factualism. The explanation, they say, is that once I learn that the colloquium is at 4:30, I don't want to implicate that I still believe it's at 4:00. Thus, I'll weaken my report by saying things like 'I thought colloquium was at 4:00.' Why I would do this, claim the non-factualists, can be explained on basic Gricean grounds. I don't want to implicate that I think p when I think $\neg p$. Thus, I use the weaker 'I thought . . . ' construction. This explanation of the retraction data is compatible with non-factualism.[34]

At first blush, this doesn't seem to be enough. This is because these implications should be cancelable. Of course I do implicate that I believe that colloquium starts at 4:00 when I say 'I'm going to Robertson because colloquium starts at 4:00.' And I don't when I say 'I'm going to Robertson because I thought colloquium starts at 4:00.' But if it's really the case that I'm going to Robertson because colloquium starts at 4:00, then I should be able to say as much *while also* canceling the implication. I should be able to felicitously say, for example, 'I no longer believe that colloquium starts at 4:00, but I was going to Robertson because colloquium starts at 4:00.' To my ear this still sounds awful.

Suppose I'm right and these things are infelicitous. This is some reason to think that non-factualism is false—perhaps even a very strong reason. But, the non-factualist might contend, this isn't the end of the story. For we know that there are some true sentences that are never felicitous. Perhaps the most famous examples are Moorean absurdities. For example, it's never felicitous for me to say (nor is it ever rational for me to believe) 'I believe I'm writing, but I'm not writing.' This very well might be true, though. So the non-factualists might take recourse in the fact that Moorean absurdities are infelicitous even though they can still be true. Perhaps our normative achievement explanations are like that, at least in the bad cases.

Perhaps. But as Littlejohn (2012) has pointed out, this is too quick. For there is at least one test for truth that Moorean absurdities pass that our normative because explanations don't seem to pass. Namely, when it comes to Moorean absurdities, there is nothing wrong with third-personal reconstructions. There is nothing wrong with saying 'EL believes he is writing, but he's not.' However, it still seems infelicitous to say 'EL was going to Robertson because colloquium starts at 4:00, but colloquium

of takes place in the comment thread of a Pea Soup post written by Clayton Littlejohn. See http://peasoup.typepad.com/peasoup/2010/02/thoughts-as-motivating-reasons.

[34] Here's Mark Schroeder in the aforementioned Pea Soup post: 'The fact that when I don't believe that p, I can't aptly describe Sue's reason for ϕ-ing by saying that her reason for ϕ-ing was that p, doesn't show that her having the motivating reason for ϕ-ing that she did doesn't consist in her bearing the had-as-her-motivating-reason relationship to the proposition that p. It just shows something about the further commitments of saying "her motivating reason was that p".'

starts at 4:30.' This, I think, make the prospects of saving the non-factualists by drawing some analogy with Moorean absurdities much dimmer.

For these reasons, I am far from convinced that non-factualists can save their theory from the data provided by our explanatory practices. Still, I also do not think that the linguistic data should settle the matter. This is because the concepts that we are using to theorize about the relevant phenomena are technical. While I think that English allows us to track the phenomena by and large, there is not compelling reason to think that English will track it perfectly. This is why the linguistic data is unlikely to settle the debate between factualists and non-factualists.

A better tack, I suggest, is to investigate the roles that reacting for possessed reasons is supposed to play. Similarly, we should investigate what exactly we need in order to maintain the thought that there is some sense in which my reason for going to Robertson is that colloquium starts at 4:00 in Unusual Colloquium. When we do this, I think it will become clear that there are two very different relations in play, and the one that is associated with possession is factive.

To warm up to this, let me consider some of the standard objections to factualism. I think the core intuition driving non-factualism is a sort of internalism about the reasons we base our reactions on. The thought is that the reasons for which we react supervene on our non-factive internal states. The internalist idea that drives non-factualism is that the mere fact that colloquium starts at 4:00 in Normal Colloquium can't change whether I act for the same reason in Unusual Colloquium and Normal Colloquium. Nor does it matter that in one case I have a true belief and in the other I have a false belief, and likewise for the fact that in one case I know that it starts at 4:00 and in the other I don't. None of these facts make a difference to which reasons I act on when I start walking towards Robertson.[35]

One way to motivate the internalist view is to think about things first-personally. It *seems* like I have unproblematic access to the reasons for which I react. When I start walking towards Robertson, it seems bizarre to think that I could be easily mistaken about why I was leaving my office, walking down the stairs, etc.[36] But, the thought goes, this is only true if the internalist view is true. For it will seem like I know what my reasons are whether my beliefs are true or not. So in order to hold onto the thought that we have unproblematic access to the reasons for which we act and believe, we better be internalists.

This general line of argument is often bolstered by the thought that to deny the internalist view would be to embrace the thought that one doesn't react for any reason

[35] Williams (1981) famously says that the truth-value of the beliefs we reason from don't affect the structure of the explanation given. This idea runs rampant in the philosophy of action. As we'll see, I think it's true for a particular kind of action explanation, but not the kind theorists of rationality should be primarily interested in.

[36] Of course, the linguistic data—especially the retraction data—seems to cut against this. I'm probably blinded by theory, but I have a hard time feeling the pull of these thoughts. In general, I think we are apt to be mistaken about all sorts of things internalists think we have unproblematic access to.

in the bad cases.[37] And this suggests that when one is in the bad case one's actions and beliefs are simply inexplicable.[38] This thought, I think, is what Dancy is getting at when he says that non-internalist views are 'too harsh.'[39]

The internalist picture emerging, then, holds that I act for the same reason in both Normal Colloquium and in Unusual Colloquium. The general strategy for defending this picture relies on claims about what Normal Colloquium has in common with Unusual Colloquium. Both seem to be the same from the inside and my action in both seems to be rationalized by the claim that colloquium starts at 4:00.

As we will see in chapter 6, these sorts of similarity arguments bear a striking resemblance to the so-called argument from illusion in the philosophy of mind. That argument seeks to show that the kind of mental state we are in when we have veridical perceptual experiences is the same kind of mental state we are in when we have non-veridical experiences (e.g., hallucinations and illusions). Arguments from illusion are shaky. I think the sort of similarity arguments given in favor of internalism are equally shaky. I will just sketch part of my view here. I will go through this in great detail in chapter 6.

The most important aspect of my view right now is that I think that in both cases I go to Robertson on the basis of the consideration that colloquium starts at 4:00. Thus, I think that there is a way in which I act on the basis of the consideration that colloquium starts at 4:00 (*pace* the first objection to factualism above). This is because in both cases my *rationale* for going to Robertson is the consideration that colloquium starts at 4:00. Rationale explanations are not factive. It seems felicitous to say 'EL's rationale for going to Robertson was that colloquium starts at 4:00, but he didn't read his emails closely enough so he was mistaken about that.' Why is this? It is because rationale explanations are in the business of making attitudes and actions *intelligible*. And intelligibility comes cheap. Some consideration can make an attitude or action intelligible even if it is false. When r is one's rationale for ϕ-ing, I will say that r is one's *motivating reason* for ϕ-ing. By contrast, when we can provide a rational achievement explanation of someone's ϕ-ing by citing r, I will say that one ϕs for a *normative reason* to ϕ.[40]

The rub—and this is really important—is that rationale explanations *don't* entail normative achievement explanations. It might be that my rationale for walking to Robertson is that colloquium starts at 4:00; it doesn't follow that my action is a rational achievement.[41] This is because intelligibility comes cheap. The acts and attitudes of

---

[37] Some non-internalists embrace this conclusion (see especially Alvarez (2010), Littlejohn (2012)).

[38] Although Littlejohn thinks you don't act for a reason in the bad case, he doesn't think your actions are completely inexplicable.

[39] This was in conversation. For more, see Littlejohn (2012).

[40] This is just a stipulation of terminology at this point. I will argue in chapter 6, though, that this is the best use of the terms 'motivating reason' and 'reacting for a normative reason.'

[41] It should be noted that Dancy (2004a) makes the exact opposite inference. He infers that normative achievement explanations aren't factive because something like rationale explanations aren't factive and

even the most deluded amongst us can be made intelligible. That is, their reactions have rationales. But it is implausible that their reactions are rational achievements or are rationally creditworthy.[42]

At the very least, this is a substantive issue, and thus non-factualists need to argue that the rationale explanations entail the normative achievement explanations. This shows that the following position is open to the factualist: The epistemic condition on possession is factive. This follows from the fact that possessing r as a reason to ϕ enables one to ϕ because r. Nevertheless, one can have r as their rationale for ϕ-ing even when $\neg r$. Rationale explanations are what non-factualists are getting at. Their mistake is to think that rationale explanations are the same thing as normative achievement explanations.

The flip side of this is that non-factualists might agree that there are these two kinds of explanations and then use the distinction to argue against (1). They might say, that is, that the only kind of explanation associated with possession are rationale explanations. This would give them a way out of the argument even though they accept (2) as a claim about normative achievement explanations. Given this, let's now turn back to (1) to see if possession is linked with rationale explanations or normative achievement explanations.

3.5.2 Back to (1)

Everyone agrees that there is some *Acting On Condition* when it comes to reasons that are possessed.

Acting On Condition: If A possesses r as a reason to ϕ, A can ϕ on the basis of r.

The reason why the Acting On Condition is plausible is that it is plausible that we can *use* the reasons we possess. That is, it is plausible that when we possess some reason to ϕ, we can be guided by that reason in ϕ-ing. The last section argued that there are two different ways to understand ϕ-ing on the basis of r. On the one hand, r might be my motivating reason for ϕ-ing—it might be my rationale for ϕ-ing. On the other hand, I might ϕ for r qua normative reason to ϕ—I might ϕ because of r. This gives us Acting On Rationale and Acting On Achievement:

Acting On Rationale: If A possesses r as a reason to ϕ, A can ϕ with r as her rationale for ϕ-ing.

Acting On Achievement: If A possesses r as a reason to ϕ, A can ϕ for r qua normative reason to ϕ.

---

they entail the normative because explanations. He doesn't argue for this beyond reporting intuitions I (and others) simply don't have.

[42] It's natural to respond to this by claiming that the problem with the deluded is not with the relation they stand in with their motivating reasons. Rather, it is a problem with *what* their motivating reasons are. This is a tempting thought, but as I argue in the next subsection and in chapter 5, this will not ultimately work.

Right now Acting On Rationale is not in dispute, and I will grant it for the sake of argument here.[43] The question is whether Acting On Achievement is also true. I hold that Acting On Achievement is also true. In this subsection, I will present two arguments against the claim that only Acting On Rationale is true.

The first reason why we need more than Acting On Rationale is that there is also a Reverse Acting On condition.

> **Reverse Acting On Condition:**   If A can ϕ on the basis of r (in the sense relevant to the Acting On Condition), then A possesses r as a reason to ϕ.

The Reverse Acting On Condition holds that having the ability to ϕ on the basis of r in the way required by the Acting On Condition is sufficient for possessing r as a reason to ϕ. The Reverse Acting On Condition is plausible because it seems like having the ability to stand in the relation required by the Acting On Condition is sufficient for possession. After all, if I can be guided by some consideration r in the way that is required by the Acting On Condition, then r is the kind of thing that can rationally guide me. If it is, then it seems like I possess r. If you think that only Acting On Rationale is true, then you'll flesh out the Reverse Acting On condition via Reverse Acting On Rationale.

> **Reverse Acting On Rationale:**   If A can ϕ with r as her rationale for ϕ-ing, then A possesses r as a reason to ϕ.

If Acting On Achievement is also true, then we can flesh out the Reverse Acting On condition via Reverse Acting On Achievement:

> **Reverse Acting On Achievement:**   If A can ϕ for r qua normative reason, then A possesses r as a reason to ϕ.

Reverse Acting On Achievement is plausible. Reverse Acting On Rationale is surely false. Thus, in order to hold on to the Reverse Acting On condition, we'll need to appeal to reacting for normative reasons. Let me explain each claim in turn.

If you are able to ϕ because of r, then it's very plausible that you possess r. In order for r to be able to provide a normative achievement explanation of your ϕ-ing, it has to be that you are in a position to be sensitive to r as the reason that it is. Given this, if r is completely outside of your epistemic ken, or if you don't even implicitly see the appropriate connection between r and ϕ-ing, then it's hard to see how r could provide a normative achievement explanation of your ϕ-ing.

On the the other hand, it's not plausible that if you are able to ϕ with r as your rationale, then you possess r as a reason to ϕ, at least not on any view about possession on the table. Take the consequent affirmer. Let's call him Jimmy. Jimmy knows if p,

---

[43] In chapter 6, I will suggest that it is not particularly important to hold that one always reacts for a normative reason when one reacts for a motivating reason. Right now I will assume this is true, though.

then q and he's just learned q. He then infers p from q and if p, then q. It's plausible that his rationale for believing p is q and if p, q. But he doesn't thereby possess q and if p, then q as reasons to believe p. On high bar views (at least as we've understood them), some reason r to ϕ is a reason you possess only if r is an objective reason to ϕ. And obviously q and if p, then q aren't objective reasons to believe p in this case. On low bar views, some reason r to ϕ is a reason you possess only if r is an objective reason to ϕ if true. But by stipulation q and if p then q are not objective reasons to believe p if true because they are true and they aren't objective reasons to believe p. So Reverse Acting On Rationale is false.

The non-factualist might object to this argument by claiming that the problem with Jimmy is not that q and if p, q are his rationales for believing p. The problem is that q and if p, q are not reasons to believe p. Jimmy shows that Reverse Acting On Rationale is false, they might continue, but he doesn't show that the Reverse Acting On Rationale+ is false:

> **Reverse Acting On Rationale+:** If A can ϕ with r as her rationale for ϕ-ing and r is a reason to ϕ, then A possesses r as a reason to ϕ.

The non-factualist is right that Jimmy's case is not a counterexample to Reverse Acting On Rationale+, but Jimmy+'s case is a counterexample to Reverse Acting On Rationale+.[44] Jimmy+ believes that Barcelona won. He also believes that Real Madrid lost. As it happens, it is true that if Barcelona won, then Real Madrid lost. Thus, in the actual world the fact that Barcelona won is a reason to believe that Real Madrid lost. However, Jimmy+ did not infer that Real Madrid lost from the fact that Barcelona won and if Barcelona won, then Real Madrid lost via modus ponens. Instead, he inferred that Real Madrid lost from the claim that Barcelona won using inference rule Explosion:

> **Explosion:** For any p, infer <REAL MADRID LOST> from p.

The claim that Barcelona won is Jimmy+'s rationale for believing that Real Madrid lost. It is also a reason to believe that Real Madrid lost. But it doesn't follow that Jimmy+ possesses the claim that Barcelona won as a reason to believe that Real Madrid lost. He might not know anything about the relationship between Barcelona and Real Madrid. He might irrationally think, for example, that Real Madrid plays in the second division (if only!) and thus that Barcelona and Real Madrid very rarely play each other. Given all of this, it is implausible that Jimmy+ possesses the claim that Barcelona won as a reason to believe that Real Madrid lost. He is not at all sensitive to that claim qua the reason that it is.[45]

---

[44] This kind of case has been in the epistemology literature for a long time (see chapter 5 for many citations). It is the centerpiece of Turri (2010). Cases of this kind will play a large role in chapters 5 and 6. See also Lord & Sylvan (FC).

[45] There is more to be said about this argument. I won't say it here because there is an extended discussion of this issue in chapters 5 and 6 (see §§5.5.3 and 6.4.2).

That's the first reason to be skeptical that only Acting On Rationale is true. The second reason is that once you adopt a non-factive understanding of the Acting On Condition, you've got to give up on the idea that those in favorable epistemic environments are in an importantly different situation from those in the depraved epistemic environments. In particular, you're committed to thinking that the facts that, in the favorable case, you know, or truly believe, or truly justifiably believe, aren't important when it comes to the explanation for why you are rational. For you could have possessed the relevant reasons even if you didn't stand in any of those relations with the reasons that explain why you are rational. This is because the explanation of your actions and attitudes relevant to whether you're rational are just rationale explanations. But the rationale explanations are the same in the favorable conditions and the depraved conditions, even if the normative achievement explanations are different.

I'm assuming here that the Acting On Condition is important because it tells us something important about what it is to *correctly respond to reasons*. This is because it tells us the connection between possessing reasons and a certain kind of normative explanation. Plausibly, what it is to correctly respond to a reason r to ϕ when you ϕ is for r to (at least partially) explain why you ϕ-ed, where this is the kind of explanation possessed reasons are linked to via the Acting On condition. The rationale explanation will be the same whether you are in the good environment or the bad environment. And thus, knowing p, or truly believing p, or truly believing with justification doesn't matter when it comes to correctly responding to reasons.

This is objectionable because it seems like there is a important rational difference when a normative achievement explanation can be given rather than merely a rationale explanation. When a normative achievement explanation is available, I'm connected to a (normative) reason to ϕ in a way that I'm not in cases where merely a rationale explanation is available.[46] The fact that you know certainly seems relevant when you're explaining yourself to other people. At least when I know that I know p, I will often find it essential to explain myself in terms of the fact that I know p when I am really pushed to explain myself.[47]

It's important to stress that I'm not objecting to the fact that the internalist holds that you are rational in both the good and the bad case. I agree with this; chapter 7 is devoted to arguing that you are rational in both cases. Rather, I'm objecting to the fact that the internalist view commits us to thinking that, as far as rationality is concerned, both the deceived subject and the knowing subject are *on a par*. This is what seems objectionable to me. It seems essential to explaining the rationality of the knowing to appeal to the fact that they know, even if the deceived are also rational.

---

[46] For more detailed arguments for this, see. Gibbons (2001), Hyman (2006), Hornsby (2007, 2008).

[47] Objection: Your view doesn't explain *this*. After all, you think the Acting On condition just comes to p being able to explain your action, not the fact that you know that p. Reply: This is a canard. Given plausible assumptions about assertion, when I offer up a normative because explanation of the form 'I ϕ-ed because of p,' I am expressing my knowledge that p (or at least I think I am). Often when I am pushed harder to explain myself, I will explicitly say that I knew p. This is not to say that I wasn't expressing my knowledge all along.

Here's how I see the dialectic, at this point. The initial linguistic data suggests that normative achievement explanations are factive, and the most obvious non-factualist stories don't seem compelling. Still, there is intuitive force behind the type of internalism that underwrites non-factualism. This force is especially acute if the non-factualist is right to think that factualism commits one to the view that in the bad cases one's reactions are not based on reasons. There is a sense in which one can base reactions on considerations that are false. False considerations can be one's rationale. Given this, I see little reason to overturn the initial presumption in favor of (2)—i.e., in favor of thinking that the 'because' explanations in question are, like the rest of 'because' explanations, factive.

That said, an appeal to both rationale and normative achievement explanations opens the door for the non-factualist to deny (1)—i.e., to deny that we need to be able to ϕ because of the reasons we possess. Perhaps it is enough that the reasons we possess can be our rationales. This is implausible, as well. This is because we want the Acting On condition to tell us something about what it is to correctly respond to reasons. Because of this, it's plausible that there is a Reverse Acting On condition. It should be that when I have the ability required by the Acting On condition with respect to some consideration p, I possess p. But the Reverse Acting On condition is false if we only need to have the ability to act with p as a rationale. We can act with p as a rationale much more often than we possess p. This, I think, provides a compelling case for (1). It follows from (1) and (2) that non-factive views are false.

3.6 Against P→TEAR

I've now argued against Low Bar views, Holding views, and Non-Factive views. If those arguments are sound, then the correct view about the epistemic relation must be a High Bar, Non-Holding, and Factive view. Our chart now looks like this (the views that have been eliminated via previous arguments are crossed out; the features of the views that led to their rejection are bolded).

Table 3.2. Updated Epistemic Condition Taxonomy

View	High Bar v. Low Bar	Holding v. Non-Holding	Factive v. Non-Factive
P→B	Low Bar	Holding	Non-Factive
P→Pres	Low Bar	Holding	Non-Factive
P→RB	High Bar	Holding	Non-Factive
P→EAR	High Bar	Non-Holding	Non-Factive
P→TRB	High Bar	Holding	Factive
P→TEAR	High Bar	Non-Holding	Factive
P→K	High Bar	Holding	Factive
P→PTK	High Bar	Non-Holding	Factive

As you can see, there are two High Bar, Non-Holding, Factive views: P→TEAR and P→PTK. P→TEAR holds that you possess a reason r only if the proposition p that constitutes r is true and you are *ex ante* rational in believing p. P→PTK holds that you possess r only if you are in a position to know p. In this final subsection, I will first try to allay skepticism about the notion of being in a position to know, and then I will offer two arguments against P→TEAR in favor of P→PTK.

Position to Know, What

The notion of being in a position to know is common in contemporary epistemology. Epistemologists rarely bat an eye when it is used on the periphery. However, I've found that when you place it at the forefront of your theory, philosophers will quickly become skeptical. In this case this seems fair enough, for the notion is obviously vague. To see this, we needn't look past my paradigm case in §3.3.3.

In that case, I believe that my wife will pick up my son at the normal time, despite the fact that she just told me that she can't pick him up that day. Despite the fact that she told me this, I was engrossed in my magazine just enough not to take the information in to form the belief that she can't pick him up that day. I am, at least when she tells me this, in a position to know my wife can't pick him up that day. This is why, I claim, I'm not rational in believing that she will pick him up at the normal time. Now consider this feature of my situation: 'I ate pizza on January 3rd, 2004' is written on a piece of paper stuck between pages 192 and 193 of my copy of *American Psycho* on the bookshelf behind the kitchen table. Good question: Am I in a position to know that I ate pizza on January 3rd, 2004?

I hope not, and I think not, too. I think there is a way to precisify 'position to know' such that I am in a position to know that I ate pizza on January 3rd, 2004. But this is not the precisification used here. Roughly, in order to be in a position to know p, you have to be able to learn that p without a significant change in your epistemic situation.[48] What constitutes a significant change is also vague (which isn't in-itself objectionable). I'm happy to adjudicate this question in the normal way we do with vague concepts. Plus, since 'rational' itself is vague, we shouldn't be too surprised if some of the analysans of what it is to be rational are also vague.

Still, I sense hostility towards this strategy. So let me precisify some more.[49] To start, compare being in a position to know with being *ex ante* rational. When you are *ex ante* rational in believing p, all of what we can call the impersonal conditions for *ex post* rationality are met. The personal conditions are believing p and believing p for the right reasons. The impersonal conditions are just whatever is left. There are two different kinds of cases where you are *ex ante* rational. The first kind of cases are *inferential*, while the second kind of cases are *uninferential*. In the inferential cases,

---

[48] Compare with Williamson (2000) and Gibbons (2006).

[49] What follows was partially inspired by Smithies (2006). I'm confident Smithies wouldn't be all that happy with the product of my inspiration (or at least the use I put it to).

you are *ex ante* rational in virtue of some of your other beliefs. In the uninferential cases, you are *ex ante* rational in virtue of some other kinds of states—e.g., perceptual states.[50]

Since believing *p* is a personal condition, it's possible to be *ex ante* rational without believing *p*. When this happens, what is it about the facts that ground your *ex ante* rationality that puts you in a position to meet the personal conditions? Here's a stab at an answer: In the inferential cases, it's the fact that you have some beliefs with contents such that, if you could and did attend to those contents and inferentially form a belief that *p* in the right way, you would have an *ex post* rational belief that *p*. In the uninferential cases, it's the fact that you have some experiences such that, if you could and did attend to certain features of those experiences and uninferentially form a belief in the right kind of way, then you would have an *ex post* rational belief that *p*. Of course I haven't told you what the right way is, but presumably my burden isn't that heavy.

Being in a position to know works in an analogous way. You are in a position to know *p* when all the impersonal conditions for knowledge are met. The personal conditions are (1) believing *p* and (2) believing *p* for the right reasons. The impersonal conditions are just whatever are left over. There are also inferential cases and uninferential cases. Since believing *p* is a personal condition, it's possible to be in a position to know *p* when you don't believe *p*. In cases like this, what is it in virtue of which you are in a position to know *p*? In the inferential cases, it's the fact that you have some beliefs with contents such that, if you could and did attend to those contents and inferentially form a belief that *p* in the right way, you would know that *p*. In the uninferential cases, it's the fact that you have some experiences such that, if you could and did attend to certain features of those experiences and uninferentially form a belief that *p* in the right kind of way, then you would know that *p*. Again I haven't told you what the right way is, nor I have told you what impersonal condition or conditions must be added to go from being *ex ante* rational to being in a position to know. But I think that I needn't solve the problem of the basing relation or the Gettier problem in order for the average reader to glob onto what I mean by 'position to know.'[51]

In my paradigm case, I have an auditory experience that is such that were I to attend to certain features of it—the feature of it that sounds like my wife telling me she can't pick up my son that day—and formed a belief that *p* in the right way, then I would

---

[50] Note that I'm using 'in virtue of' in its usual broad sense. I'm not committing myself to the claim that *the beliefs themselves* or the *experiences themselves* are the *justifiers*. On my view, a *background condition* on the contents of the beliefs/perceptual states being the justifiers is that you have the belief or perceptual state.

[51] I offer my own account of the basing relation in chapter 5 (don't ask for a solution to the Gettier problem).

know that my wife can't pick up my son that day.[52] It's not the case that I have any such experiences when it comes to what is written on that piece of paper inside *American Psycho*, nor do I have any beliefs that play the analogous inferential role. So I'm not in a position to know that I ate pizza on January 3rd, 2004.

Let me stress that, in some moods, I think being in a position to know is broader than this characterization. For example, it doesn't seem like having my eyes closed when I enter a room I've never been in before changes the fact that I'm in a position to know the color of the room's walls (assuming that the room is lit in a normal way). But if this characterization is correct, then having my eyes closed would make a difference. The problem is that I don't know of any characterization specific enough to allay the doubts of a skeptic that captures these cases. This is why I'm happy enough to work with the more specific version above, at least for the time being. I think there will be plenty of progress to be made even if we fix position to know in this way.

Now let's see why we should accept P→PTK over P→TEAR.

The Circularity Objection

One cannot accept P→TEAR and analyze rationality in terms of possession. For if one did, then one's analysis of rationality would be viciously circular. It would say, partly, that what it is to be rational is to correctly respond to the reasons you are *ex ante* rational in believing that are true. Since *rational* is one of the analysans and is the supposed analysandum, it's very plausible that the analysis is viciously circular.[53]

Many will think that the same objection applies to P→PTK. After all, they'll say, knowledge is analyzed in terms of rationality. And thus being in a position to know will be analyzed in terms of rationality. So if rationality is analyzed in terms of being in a position to know, *rationality* will end up being one of the analysans, albeit in a more round about way. Thus, if you accept P→PTK, then you can't give a non-circular analysis of justification/rationality.

No doubt this has its *prima facie* appeal. It is an orthodox view that knowledge can be analyzed in terms of rationality. Nevertheless, it is an orthodoxy that I reject. Instead, I think that it is rationality that is to be analyzed by knowledge. Since I think this, it's no surprise that knowledge will be one of the analysans in my analysis of rationality!

---

[52] One might think this way of characterizing this case opens the door for the Holding view to resist my counterexample in §3.3.2. The thought is that one's auditory experience has the relevant reason as its content. This is not how I'm thinking of the auditory experience. As I'm imagining the case, I do not have an experience that has propositional content. It's rather that the experience puts me into a position to be in a state with propositional content if I were to attend to the right features. Much of our perceptual experiences are like this. Right now there are many things in my visual and auditory field that are such that if I attended to them, I'd have a perception with propositional content. But without attending to them I don't have such a perception. Thanks to Shyam Nair for raising this objection.

[53] Beddor (2015) independently makes a similar point. He thinks the objection extends to P→PTK as well. For reasons I give in the next paragraph, I disagree.

Defending my knowledge-first methodology is outside the scope of this chapter.[54] I think that it's independently interesting to work out a view using this method in order to see what fruit it bears. That is, I think this book has merit even if I don't defend the knowledge-first methodology. The devil is in the details, and thus progress will be made by working out the details. I'm happy to write this promissory note here. The important point for our purposes is that there's simply no way for the defender of P→TEAR to accept that rationality is analyzed in terms of the reasons that are possessed without thereby accepting a circular analysis. It is possible for the defender of P→PTK to do this by denying that knowledge is analyzed in terms of rationality. This gives those who think that rationality is analyzed in terms of the reasons that are possessed decisive reason to reject P→TEAR. Given the other arguments, one who accepts that rationality is analyzed in terms of the reasons that are possessed has very strong reason to accept P→PTK and the claim that rationality is analyzed in terms of knowledge.

The Naturalness Objection

Although the Circularity Objection provides a decisive reason to reject P→TEAR for those who think that rationality is analyzed in terms of the reasons that are possessed, its force only extends that far (or at least the *decisive* nature of its force). It would thus be nice to have something to say to those readers who aren't on board with my particular project of analyzing rationality in terms of the reasons that are possessed. I should say up front to readers in that position that I'm not too concerned if you get off the boat here (of course, I will be concerned with your upstream decision to not think that rationality is analyzed in terms of the reasons that are possessed!). You will agree with me on much of what is important to me in this chapter if you accept P→TEAR. Moreover, if I've shown that everyone who accepts that rationality is to be analyzed in terms of the reasons that are possessed must accept P→PTK, then I'll consider today a pretty great day for the advancement of my view.

Those caveats aside, there is at least one thing that can be said in favor of P→PTK over P→TEAR. Namely, the property of being in a position to know is much more natural than the property of being *ex ante* rational in believing a truth.[55] Think of

---

[54] The *locus classicus* defense of the knowledge-first approach is ch. 1 of Williamson (2000). For Williamson's remarks on how this relates to analyzing rationality (or at least justification) in terms of the evidence that is had, see §9.1 of Williamson (2000).

[55] Here's Williamson (2009) making the same point against a similar proposal advocated by Goldman (2009) (Goldman's view, for what it's worth, faces the Circularity Objection): 'Such a view is a rather unnatural hybrid; the truth condition is an *ad hoc* afterthought, not an organic consequence' (311).

And here's Weatherson (2012) making a similar point: 'To put the point in Lewisian terms, it seems that knowledge is much more *natural* relation than rational true belief.' In a footnote he says 'What is important here is that on sufficient reflection, the Gettier cases show that some rational true beliefs aren't knowledge and that the cases in question also show that being a rational true belief is not a particularly natural or unified property' (7).

it this way:[56] Suppose we decide that the relevant epistemic condition is factive, and then we ask what the explanation is of this fact. Both P→PTK and P→TEAR offer an explanation. The P→PTK theorist explains the factivity by appealing to the factivity of being in a position to know. The P→TEAR explains factivity by pointing out that all the truths you are *ex ante* rational in believing are true.

It's plausible that the former explanation appeals to more a natural or unified property than the latter. An *essential* property of the state—being in a position to know—posited by the P→PTK theorist is that you can be in that state only if the content of the state is true. It's true that you can't be *ex ante* rational in believing a truth without the content being true. But you can be in the same state you're in when you are *ex ante* rational in believing a truth even when that proposition is false. Adding the truth condition to P→EAR, in other words, seems *ad hoc*. And thus the factivity of the possession relation turns out to be, in Williamson's words, 'an *ad hoc* afterthought, not an organic consequence.' But the factivity of the possession relation *is* an organic consequence of P→PTK.[57]

The fact that being in a position to know is more natural than being *ex ante* rational in believing a truth gives us some reason to prefer P→PTK over P→TEAR. I spelled this out via illustration. It seems like the factivity of the possession relation is better explained by P→PTK than P→TEAR precisely because being in a position to know is essentially factive and it being *ex ante* rational to believe a truth isn't. Better explanations make for a better theory.

3.7 Conclusion

In this chapter, I have argued that the epistemic condition on possession is being in a position to know. I have argued for this view by arguing that it is the most plausible Non-Holding, High Bar, Factive view. Nearly everyone in the literature on possession would assume that my task should now be done. This is because they assume that

---

[56] I don't think this is the only way to think of it. I give another way in n. 57 below. The way of putting it in the text seems to me to be one of the more simpler ways of putting it, and that's why I use that way of putting the point.

[57] I think the lesson we should take from Williamson's primeness argument (see Williamson (2000, ch. 3)) is not that knowledge is unanalyzable (this is the conclusion that many readers of Williamson draw), but that knowledge is unified in a way that composite states aren't. This doesn't show that knowledge is unanalyzable because it's possible for knowledge to be both prime and analyzable (this is forcefully shown in Brueckner (2002). I also heard the point independently made by Ernie Sosa). In general, I think we should expect the prime states to be more explanatorily basic than the composite ones. Since being in a position to know is a prime state and being *ex ante* rational in believing a truth is a composite one, I think we should expect the former to be more explanatorily basic than the latter. I also think this provides some independent motivation for a knowledge-first methodology. Williamson does make a point close to this in Williamson (2000, §3.6–3.7), but he doesn't think this is the grandest conclusion one can draw from the primeness arguments.

meeting the epistemic condition is both necessary and sufficient for possession. It is a demonstrable mistake, in my view, to think that meeting the epistemic condition is a sufficient condition for possession. Thus, I think that our inquiry into the nature of possession must continue. Not only is there an epistemic condition, there is also a practical condition. Chapter 4 is dedicated to the practical condition. Onward!

4

What it is to Possess a Reason
The Practical Condition

4.1 The Insufficiency of the Epistemic Condition

In chapter 3, I argued that in order for an agent A to possess a reason r to ϕ, A has to be in a position to know r. Most participants in the literature on possession think that this itself amounts to a view of possession. This is because nearly all participants assume that meeting the epistemic condition is both necessary and sufficient for possession.[1]

Some examples: Williamson (2000) boldly declares that evidence *is* knowledge. By this he means that the evidence that is possessed is the evidence that one knows. More precisely, r is a piece of evidence that p that A possesses just in case r is evidence that p and A knows r.[2] Schroeder (2008, 2011b), Way (2010a, 2009), Parfit (2011) hold that the reasons that are possessed are (i) considerations that would be objective normative reasons if they were true that (ii) one believes or perceives.[3] According to Feldman (1988), your possessed reasons for belief consist in what you are currently thinking about. And, according to Lewis (1996), the evidence you possess consists in your perceptual experiences and 'apparent memories.'

As we saw in chapter 2, I think that all of these views are open to simple counterexamples. These counterexamples show that meeting the epistemic condition is not sufficient for possession. Let's start with a simple epistemic case:

The Murderer's Boots

Sherlock's analysis is complete. The bootprints were created by Red Wing Iron Rangers. He excitedly tells this to Watson. Watson looks confused. With a sigh, Sherlock informs Watson that the cabby wears Red Wing Iron Rangers.

---

[1] There are some notable exceptions. Whiting (2014) and Sylvan (2015) both confront some of the data I will appeal to below. Their focus is slightly different, though. They are each solely focused on counterfactual accounts of non-factive subjective (or apparent) reasons. They use some of the kinds of cases I appeal to below to show that these views are in trouble. They don't point out, however, that these cases have much larger consequences—viz., they show that meeting the epistemic condition, no matter what it is, is insufficient for possession. Sylvan (MSa) does do this. He goes on to develop an account of the practical condition that is in many ways similar to the view I will defend here (this is not surprising given Lord & Sylvan (FC)).

[2] See Williamson (2000, ch. 9, §2).

[3] Vogelstein (2012) defends a similar idea.

In this case, Watson knows something (and thus believes something, justifiably believes something, truly believes something, etc.) that is an excellent reason to believe that the cabby did it. Namely, the fact that the bootprints were created by Red Wing Iron Rangers. However, until Sherlock fills him in on the cabby's choice of boot, Watson intuitively doesn't possess that fact as a reason to believe the cabby did it. We can confirm this by considering chapter 3's Working Hypothesis:

> **Working Hypothesis:** You possess reason r to ϕ iff r affects the rational merits of ϕ-ing.

The left-to-right direction holds that if one possesses a reason r to ϕ, then r affects the rational merits of ϕ-ing. If this is right, then Williamson's, Schroeder's, Parfit's, Way's, Feldman's, and Lewis's views predict that the fact that the prints were caused by Red Wing Iron Rangers affects the rational merits of believing the cabby did it for Watson. But, given reasonable background conditions, this is not so. A reasonable way to interpret the case (one which I am henceforth stipulating) is to think that Watson, unlike Sherlock, does not see the connection between the cabby and Red Wing Iron Rangers. Given this, it's very plausible that the fact that the prints were created by Iron Rangers doesn't affect the rational merits of believing the cabby did it for Watson. Thus, Watson doesn't possess that fact as a reason to believe that the cabby did it. Thus, Williamson's, Schroeder's, Parfit's, Way's, Feldman's, and Lewis's views are false.[4]

If there is one counterexample, there are many. Here's the case discussed in chapter 2 involving action (inspired by Broome (2007a)):

Lois's Fish

Lois just ordered fish from her favorite seafood restaurant. Right before she digs in, the waiter comes out to inform her that the fish contains salmonella. Lois has the unfortunate belief that salmonella is one of the many bacteria found in food that is harmless to humans. And, indeed, this belief is rational. A renowned food scientist told her so. So she goes ahead and forms an intention to eat the fish and eats the fish.

In this case Lois knows (and thus justifiably believes, believes, truthfully believes, etc.) that the fish contains salmonella. This fact is also a very strong reason not to eat the fish. Thus, Williamson's, Parfit's, Feldman's, Way's, Lewis's and Schroeder's views predict that Lois possesses that fact as a reason to not eat the fish. Given Working Hypothesis, these views predict that the fact that the fish contains salmonella affects the rational merits of not eating. Intuitively, this is not right. If that fact affected the rational merits of not eating, it would be irrational to eat—it is a very strong reason, after all. But Lois is rational to eat. So it's plausible that that fact doesn't affect the rational merits of not eating despite the fact that Lois meets the epistemic condition for possession.

---

[4] A more local version of this objection has been pressed by Whiting (2014) and Sylvan (2015) against views like Schroeder's and Parfit's. Sylvan calls it the unapparent reasons problem.

In case you are worried that all cases of this type turn on false beliefs like Lois's, consider Thirsty Billy:

Thirsty Billy

Billy is a thirsty 8-year-old. The bottle in front of Billy contains H_2O. Billy's wisecracking chemist for a father tells him that the bottle contains H_2O knowing full well that Billy doesn't know that H_2O is thirst quenching.

Billy knows that the bottle contains H_2O. That fact provides a reason for Billy to drink from the bottle. Thus, Williamson's, Parfit's, Way's, Schroeder's, Feldman's, and Lewis's views predict that Billy possesses that fact as a reason to drink. Given Working Hypothesis, these views thus predict that the rational merits of drinking what's in the bottle are affected by the fact that the bottle contains H_2O. This is a bad prediction. For if that fact did affect the rational merits of drinking from the bottle, it would be irrational for Billy not to drink. But it is rational for Billy to refrain from drinking. Thus, he doesn't possess that fact as a reason despite meeting the epistemic condition.

The task now becomes figuring out what else needs to obtain in order for one to possess a reason. Notice that in each counterexample, there is an obvious sense in which the characters don't 'see' the connection between the fact in question and the reaction that that fact speaks in favor of. In other words, they don't comprehend *how* the relevant fact is connected to the relevant reaction. They don't see the *practical* upshot of the relevant fact. For this reason, I will say that what's missing is that these characters don't satisfy the practical condition for possession. Note that this does not mean that I think that their problem is always a practical *rather than* an epistemic one. In Watson's case he is not practically deficient in the sense in which he is failing to do or intend to do something. Rather, it is just that he cannot rationally get himself from a belief about what caused the prints to a rational belief that the cabby did it. The fact that Iron Rangers caused the prints thus doesn't have the right motivational upshot, in a broad sense of 'motivational.'

This is just to give a name to what needs to be explained. It is not to explain it. The rest of the chapter is dedicated to defending my view of the practical condition. On my view, in order to meet the practical condition for some reason r to ϕ, one must be in a position to manifest knowledge about how to use r to ϕ. On my view, then, the practical condition is very practical—it's all about knowing how to do various things with reasons. While not much has been said in the literature about possession about the practical condition, there has been some discussion of it. As we'll see, some think that the practical condition is less practical and more theoretical than my condition. Some think of it more literally as a matter of seeing the connection (see especially Whiting (2014)). I will argue that those views don't provide the best explanation of all of the relevant data.

The plan is this. In the next section, I will provide a more rigorous diagnosis of the counterexamples. According to this diagnosis, the problem with the characters can be traced to the fact that they aren't in a position to react in the various ways in an *ex post* rational way. The practical condition, in effect, fills this practical gap. Thus, when one meets the practical condition, one is in a position to have an *ex post* rational reaction. This focuses the debate about the practical condition on what we need to add to put our characters in a position to have an *ex post* rational reaction. With this in hand, I will argue against three rival views to my own. After doing that, I will be in a position to defend my own proposal. To finish I will consider the question of whether the right view of possession is conjunctive—i.e., whether the right analysis is a conjunction of the epistemic and practical conditions. I will argue that the right analysis is not conjunctive. This is because it turns out that being in a position to know the fact that provides a reason is a *background condition* for being in a position to manifest knowledge about how to use a fact as a reason. Thus, I will conclude that what it is to possess a reason r to ϕ is to be in a position to manifest knowledge about how to use r as a reason to ϕ.

4.2 The Counterexamples: A Diagnosis of What's Going Wrong

In order to focus discussion, it will be helpful to have a diagnosis of what is going wrong in the counterexamples. I claimed that it's not plausible that the relevant characters possessed the relevant facts as reasons because if they did possess them, then they'd be rationally required to react in ways that are intuitively irrational. Watson, for example, would be required to believe that the cabby did it if he possessed the fact that the prints were caused by Iron Rangers *as a reason to believe the cabby did it*. Similarly, Lois would be required to refuse to eat the fish if she possessed the fact that the fish contains salmonella *as a reason not to eat*. Finally, Billy would be rationally required to drink from the bottle if he possessed the fact that the bottle contains H_2O *as a reason to drink from the bottle*. But, I claim, these characters are obviously not rationally required to react in those ways. It's rationally permissible for them to have different reactions—Watson should remain agnostic about who did it, Lois can dig in, and Billy can refrain from drinking from the bottle.

All of this can be established by reflecting on the cases. Now I want to ask *why* those things are true. The explanation I will explore holds that those things are true because there is no *route* that the characters can take to an *ex post* rational reaction. Since there would be a route they could take if they possessed the relevant facts as reasons for the relevant reactions, this amounts to an explanation for why they don't possess those reasons. This explanation relies on the following principle:

> **Possession Enables Rational Routing:**   If A possesses r as a sufficient reason to ϕ, then there is a route that A can take to *ex post* rational ϕ-ing on the basis of r.

Possession Enables Rational Routing is merely a special case of something much more general. Possessing reasons—whether they are sufficiently weighty or not—puts one in a position to react in a way that has at least *some* rational merit. If you ϕ on the basis of a possessed but defeated reason r, you act in a way that is less than perfectly rational, but your token act has some rational merit. After all, it was sensitive to an honest to goodness normative reason.

Possession Enables Rational Routing is plausible because of the connection between *ex ante* and *ex post* rationality. Whenever you are *ex ante* rational in ϕ-ing, you can be *ex post* rational. And this 'can' is quite fine grained. Roughly, you can in the sense that there is a path you can take from what you are like now to *ex post* rational ϕ-ing.[5] This is at least tacitly assumed by every discussion of *ex ante*/ *ex post* rationality that I am aware of.[6]

Now we can give a proper argument against all of the views that hold that meeting the epistemic condition is sufficient:

1. If A possesses r as a sufficient reason to ϕ, then there is a route that A can take to *ex post* rational ϕ-ing on the basis of r.
2. There is no rational route that Watson can take to an *ex post* rational belief that the cabby did it on the basis of the fact that the prints were caused by Iron Rangers.
3. Therefore, Watson doesn't possess the fact that the prints were caused by Iron Rangers as a sufficient reason to believe the cabby did it.
4. If meeting the epistemic condition is sufficient, Watson possesses the fact that the prints were caused by Iron Rangers as a sufficient reason to believe the cabby did it.
C. Therefore, meeting the epistemic condition is not sufficient.

My hypothesis is that by meeting the practical condition on possession, one fills the gap that exists in the counterexamples. That is, when one meets the practical and epistemic condition at the same time for some sufficient reason r to ϕ, there is a route one can take to *ex post* rational ϕ-ing on the basis of r. Now we have a concrete philosophical task: Figure out what fills the gap.

I will split the discussion into three parts. In the first part, I'll discuss views that hold that the practical condition is cashed out in terms of something broadly epistemic. I will argue that these views both overintellectualize and don't guarantee the right kind of (re)action guidance to fill the gap. In the second part, I will consider views that hold that the practical condition is a matter of having one's motivation directed at the right things. I will argue that this view also overintellectualizes the

---

[5] Of course, ability talk is context sensitive. This allows my opponents a classic line of defense: They can agree that the claims I make about abilities are true, but only because they involve more liberal abilities (i.e., more possible worlds are relevant than I am assuming). I am trying to head this off explicitly here. For related discussion, see §8.4.2.

[6] Turri (2010) analyzes *ex ante* rationality in terms of *ex post* rationality. He claims: 'Necessarily, for all S, p, and t, if p is [*ex ante*] justified for S at t, then p is [*ex ante*] justified for S at t because S currently possesses at least one means of coming to believe p such that, were S to believe p in one of those ways, Ss belief would thereby be [*ex post*] justified' (320). For reasons to reject Turri's view, see chapter 5 and Lord & Sylvan (FC).

practical condition. Further, it doesn't hold much promise as a fully general account of what's going on. The failures of these views will motivate my view, which will be discussed in §4.4.

4.3 Filling the Gap

4.3.1 First attempt: missing beliefs(ish)

The flat footed thought

A natural starting point for filling the gap would to be hold that what's going wrong with our characters is that they fail to believe that the relevant considerations are reasons for the relevant reactions.[7] Watson doesn't believe that the fact that the prints were caused by Iron Rangers is a reason to believe that the cabby did it. Further, Lois doesn't believe that the fact that the fish contains salmonella is a reason not to eat it. And Billy doesn't believe that the fact that the bottle contains H_2O is a reason to drink what's in the bottle. Moreover, it's plausible that once they are filled in about the normative upshot of those facts—once Watson finds out that the cabby wears Iron Rangers, Lois finds out salmonella makes you sick, and Billy finds out H_2O is thirst quenching—they will come to have those beliefs about reasons. Thus, what we might call the Reasons Belief condition does seem to match up in the right ways with our characters.

I grant that all of that is true about our characters. Nevertheless, I think that having explicit beliefs about one's reasons is neither necessary nor sufficient for meeting the practical condition. I'll start with the necessity claim. According to this claim, if you meet the practical condition for some reason r to ϕ, you believe that r is a reason to ϕ. I don't think this is a necessary condition because that involves objectionable overintellectualization. Parfit (2011, p. 118) puts the point nicely:

We can have rational beliefs and desires, and act rationally, without having any beliefs about reasons. Young children respond rationally to certain reasons or apparent reasons, though they do not yet have the concept of a reason. Dogs, cats, and some other animals respond to some kinds of reason . . . though they will never have the concept of a reason. And some rational adults seem to lack this concept . . .

The Reasons Belief view gives rise to two forms of overintellectualization. The more extreme kind of overintellectualization is that this view rules out that creatures that lack the concept of a reason can possess reasons. This is because one needs to possess the concept in order to have beliefs about normative reasons. I find it implausible to think that there is this strong a conceptual condition on possession. It seems plausible to me (and to Parfit) that small children and some animals can meet the practical

---

[7] Sylvan (2015) calls this the *de dicto* view. He argues against it in a similar way that I do. The *de dicto* view seems to tempt Scanlon (1998), Kolodny (2005), Broome (2007a, 2013).

condition on possession. This is because they can recognize that certain facts support certain reactions. But I take it that it's very implausible to suppose that they can have explicit beliefs about normative reasons.

One might think that this objection turns on a view of concept possession and hence normative beliefs that is too demanding. Perhaps all that is obvious is that small children and animals cannot express their normative beliefs the way that fully capacitated agents can. If this is right, then they could have the beliefs in question. Perhaps this is correct. I doubt it because I think it's plausible that beliefs *represent contents*. Further, Frege's puzzle shows us that these contents have to be fairly fine grained. This rules out the obvious candidates that would save Reasons Belief from this objection—e.g., the view that it is sufficient for believing p that you behave as if p. These views will have a very hard time explaining how it is that I can believe that there is water in my glass without believing that there is H_2O in my glass.[8]

Even if Reasons Belief could be fixed so that it avoids the extreme overintellectualization objection, there is a less extreme overintellectualization objection lurking. Reasons Belief requires that one have beliefs about normative reasons each time one meets the practical condition. It seems to me that this requires us to form too many beliefs. Imagine a case of inference. I know p, if p, q, and I infer q from those known facts. This flat footed view requires that in order to possess p as a reason to believe q in this case, I need to believe that p is a reason to believe q. That seems like one thought too many.[9] If I'm competent with modus ponens, it's plausible that I possess those reasons in virtue of knowing those facts. I needn't have other beliefs about reasons in order to meet the practical condition.

The overintellectualization worries threaten the necessity claim. There are also serious worries about the sufficiency claim. First, as it's been stated so far, the Reasons Belief condition is obviously insufficient. To see this, let's think about a variation on Lois's case. Suppose that Lois does in fact meet the Reasons Belief condition. She does believe that the fact that the fish contains salmonella is a reason not to eat the fish. However, the reason why she has this belief is because she falsely (yet rationally) believes that the presence of salmonella has a negative effect on the flavor of the fish. Now, she doesn't think it affects the taste very much and thus doesn't think that this reason is very strong. Even if you think that Lois possesses some reason not to eat in this case (which is itself controversial), it is *not* the reason grounded in the fact that salmonella will make you very ill. It is still rational for Lois to eat in this version of the case. Again, if she possessed the reason grounded in the fact that salmonella makes you very ill, it would not be rational for her to eat. So she must not possess that reason.

[8] Cf. Sylvan (2015).

[9] Most participants in the literature on inference agree. For a nice overview, see Boghossian (2014), Broome (2014). Valaris (2014) argues that reasoning requires beliefs about what follows from what. See Dogramaci (2016) for a reply and Valaris (2016) for a reply to the reply.

We might use this case as motivation for a modification of the Reasons Belief condition. One modification that would help in the above case is to insist that one needs to believe that the reason is sufficient. I don't think this will be right extensionally, either. We needn't to go into why not because it fails for a much simpler reason.[10] It fails because we can possess insufficient reasons. When we do, it's very implausible that we're *required* to believe they are sufficient. Thus, this modified view is false.

It's not clear how one might modify the belief condition in order to meet the twin demands of allowing possessed insufficient reasons and avoiding the incongruous weight problem posed by Lois's case. One could hold that one must have a belief about a reason *and* its (approximate) weight. But I take it that that view clearly overintellectualizes. Further, it's not clear what content should be required. Does one need to explicitly quantify the weights? Do they employ some mushier concept of weight? What is that? These all seem like very hard questions.

I think that this problem for the Reasons Belief condition raises a more general problem. The problem is anchored in the fact that it does seem like one needs to have some sensitivity to the way in which something is a reason in order to posses it. This is especially plausible if we go in for Possession Enables Rational Routing. Given this principle, any view that allows one to possess reasons without some sensitivity to their grounds is liable to run into extensional problems. To see this, think of inductive reasons for belief. Suppose p provides an inductive reason to believe q—the fact that there are 5,000 tickets in the lottery is a reason to believe ticket number 6 will not win. Now suppose that Al believes the fact that there are 5,000 tickets in the lottery is a reason to believe ticket number 6 will not win. However, he believes this because he has the crazy background belief that all tickets will lose in a lottery with 5,000 tickets or more. In other words, he thinks that the fact that number 6 will not win is deductively entailed by the fact that there are 5,000 tickets in the lottery. I submit that Al does not have a route to an *ex post* rational belief in this case. The reason why is that he is not at all sensitive to the way in which the relevant fact is a reason. Thus, if Possession Enables Rational Routing is true, I think that possession requires some sensitivity to the way in which something is a reason.

The general problem is explaining how one can meet this sensitivity requirement without some impressive intellectual powers. It seems like one might have to have the ability to know rather complex normative facts in order to meet the sensitivity requirement. This threatens to divorce possession from the intellectual powers of

---

[10] Here's why it fails extensionally. Take Watson. Suppose that he does believe that the fact that the prints were caused by Iron Rangers is a sufficient reason the cabby did it. Further, suppose he has that belief because he has the background belief that all cabbies wear Iron Rangers. Even if you think he possesses some reason to believe the cabby did it (which is controversial and, I think, implausible), he doesn't possess the reason that's grounded in the fact that the particular cabby wears Iron Rangers. Watson is plausibly not disposed to be sensitive to that reason. Think of it this way: It seems like he'd make an inference from the boot fact to the cabby claim even if the cabby in question didn't wear Iron Rangers because of his strange background belief about what cabbies in general wear.

ordinary people. That would be a massive problem. I'll call this the Intellectual Problem and return to it throughout this chapter.

I think that these problems show that the prospects for any kind of Reasons Belief condition are quite dim. I will thus move onto a view that seems, at least at first, to be more promising.

Whiting's *a priori* Knowability

Whiting (2014)'s view offers up a more sophisticated missing beliefs view. According to Whiting's theory, 'a subject has a [possessed] reason to ϕ if and only if it is a priori that, if the facts of the situation are as they [rationally] appear to her to be, those facts give her an objective reason to ϕ' (12). Let's start with two clarifying remarks about this analysis. First, Whiting holds that rational belief is the epistemic condition on possession. Thus, only rational beliefs and the rational lack of beliefs counts for determining what 'the facts of the situation are as they appear' to be for some particular agent. This saddles Whiting's view with the Circularity Objection from chapter 3. He recognizes this and is fine with it because he lacks 'reductive ambitions.' Regardless, Whiting's view is compatible with all of the epistemic conditions. So one could accept his view and hold that the epistemic condition is being in a position to know. The way in which one goes on this point won't affect my remarks below.

A second clarificatory point is that it is important for Whiting's view that the conditional involved is an indicative conditional, not a counterfactual conditional. This is because Whiting wants the relevant modality to be epistemic, not metaphysical. This won't affect my discussion of the view too much, for I am mostly interested in the knowability claim that is at the heart of Whiting's account. Whiting holds that the claim that r is an objective reason if the facts of one's situation are as they appear to be must be *a priori* knowable in order for r to be a possessed reason. He doesn't take a definite stand about which agent(s) this condition applies to. But he seems most confident in the claim that the agent that possesses the reason must be able to know the relevant claim *a priori*. Let's start with this version of the view.

This version of the view holds real promise when it comes to the letter of the problems for the Reason Belief view. First off, it straightforwardly avoids the second type of overintellectualization. It does not require one to have any beliefs about reasons in order to possess reasons. It just requires that one be *able* to know a priori that the relevant consideration is a reason given one's perspective.

That said, it is saddled with the first type of overintellectualization. In order to possess reasons, one will have to be able to have beliefs about reasons. Otherwise, I take it, the claims about reasons will not be knowable *a priori*. So small children and sophisticated animals likely cannot possess reasons. While that strikes me as an implausible overintellectualization, it's a virtue of Whiting's account that it's not committed to the claim that one has to have explicit beliefs about reasons in order to possess them.

Whiting's account holds promise when it comes to the examples. It looks like it is not knowable *a priori* for Watson that if the world is as it appears to him to be, the fact that the prints were caused by Iron Rangers is a reason to believe the cabby did it. Further, it doesn't look like it is knowable *a priori* for Lois that if the world is as it appears to her to be, then the fact that the fish contains salmonella is a reason to refrain from eating. Finally, it doesn't look like it is knowable *a priori* for Billy that if the world is as it appears to him to be, then the fact that the bottle contains H_2O is a reason to drink from the bottle. Further, one might think—although more would need to be said—that one would have to be somewhat sensitive to the kind of reason a reason is in order for it to be *a priori* knowable for her that it is a reason given her perspective on the world.

This last point is the key point in this context. For recall my diagnosis of what's going wrong in the counterexamples. What's going wrong is that the characters don't have a route to an *ex post* rational reaction. The sufficiency problem for the Reasons Belief condition was that it seems possible to meet that condition even though you lack a route to an *ex post* rational reaction. In order for Whiting's view to fill the gap that needs filling, his view needs to be able to fit the data about when agents have a route to an *ex post* rational reaction. That is to say, it needs to be that whenever the relevant normative fact is knowable *a priori* by some agent *A*, *A* has a route to an *ex post* rational reaction.

While I agree that the view holds some promise when it comes to the problems with the sufficiency claim, I think that there will be serious implementation problems. The first problem—the problem of grounds—threatens the sufficiency of *a priori* knowability. As we saw, Lois can believe that the fact that the fish contains salmonella is a reason not to eat the fish but fail to possess the *actual* reason provided by that fact by having false background beliefs about *why* that fact is a reason. The most natural way to avoid this problem, on Whiting's view, is to hold that when Lois has those false background beliefs, she's not in a position to know *a priori* that the relevant fact provides the objective reason it in fact provides.[11]

I grant that the natural way to interpret Lois's case is such that she is not in a position to know *a priori* that the salmonella fact is a reason to refrain from eating in the way it actually is. But I don't think the natural interpretation is the only interpretation. It might be that Lois is in a position to know the relevant claim *a priori*. So, for example, it might be that Lois knows that pathogenic members of Enterobacteriaceae usually make people ill. And she might even know—implicitly and deep down—that salmonella is a pathogenic member of Enterobacteriaceae. Her

---

[11] I am assuming that Lois's false background beliefs are also irrational. This is important because if I didn't assume this, then Whiting's view would predict that the relevant fact would provide a reason 'grounded' in the claim that salmonella makes the fish taste worse. But if the relevant beliefs are irrational, Whiting's view does not predict that Lois possesses the relevant fact as a reason that's 'grounded' in the claim that salmonella makes the fish taste worse.

high school microbiology class wasn't for nothing. Finally, as we've imagined all along, she has completely pedestrian views about becoming ill—she doesn't like it and she thinks she has strong reasons to avoid it. However, while it is possible for her to put all of these thoughts together in the right way, it is extremely unlikely she will. This is partly because she already has a strong conviction that salmonella will not make her ill and that it's only negative side effect is that it makes the fish taste slightly worse than it normally does. She believes that this is some reason not to eat, but it's not sufficiently weighty.

In this version of the case, it seems quite plausible that the following claim is knowable *a priori* by Lois: <THE FACT THAT THE FISH CONTAINS SALMONELLA IS A REASON TO NOT EAT THE FISH>. Further, it's plausible that it's possible for the resulting *a priori* knowledge to be based on the proper grounds. So, it looks like Lois meets Whiting's condition in this case. She also meets the epistemic condition since she rationally believes that the fish contains salmonella. Yet, I still think it's implausible to hold that she possesses that fact as a reason in this case. While it's possible for her to put two and two together, she is very unlikely to do this. Any deliberative path she takes to refraining from eating is rationally deficient. Or, at the very least, she can't get to a rational refraining on the basis of the fact that the fish contains salmonella.

What this version of the case shows, I think, is that one can meet the epistemic conditions required for some fact to be knowable *a priori* without being in a position to manifest the motivational capacities that are required to count as being sufficiently sensitive to the normative dimensions of one's environment. Lois meets the epistemic conditions. Nevertheless, she still doesn't seem to stand in the right relationship with the salmonella fact to have a good route to an *ex post* rational reaction.

One might worry that this kind of example crucially turns on Lois being inconsistent. She's inconsistent because she believes that salmonella is harmless, she believes that pathogenic members of Enterobacteriaceae usually cause humans to be ill, and she believes that salmonella is a pathogenic member of Enterobacteriaceae. One might think that Whiting can get out of this problem by somehow restricting the information that makes it into one's perspective in a way that eliminates some of these beliefs.[12] I'm not confident that this can be done in a plausible way. This doesn't matter, though. While including the belief that salmonella is harmless helps elicit the intuition that Lois is rational to intend to eat (and thus doesn't possess the salmonella fact as a reason not to eat), we can construct analogous cases that don't involve inconsistent beliefs.

To see this, consider Grace. Grace is an engineer at a nuclear facility. One of the reactors might be malfunctioning and Grace needs to decide whether to shut it down. She knows that if the answer to a particular calculation is less than 1,500,000, then she doesn't need to shut down the reactor. The only way she can figure out the answer, given her circumstances, is to do the calculation in her head. She knows how to do

---

[12] Thanks to Sam Fulhart for this suggestion.

the calculation due to her training. Further, she knows all of the facts that would allow her to do the calculation—i.e., all that is required is applying some functions to information she already has. Call this information I. However, the calculation is extremely difficult. It is so difficult that there is no way she can do it before she has to decide. Suppose the correct answer is greater than 1,500,000.

In this case, the following claim is knowable *a priori* for Grace: <I IS A REASON TO SHUT THE REACTOR DOWN>. Thus, Grace meets Whiting's knowability condition. Further, she knows I. Whiting's view thus predicts that Grace possesses I as a reason to shut the reactor down. This is a bad prediction. Grace is not in a position to shut the reactor down in an *ex post* rational way on the basis of I. She has the ability to *come* to be in this position by doing the calculation. Unfortunately, there is no way she can do that in time. Thus, she seems to be in a position to be in a position to be sensitive to I in the right way. That is not to say that she is in such a position now.

I expect that those sympathetic to Whiting's view will be unmoved by this. They will insist that if the relevant fact is truly knowable *a priori* for Grace, then she possesses that fact as a reason to refrain. They will likely point out that the mere fact that it is unlikely that she'll shut down the reactor for the right reason does not by itself show much of anything. After all, it might just be very likely that she'll be less than perfectly rational. This is no theoretical problem.

This response is appealing because it does rely on a truth. Namely, that the mere fact that it's unlikely that Grace will shut down the reactor for I is no reason to think that she fails to possess. The problem for the response, though, is that the objection does not derive solely from the fact that Grace is unlikely to shut the reactor down for I. The problem can be put like this: In some cases—cases like Lois's and Grace's—some normative claim being knowable *a priori* puts one *in a position to be in a position* to manifest a capacity to react in an *ex post* rational way. Grace is in no position to refrain in an *ex post* rational way as she is. She is in a position to be in that position. In a very remote world where she has the time to do the calculation, she figures out that the answer is greater than 1,500,000 and thus she has a strong reason to shut the reactor down. *In that world* she possesses the mathematical fact as a reason to shut down the reactor. *In this world* the relevant fact is knowable *a priori* because of what happens in that world. But, I claim, it doesn't follow that Grace meets the practical condition because of what happens in the distant possible world where she has the time to work out the answer. This is why Whiting's view cannot fill the gap.

To be clear, the mere fact that it is unlikely that Grace will shut down the reactor is not the relevant fact. It's important why this is so unlikely. It is so unlikely because it's very unlikely that she'll do what is required to *be in a position* to manifest a capacity to refrain in an *ex post* rational way. This is true, in turn, because it's so unlikely that she'll reason in a way that would deliver the relevant *a priori* knowledge. If she did do this then she'd meet the practical condition, but since she doesn't, she doesn't.

An important factor in both Grace's and Lois's cases (in this section) is that neither of them are in a position to know (in the sense I elucidated in chapter 3) the relevant normative facts even though those facts are *a priori* knowable. This seems to be playing a crucial role to the success of these examples. This, it seems, is what explains why they are merely in a position to be in a position to manifest some ability. They are merely in a position to be in a position because in order to be in a position to manifest the ability, they'd need to come to know the truths that are merely *a priori* knowable. Given this feature of the cases, one might think that a more plausible version of Whiting's view appeals to being in a position to know *a priori* rather than to being knowable *a priori*.[13] On this view, then, one meets the practical condition for some reason *r* to ϕ just in case one is in a position to know *a priori* that given one's perspective, *r* is a normative reason to ϕ.

Grace and Lois are not counterexamples to this revised view. So this view is clearly an improvement. However, I still think this view is open to counterexample for the simple reason that being in a position to know certain facts does not guarantee that one is in a position to manifest an ability to respond to those facts in an *ex post* rational way. To see this we need to think of characters who are good at thinking about the normative facts but bad at using the normative facts. Here are two cases. The first is Eddie the epistemologist. Eddie is an expert about evidence. Thus, he is good at thinking about which facts count in favor of belief. However, he is not a good applied logician. In fact, he is very bad with modus ponens—in day to day life he is more likely to affirm the consequent than use modus ponens. Now suppose he is in an epistemology seminar that is considering whether *p* is evidence for *q*. Suppose that Eddie knows that if *p* then *q* and knows that if <*p*> and <IF *p*, THEN *q*>, then *p* is a reason to believe *q*. He's thus in a position to know that *p* is a reason to believe *q*. This does not guarantee that Eddie is in a position to have an *ex post* rational belief that *q*. For it might be that given his poor reasoning skills he is not able to infer *q* from *p* in this case. If that's so, then Eddie doesn't meet the practical condition even though he meets the revised version of Whiting's condition.[14]

Here is a practical version of the case. Keith the Kantian is a prominent moral philosopher. He has developed a particularly compelling Kantian view about normative ethics. In fact, we can suppose that Keith has developed the true normative ethical view. A central feature of this view is that it is always wrong to fail to respect the dignity of others. Unfortunately, despite being a very good moral philosopher, Keith is not a good person. One particular way in which he is a bad person is that he almost never respects the dignity of restaurant workers. Suppose he is out to eat with a colleague. They begin to discuss what it takes to respect restaurant workers. Suppose Keith knows

---

[13] I thank Daniel Whiting for raising this possibility.

[14] I realize that my use of this case here is in stark tension with my discussion of inferentialism and practical condition failures in chapter 2. My official view is that Eddie is unlikely to be possible as described. However, more complicated versions of Eddie are possible. Just imagine that Eddie is an expert not at deductive relations but inductive ones. He might be able to learn that a complicated inductive relation obtains between *p* and *q* without being able to get an *ex post* rational belief that *q* from *p* (this mirrors the next case).

that failing to tip the server will thwart a social norm that the waiter relies upon and he knows that thwarting a social norm that another person relies upon is a way of failing to respect dignity. He is thus in a position to know *a priori* that it follows from his perspective that there is a reason to tip the server. However, this doesn't *guarantee* that Keith is in a position to tip the server in an *ex post* rational way on the basis of the relevant reasons. Keith might find the server so contemptible that he simply cannot tip him on the basis of the relevant facts. If this is right, then Keith doesn't meet the practical condition even though he meets the revised version of Whiting's condition.

These cases bring out a fundamental problem with the Missing Belief views, which is that upon reflection it doesn't seem like the motivational deficit can be overcome *simply* by gaining propositional knowledge (or being in a position to gain it).[15] No matter what further (purely[16]) epistemic condition one adds, we can think of characters who meet that condition but lack the right motivational abilities. Those characters will be counterexamples to the relevant Missing Belief view.

The last reply I'll consider on Whiting's behalf is the thought that the characters in these cases are at least partially irrational for not having the relevant abilities. Perhaps it is this irrationality that is driving our intuitions. Perhaps the relevant characters really do meet the practical condition, but they can only manifest the relevant capacities if they purge themselves of the relevant irrationality. A supporter of Whiting's view might charge me of letting people off the hook for certain reasons by allowing them to avoid possessing them by being irrational in this way.

I have two replies to this. First, I do not think it's plausible that Lois or Grace (I'll get to Eddie and Keith in a moment) are necessarily irrational in any interesting sense just because they fail to put the relevant beliefs together, especially in context. To think this is to commit oneself to an onerous view about rationality. At any given time there might be many things we know that *might* be fruitfully brought to bear on our current decision problem. Nevertheless, our resources are finite and we thus cannot be rationally required to always see the often complicated interaction between the things we believe.

This point is particularly plausible when the relevant inferences are *a priori*. A vast amount of facts are knowable *a priori* by many people. Nevertheless, getting this knowledge is often very hard. It is very implausible, I think, to hold that we are all rationally required to come to know these things whenever they have some practical upshot.[17] To make this vivid, think about the fact that normative ethics itself is

---

[15] Sylvan (2015) makes a similar point about what he calls *de dicto* views.

[16] I make this qualification because if certain views of know-how are true (so-called intellectualist views), then gaining know-how will be to gain propositional knowledge. However, this is very special propositional knowledge because it is *essentially practical*. Accounting for the essential practicality of know-how has long been intellectualism's stumbling block. See Stanley (2001, 2011), Bengson & Moffett (2011), Pavese (2015) for defenses of intellectualism. See Glick (2015) for a very nice articulation of a central problem.

[17] Some think (e.g., Ichikawa & Jarvis (2013)) that rationality requires us all to know all of the *a priori* truths. Importantly, though, the notion of rationality they are invoking is *not* the notion at issue here. They

plausibly *a priori*. Further, many philosophers are competent with all the concepts that are needed to have such *a priori* knowledge. This does not mean that all of these philosophers are *irrational* because they've failed to work out the truth of normative ethics for themselves. Philosophy is demanding work, but it's not *that* demanding. Thus, I don't think it's plausible that Lois and Grace are irrational for not putting it all together.

That said, there is an obvious gap in Lois's perspective. And she'd be intellectually better off if she plugged that gap. In other words, she is deficient in some way because she hasn't put things together. She will not be pleased at herself tomorrow for failing to put things together! This does not mean she was being irrational at the restaurant.

It's more plausible that Eddie and Keith are being irrational insofar as they lack the requisite motivational abilities. I think most versions of Eddie and Keith are irrational. That said, I don't think they are *necessarily* irrational. There are a variety of ways they could have ended up with the deficits they have in rational or arational ways. Their incapacitations might be a result of factors completely outside of their control and thus they might not be irrational for having them.

That said, even if you think that Keith and Eddie are necessarily irrational, you still shouldn't buy this defense of Whiting. This brings me to the second reply. The second reply to this takes issue with the principle that we always possess r to ϕ when we are required to ψ and by ψ-ing we'd be in a position to manifest a capacity to ϕ in an *ex post* rational way. The reply tacitly assumes this principle because it assumes that (for example) Keith possesses the social norm fact as a reason to tip because he's rationally required to be sensitive to such facts and if he were, then he'd be in a position to exercise a capacity to tip in an *ex post* rational way.

To see that this is false, let's think about affective and emotional reactions. To take an extreme example, consider a first time parent—Pat—who has the choice to go see her child for the first time. We can safely assume that Pat is rationally required to go see her child. Further, if she does go see her child, she will be in a position to have *ex post* rational affective and emotional reactions. She will be in a position to rationally be in awe of her child's innocence (just to take one example). Before she goes into the room, however, she does not possess this fact as a reason to be in awe. This is so even though she might know that her child is completely innocent. Before she is acquainted with her child, she cannot rationally be in *awe* of her child's innocence.[18]

Yet, if the transfer principle above is true, Pat does possess that fact as a reason to be in awe of her child's innocence. This is because Pat is required to do something (go into the room) that is such that were she to do it, then she would be in a position to

---

are explicit that their notion is a notion of *ideal* rationality. Ideal rationality requires many things that the type of rationality Whiting and I are concerned with does not require. So appealing to Ichikawa & Jarvis's notion will not cut any ice here.

[18] For discussion of the conditions under which we possess reasons for emotional and affective responses, see Lord (2016b), Lord (2018c), and Lord (MS).

rationally be in awe of her child's innocence. For this reason, I reject that principle. Without it, the final defense of Whiting does not go through.

To recap: Whiting's view tries to fill the gap by positing an *a priori* knowability constraint on possession. In particular, he thinks that in order for A to possess r to ϕ, it needs to be *a priori* knowable for A that if A's (rational) perspective is as it appears, then r is an objective normative reason to ϕ. I do not think that this condition ensures that Possession Enables Rational Routing is true. This is because the capacity to know the normative facts *a priori* and the capacity to be sensitive to the normative facts in one's reactions can come apart. When they do, Whiting's view predicts that one possesses reasons to ϕ even though one does not have any routes to *ex post* rational ϕ-ing.

4.3.2 Second attempt: attitudinal orientation towards the right and good

The first attempt to fill the gap required that some broadly *epistemic* condition be met. The first view held that what was missing were some beliefs about reasons. The second view held that one needed to be in a position to have some *a priori* knowledge about the normative facts given one's perspective. I found both attempts wanting because it didn't seem like these further epistemic conditions would guarantee that whenever one possesses a reason to ϕ, there is a route to *ex post* rational ϕ-ing. Without such a guarantee, it's hard to explain what is going wrong in the counterexamples to the epistemic condition.

Given this, we are now going to switch tacks and try to more directly build in the relevant kind of sensitivity. We will start with a familiar idea. This is the idea that what it is to have a good character is to be attitudinally oriented towards what is normatively relevant. Now the idea pitched at this level of abstraction borders on truistic. There are several familiar implementations of the idea that are far from truistic. I will focus my attention on the most popular version of this idea from moral psychology.[19] According to this theory—the Desire-Based theory—what it is to have a good character is to have intrinsic desires about the good and the right.

The Desire-Based theory has many prominent defenders: Smith (1994), Markovits (2010), and Arpaly & Schroeder (2014).[20] I will focus my attention on the most worked out view; namely, the view defended in Arpaly & Schroeder (2014). Now, to be clear, none of the views just cited defend views about *possession*. They are concerned with different topics. The topic they are all concerned with is what it takes to be a *good moral agent*. In the service of theorizing about this topic, they theorize about what it takes to be sensitive to moral reasons in ways that count as creditworthy. This is why these views are of interest to us. We want to understand what it takes to be sensitive to normative reasons more generally in ways that generate *ex post* rational reactions.

---

[19] For another sort of view of this type, see Sylvan (2015).

[20] Smith doesn't focus on character. Instead, he focuses on good moral thinking.

It will be fruitful, then, to see how plausible it is to take some of the machinery of Desire-Based theories and apply it to our problem.

The basic idea that I will work with is the claim that in order for one to have a route to an *ex post* rational reaction, one needs to stand in some desiderative relation to facts that provide normative reasons. The trick is working out a plausible view about what this desiderative relation is. Arpaly & Schroeder offer up two different proposals. The first concerns what they call the *ideal good will*. When someone has an ideal good will, one intrinsically desires the good and right via the concepts that figure in the correct moral theory. So, for example, if maximizing consequentialism is true and what is good is pleasure, then one has an ideal good will insofar as one intrinsically desires <THAT ONE MAXIMIZE PLEASURE>. If some version of Kantianism is true, then one has an ideal good will insofar as one intrinsically desires <THAT AUTONOMY BE RESPECTED>. One uses one's ideal good will when one combines these intrinsic desires with beliefs (perhaps justified beliefs, perhaps pieces of knowledge) about which actions will satisfy these desires. When one's action is caused by these beliefs and desires in the right way, one expresses one's good will in action and is creditworthy.

I do not think that this first notion can be fruitfully applied to our problem. First off, the attitudes that are relevant to the ideal good will are not attitudes directed at the facts that provide reasons. The attitudes are about very general facts—facts about maximizing pleasure, respecting autonomy, etc. What we want to know is when one possesses the facts that provide reasons *as reasons*. Most of the facts that provide reasons are specific descriptive facts—facts about salmonella, the cabby's choice of boot, the contents of the bottle, the location of the next World Cup etc. While Arpaly & Schroeder's notion of an ideal good will might be important for some purposes, I don't think it is important for ours.[21]

Their second proposal is helpful, though. This is a proposal about what they call a *partial* good will. When one merely has a partial good will, they have attitudes about some of what's right and good, but lack a general intrinsic desire for what is right or good. Further, Arpaly & Schroeder maintain that one has a partial good will (partially) in virtue of having beliefs and desires about descriptive matters. Indeed, they analyze partial good will in terms of the notion of a *pro tanto* moral reason. They write that one has a partial good will when one has 'an intrinsic desire for something that there are *pro tanto* moral reasons to bring about' (166). This has obvious application to our problem, for one might think that one does have a route to *ex post* rational ϕ-ing on the basis of some normative reason r if one both meets the epistemic condition with respect to r and intrinsically desires what would be brought about by ϕ-ing.

This clearly won't do as it stands. This is because there are many ways of intrinsically desiring something there is reason to bring about. That is, one can desire things there

---

[21] See Lord (2017a) for a sustained argument against the relevance of Arpaly & Schroder's view to responsibility.

is reason to bring about under many different *guises*. Some intrinsic desires that are about things there are reasons to bring about do not count as sensitivities to the normative facts. We again needn't look past the version of Lois's case discussed in the last section. Lois knows that the fish contains salmonella. She also intrinsically desires a state of affairs there is reason to bring about—viz., the state of affairs where she refrains from eating the fish. But she doesn't possess the salmonella fact as the reason it is.

This is of course not the end of the story. There is work to be done to see if a more sophisticated account is plausible. Notice first that Lois has her intrinsic desire *because* she believes that the fish contains salmonella. So the problem isn't that there isn't a connection between the belief about the fact that provides the reason and the intrinsic desire. Nevertheless, the explanation for why she has the desire because of the belief appeals to the belief that salmonella makes the fish taste worse. It *doesn't* appeal to the fact that salmonella makes you ill. So perhaps this is where things go wrong. Perhaps what is needed is that you base your desire on your belief because of an accurate view about why the state of affairs you desire is desirable.

This gives us the Sophisticated Desire Based Practical Condition:

Sophisticated Desire Based Practical Condition: *A* meets the practical condition with respect to a reason *r* to ϕ just in case (i) *A* intrinsically desires ϕ-ing and (ii) *A* desires this on the basis of an accurate view about why ϕ-ing's outcome is desirable.

The key notion here is what it takes for one's desire to be based on an accurate view about why what one desires is desirable. We've already seen good evidence against some natural contenders. These are views that require one to have explicit beliefs about normative matters. One possible view holds that one needs a belief that there is reason to desire what is desired. Another possible view holds that one needs to have a belief that what is desired is desirable. I take it that both of these views will fall prey to the problems that plague the missing beliefs views outlined above. These views overintellectualize—i.e., these types of beliefs aren't necessary. Moreover, they don't guarantee the right kind of sensitivity since one can have the beliefs without being sensitive—i.e., having these beliefs isn't sufficient.

Those views are out. What else is there? Let's think of a version of Lois's case where she does meet the Sophisticated Desire Based Practical Condition. In this version of the case, she does know that salmonella makes you sick. She knows that the fish contains salmonella. On the basis of these beliefs, she intrinsically desires to refrain from eating. What is needed is a story about how the basing works between the beliefs and the desire.

It's implausible that Lois has to *infer* the desire from both of the beliefs. In the normal case this is likely not what happens. Instead, Lois infers the desire just from the belief that there is salmonella in the fish. This doesn't mean that the other belief plays no role. In the normal course of things, Lois infers the desire from the belief that the fish contains salmonella *because* she knows that salmonella makes one ill. That is, the fact that she makes that inference is itself explained by the fact that she knows that salmonella makes one ill. But how?

It's helpful to think about inferences from beliefs to beliefs. This is because we know from Lewis Carroll that not all claims relevant to deliberation can be a premise.[22] If everything had to be a premise, then we'd never get anywhere inferentially. So, for example, it's clear that I can reason from p and if p, then q to q without having to have as a premise $(((\text{if } p, \text{then } q) \wedge p) \rightarrow q)$. Nevertheless, it can be that what explains why I make the inference is the fact that there is a logical relationship between the ps and qs. It turns out to be a very hard philosophical problem figuring how this all works.

Now, for a twist: I am not going to argue that the spirit of Sophisticated Desire Based Practical Condition is mistaken. It turns out that the basic idea is compatible with the view that I want to defend. In fact, I think that defenders of the Sophisticated Desire Based Practical Condition have to appeal to my view in order to explain how Lois's inference works.

Before we get to that, let me first argue that the letter of the Sophisticated Desire Based Practical Condition cannot be right. This is for two reasons. The first is that it cannot explain all cases of possession. The second reason it is false is that it's not plausible that one needs to *actually* be motivated to do what they possess a reason to do. If this were so, people could get off the hook too easily. Nevertheless, I think something in the spirit of the view might be true when it comes to possessing reasons for *actions*. Given that its defenders are primarily interested in actions, I take it that the spirit of the view can survive. Let me say a bit more about each reason to think it is false.

The reason why it doesn't explain all cases of possession is that desire does not play a central psychological role for many reactions we can possess reasons for.[23] Just consider the modus ponens case of inference. It's not plausible that one possesses p and if p, then q as reasons to believe q because one desires to believe q and has such a desire because she has the right view about why believing q is desirable. It might be that believing q is *not* desirable. Still, one can possess p and if p, then q as reasons to believe q (so long as p and if p, then q are true).

This point actually generalizes to *all* propositional attitudes. One can possess reasons to intend to ϕ even if one doesn't desire to intend to ϕ. It might be that intending to ϕ itself is not desirable. Similarly, one can possess reasons to desire p without desiring to desire p. Desiring to desire p might not be desirable even if p is. The practical condition on possession should not require you to desire things that are not desirable. And, in fact, it doesn't seem very plausible that it does so require. The Desire Based view of possessing reasons for belief looks like an utter failure.

---

[22] See Carroll (1895).

[23] Kurt Sylvan pointed out to me that attraction might be a more generic mental state that has a better chance of explaining all of the cases (cf. Sylvan (2015)). I agree that this is an interesting idea, but it will still fall prey to the second problem for the Sophisticated Desire Base Practical Condition spelled out below.

The second reason why the Sophisticated Desire Based Practical condition is false as it stands is that it is not plausible that one needs to actually be motivated to act in the ways in which they possess reasons to act.[24] This would rule out a certain kind of irrationality. Imagine Lois has a dinner companion, Bob. Bob knows that salmonella makes one ill and is generally disposed to be very averse to being ill. Further, he just heard that the fish contains salmonella. Nevertheless, he hasn't formed a desire to refrain from eating on the basis of this information. He was slightly distracted by his telephone when the waiter said that the fish contains salmonella. He still hears what the waiter says, but doesn't properly attend to the upshot of what was said. In this version of the case, it's plausible that Bob does possess the salmonella fact as a reason to refrain from eating. If he picked up his fork to eat, it would be appropriate for Lois to scold him: 'Didn't you just hear what he said, you idiot!' Since he did hear what was said, the right response to this would be sheepishness.

This raises a puzzle for the Desire Based view. On the one hand, actually having the motivation does not seem necessary. Bob shows this. On the other hand, there is some type of restriction. This is what the original Lois case shows (plus Billy's case from the introduction). So the desire based theorist needs to have some notion that explains the cases from the beginning of the chapter without demanding that one have the motivation.

Given a solution to this problem (which will be given in the next section), the Sophisticated Desire Based Practical Condition looks plausible for the special case of possessing reasons for action just so long as we understand 'desire' in a broad, Davidsonian, way.[25]

My plan now is this. In the next section, I will introduce my view by showing how one can use the basic machinery to explain how Lois bases her desire on her knowledge in the good case and how it can solve the puzzle just mentioned. I will then generalize the view.

4.4 The Practical Condition and Know-How

4.4.1 Inferring desires from knowledge

Our dear Lois has been through the ringer in this chapter. Fortunately for her we are now considering the good case; that is, we are considering what is going on when she gains a desire not to eat the fish when she finds out that the fish contains salmonella. Further, this transition—the transition from knowledge to desire—is in some way mediated by her knowledge that salmonella will make you ill. The problem for the desire based theory is explaining how this mediation works.

---

[24] This was made quite clear in the last section, I think, but it's worth saying again in this context.
[25] Davidson (1963) stipulates that the extension of 'desire' in his broad sense is any pro-attitude.

Several views look unpromising. These are views that require Lois to have explicit beliefs about the mediation or about the relationship between the fact that salmonella makes you ill and the fact that the fish contains salmonella. We likely often have those beliefs, but we needn't. Further, even when we do have those beliefs, they needn't play any role in explaining why we make the transition. The more usual course of events is that we immediately move from our knowledge to our motivation.

I think the explanation of what is going on in these cases is that we are *manifesting knowledge about how to use* certain facts as reasons.[26] Lois knows how to use the fact that the fish contains salmonella to inform her desires. She knows how to move from knowledge that this piece of fish contains salmonella to a desire to refrain from eating this fish. Further, when she makes this transition in normal conditions, she manifests this know-how.

Importantly, this know-how is a *competence*. It disposes one to get things right. Because of this, Lois cannot have this know-how without being sensitive to the grounds of the reason provided by the fact that the fish contains salmonella. If she isn't sensitive (at least partially) to the grounds of the reason, then she won't know how to use it as a reason for desire. Part of what this means is that she won't be in a position to reliably form rational desires on the basis of that knowledge. This is the problem with Lois in the earlier case where she thinks the only problem with salmonella is that it makes fish taste slightly off. That version of Lois doesn't know how to use the fact that the fish contains salmonella as a reason to desire not to eat the fish.

It's natural to ask at this point whether one needs to have the kind of background beliefs I objected to above in order to know how to use certain facts as reasons. If this was required, then my view wouldn't have any advantages to the views that don't appeal to know-how. Fortunately, it's not plausible that such beliefs are required. I'll argue for this in two stages. First, I'll argue that the know-how view gives a plausible story of the belief to belief case and that in that case it is not at all plausible that the further beliefs are needed. Second, I'll argue that know-how in general doesn't require these types of beliefs. Since we have no reason to think that knowing how to use facts as reasons is different from the normal case of know-how, we should conclude that these beliefs are not needed.

Let's start with the purely epistemic cases. Billy comes to know that Julia is at The Royal Oak. He knows that if she is at The Royal Oak, then she is not at The Rose and Crown. He comes to know that she is not at The Rose and Crown via an inference.

---

[26] Objection: My use of the word 'use' suggests that the thing that one knows how to do is the sort of thing that is itself governed by rationality. If that is right, then there is a regress worry looming. After all, if using reasons is governed by rationality, then my view predicts that in order to permissibly use reasons, we need to possess reasons to use. But then we would need to know how to use *those* reasons as reasons to use. This looks like the start of a regress. Reply: I don't think that using reasons in the relevant way is something that is itself governed by rationality. This will become clear in chapter 5 when I analyze what it is to know how to use facts as the reasons they are. According to that view, having the relevant know-how is a matter of having certain dispositions. I don't think those dispositions are governed (directly) by rationality. So, in the end, I do not think that the regress gets started. Thanks to a referee for raising this issue.

The inference is mediated by a sensitivity to the logical relationship between being at The Royal Oak and not being at The Rose and Crown. For comparison, imagine that John also infers that Julia is not at the Rose and Crown. However, he infers this from his belief that she is at The Royal Oak and his belief that if she is not at the Rose and Crown, then she is at The Royal Oak. In other words, John affirms the consequent.[27] His inference is not sensitive to the logical relationship between being at The Royal Oak and not being at the Rose and Crown.

By now you can anticipate what I think the difference is between Billy and John. Billy manifests knowledge about how to use the upstream facts as reasons to believe Julia isn't at the Rose and Crown. John does not. This is why it's so natural to say that Billy's inference is *competent* whereas John's is not.

Despite all of this, it is not plausible to think that Billy needs to have background beliefs about the relationship between the upstream facts and his inferred belief, nor need he have beliefs about how the transition is being mediated by a sensitivity to the underlying logical facts. Some very good evidence for this is the lesson from Carroll. We know that such beliefs are not required as *premises*. If they were, then inference would fail to get off the ground. But that is the most natural place for them to go. If they don't play the premise-role, it's not clear what other role they could play. It seems like any alternative would make it seem as if they played a merely subliminal role. This is not plausible.

It's more plausible to think that his sensitivity to the logical facts are not directly dependent upon any beliefs about reasons or the logical facts or the relationship between them. The sensitivities work independently of any beliefs about them or about the things they are sensitive to. This doesn't mean that they are *completely* immune from the influence of beliefs. That is not the case. We've already seen one way in which this true. In order for Lois to manifest her know-how, she needs to know that the fish contains salmonella—her psychology needs to mediate between her reaction and the external facts. Nevertheless, beliefs about how the premises fit together or support the conclusion are superfluous when it comes to manifesting the relevant competences.

Upon reflection on these types of thoughts, some epistemologists posit that the competences I've been appealing to are psychologically basic and thus part of the normative bedrock.[28] I share some sympathy for this view.[29] Right now it's not important how fundamental the competences are. What's important is that it is not plausible that normative or logical beliefs are needed in order for one to possess or manifest competences of this type.

---

[27] Further, we can imagine that the conditional John believes is not only false, it's not even very likely that she'll not be at the Rose and Crown in virtue of being at The Royal Oak. Thus, it's not plausible that what John is *really* doing is making an abductive inference. He is simply affirming the consequent.

[28] See especially Sosa (2015).

[29] Although, as we'll see below and in chapters to come, I do think that we can understand the relevant know-how at least partially in terms of reasons.

That's the first argument that extra beliefs are not needed to have or manifest the relevant competences. There is a way in which this argument is question begging. Namely, those who are thoroughly convinced that extra beliefs are needed when it comes to manifesting competences to desire will likely think that they are needed in the epistemic case, as well. The argument I just gave pointed to some large intuitive costs of holding this view. But the most diehard of my opponents will likely be willing to bear these costs (or don't see them as costs). For this reason, it would be good to have evidence for my view that does not turn on cases of reacting for reasons.

I think such evidence is not hard to find. We just need to look at other competences. Let's consider one that we are all familiar with: Linguistic competence. Consider Rachel. Rachel is a native speaker of English. She knows how to use her language to communicate with people in multitudinous ways. Consider one simple manifestation of her competence. Her young son is learning his colors. He is very interested in red today. He is asking her whether objects they encounter through the day are red. Rachel gets all of her son's questions right. She says 'Yes' whenever the object is red and 'No' whenever it is not. In so doing, she manifests her linguistic competence with 'red' (and conceptual competence with RED). Because of this, it's plausible to say that she says 'Yes' when she says 'Yes' *because* the relevant objects are red and she says 'No' when she says 'No' *because* the relevant objects are not red. The fact that a competence is manifested enables a certain kind of explanation.

Does being semantically sensitive in this way require that she have beliefs about the semantic relations between objects with a certain hue and the word 'red'? No, it most certainly does not. That would be an overintellectualization. It's hard to see how we could be so good at becoming competent if competence required beliefs about semantics. Instead, the competences work at a level below belief. They are directly sensitive to facts about the hue of things (when appropriately mediated through our senses). In other words, Rachel is disposed to say Yes when the hot wheels car is red in virtue of her competence. This is why she says 'Yes' in reply to the question because the car is red.

Obviously this is just one case, but the lessons generalize. Linguistic competence in general does not demand beliefs about meaning. It would be cognitively bad if it did. The amount of operative beliefs would rapidly multiply. It is much more plausible that we are directly disposed to react in various ways (say certain things, think certain things, etc.) in virtue of our linguistic competence.

So it looks like in at least one prominent domain, competence does not require background beliefs. As you might suspect, I think that this is very generally true. While some competences might require these types of belief, I suspect most of them do not. If this is right, then we need independent reason to think that a particular competence requires background beliefs in order for it to be justified to posit the need for background beliefs. Since we don't have independent reason to think that inferential competences are like this, I think we can conclude that we can have and manifest inferential competences without having beliefs about reasons, logic, or the relation between the two. Thus, my view can explain the difference between Billy and John without appealing to those types of background beliefs.

We have good reason, then, to think that it can also explain what is going on with Lois without appealing to those background beliefs. Lois is manifesting her knowledge about how to desire to refrain when the fish contains salmonella. This competence is (at least partially) sensitive to the way in which that fact is a reason to refrain. Those who defend a Desire Based view about possessing reasons for action should hold that the practical condition is met when it comes to a reason for action when one is motivated to perform the action and that motivation is the manifestation of knowledge about how to use the fact that provides the reason as a reason to be motivated to act.

That's the explanation, then, of what is going on in the very best of cases. But what about a good but not great case like Bob's? Bob is in a way properly oriented to the normative world. He has the right conception of the relationship between salmonella, illness, and his reasons. He also knows that the fish in front of him contains salmonella. But he hasn't properly taken up that specific fact due to distraction. Intuitively Bob is irrational for failing to desire to refrain. If he is, though, then it better be that he possesses the fact that there is salmonella in his fish as a reason to refrain. If he does possess that fact as a reason to refrain, though, then he needs to meet the practical condition. We can make the point sharper by asking the following question: What do Bob and Lois have in common such that they both meet the practical condition?

What they have in common is that they are both *in a position to manifest* knowledge about how to use the salmonella fact as a reason to be motivated to refrain. Lois is obviously in such a position since she actually manifests that know-how. Bob doesn't manifest it, but he is intuitively in a position to manifest it. Being in a position to manifest know-how is similar to being in a position to know that something is the case. Not only do things need to be right with you, things also need to be right around you. In this case, not only does Bob need to know how to use the fact as a reason, Bob's environment needs to be conducive to him manifesting his know-how. Perhaps the most obvious way in which Bob's environment needs to be conducive is that he needs to (be in a position to) know the fish contains salmonella. If he doesn't, then he won't be able to manifest his know how.

In this case, Bob is in a position to manifest his know-how. Indeed, once Lois scolds him, he immediately changes. He immediately manifests his know how by forming the relevant desire. It's not as if Lois gives him the know-how that he manifests when she scolds him. He already had it. Nor does she give him any important materials needed to manifest the know-how. He already had those too. She just draws his attention to those materials. That is why, I claim, it is natural to say that he was in a position to manifest the know-how all along.

Notice that in the original version of Lois's case, Lois is not in a position to manifest knowledge about how to use the salmonella fact as a reason to refrain. This is because she doesn't have this know-how. She has an inaccurate conception of the normative upshot of salmonella. So the difference between Bob and Lois in the bad case is that Bob is in a position to manifest know-how and Lois isn't. The difference between Bob and Lois in the good case is that Bob is in a position to manifest know-how and Lois actually does manifest know-how. Thus, we can use the notion of being in a position to manifest know-how to divvy up the cases in the right way.

4.4.2 Generalizing

The aim of the last section was to show that the Desire Based view can solve some problems by appealing to know-how. The main virtue of appealing to know-how is that it is natural to think that the kind of competence involved in know-how involves a sensitivity to the grounds of the various reasons without demanding that one have explicit beliefs about reasons. In this section, I will extend this thought to the practical condition itself.

My view is that one meets the practical condition for some reason r to ϕ just in case one is in a position to manifest knowledge about how to use r as a reason to ϕ. As we saw in the last section, one isn't in a position to manifest know-how just by having the know-how. The environment needs to be friendly as well. Before Lois and Bob hear about their particular fish containing salmonella, they both know how to use the fact that a piece of fish contains salmonella as a reason to not eat. They are not in a position to manifest this know-how when it comes to their particular fish until the waiter tells them about their particular fish being contaminated.

Although I will say much more about this in chapters 5 and 6, it will be helpful now to say something about what I take to be constitutive of the relevant know-how. The most important aspect of the know-how for this chapter's purposes is that when you know how to use r as a reason to ϕ, you are disposed to ϕ when r is a reason to ϕ. Now this is only a rough formulation of the triggering conditions of the disposition. This is because the disposition won't manifest whenever r is a reason to ϕ. To see this, we just need to return to the examples we used to motivate the notion of possession to begin with. Suppose that the fact that Anne is smiling is a reason to believe she's pleased. Suppose she's smiling right now but I'm halfway around the world. There is no disposition that I have that will trigger just in virtue of the fact that the fact that she's smiling is a reason to believe she's pleased.

Fortunately, we needn't do much more work to solve this problem. Chapter 3 did the work. Meeting the epistemic condition is what is needed in order for the triggering conditions to be met for the relevant disposition. Taking my view of the epistemic condition, the relevant disposition is the disposition to ϕ when r is a reason to ϕ that you are in a position to know. Notice that these dispositions are triggered by the normative facts themselves. They are not triggered by the descriptive facts that provide the reasons. They are triggered by the fact that some descriptive fact provides a reason. As we'll see in the next section, this is important when it comes to reacting *for* normative reasons. Part of why this is true is important for our purposes here. By insisting on dispositions that are triggered by the normative facts directly, you are ensuring that the relevant dispositions are true sensitivities to the normative facts. This is why it was plausible to say of Lois in the good case that her motivation is sensitive to the normative facts. It is because it was the manifestation of a disposition that is directly sensitive to such facts.

As I said, much more will be said about the nature of the relevant know-how in chapters 5 and 6. Right now I am just interested in showing how my view can explain all of the cases without incurring the costs of the other views we've discussed.

We can group the cases into two main categories. In the first category we have cases where the characters lack the relevant know-how. The exemplars of this category are all of the bad versions of Lois. The first version of the case is one of these. This is the version where Lois thinks that salmonella is completely harmless and has no ill effects whatsoever. The second version of the case is the version where she thinks that salmonella does have one ill effect: viz., that it makes the fish taste worse. She doesn't know how to use the fact that the fish contains salmonella as a reason to refrain from eating in this case, either. Billy and the bottle full of H_2O is a second case in this first category. He doesn't know how to use the fact that the bottle is thirst-quenching as a reason to drink because he doesn't know whether H_2O is thirst quenching.

In the second category we have cases where the agents do possess the relevant know-how but they are not in a position to manifest that know-how. The case of Watson and the boots is a paradigmatic instance of this kind of case. Watson does know how to use the fact that the print was created by a size 9 Iron Ranger as a reason to believe the cabby did it. We can see this by noting that he immediately sees the relevance of the boot print to the case. Even Watson comes to know that the murderer wears size 9 Iron Rangers. What Watson fails to know is which suspect wears the Iron Rangers. Once Holmes tells him about the cabby, Watson is in a position to manifest his knowledge about how to use the boot print fact as a reason to believe the cabby did it, and he does.

So my view can explain why the characters in the cases don't meet the practical condition on possession. Further, it can do this without incurring the vices of the Missing Beliefs views. Those views overintellectualized by positing requirements that those who possess either have certain epistemic beliefs or be in a position to know certain normative facts *a priori*. I argued further that it's also plausible that those epistemic requirements are not particularly relevant to the practical condition on possession. My view avoids these problems because we can have the relevant know-how without having the beliefs that the Missing Beliefs views require. At the very limit, I think we could have much of the relevant know-how without even being capable of having the relevant beliefs due to a lack of full conceptual competence with NORMATIVE REASON. Most of us aren't this extreme. We are competent with that concept and have many beliefs that token it. But we needn't have these beliefs to meet the practical condition, nor do we need to use these beliefs when we have them when we meet the practical condition.

Since it seems to make the right predictions about the cases, it is natural to wonder at this stage how well it meshes with Possession Enables Rational Routing. Recall that principle:

Possession Enables Rational Routing: If A possesses r as a sufficient reason to ϕ, then there is a route that A can take to *ex post* rational ϕ-ing on the basis of r.

While we won't be in a position to fully appreciate this for a few chapters, it turns out that my view of possession meshes very well with a plausible view of what it takes to ϕ in an *ex post* rational way. As I'll argue in chapters 5 and 6, what it is to ϕ in an *ex post* rational way is to ϕ *for* sufficient reasons to ϕ. And what it is ϕ for sufficient reasons to ϕ is to manifest knowledge about how to use the particular sufficient reasons to ϕ. My practical condition insists that when you possess a reason, you are in a position to manifest such know-how. Thus, if my practical condition is right and my view of *ex post* rational ϕ-ing is right, then the practical condition on possession ensures that whenever you possess r as a sufficient reason to ϕ, there is a route to *ex post* rational ϕ-ing. That route flows through the manifestation of the relevant know-how. Thus, my practical condition plus my account of *ex post* rational ϕ-ing explains Possession Enables Rational Routing. That is a strong reason to accept the package of views.

4.5 Is Possession Composite?

I'll end by asking whether the analysis of possession is composite. That is to say, is the right hand side of the analysis of the possession relation a conjunction? Given the arguments of chapters 2 and 3, it's tempting to think that Composite Possession is true:

Composite Possession: What it is for agent A to possess reason r provided by fact f to ϕ is for (i) A to be in a position to know f and (ii) A to be in a position to manifest knowledge about how to use r to ϕ.

My overall purposes in this book would not be undermined if we were to accept Composite Possession. Nevertheless, I don't think that we should. Instead, I think that what we've been calling the epistemic condition on possession is really a *background* condition on possession. This is because meeting the epistemic condition is necessary *to be* in a position to manifest the relevant know-how. The epistemic condition being a background condition on the practical condition is really not surprising. If you read chapter 3 with the practical condition in mind, it's very plausible that the debates that are relevant to the epistemic condition are driven by intuitions about when a reason is useable in a certain way. But a reason is usable in the relevant way, I claim, only when the practical condition is met. The mistake that has been made by many in the literature is thinking that it being useable in the relevant way is just a matter of meeting the epistemic condition. This is not right. Meeting the epistemic condition is just part of this. We now know why. It is because meeting the epistemic condition is a background condition for meeting the practical condition, which is directly about useability.

For these reasons, I think we should prefer Possession to Composite Possession:

Possession: What it is for agent A to possess reason r to ϕ provided by fact f is for A to be in a position to manifest knowledge about how to use r to ϕ.

Being in a position to know f is a background condition on being in a position to manifest knowledge about how to use r as a reason to ϕ. This is how the view defended in chapter 3 fits into the view defended in this one.

This ends my defense of a view of possession. I now turn to the second main notion appealed to in my account of rationality, which is the notion of *correctly responding to reasons*. In chapters 5 and 6, I will defend the view introduced above; namely, that to correctly respond to reasons is to manifest knowledge about how to use the facts that provide those reasons as reasons for the reactions they are reasons for. It turns out that reacting for normative reasons is intimately connected to the broader notion of reacting for (motivating) reasons. So in the course of defending my view of correctly responding to reasons I will grapple with views of what it takes to react for (motivating) reasons. In the end, I will defend both a view of reacting for normative reasons and a view of reacting for (motivating) reasons.

PART III

Correctly Responding to Reasons

Summary of Part II and Introduction to Part III

Part II defended my view of possession. On my view, what it is to possess a reason r to ϕ is to be in a position to manifest knowledge about how to use r as the reason it is to ϕ. I defended this view directly in chapter 4, which was about how to fill the gap created by counterexamples to the claim that meeting the epistemic condition is necessary and sufficient for possession. Chapter 3 defended a view about the epistemic condition. I argued that the epistemic condition is being in a position to know.

This Part will defend my view about correctly responding to reasons. This again will come in two stages. Chapter 5 is a defense of my view of responding to *normative* reasons. This view is intimately connected to my account of possession. When one possesses a reason r to ϕ, one is *in a position* to manifest knowledge about how to use r as the reason it is to ϕ. When one responds for r, one *manifests* this know-how. I spell this out in terms of *essentially normative dispositions*, which are dispositions that are essentially sensitive to some normative facts. I defend the view by showing how it (i) explains core data about responding for normative reasons and (ii) solves problems involving deviant causal chains. This view provides my view about what it is to *correctly respond* to the reasons one possesses.

Despite the virtues of my account of responding for normative reasons, the type of view that I defend doesn't fit nicely into the landscape of views in the philosophy of mind and action about reacting for reasons. This is because it does not account for cases where we react for reasons that are not normative reasons—i.e., cases where we merely react for motivating reasons. This is a central phenomenon for the philosophy of mind and action. Chapter 6 defends a view about what it is to react for motivating reasons and situates it with respect to my view of reacting for normative reasons. I argue that reacting-for-reasons is a *disjunctive* phenomenon, which is to say that the relation we stand in with normative reasons when we react for normative reasons is different in kind from the relation we stand in when we merely react for motivating reasons. I defend a new view of reacting for motivating reasons. According to this view, what it is for A to ϕ for a consideration r is for A to ϕ in virtue of the fact that A conceives of r as a normative reason to ϕ. I argue that this account solves the classic deviant causal chain problems for causal theories of reacting for reasons.

5

What it is to Correctly Respond to Reasons

5.1 Introduction

The basic idea defended in this book is that being rational is a matter of correctly responding to normative reasons. As we saw in chapters 2, 3, and 4, this basic idea needs to be refined in an important way. This is because it's simply not true that we are on the rational hook for all of the normative reasons. We are just on the hook for the ones that we possess. In chapters 3 and 4, I defended an account of possession. According to this account, what it is to possess a normative reason for a particular reaction is to be in a position to manifest knowledge about how to use the fact that provides the reason as the reason that it is for that reaction.

So chapters 3 and 4 took care of the first important part of my ideology. This chapter and chapter 6 will tackle the second important part of my ideology. This is the notion of *correctly responding* to reasons. Unlike possession, this notion has been theorized about in one way or another for a very long time. This is because many normative philosophers have realized that it is not only important to react in ways that are right, good, or required. It is also important to react in the right, good, or required ways as a result of some type of sensitivity to the right, good, or required.

This thought has been had by many philosophers spanning the whole gamut of normative theory. In ethics we can trace the idea back to the ancients via the notion of acting out of virtue. That basic thought was appropriated by Kant and put at the forefront of his theory of *moral worth*. Various contemporary theorists have incorporated something like the Kantian idea into their theories of moral worth, virtue, or creditworthiness.[1]

In epistemology the idea has come up in several places. The debate in which it has had the most influence is the debate about so called doxastic justification, or what I have been calling *ex post* rationality. It's very plausible that not all beliefs that are supported by sufficient reasons are rational. To see this, imagine that Jack has excellent reasons to believe that the temperature will be between 40 and 70 degrees tomorrow—five reliable forecasts predict it will be between 50 and 60 degrees. Jack

---

[1] See, for example, Arpaly (2006), Markovits (2010), Arpaly & Schroeder (2014), Lord (2017a, 2015).

also believes the temperature will be between 40 and 70 degrees. However, his reasons for believing this are that tomorrow is April 12th, that the temperature of any given day will be the product of the month and the day, and that $4 \times 12 = 48$. He infers from these beliefs that the temperature will be between 40 and 70 degrees.

Jack's token belief is not rational given its inferential source. Yet, he does possess sufficient normative reasons to believe that the temperature will be between 40 and 70 degrees. The common way of explaining this is by saying that while Jack's belief is *ex ante* rational, it is not *ex post* rational. On the most commonly held view, being *ex ante* rational is a matter of one's evidence sufficiently supporting the attitude in question. In order for a reaction to be *ex post* rational, it needs to be connected to the evidence in some way. The trick is to figure out what the connection needs to be.

My view of correctly responding is a generalization of a view about this epistemological problem. My view is also intimately connected to my view of possession. When you possess a reason to ϕ, you are in a position to manifest knowledge about how to use that reason as a reason to ϕ. When you correctly respond to the reason, you manifest this know-how. The problem with Jack is that he doesn't manifest the know-how that he is in a position to manifest even though he believes something that he possesses sufficient reason to believe.

This chapter is dedicated to further fleshing this view out and arguing that it can solve a version of a classic problem for (broadly) causal accounts of reacting for reasons.[2] I will start, though, by situating the task of chapters 5 and 6 within the debate about reacting for reasons. As we'll see, there are at least two things that are of interest. The primary focus for my purposes is reacting for *normative* reasons. But there is a much more common phenomenon that plays a massive role in the philosophy of action and mind. This is the notion of reacting for *motivating* reasons. The debate about reacting for normative reasons has unsurprisingly been intertwined with the debate about reacting for motivating reasons. The first main argumentative task of this chapter is to argue that we need to pull these notions apart in an important way. After that I will be in a position to flesh out my view of reacting for normative reasons before showing that it offers an elegant solution to a version of the problem of deviant explanatory chains. Chapter 6 will take up more directly what it is to react for a motivating reason and the relationships between reacting for normative reasons and reacting for motivating reasons.

---

[2] I have the 'broadly' qualification because some in the literature reserve the term 'causal account' just for views that appeal to event-event causal relations (or something near enough). This is particularly explicit in Mantel (2018). Mantel develops a view of acting for normative reasons that is similar to the view defended here. She denies it is a causal account. I think this is a confusing way to frame the issue given the connection between dispositions and causation. See Wedgwood (2006b) for further defense of my framing.

5.2 Acting for Motivating Reasons, Believing for Motivating Reasons, and Being Deviant

In this section, I will introduce the notion of reacting for motivating reasons and explicate the famous problem of deviant causal chains for causal accounts of reacting for motivating reasons. I do this here and now because it will help illuminate the topic of this chapter, which is causal accounts of reacting for normative reasons. In chapter 6, I will return to reacting for motivating reasons in order to defend an account that I claim solves the classic problem of deviant causal chains.

Now, some examples: I just bought my son an ice cream cone. Why? Because he has been well behaved today. Rose went to room 201 on May 10th, 2012. What motivated her to go? Answer: her sociology lecture was held in that room at that time. Bart believes that Andrew Wiles proved Fermat's last theorem. What motivates Bart to so believe? Answer: his math textbook says so. Sally always smokes cigarettes at parties. What motivates her to smoke? Answer: it makes her look cool (or so she thinks). Louis believes he will be lucky this year. What motivates this belief? Answer: his horoscope says he will be lucky.

These are all cases of reacting for motivating reasons. Interesting question: What is it in virtue of which the cited considerations motivate our characters? What is it about me that makes it true that the reason for which I bought my son an ice cream cone is that he has been well behaved today? And what is it about Rose that makes it the case that the reason for which she went to 201 on May 10th, 2012 is that her sociology lecture is held in that room on that day?

Nearly all accounts hold that in order for some consideration p to be the reason for which A ϕs, p must explain A's ϕ-ing. We'll call these *explanatory accounts*. A central debate in the literature is about whether the relevant kind of explanation is *causal*. According to causal accounts, the reasons for which we react cause our actions and beliefs. Not just any old cause will do, though. This is because there are clearly deviant causes. Here's a version of Chisholm (1966)'s famous example:

Dead Uncle

Dan has decided to kill his uncle Fred because he is set to inherit a vast amount of money from his uncle. The thought of inheriting the money excites him so much that he loses control of his car and kills a pedestrian. The pedestrian happens to be his uncle. He inherits the fortune.

In Dead Uncle, some consideration—viz., that he is set to inherit a fortune from his uncle—causes Dan to do something that leads to the death of his uncle. However, it doesn't seem like the reason for which Dan kills his uncle is that he is set to inherit a fortune from him. Indeed, it doesn't seem like Dan performs any action at all. Thus, causing the outcome is not sufficient for some consideration to be the reason for which some agent acts.

Here's a version of Davidson's most famous deviancy case (originating in Davidson (1980)):

Dead Climber

Dan and Fred are climbing an arduous mountain together. Dan decides that he will only survive the climb if he rids himself of the burden Fred brings to the project. He thus believes that he must get rid of Fred in order to survive. This thought so terrifies him, though, that it causes him to loosen his grip on the rope that is supporting Fred. Fred falls to his death. Dan survives.

In Dead Climber, there is some consideration—that Dan will survive only if Fred dies—that causes Dan to do something that leads to Fred's death. However, it doesn't seem like the reason for which Dan loosens his grip is that he must kill Fred in order to survive. Once again, it doesn't seem like Dan performs an action at all. Thus, causing the outcome isn't enough to count as a reason for which one acts.

Cases with the same structure litter the literature on believing for reasons found in epistemology. Here's one from Pollock & Cruz (1999):

Late for Class

Joe is late for class. This causes him to quicken his pace. This causes him to slip, which causes him to fall on his back and look skyward. This causes him to believe there are birds in the tree.

In Late for Class, there is some consideration—that Joe is late for class—that causes him to believe that there are birds in the tree. However, it's clear that the reason for which Joe believes there are birds in the tree is not that he is late for class. So some consideration causing a belief isn't enough for that consideration to be a reason for which the belief is held.

Some have thought that deviancy problems are unsolvable and thus think we should reject causal theories of reacting for reasons.[3] Others are convinced that only a causal theory will do and have faith that even though all proposed solutions are false, some solution must be out there.[4] In chapter 6, I will offer an analysis of reacting for motivating reasons that I think solve these problems. This chapter, though, is about reacting for normative reasons. To this we now turn.

---

[3] See, for example, Swain (1981), Ginet (1990, 2008).

[4] See, for example, Davidson (1980), Pollock & Cruz (1999), Arpaly (2006). In the epistemology literature one gets the sense that trying to solve the deviancy problems is a bit passé. Some evidence for this: Nearly all of the more recent work on the problem in epistemology devote large amounts of space in the introduction justifying the importance of the topic to other issues in epistemology (see, e.g., Turri (2011) and especially Evans (2013)). Apparently epistemologists need constant reminding that a lot of things hang on the right answer. Even though the problem has not been solved and most theorists are card-carrying causal theorists, solving the problem doesn't seem to be high on most people's to-do list.

5.3 Reacting for Normative Reasons

Although we almost always react for motivating reasons when we act and believe, we don't always react for normative reasons. We often, although not as much as one would like, react for normative reasons. I might refrain from jumping off the building because it's so tall. I might believe Anne is amused because she's smiling. I might start walking at 3:55 because the talk starts at 4:00 (alas, I'm not so good at doing this).

It's natural to think that when I react for normative reasons, I'm not doing anything over and above reacting for motivating reasons. It's just that, when I react for normative reasons, the motivating reasons for which I'm reacting are also normative reasons. If this were right, then once we worked out both what it is to react for a motivating reason and what it is for something to be a normative reason, we'd know what it is to react for a normative reason. One upshot of this would be that there is just a problem of deviant causes for accounts of reacting for motivating reasons. Once we solve that problem, we will have solved any deviancy problems for the notion of reacting for normative reasons.

The view that reacting for normative reasons is a special case of reacting for motivating reasons is nearly always assumed in the literatures on reacting for normative reasons. Audi (1993) eloquently gives voice to the view. The pages preceding this quote are spent defending a view of what it is to believe for motivating reasons.

Since believing for a good reason is believing for a reason (one that is good), the account clarifies believing for a good reason. [. . .] Indeed, if an indirectly (prima facie) justified belief is simply a belief held for at least one good reason, then if our conditions are supplemented with an account of what constitutes a good reason, we shall have all the materials we need to understand one of the main kinds of justified belief and, in good part, one of the main kinds of knowledge. (267)

Here is Dancy (2000) explaining the connection between acting for reasons and acting for normative reasons.

It seems, then, that the explanation of action [. . .] can always be achieved by laying out the considerations in light of which the agent saw the action as desirable, sensible, or required. If things were as the agent supposed, there is no bar against the agent's reasons being among the reasons in favor of doing what he actually did. [. . .] The reasons that motivated the agent can be among or even identical with the good reasons in the case. (136–7)[5]

This suggests Composite:

Composite Account: What it is for A to ϕ for a normative reason r is for r to be A's motivating reason for ϕ-ing and for r to be an objective normative reason to ϕ.

[5] There are several others who explicitly endorse the thought. See, for example, Armstrong (1973), Swain (1988, 1981), Schossler (2012). Over and above these examples, the thought often functions as a basic presupposition of the debates, as evidenced by the fact that nearly everyone thinks the key thing to explain is reacting for motivating reasons even in contexts when they are searching for the connection that must hold between normative reasons and reactions in order to be rational.

Despite the fact that Composite is often taken as an axiom in the debates about believing and acting for normative reasons, it is false.[6]

The problem is that it's possible for r to be A's motivating reason for ϕ-ing and for r to be a normative reason to ϕ even though A doesn't intuitively ϕ for the normative reason r. Cases that show this have been around in epistemology since at least Swain (1988), even though no one has fully appreciated what they show.[7] In fact, in chapter 3, I sketched a case that is a counterexample to Composite. This is El Clasico (I am changing the protagonist's name):[8]

El Clasico

Sam is wondering whether Real Madrid lost yesterday. She believes that Barcelona won yesterday. This is, as it happens, a strong normative reason to believe that Real Madrid lost, as yesterday was the El Clasico game between Barcelona and Real Madrid. Sam infers that Real Madrid lost from her belief that Barcelona won. The inference rule she follows is Explosion: Infer <REAL MADRID LOST> from any proposition p.

El Clasico is, I submit, a deviance counterexample to Composite. First things first, let's confirm that the two conditions of Composite are met. By stipulation, the fact that Barcelona won is a sufficient normative reason to believe Real Madrid lost. This is just to say that it is stipulated that the fact that Barcelona won is a reason to believe that Real Madrid lost and that it is stipulated that there are no defeaters of

---

[6] I should flag that it is complicated exactly what Dancy's view is about Composite, despite the quote above. As I read the Dancy quote above, he is endorsing the thought that when we act for normative reasons, the considerations that explain our action are also facts that justify our action. This by itself is weaker than Composite. However, he also seems to assume that when we act for normative reasons, the considerations explain them in the same way considerations that fail to justify can also explain actions (he clearly thinks these cases are possible). Further, he doesn't consider the sorts of cases that cause trouble for Composite. So I think it's fair to infer that he thinks (or least thought in Dancy (2000)) that when we act for normative reasons we are motivated by considerations that are normative reasons. With all of that said, it is a central tenet of Dancy's view that there is no difference in *kind* between normative and motivating reasons. Composite isn't supposed to conflict with that view. In order to accept Composite you just need to accept that there are some cases where one reacts for motivating reasons even though one does not react for normative reasons. Dancy clearly accepts this (some more recent defenders of views in a Dancyean spirit do not—e.g., Alvarez (2010)).

[7] See Turri (2010) for many cases of this kind. Alston (1988), Millar (1991), Goldman (2012) discuss the same type of cases. I will return to Turri and Millar below. See also Lord & Sylvan (FC).

[8] An important qualification: I will assume that the only normative reasons that are relevant here are possessed normative reasons. I will be officially neutral in this chapter about what the possession relation is. I will, however, make the simplifying assumption that characters in my stories know all of the relevant facts. As we saw in chapter 3, on any plausible view about possession, knowing the fact is sufficient to meet the epistemic condition.

It is also important to note that this doesn't mean that I am assuming that Sam possesses the relevant reason in the case below. She probably doesn't. This doesn't spoil the point because she does believe for the consideration that is the normative reason. If Composite is true, then this should be sufficient for reacting for a normative reason. Moreover, I think you can get cases with the same structure as El Clasico where the character possesses the reasons. These cases are not as clear as El Clasico, though. Thanks to Shyam Nair for pressing me to clarify this.

this reason. Moreover, Sam's motivating reason for believing that Real Madrid lost is that Barcelona won. After all, she inferred that Real Madrid lost from the claim that Barcelona won. Nonetheless, she intuitively doesn't believe *for a normative reason*. For one thing, she follows the absurd inference rule Explosion! More importantly, notice that she is actually insensitive to whether the fact that Barcelona won is a reason to believe that Real Madrid lost.[9,10]

To see this, note that the fact that Barcelona won is not always a reason to believe that Real Madrid lost. In particular, on match days where they don't play each other, the fact that Barcelona won is not a normative reason to believe Real Madrid lost. Nevertheless, given the nature of the inference rule Sam uses, it seems like even on match days where they don't play, Sam would take the fact that Barcelona won as a reason to believe Real Madrid lost. This is very good evidence that Sam is not sensitive to the actual reason provided by the fact that Barcelona won; that reason is dependent on it being a match day on which there is an El Clasico game.

If you don't find this immediately intuitive, fear not. For I think two platitudes about ϕ-ing for normative reasons predict that Sam isn't believing for a normative reason. The first platitude is that when one ϕ-s for a normative reason r, one is sensitive to r *qua* normative reason. Call this The Sensitivity Platitude. The Sensitivity Platitude is a platitude because it is extremely plausible that reactions for normative reasons *track* the normative facts. Those are the features of the considerations we ϕ for that

---

[9] Objection: The problem here is that Sam is also believing for another reason—viz., that if anything is true, then Real Madrid lost. In order to believe for a normative reason r, one might think, it has to be that one doesn't also believe for a consideration that isn't a normative reason. I have two replies to this objection. First, this would underdetermine the extension of believing for normative reasons. We often believe for multiple reasons. Sometimes some of those reasons aren't normative reasons. But that doesn't automatically entail that our beliefs aren't based on any normative reasons (cf. Turri (2010)). Second, *and most importantly*, this objection does violence to the case. Given the description of the case, it is implausible that Sam uses the claim that it follows from anything that Real Madrid lost *as a premise*. Instead, she is following the explosion inference rule. As Lewis Carroll made clear (Carroll (1895)), there is an important difference between these things. Given this, I do not think it's plausible that one of Sam's motivating reasons is the claim that it follows from anything that Real Madrid lost.

[10] Objection: We can't factor out Sam's reasons like this. Instead, Sam only has one reason, which is a conjunction of all the claims that Sam's belief that Real Madrid lost depends on (for a reply like this to a similar kind of case, see Alston (1988)). Since this conjunction isn't a normative reason to believe Real Madrid lost, this isn't a potential counterexample to Composite. Reply: This assumes both an implausible view about normative reasons and an implausible view of believing for (normative) reasons. First, it annihilates the difference between background and foreground conditions on normative reasons. To take an uncontroversial example, the fact that the wall seems red is a normative reason to believe the wall is red. But this normative fact depends on other facts in certain ways. For example, the fact that it seems red is not a reason to believe it's red if you know that there is a red light shining on it. This doesn't show, though, that when it is a reason the normative reason is actually constituted by the fact that it seems red *and* the fact that it is not the case that a red light is shining on it. The latter fact is just a background condition for the former fact being a normative reason. Second, there are similar problems for the account of believing for motivating reasons that is assumed by the objector. Sam's belief that Barcelona won might depend on a very large amount of things. It might be that Sam will give up that belief if she comes to believe all sorts of things. It doesn't follow from this that her reason for believing that Real Madrid lost is that Barcelona won *and* she doesn't believe p *and* she doesn't believe q *and* she doesn't believe x...

we seek to track when we ϕ for normative reasons. The rub is that Sam is *not* sensitive to the relevant fact *qua* normative reason. This is shown by the fact that she would continue to believe Real Madrid lost, and for the same reason, even when they didn't play Barcelona that day. If this is right, then she doesn't believe for a normative reason.

The second platitude is that when one ϕ-s for a normative reason r, one's ϕ-ing is explained by r *qua* normative reason. This is plausible for similar reasons to the first platitude. When we ϕ for normative reasons, our ϕ-ing is explained by some normative facts. This, I think, follows from the fact that we are sensitive to the normative facts when we ϕ for normative reasons. Once again, though, Sam's belief is not explained by the relevant fact *qua* normative reason. Thus, it is not held for a normative reason.

It is important to note that it looks like El Clasico is a deviant causal chain counter-example to a view of reacting for normative reasons—viz., Composite. Further, it looks to be a *direct* counterexample. That is, it is not a counterexample to Composite just because the deviant causal chain affects what Sam's motivating reason is. There is no causal problem when it comes to her motivating reason. She believes for a motivating reason. That consideration also happens to be a normative reason. But she doesn't believe for a normative reason. Thus, solving the problem of deviant causal chains when it comes to reacting for motivating reasons is not enough to solve the problem when it comes to reacting for a normative reason.

The lesson to learn from cases like El Clasico, I think, is that we need a separate analysis of what it is to react for a normative reason. We can't get by just with analyses of normative reasons and reacting for motivating reasons. This point has been, as far as I can tell, unappreciated.

These cases not only show this, they also tell us a bit about what the right kind of view must look like.[11] They show that the correct view must respect Prime:

Prime: What it is for A to ϕ for some normative reason r is not just a matter of r being A's motivating reason for ϕ-ing and r being a normative reason to ϕ.

Prime on its own isn't very illuminating. It is, after all, equivalent to the negation of Composite. We do better by thinking of what failure the cases point to. They point to what all deviancy counterexamples point to, which is a failure of the analysis to account for some type of connection between the parts. The problem highlighted by the cases is that Composite doesn't specify what relation must obtain between the fact that A ϕs with r as her motivating reason and r being a normative reason to ϕ. Since it doesn't do this and there is more than one way one can ϕ with r as her motivating reason, there are cases where both conditions of Composite are met that are intuitively not cases of reacting for normative reasons. Since it will be helpful later, let's say that

---

[11] I don't believe anyone has made this lesson explicit (again, besides Lord & Sylvan (FC)), but several accounts in the literature have the relevant feature (e.g., Wedgwood (2006b), Arpaly (2006), Turri (2011)).

an analysis is *prime* just in case the analysis holds that some connection must hold between the various parts of the analysis.

My reaction to the failure Composite is to explore analyze reacting for normative reasons *directly*.[12] I don't think we will make progress by simply thinking about the more common phenomenon of reacting for motivating reasons. Given this, for the rest of this chapter, I will focus my attention solely on reacting for normative reasons. In chapter 6, I will consider reacting for motivating reasons and the relationship between reacting for normative reasons and reacting for motivating reasons.

5.4 Reacting for Normative Reasons, Essentially Normative Dispositions, and Know-How

The last section showed that reacting for normative reasons is a subject in its own right. Reacting for normative reasons isn't merely reacting for motivating reasons plus something else—viz., the consideration for which one reacts being a normative reason. In this section, I will explicate and defend my preferred analyses of reacting for normative reasons. I will break the discussion up into two parts. In the first subsection, I will introduce the machinery I will use to solve the deviancy problem. In the second subsection, I will tie this machinery to know-how. The third and final subsection will introduce a complication and important refinement.

5.4.1 Essentially normative dispositions and deviancy

The lesson we should draw from the counterexamples to Composite is that the correct analysis of reacting for normative reasons holds that when A ϕs for a normative reason r, there is some connection between the fact that A ϕ-ed and the fact that r is a normative reason for A to ϕ. On my view, the right kind of connection is a *causal* connection. The relevant kind of causal connection is what Paul (2000) calls *aspect* causation. This is the kind of causal connection we talk about when we talk about things happening *in virtue of* certain aspects of things. Here are some examples: The towers collapsed in virtue of the heat (as opposed to the force of the collision). The grass grew in virtue of the rain (as opposed to the sprinklers). The computer broke in virtue of the water that was spilled on the keyboard.

The relevant connection that needs to obtain in order to react for normative reasons is captured by Normative:

Normative: A ϕs for a normative reason r just in case A ϕs in virtue of the fact that r is a normative reason to ϕ.

---

[12] Prime does not *entail* that we must proceed this way. We could, of course, add more conditions. I won't pursue views of this type here. See Lord & Sylvan (FC), Sylvan (MSa), and Way (2017) for some discussion. Thanks to a referee for help here.

The problem with Sam in El Clasico is that while she believes Barcelona won on the basis of the claim that Real Madrid lost, she doesn't believe Barcelona won in virtue of the fact that <REAL MADRID LOST> is a normative reason to believe Barcelona won.[13] We can see this when we notice that Sam would continue to hold the belief on the basis of the claim that Real Madrid lost even if that fact were no longer a reason—e.g., when Real Madrid plays someone else.

This is, I think, a very intuitive explanation of what's going wrong in cases like El Clasico. The short version of the explanation is that in these cases the subjects aren't sensitive to the normative aspect of the fact that provides the reason. However, this is clearly less than fully satisfying without some story of how the relevant causal relation works. At least one theorist who defends this type of view refuses to give an account of this, claiming that it is a task for the metaphysicians (see Arpaly (2006), Arpaly & Schroeder (2014)). But the project of fleshing out what it is to act for normative reasons *is metaphysics*. We're all metaphysicians, whether we like it or not.

My view of the causal relation is dispositional.[14] Before I get to the details of the account, it's important to be clear that in fact there are two different sorts of causation that are relevant. On the one hand, we have *productive* causation. Productive causation produces reactions. For example, my judgment that Arzak is closed is produced when I infer that Arzak is closed from the fact that Maizea is closed and the fact that if Maizea is closed, then Arzak is closed. Similarly, my act of pushing the button is produced when I see that that is the button that needs to be pressed when I want $20. On the other hand, we have *sustaining* causation. Sustaining causation sustains reactions. For example, my belief that Arzak is closed is sustained by the fact that Gambara is closed when I learn that Gambara is closed *after* I form the belief that Arzak is closed. Similarly, my baking of the pie comes to be sustained by the fact that my friend is coming for a surprise visit *after* I start baking the pie for another reason (e.g., to have something special for dessert).

Many have thought that only one kind of causal relation is relevant for reacting for normative reasons. For example, a dominant view in philosophy of action holds that *all* actions are produced by the reasons for which they are done.[15] Many accounts of

---

[13] A note about the causal relata here. Aspect theorists usually think causes are properties. While this is compatible with my claims, I don't think one needs to think this in order to hold my view. One could also think of the causes as facts (the fact that some fact is a reason to ϕ) or think in more purely dispositional terms (the disposition manifested is the disposition to...). I will use all three idioms in what follows. At the end of the day, I think that dispositions must play a role. Nevertheless, I think we can still incorporate properties or facts into the picture by having them play important roles in the manifestation conditions of the dispositions. For similar discussion, see Wedgwood (2006b).

[14] There is a good reason why I don't jump directly to my dispositional account. I think that Normative would be true *even if* the following dispositional account failed. This is why I introduce Normative before explicating my dispositional theory of the causal relation.

[15] This has become dominant because of the influence of Davidson (1963). Other prominent production accounts of acting for reasons are Smith (1994), Fischer & Ravizza (1998), and Arpaly & Schroeder (2014).

reacting for reasons in epistemology make a similar assumption.[16] That said, some in epistemology have thought that believing for reasons is only a matter of sustaining.[17]

My view is that both kinds of causation are relevant for both attitudes and actions. Thus, I think that the causal in virtue relation is something like a genus and that production and sustenance are species belonging to this genus. Most who explicitly argue that only one kind is relevant are motivated by arguments designed to show that the other kind of causation cannot avoid the problem of deviant causal chains.[18] I think that these arguments fail. I think the views given below are successful accounts of both kinds of causation.[19]

Now to my dispositional account of the in-virtue-of relation. Unsurprisingly, the dispositions one must have in order to count as reacting in virtue of the fact that something is a normative reason differs depending on whether the reaction is being produced or sustained. For illustration I will use belief for sustaining and action for production.

To see how my account of sustaining works, notice that a common feature of normative reasons is that the facts that constitute them aren't always reasons in worlds in which they obtain.[20] There are at least two ways in which this works.[21] First, sometimes a fact that otherwise would provide a reason to ϕ doesn't because a *disabling* condition is met or an *enabling* condition is not met. This latter phenomenon can be illustrated by El Clasico. Given normal background conditions, in order for the fact that Barcelona won to be a reason to believe that Real Madrid lost, it has to be that Real Madrid and Barcelona played each other. An enabling condition for the fact that Barcelona won to provide a reason to believe Real Madrid lost is that they played each other. Thus, when they don't play each other, the fact that Barcelona won doesn't provide a reason to believe Real Madrid lost.

The second way in which some fact can cease providing a reason is for there to be what Pollock (1974) calls *undercutting* defeaters. Suppose I look at the table and it appears red. Given normal background conditions, the fact that it appears red is a reason to believe that it is red. But background conditions aren't always normal. Suppose I then find out that there are red lights shining on the table. This fact

---

[16] See, for example, Swain (1981), Wedgwood (2006b).

[17] See, for example, Harman (1976), Dretske (1981), Kelly (2002), Turri (2011), Evans (2013).

[18] See, for example, Harman (1976), Turri (2011), Evans (2013).

[19] It should be noted that the account I defend below is, in a particular way, maximally ambitious. This is because it aims to provide a satisfactory account of both relations. This is a dialectical advantage because I will have some account even if only one kind of causation is relevant to reacting for (normative) reasons.

[20] Of course, this is not to say that there aren't some facts that are necessarily reasons for certain things. It's plausible that some facts are (to use terminology I'm about to introduce in the main text) reasons that cannot be undercut or disabled. I of course think you can act and believe for those reasons. I'm thus committed to thinking that one can have dispositions that can never be manifested (viz., the disposition to revise if the reason is undercut). Fortunately, I think everyone has to think that there are dispositions that can't possibly be manifested. For a plethora of examples, see Jenkins & Nolan (2012).

[21] Some think enabling and disabling are not distinct. See Bader (2016) for citations and compelling arguments that they are distinct.

undercuts the normative power of the first fact. The fact that the table appears red no longer makes it rational for me to increase my confidence that it is red.[22]

With these phenomena in mind, we can get a grip on what the relevant dispositions need to be. In order for some normative reason p to sustain a belief of A's that q, it needs to be that A is disposed to revise q if p ceases to be a possessed reason to believe q. It's very important that the manifestation condition of this disposition is the fact that p ceases to be a possessed reason to believe q. If A has this disposition, then her belief that q is sensitive to the fact p is a reason to believe q. This is what we want.

Now onto production.[23] When one's reaction is produced by the normative reasons for which it is done, it is the result of a certain kind of disposition manifesting. These dispositions are sensitive to normative reasons *qua* normative reasons. When A ϕs for the normative reason r, one's ϕ-ing is the manifestation of a disposition to ϕ when r is a reason to ϕ. Thus, when A ϕs for some normative reason r, it's (usually) true of A that if r hadn't been a normative reason to ϕ, A wouldn't have ϕ-ed.[24] If A's ϕ-ing is a manifestation of such a disposition, then intuitively A is sensitive to the fact that r is a normative reason. This is precisely what we want.

One objection to the way I've set things up holds that I've just reintroduced the deviancy problem by ultimately analyzing what's going on in terms of sustaining and production. This is not right, though. What I've done is *isolated* where the problem lies. The solution to the deviancy problem is found by figuring out which aspect of the fact doing the causal work must do the causing in order for it to be causation of the right kind. The aspect of the fact that must play the relevant causal role, on my account, is a normative aspect of the fact. It is the property of being a normative reason that is relevant to the dispositions involved in reacting for normative reasons. For this reason, we can, following Ralph Wedgwood, call these *essentially normative dispositions*. They are essentially normative because it is part of the essence of these dispositions to be sensitive to normative features of facts. This is precisely what allows them to deliver the correct results.

I can now state two more fleshed out versions of Normative:

Normative–Sustaining: A ϕs for a normative reason r if A is disposed to revise her ϕ-ing if r ceases to be a normative reason to ϕ.

---

[22] As a referee pointed out to me, my descriptions of disablers and undercutters are very similar. That raises the question of whether they are the same. The short answer is that it is controversial. For a third notion is also relevant, which is attenuation (discussed at great length in chapter 2). Some see undercutting as a special case of attenuation (e.g., Schroeder (2011a), Bader (2016)). If that view is right, then it's plausible that disabling is distinct from undercutting since disabling is non-gradable and attenuation is (although, see Horty (2007)). For arguments that disabling is distinct from undercutting, see Bader (2016).

[23] I'm deeply indebted to Wedgwood (2006b, 2007) here.

[24] Two things to note about this. First, it's not meant to imply a counterfactual account of dispositions. I think all such accounts are false. Second, despite the falsity of counterfactual accounts, the counterfactuals are usually true when one has the dispositions. This makes the counterfactuals a good (but fallible) guide to whether one has the relevant dispositions.

Normative–Production: A ϕs for a normative reason r if A's ϕ-ing is the manifestation of a disposition to ϕ when the fact that constitutes r is a normative reason to ϕ.

When we combine these two claims with Normative–Fleshed Out

Normative–Fleshed Out: A ϕs in virtue of the fact that r is a normative reason to ϕ just in case A's ϕ-ing is produced or sustained by r (in the ways specified by Normative–Sustaining and Normative–Production).

we have necessary and sufficient conditions for reacting for a normative reason.

5.4.2 Essentially normative dispositions and know-how

Notice that Normative–Fleshed Out is only a biconditional. I thus do not take it to state a real definition. This is for good reason. I do not think it is a real definition.[25] Instead, I think that Manifest is the real definition of reacting for normative reasons:

Manifest: What it is for A to ϕ for a normative reason r is for A's ϕ-ing to be a manifestation of A's knowledge about how to use r as the reason it is to ϕ.

Putting Normative–Sustaining together with Manifest, we get the prediction that r sustaining A's ϕ-ing is sufficient for A to manifest knowledge about how to use r as a reason to ϕ. Putting Normative–Production together with Manifest, we get the prediction that A's ϕ-ing being produced by r is sufficient for A to manifest knowledge about how to use r as a reason to ϕ.

This latter prediction—the prediction about production—is intuitively very plausible. Manifesting a disposition to ϕ when r is a normative reason certainly seems sufficient for manifesting knowledge about how to use r as a normative reason to ϕ. It seems especially plausible when the reasons in question are reasons for *action*. It is not clear how one can *manifest* knowledge about how to *act* for a normative reason if one does not thereby act. There are various ways in which one might *express* such know-how without acting—e.g., if one is prevented from ϕ-ing by unfavorable circumstances. But manifestation plausibly requires the relevant output obtains.

The plausibility of the prediction about manifesting know-how when one's ϕ-ing is sustained by normative reasons is less clear. Sustenance is a matter of being disposed to react if conditions change, not a matter of reacting in light of changes. Thus, when one's reaction is sustained by a normative reason r, there is nothing that one is *doing*. One is poised to do something if conditions change; but if they don't, then one's reaction will continue along unchanged. Given this, it's unclear that one is really manifesting know-how when a normative reason is sustaining a reaction. This is a challenge for Manifest given the plausibility of Normative–Sustaining.

---

[25] This is part of the reason why I do not think it is worrisome that Normative–Fleshed Out is disjunctive.

The question is whether one can manifest know-how by sustaining some state. While cases like this are not the ones we normally think of when we think of the manifestation of know-how, I think it is plausible that there are such cases. Consider Alfred the archer. Alfred is lining up a shot. He pulls the string back and holds it in position for five seconds. We can imagine that the arrow is positioned to hit the bullseye. For the five seconds that he holds the string's position, the arrow's positioning is sustained by Alfred. The position is sustained, at least in part, by Alfred's dispositions to adjust if conditions change. Alfred is disposed to tighten his grip under certain conditions, disposed to move his arms in certain ways if the wind picks up, etc. He maintains the arrow's position intelligently, which is to say that he maintains the arrow's position by manifesting his knowledge about how to aim. He does this in those five seconds in virtue of having the various dispositions that play a role in the sustenance of the arrow's position.

Now consider Eden. Eden knows how to meditate. When Eden meditates, his mind is blank. He thinks of nothing. Consider one token instance of Eden meditating. At *t* his mind is blank. He intelligently sustains that state through time. At least part of the explanation of why he intelligently sustains that state is the fact that he is disposed to maintain that state if certain things happen. He is disposed to go back to the blank state if thoughts start to bubble up, he is disposed to fight off the distractions of noise or light, etc. By having these dispositions in this context, Eden is manifesting his knowledge about how to meditate.

These examples provide evidence that someone can manifest know-how by having dispositions to change if conditions change. This, I claim, is precisely what happens when our reactions are sustained by normative reasons. We manifest knowledge about how to use those facts as reasons by being disposed to revise our attitudes if those reasons cease to be possessed.

One further way to make this more palatable is to think about the fact that the particular dispositions are usually grounded in more *general* know-how. Suppose that Andy finds out that Bar Haizea is closed and that Bar Haizea closes later than Arzak. His belief that Arzak is closed comes to be sustained by the fact that Bar Haizea is closed. He's thus disposed to revise his belief that Arzak is closed when the fact that Bar Haizea is closed ceases to be a possessed reason to believe Arzak is closed. This disposition didn't come from nowhere. It was generated by a more general piece of know-how. This is Andy's knowledge about how to use facts that entail other facts as reasons. By having these dispositions, one is manifesting this more general know-how. Further, in having these dispositions, one is manifesting the more specific know-how. There is a tight connection between the manifestation of the general and the specific. The way in which one manifests the general know-how is itself manifestation of the more specific.

For these reasons, I think we should accept the prediction generated by Normative–Sustaining and Manifest. What it is to react for a normative reason is to manifest knowledge about how to use the fact that provides the reason as a reason.

5.4.3 Why this is, alas, not enough to get all that we want

I think Manifest is the correct account of what it is to react for a normative reason. It would be natural to think that I thus hold that to correctly respond to possessed reasons is to react for a normative reason. That is, to react in an *ex post* rational way is to react for the normative reasons that make the reaction rational. Unfortunately things are not so simple.

The preceding accounts aren't enough to give us a successful account of *ex post* rationality. The problem stems from the fact that when ϕ-ing is *ex ante* rational, it is supported by *sufficiently strong* normative reasons. Not all reactions supported by normative reasons are rational. Only the ones that are supported by sufficiently strong normative reasons are.

This will lead to yet another batch of deviancy counterexamples—cases where one reacts for some normative reason r, but doesn't react for a sufficient normative reason. To see this, let's modify El Clasico a bit. Suppose that Sam knows that Real Madrid lost and she believes Barcelona won. Moreover, she is disposed to revise her belief that Barcelona won if the fact that Real Madrid lost ceases to be a reason to believe Barcelona won—e.g., if it's a match day where they don't play.

Thus, Sam believes Barcelona won for the normative reason provided by the fact that Real Madrid lost. However, it doesn't follow that she believes Barcelona won for the *sufficient* normative reason provided by the fact that Real Madrid lost. Lying Friend shows this:

Lying Friend

In the actual world, the fact that Real Madrid lost is a sufficient reason to believe that Barcelona won. However, consider the world where it isn't a sufficient reason even though it's still a reason. Suppose Sam calls her friend Mikkel to talk about El Clasico. Mikkel says that El Clasico was last weekend and that Sam must have watched the game on replay (further, he says, falsely, that Barcelona lost this match day). This defeats the reason provided by the fact that Real Madrid lost. However, suppose that Sam, despite being disposed to revise her belief if the reason ceased being a reason, isn't disposed to revise when she finds out this new information, and thus does nothing.

In Lying Friend, Sam does in fact believe for a normative reason that happens to be sufficient. This is because she believes for a normative reason and, in the actual world, that reason is sufficient. However, it doesn't seem like she believes for a sufficiently strong normative reason. This is because she isn't sensitive to the fact that it's a sufficiently strong normative reason, as is shown by her behavior in the world where the reason in question stops being sufficiently strong. Thus, believing for a normative reason that happens to be sufficiently strong isn't enough for believing for a sufficiently strong normative reason.

Just to be clear, in Lying Friend Sam is sensitive to undercutting defeaters and enablers/disablers—this is what it is to believe for a normative reason. She is, in other words, sensitive to whether the fact in question is a reason. But she's not sensitive to the fact that the normative reason for which she believes is sufficient. We can see this by noting that she is not disposed to revise her belief when the reason is outweighed—i.e., when there is an overriding defeater. It seems like you need to be sensitive to both kinds of defeat (and enablers/disablers) in order to believe for a sufficient normative reason.

The form the proper response should take is exactly the same as our response to the deviancy problems from §5.3.3. The problem with the view that what it is to react for a sufficient normative reason is to react for a normative reason that happens to be sufficient is the same problem we saw for the account that holds that what it is to react for a normative reason is to react for a reason that happens to be normative—they are both composite accounts. The proper way to solve the deviancy problems in both cases is to move to a prime account.

Just as in the previous section, I think the correct account holds that when A ϕs for a sufficiently strong normative reason r, there is a tight connection between the fact that A ϕs and the fact that r is a sufficiently strong normative reason to ϕ. On my view, the relation is the causal *in virtue of* relation. I think Sufficient Normative is true:

Sufficient Normative: A ϕs for a sufficient normative reason r just in case A ϕs in virtue of the fact that r is a sufficient normative reason to ϕ.

I spell out this *in virtue of* relation dispositionally, just as before. The only difference being that the disposition involved with reacting for a sufficient normative reason is not only sensitive to whether the consideration in question is a reason—i.e., to whether it has been undercut—but also to whether the reason is a sufficient reason—i.e., it is sensitive to whether it has been outweighed by stronger reasons on the other side. Thus, when one reacts for sufficient normative reasons, one is sensitive to both kinds of defeaters, which is intuitively what we want from an agent who acts and believes rationally or justifiably.

The difference between production and sustaining applies here, as well. The relevant dispositions will be different depending on whether the reaction is produced or sustained. Rather than going through all the details of this again, I give you Sufficient Normative–Sustaining and Sufficient Normative–Production:

Sufficient Normative–Sustaining: A ϕ-s for a sufficient normative reason r if A is disposed to cease ϕ-ing when r ceases to be a sufficient normative reason to ϕ.

Sufficient Normative–Production: A ϕs for a sufficient normative reason r if A's ϕ-ing is the manifestation of a disposition to ϕ when the fact that constitutes r is a sufficient normative reason to ϕ.

We get necessary and sufficient conditions for reacting for a sufficient normative reason when we add Sufficient Normative–Fleshed Out:

Sufficient Normative–Fleshed Out: *A* ϕs for a sufficient normative reason *r* just in case *A*'s ϕ-ing is sustained or produced by the fact that *r* is a sufficient normative reason to ϕ.

Finally, just as before, I think that the real definition of reacting of sufficient normative reasons is spelled out in terms of know-how. This gives us Manifest Sufficient:

Manifest Sufficient: What it is for *A* to ϕ for a sufficient normative reason to ϕ is for *A* to manifest knowledge about how to use *r* as the sufficient reason it is to ϕ.

On my considered view, then, one's token ϕ-ing is *ex post* rational when and only when one manifests knowledge about how to use a possessed sufficient reason as a possessed sufficient reason. This gives us the following real definition of *ex post* rationality:

Correctly Responding: What it is for *A*'s ϕ-ing to be *ex post* rational is for *A* to possess sufficient reason *S* to ϕ and for *A*'s ϕ-ing to be a manifestation of knowledge about how to use *S* as sufficient reason to ϕ.

5.5 Further Upshots

In addition to offering a plausible solution to the deviancy problems, I think there are several important upshots of the views defended here. I'll start with two debates in epistemology before moving on to two debates in practical philosophy.

5.5.1 *The relationship between* ex post *and* ex ante *rationality*

As we've just seen, the view defended here provides the basis for an interesting and plausible account of *ex post* rationality. It is common to think that we can understand *ex post* rationality in terms of *ex ante* rationality plus believing for normative reasons.[26] That is to say, what it is for *A*'s belief that *p* to be *ex post* rational is for the proposition believed to be *ex ante* rational—i.e., for there to be some set of reasons *S* that sufficiently supports *p*—and for *A* to hold her belief that *p* for the members of *S*.

On the common picture, then, *ex post* rationality can be understood just in terms of *ex ante* rationality and believing for (normative) reasons. Two of the more forceful challenges to this traditional view, it turns out, try to create problems for it by appealing to cases with the same structure as El Clasico. These are the arguments of Millar (1991) and Turri (2010). Millar argues in light of the cases that we need some other condition above *ex ante* rationality and believing for the reasons that confer *ex ante* rationality, while Turri argues that we need to analyze *ex ante* rationality in terms of *ex post* rationality. Both Millar's and Turri's arguments share a common premise. Namely, that believing for a normative reason is a matter of believing for a reason

---

[26] In epistemology, the focus is usually on justification rather than rationality. I will follow the majority of epistemologists in thinking these are the same. If they aren't, you can read this subsection as being just about justification.

that happens to be normative—both assume that the correct view of believing for normative reasons is a composite one.

Turri appeals to two cases.[27] The second case he uses is very close to El Clasico. I'll call it Spurs Win (see p. 317 of Turri (2010)):

Spurs Win

Both Mr. Ponens and Mr. F.A. Lacy know that the Spurs will win if they play the Pistons and know that the Spurs will play the Pistons. They are both thus propositionally [i.e., *ex ante*] justified in believing that the Spurs will win. They also both infer that the Spurs will win from those two propositions (and only those two propositions). However, Mr. Ponens uses *modus ponens*, whereas Mr. F.A. Lacy uses *modus profusus*: For any p, q, and r, $(p \land q) \rightarrow r$.[28]

Obviously Mr. F.A. Lacy lacks an *ex post* rational belief. Moreover, it is obvious that the reasons for which he believes the Spurs will win is that they will play the Pistons and that if they play the Pistons, they will win. Finally, it is obvious that those facts constitute sufficiently strong reasons to believe the Spurs will win. But this doesn't mean the common view is false. My view predicts that Mr. F.A. Lacy's token belief is not *ex post* rational. This is because, according to my view, Mr. F.A. Lacy doesn't believe for sufficiently strong normative reasons—he merely believes for reasons that happen to be normative (and sufficient). He is just like Sam in El Clasico. If this is right, then cases like Spurs Win are no threat to the traditional view of *ex post* rationality. The key is understanding what acting and believing for reasons actually amounts to.

Millar's and Turri's arguments get traction against the traditional analysis of *ex post* rationality only if the cases in question truly are cases of believing for normative reasons. Since they're not, they pose no challenge to the claim that *ex post* rationality is analyzed in terms of *ex ante* rationality and acting and believing for normative reasons. Thus, a virtue of my view is that it allows us to hold onto the common analysis of *ex post* rationality.

5.5.2 Speckled hens and the epistemology of perception

It's plausible that experience provides us with reasons. When I see that the table is red, I gain a reason to believe that the table is red. Moreover, it seems like I can gain *ex post* rational beliefs when I experience the table as red and believe for the reason provided. An objection to these thoughts runs through the fact that experience can represent very specific things. Moreover, sometimes it seems like beliefs that those specific things obtain can be caused by experiences that represent those specific things *even*

---

[27] I won't mention Millar's cases because he unfortunately never gives any. He only refers to cases with this structure (see Millar (1991, pp. 57–64)). Turri's argument was anticipated by Swain (1988).

[28] I'm following Turri here by making this a conditional. I assume he meant to make this an inference rule. Otherwise Mr. F.A. Lacy is just using modus ponens from a particularly dumb conditional premise.

though it's intuitively clear that those beliefs are not *ex post* rationalized by reasons provided by the experiences.

The case of the speckled hen brings out the problem.[29] Suppose you have a visual experience of a speckled hen. This visual experience represents the hen's 106 spots. It also causes you, suppose, to form the belief that the hen has 106 spots. According to a naïve causal view about believing for normative reasons, this is sufficient for your belief to be held for the reason provided by the visual experience. So it seems like the view that holds that having an *ex post* rational belief is a matter of believing for a sufficient normative reason predicts that this belief is *ex post* rational. But it doesn't always seem to be *ex post* rational.

This is just another deviancy case. Your belief might be caused in some way by the experience, but it won't be sustained by the right feature of the experience, which is the fact that it is a sufficient reason to hold the belief. Since your perceptual apparatus lacks certain discriminatory abilities, it's plausible that your belief is not produced by the normative feature of the content of your experience. Further, it's plausible you aren't disposed to revise the belief if the reason in question ceases to be sufficient. For example, suppose that your initial perception was non-veridical—the hen has another spot that was hidden from view at first. Suppose the hen changes positions and reveals the 107th spot. The reason provided by the first experience is now defeated. But it's plausible that you won't revise your belief, given your lack of discriminatory abilities. This is strong evidence that you don't actually believe for a sufficient normative reason, and hence my view doesn't predict that you are *ex post* rational. Thus, my view can explain what's going wrong in the speckled hen case. This is a virtue.[30]

5.5.3 *The causal efficacy of the normative*

It has been highly contentious since at least Harman (1984) whether normative properties—if they exist at all—are *causally efficacious*. Although there is some dispute as to what it would take for them to be causally efficacious, most seem to think that they would need to play an essential role in some correct causal explanation in order to be causally efficacious.

As Wedgwood (2007) has pointed out, views about acting and believing for normative reasons like the one defended here (and the one defended by Wedgwood himself) do seem to vindicate the causal efficacy of the normative. Let me explain.

Suppose I know *p* and if *p*, then *q* and I infer *q* from these two known facts. Suppose also that I believe *q* for the sufficient normative reasons constituted by those two facts. Thus, I believe *q* in virtue of the fact that the set of reasons containing just those two reasons is sufficient. This means that we can explain why I have that belief by appealing to a certain normative property of that set—the property of being sufficiently strong. This looks like a causal explanation. Moreover, the property of being sufficiently

---

[29] See Sosa (2003), Pace (2010).   [30] For more on this, see Lord & Sylvan (FC).

strong is a normative property. Thus, it looks like we have a case where a correct explanation of how my belief is caused essentially appeals to a normative fact.

The most common strategy for resisting the causal efficacy of the normative runs through the idea that the normative supervenes on the descriptive. This means that for any normative property P, there will be some descriptive fact D that P depends upon.[31] This means that for any correct explanation that appeals to P, there will be some other correct explanation that only appeals to D. Following Harman (1984), many have taken this to show that the normative is causally idle. We can just explain everything in terms of the descriptive properties that the normative ones supervene on.

I think the proper way to respond to this argument is to deny that there can only be one correct explanation.[32] There is some correct explanation that only refers to the descriptive properties that the normative ones supervene on. Fair enough. But that doesn't show that the causal explanations that appeal to the normative aren't also correct. The rest of this chapter provides evidence that they are correct.

In fact, I think the rest of the chapter provides evidence that they must be correct if there is any acting or believing for normative reasons at all. Recall that I argued that in order to solve the deviancy problem, one must pick out the property that must do the causing in order for it to be causation of the right kind. This property, I've argued, must be the property of being a normative reason. The explanation of the action or attitude that appeals to the descriptive properties that the normative properties supervene on won't always explain acting for normative reasons. This is because those descriptive properties need not ground the normative properties. Thus, appealing to the normative is essential to fully explaining our acts and attitudes when we perform them or hold them for normative reasons.

One might think this argument shows too much.[33] More specifically, one might think this argument, if successful, would also vindicate the causal efficacy of the arithmetical. For there are all sorts of true counterfactuals that have arithmetical concepts in their antecedents. For example, suppose my kitchen backsplash contains seventeen rectangular tiles. It might be true that if my backsplash were to have eighteen rectangular tiles, then I would be able to make a square. One might think this true counterfactual is analogous to counterfactuals I appeal to in my account of believing for normative reasons—e.g., usually when one ϕs for a normative reason r, it will be true that if r weren't a normative reason, one wouldn't ϕ.[34] If the claims were analogous, then one might think my argument in this section could be extended

---

[31] As Berker (FC) demonstrates, this use of supervenience is both oldschool and largely ignored in the booming literature on metaphysical dependence.

[32] This is following (Wedgwood, 2007, ch. 8). See that for much more discussion and defense of this type of account of the causal efficacy of the normative.

[33] Thanks to Gideon Rosen for raising this objection and discussing it with me.

[34] It's important to remember that I don't think that the claim that one ϕs for a normative reason r is made true by the counterfactual. It's made true by one's dispositions (which aren't made true by counterfactuals, either). I'll just ignore this important feature of my view for the sake of argument.

to show that the arithmetical is causally efficacious. Since it's (supposedly) not, this would be a major problem for the argument.

Fortunately, the two cases aren't analogous. The important point is that my claim about the normative is stronger than the claim that the various counterfactuals are true. It is possible for the various counterfactuals to be true even if the normative is causally inefficacious. The truth of the counterfactuals follows from the causal efficacy of the normative, but it could also follow from claims that are compatible with the causal inefficacy of the normative. Similar things can be said about the arithmetical. The counterfactuals follow, in our case, from claims that are compatible with the causal inefficacy of the arithmetical. Namely, they follow from claims about *the tiles*. No purely arithmetical fact is shown to be causally efficacious by the truth of the counterfactual. So my argument doesn't overgenerate in this way.

Still, even if it doesn't overgenerate in that way, it might overgenerate in a more obvious way.[35] Let's take an example involving arithmetic more analogous to paradigm cases of acting for normative reasons. Suppose Michael is taking an arithmetic exam. Question number 28 asks what 212+432 is. Michael comes to the conclusion that the answer is 644. He then writes '644' in the appropriate place. One might think that if my argument above is sound then, in this case, the fact that the 212+432=644 causally explains Michael's writing down '644' in the appropriate spot. This would vindicate the causal efficacy of the arithmetical.

I think the right thing to say about this case is that it is not analogous to a case of acting for normative reasons. This is because it *just is* a case of acting for normative reasons. The arithmetical fact has a normative property—viz., being a reason to write '644' in the appropriate spot—that is causally efficacious in this case. Does this vindicate the causal efficacy of the arithmetical? In a sense it does. Arithmetical facts can have properties—normative ones—that are causally efficacious. But any kind of fact can have those properties as well. So it's not as if there is something special about the fact that, in this case, an arithmetical fact happens to have the property. This seems like the correct amount of generation.

5.6 Conclusion

This chapter has had several aims. The main aim was to provide an analysis of correctly responding to normative reasons, which in turn provided an analysis of *ex post* rationality. Along the way I argued that we cannot understand reacting for normative reasons just in terms of reacting for motivating reasons that are normative and argued for accounts of reacting for normative reasons and reacting for sufficient normative reasons.

---

[35] Thanks to Michael Smith for raising this objection and discussing it with me.

My final aim was to show that the views defended here have important payoffs in other parts of epistemology and metaethics. They allow us to hold onto the traditional view of the relationship between *ex ante* and *ex post* rationality, they allow us to solve the problem of the speckled hen, and they allow us to defend the causal efficacy of the normative.

6

Achievements and Intelligibility
For Disjunctivism about Reacting for Reasons

6.1 Introduction

The topic of chapter 5 was reacting for *normative* reasons. As we saw, for many theorists this notion is constitutively connected to reacting for *motivating* reasons. I provided an argument against the view that reacting for normative reasons is simply a matter of reacting for motivating reasons that happen to be normative reasons. (As we'll see, that argument is important in this chapter, as well.)

In this chapter my aim is to situate this view within the context of the philosophies of mind and action. This is because most debates about reacting for reasons have not been carried out in the normative disciplines of epistemology and ethical theory. Most debates about reacting for reasons have been carried out in the philosophies of mind and action. Further, in the philosophies of mind and action, it is common to deny that the sort of thing you do when you react for normative reasons is different in kind to the sort of thing you do when you react for motivating reasons. This is a direct challenge to the view defended in chapter 5. Further, as we will see, the kind of view that I am committed to in virtue of accepting the account defended in chapter 5 incurs extra explanatory burdens. In particular, it commits me to saying something about reacting for motivating reasons and the relationship this bears to reacting for normative reasons. I aim to start meeting these burdens in this chapter.

This chapter has three aims. The first is to situate my account of acting for normative reasons in the debates in the philosophies of mind and action. In so doing I will provide comprehensive arguments that there is no constitutive connection between reacting for normative reasons and reacting for motivating reasons. The second aim is to defend a new view of reacting for motivating reasons. The third aim is to show how the disjunctivist view can provide a nice view about the relationship between reacting for normative reasons and reacting for motivating reasons.

Let's start with a pair of examples from chapter 3. These are Normal Colloquium and Unusual Colloquium.

Normal Colloquium

Today there is a department colloquium. It is at the usual time for such events, 4:00 pm. I notice that it is 3:55, and is thus time to walk over to the building where the colloquium is taking place. On my way I see my friend Dan. He asks me why I'm going to Robertson Hall. I tell him it's because colloquium starts at 4:00.

Unusual Colloquium

Today there is a department colloquium. This talk, however, is not at the usual time. It is at 4:30. I am unaware of this fact (despite receiving numerous emails that said so). I believe it is at the usual time. So at 3:55 I start walking towards Robertson Hall. I see Dan, who asks me why I'm going to Robertson. I tell him it's because colloquium is at 4:00.

It's plausible that in both cases I act for a motivating reason. One of the main tasks—if not *the* main task—of the philosophy of action has been to determine what it is for something to be one's motivating reason. This is the debate about what it is to *act for a reason*.[1] An orthodox view in the philosophy of action—albeit one that is being challenged more and more recently[2]—holds that my motivating reason is the same in Unusual Colloquium and Normal Colloquium. This view was given eloquent expression by Williams (1981, p. 102), who said 'the difference between false and true beliefs on the agent's part cannot alter the form of the explanation which will be appropriate to his action.'

It's not just philosophers of action who are interested in acting for reasons. Theorists who work on normative ethics and practical reason have also been interested in motivating reasons. This is because it has been very popular to think that hypological notions like praiseworthiness and blameworthiness are intimately tied to the reasons for which one acts. One's action is morally worthy, a common thought goes, only if one's motivating reasons are partially made up by genuine moral reasons to act in that way.[3] More generally, it is plausible and thus popular to think that whether someone's act is creditworthy or blameworthy depends on which reasons one acts for.[4]

Those who work on the normative aspects of reacting for reasons often insist that in order for one's actions to have positive hypological properties like that of being praiseworthy, one has to react for *normative reasons*. And since permissibility is tied to sufficiency, normative theorists are interested in the idea, then, that one's acts have positive hypological properties only when one acts for sufficiently weighty normative reasons.

It is natural to think that the philosopher of action's project is in some sense prior to the normative theorist's project. This is because it is natural to think that when we

---

[1] The traditional motivation for focusing on acting for reasons has been the thought that we cannot figure out what it is for some action to be intentional without figuring out what it is for an action to be done for a reason. This has become the frame of the debate due to the fact that both Anscombe (1957) and Davidson (1963) accept that there is some constitutive connection between intentional action and acting for reasons. See Hyman (2015) for recent push back on this. I will not be concerned with the intentionality of actions here.

[2] See, for example, Hornsby (2008), Alvarez (2010), Littlejohn (2012), Hyman (2015).

[3] For contemporary expressions of this view, see Arpaly (2003), Markovits (2010), Arpaly & Schroeder (2014), and Lord (2017a). It reflects an old Kantian idea.

[4] See Lord (2015, 2017a).

react for normative reasons, we are, at bottom, just reacting for motivating reasons. To put it more metaphysically, it is natural to think that we stand in the same relation to the normative reasons we react for as we do to our motivating reasons. It is all reacting for motivating reasons. Some of it is just in tune to some of the actual normative facts. I will call this view the Univocal View of reacting for reasons:[5]

Univocal View: The only relation involved in reacting for normative reasons is the relation involved in reacting for motivating reasons.

The view I defended in chapter 5 commits me to denying the Univocal View. This is because that view predicts that I do not stand in the same relation in Unusual Colloquium as I do in Normal Colloquium. On the natural interpretation of Normal Colloquium, I act for the normative reason provided by the fact that colloquium starts at 4 pm. According to the view I defended in chapter 5, I do that when I manifest knowledge about how to use the fact that colloquium starts at 4 pm as a reason to go to Robertson Hall. And I do that when my action is a manifestation of a disposition that is sensitive to the property of being a normative reason to go to Robertson Hall. I cannot be manifesting such a disposition in Unusual Colloquium. This is because there is no fact that colloquium starts at 4 pm that has the property of being a normative reason to go to Robertson Hall. So I cannot be manifesting an essentially normative disposition with that as its manifestation condition. It follows that whatever is going on Normal Colloquium is not going on in Unusual Colloquium. The Univocal View is thus false if the view defended in chapter 5 is true.

I'll argue in this chapter that this is all to the good. The Univocal View is false. The anchor of my attack against it is the thought that there is no relation that is flexible enough to explain all of the core features of reacting for motivating reasons on the one hand and reacting for normative reasons on the other. This fact has been missed, I claim, because philosophers of action have not been sensitive enough to the normative features of reacting for normative reasons and normative theorists haven't been sensitive enough to the features of reacting for motivating reasons that are of interest to the philosophers of action.

I will also argue that in place of the Univocal View, we should accept Disjunctivism:[6]

---

[5] The key issue is whether there is only one reacting-for-reasons relation. On some non-univocal views the reacting-for-normative reasons relation will entail the reacting-for-motivating reasons relation (cf. Lord & Sylvan (FC)). I will suggest below that there isn't strong pressure to go in for this idea if we hold that reacting-for-reasons is a disjunctive phenomenon.

[6] Right now I am using 'disjunctivism' in a purely stipulative way. As we will see in §6.6 below, there are different uses of the word in the literature. One use—what I call the negative use below—is just about the number and priority of relations. This is what is at issue for the bulk of the chapter. There is another use—what I call the positive use—that has to do with whether or not there is some disjunctive phenomenon (e.g., appearing-as-if or reacting-for-reasons). Often it is assumed that if you accept the negative thesis you accept the positive one. But this is not required. For most of the chapter, I will be neutral on the positive thesis, although in §6.6 I will argue that accepting it has some virtues. It is important to keep in mind, though, that up until §6.6 everything argued for is neutral about whether there is any disjunctive phenomenon.

> **Disjunctivism:**   We stand in a different relation to normative reasons when we react for normative reasons than we do with considerations when we (merely) react for motivating reasons.

Chapter 5 defended one half of the disjunctivist view—the view of reacting for normative reasons. In this chapter, I will defend the other half, which is a view of reacting for motivating reasons.

The plan is this. In the next section, I will further explicate the core features of reacting for motivating reasons on the one hand and reacting for normative reasons on the other. In §6.3, I will lay out a tempting argument for the Univocal View. I will also show how that argument is very similar to the (in)famous argument from illusion. In §6.4, I will start my attack against univocal views. First, I will argue that univocal views that take reacting for normative reasons to be prior to reacting for motivating reasons are hopeless. Second, I will argue that univocal views that take reacting for motivating reasons to be prior to reacting for normative reasons cannot account for one of the core features of reacting for normative reasons. In §6.4, I will introduce my disjunctivist alternative, sketch a new view of reacting for motivating reasons, and explain how it holds great promise when it comes to solving the problem of deviant causal chains. In §6.5, I will discuss the varieties of disjunctivisms in order to highlight some connections between reacting for normative reasons and reacting for motivating reasons.

6.2 Reacting for Motivating Reasons and Reacting for Normative Reasons

6.2.1 Reacting for motivating reasons

It's plausible that I act for a motivating reason in both Normal Colloquium and Unusual Colloquium. In both cases I am motivated to go to Robertson Hall by the consideration that colloquium starts at 4 pm. Given this, it's plausible that the consideration <THAT COLLOQUIUM STARTS AT 4 PM> plays a central role in a particular kind of explanation of my behavior. We can cite that consideration in an explanation that makes my going to Robertson *intelligible* from my perspective. To put more flesh on this idea, notice that I have a certain outlook on the world. Given that outlook, going to Robertson is made intelligible by the claim that colloquium starts at 4. Because of this, it's natural to say that that consideration is my *rationale* for going to Robertson.

There are many other true explanations of my walking that don't make my walking intelligible in this way. The fact that Robertson Hall is at 4020'54.0"N 7439'17.5"W together with the fact that I am heading for the location at 4020'54.0"N 7439'17.5"W also explains why I'm heading to Robertson Hall. But those facts needn't make my walking intelligible in the relevant way.[7] At the time I know nothing about the coordinates of where I'm going. And even if I did, I needn't think about those facts in order for my walking to be intelligible. The claim that colloquium starts at 4 pm can play that role on its own.

Now my motivation to see the talk might be completely sensible or correct. It's important to note that one can react for motivating reasons even if one is completely unreasonable. Take Taylor. Taylor just bought $1500 worth of AK-47 ammunition. Why? It's because he thinks that a zombie insurrection is imminent and he wants to protect his home. He is thus hoarding ammunition in his basement. We can suppose that Taylor is deluded. Yet, the claim that the zombie insurrection is imminent can still make his buying of the ammunition intelligible. We can see how that act fits into Taylor's perspective by citing that consideration. It is his rationale for going to the big box store and loading up on AK-47 ammunition.

Even though we can make his action intelligible by citing that consideration, we can still condemn his act in nearly every important way. We can say that it is stupid, careless, incorrect, irrational, delusional etc. His act is, to use a phrase of Davidson (1963)'s, justified only in an anemic sense of justification. It doesn't follow from the fact that his action is intelligible that his action has anything normatively important going for it.[8]

In between the colloquium cases and Taylor's case are cases where one is non-culpably mistaken about something that makes their act objectively incorrect even though it is intelligible. Take Harry. Harry is a decent person with an unfortunate false belief. This false belief is the belief that Parisians find over-the-top American personalities charming. Harry came upon this unfortunate belief because some of her hostel-mates in London were so annoyed by her all-American personality that they decided to play a trick on her. The trick was to convince her to be even more loud, closed-minded, and inquisitive about other people's business in Paris. They were able to convince her.

Given her false belief, it is easy to make sense of some of her actions. For example, she just asked a woman on the street for directions. During the exchange, she asked the woman some very personal questions. We can make her asking of these personal

---

[7] Of course, it's plausible to think that all explanations (or all informative explanations, at least) make the explanans intelligible *in some respect*. The explanation above that appeals to Robertson Hall's coordinates makes my movement geographically intelligible. That said, the kind of intelligibility at issue when it comes to reacting for motivating reasons is tied to one's perspective on the world. I thank Daniel Whiting for pushing me to say something about this.

[8] This is a teeny bit controversial since Arpaly & Schroeder (2014) defend a view of acting for reasons according to which all acts done for reasons are at least partially rational. I will argue against their view in the next section.

questions intelligible by citing the consideration that Parisians find this kind of direct questioning charming. This consideration is what, from her perspective, counts in favor of being inquisitive in a way that Parisians actually find annoying and rude. If Parisians actually found this kind of questioning charming, then Harry's questioning would be perfectly sensible. Even though Parisians don't find it charming, from Harry's perspective this type of questioning is sensible since she thinks they do in fact find it charming.

The important feature of reacting for motivating reasons for my purposes is the fact that when we react for motivating reasons, the reasons for which we react make our reactions intelligible. This, I think, is an essential feature of the motivating reasons for which we react. In other words, without making our reactions intelligible in this way, some consideration cannot be the motivating reason for which we act.

6.2.2 Reacting for normative reasons

Now that we've seen that reacting for motivating reasons is essentially tied to intelligibility, we need to investigate some of the features of reacting for normative reasons. First off, it seems clear that we don't always react for normative reasons when we react for motivating reasons. Neither Taylor nor Harry act for normative reasons. Taylor acts for downright immoral motivating reasons. Harry is moved by considerations that turn out to not be true. If they were, Harry's motivating reasons would be normative reasons, but since they aren't, her motivating reasons cannot be normative reasons.[9]

Let's get some paradigm cases on the table. We'll start with the virtuous grocer—I'll call him Gary. Gary is a hardworking man with a strong sense of justice. He is especially concerned that his customers get a fair shake. He thus is very particular about how he and his staff treat the customers. He always goes out of his way to ensure that they are treated well. He does this out of concern of fairness. One day he rings up a customer's transaction. The correct change is $9.76. He gives the customer $9.76. The fact that $9.76 is the correct change is a normative reason to give the customer $9.76. Moreover, that is the reason for which Gary gives the customer $9.76. Given his concern for justice and fairness, it's plausible that he acts for a normative reason.

Normative reasons for which we act needn't always be moral reasons. Suppose Barry is trying to decide which professional journal to submit a paper to. He has to weigh up whether to send it to big name journal X or medium name journal Y. X will be slow, but if the paper is accepted it will be a boon to Barry's career. Y will be much faster and will provide some benefit to his career. His chances are also higher with Y. So Barry has some normative reasons to submit to both journals. Suppose he submits to Y. The fact that Y will be fast is a normative reason to submit to Y. Suppose that this is the reason that Barry submits. Plausibly, he's acted for a normative reason by

---

[9] This of course assumes that normative reasons are facts or truths. I will assume this view here without defending it.

acting for that reason. This isn't a *moral* reason. It is probably a prudential one. But it is a normative reason nonetheless.

So far we just have these cases; we don't yet have clear grip on the essential features of reacting for normative reasons. Traditionally, the notion of reacting for normative reasons has been important for normative theorists because it is very plausible to suppose that reacting for normative reasons is tied to *being rational* and *being creditworthy*. We can see this by comparing Gary's case and Barry's case to Gerald's case and Brandon's case.

Gerald is also a grocer. But he doesn't have a very refined sense of justice and fairness. In fact, he doesn't care that much about those things. What he does care about is profit. He has decided that the only way to maximize his profit is by giving his customers the correct change. One of his customers just bought some beef jerky and the correct change is $9.76. He gives him $9.76. His motivating reason is that $9.76 is the correct change.

Gerald does the thing that morality requires of him. But intuitively his action is not worthy of credit (moral credit, at least).[10] His action does not speak well of him in the way that creditworthy actions speak well of one. This is because of his selfish motives. Thus, even though Gerald does what morality requires of him, he is not creditworthy. What seems to be missing is that he doesn't act for the right reasons—i.e., he doesn't act for the normative reasons that make his act right.

Brandon is also deciding whether to send his paper to X or to Y. And the facts are the same for Brandon as they are for Barry. Brandon, however, also happens to believe that the editor at journal Y will ensure that his paper is published. He doesn't have any good reason to think this. He just believes it on an unfounded hunch. Still, he submits to Y. The reason for which he submits is that the editor will ensure publication.

Brandon, like Barry, performs an action that is rational—submitting to Y. But Brandon's token action of submitting to Y is not intuitively rational, whereas Barry's token action is intuitively rational. The difference between the cases, it seems, is that Barry's token action is connected to the reasons that make it rational, whereas Brandon's token action is not. This is why Barry's action is rational and Brandon's is not.

Intuitively, then, it seems like there is an important connection between reacting for normative reasons and hypological notions like being creditworthy and deontic notions like being rational. Whether your token actions are creditworthy or rational is partly determined by whether you act for the normative reasons that make your action right or rational. This is why normative theorists have been interested in

---

[10] I use this example given its historical roots in the debate I am engaging in. As a referee noted, though, it is easy to misuse intuitions about this case. I don't mean to say that the only sort of achievement I am interested in is this sort of moral achievement involved in Gary's case (in contrast to Gerald). That is just one species of the genus I am talking about. If it helps, just imagine that while Gerald cares most about profit, he is also not very good at knowing how to maximize profit. So it turns out that giving correct change is not the best way to get what he wants.

reacting for normative reasons. It doesn't seem like we can give a complete account of creditworthiness or rationality without appealing to this notion.

The question I am interested in is this: What is it about reacting for normative reasons that makes it intimately connected to the hypological and deontic in these ways? I think that the answer is that reacting for normative reasons is connected to the hypological/deontic in these ways because reacting for normative reasons is an *achievement*. This is because one exercises a *competence* when one reacts for normative reasons.[11]

What type of competence is this? It is a competence to correctly respond to reasons. That is, it is a competence that is sensitive to some of the facts about reasons. When one exercises this competence, one's actions are sensitive to the normative facts. One gets things *right*. Moreover, given the manifestation of a competence, it is no accident that one gets things right. This is why reacting for normative reasons is an achievement. And this is why one is creditworthy when one acts for the right reasons. It is also why one's token actions are rational only when one acts for the right reasons.

Thus, the essential feature of reacting for normative reasons that I am interested in is the fact that reacting for normative reasons is an achievement. We should think this because it offers the best explanation of why there is such a tight connection between reacting for normative reasons and hypological/deontic properties like being creditworthy and being rational.

6.3 The Univocal View and the Argument from Illusion

The first upshot of the last section is that what we want from a theory of motivating reasons is a story about how motivating reasons make the reactions they are based on intelligible. The second upshot is that what we want from a theory of reacting for normative reasons is a story about how reactions based on normative reasons are achievements. The main question animating this chapter is whether the same relation is involved in both kinds of cases. The most popular view in the literature holds that it is the same relation in both sorts of case. To use Normal Colloquium and Unusual Colloquium once more, the most popular view holds that in both cases I stand in the same relation to the reasons for which I act, even though in Normal Colloquium I act for a normative reason and in Unusual Colloquium I don't.

---

[11] It's important to note that the kind of achievement in question is *not* the sort of achievement that requires a lot of effort or (statistically) unusual skill (cf. Bradford (2015)). I grant that, in ordinary English, we usually only talk about achievements when we are talking about these sorts of achievements. Nevertheless, I think that the achievements I am talking about can be talked about using ordinary English. This is because they are the result of an exercise of skills or competences, which is tightly connected to the meaning of 'achievement' in English. Further, my usage is in line with a prominent tradition in philosophy that thinks that all exercises of competences are achievements (see, e.g., Sosa (2015), Sylvan (MSa), Miracchi (MS)).

Why is the Univocal View so popular? It is probably because there is a very tempting argument in its favor. This is what I'll call the Similarity Argument. The Similarity Argument can be put like this:[12]

1. In both Normal Colloquium and Unusual Colloquium, I act for a reason.
2. The only difference between Normal Colloquium and Unusual Colloquium is that my belief in Normal Colloquium is true.
3. The truth value of my belief does not affect the relation I stand in when I act for reasons.
C. Therefore, the relation in both Normal Colloquium and Unusual Colloquium is the same.

(1) is surely true. (2) is tempting given that the world appears to me the same in Normal Colloquium and Unusual Colloquium. As long as we are precise enough in the details, it could be that from the inside everything appears the same in the two cases. If that's right, then it's tempting to think that the only difference is one external to my perspective—viz., the truth value of my belief. (3) can be made plausible by considering the huge range of cases where someone reacts for a reason. Not only do these include cases like the colloquium cases, but also cases of systematic delusion like Taylor's. Given this range, it seems like what is important is the agent's perspective on the world, not whether that perspective lines up with the facts. It is tempting to infer via induction that the relation is the same in the two cases.

Just to be clear, this of course does not mean that there aren't differences between the two cases. You are not committed to denying that I act for a normative reason in Normal Colloquium just because you accept the Similarity Argument. You are committed to thinking, however, that reacting for normative reasons is a matter of reacting for motivating reasons plus some other condition or conditions. In other words, you are committed to thinking that there is just one reacting-for-reasons relation.

The Similarity Argument is tempting. However, it should be noted that it bears a striking resemblance to the so-called arguments from illusion and hallucination.[13] These arguments also focus on pairs of cases. In one case, I have a veridical perception of a brown table in front of me—this is the good case. In the other case, I have an illusory perceptual experience of a brown table in front of me—this is the bad case. The argument from illusion attempts to establish that the kind of mental state I am in in the good case is the same kind of mental state I am in in the bad case. It does this by relying on a similarity claim akin to (3) above. One of the more popular similarity

---

[12] Dancy (2006) warns us not to be taken in by a different argument that bears resemblance to the argument of illusion. This is not exactly the Similarity Argument. The issue Dancy is interested in is whether motivating reasons are beliefs or the contents of beliefs. He considers an argument for the former position that resembles the argument of illusion. I agree with him that that argument is misguided. However, it is not the Similarity Argument. As I read him he accepts the conclusion of the Similarity Argument.

[13] See Crane & French (2015) for a nice overview.

claims is the claim that what individuates state kinds is their phenomenology. Since the phenomenology is (seemingly) the same in the good case and bad case, the arguer from illusion concludes that you are in the same kind of state in both cases.[14]

The argument from illusion has proved to be resistible. Many have argued against it.[15] The most common way of doing this is resisting the similarity claim. Given the affinities between the argument from illusion and the Similarity Argument, one would expect similar complaints can be made against the similarity claim that the Similarity Argument relies upon. I think this is exactly right. In the next section, I will argue that this is so by arguing against several particular instances of the Univocal View.

6.4 Against the Univocal View

Univocal views hold that those who react for normative reasons and those who react for motivating reasons stand in the same relation to the reasons they react for. Those who react for normative reasons might have some other features, but when it comes to the reacting-for-reasons relation, the same relation obtains in each case.

In this section, I will argue against the Univocal View. There are two different types of univocal views. According to the first, all reacting for reasons is reacting for normative reasons. According to these views, the Univocal View is true because whenever anyone reacts for motivating reasons they react for normative reasons. I'll call this the Normative Reasons-First View. The Normative Reasons-First View is not popular. As we'll see, this is for good reason. Recently a Normative Reasons-First View has been defended by Arpaly & Schroeder (2014). Further, there is a way of interpreting a familiar view as a Normative Reasons-First View. I will argue against both views in the next subsection.

According to the second view, all instances of reacting for normative reasons are instances of acting for motivating reasons. According to this view, the Univocal View is true because whenever anyone reacts for normative reasons, they react for motivating reasons (although not vice versa). I will call this the Motivating Reasons-First View. The Motivating Reasons-First View is widely held. It is so widely held that it is rarely explicitly mentioned. Usually commitment to it is shown via one's method. Very often theorists will attempt to theorize about reacting for normative reasons by theorizing first about reacting for motivating reasons. The tacit assumption is that since reacting for normative reasons just is reacting for motivating reasons (that are normative), all of the hard work is to be done at the level of theorizing about reacting for motivating reasons.

---

[14] One sort of disjunctivist about perception holds that hallucinations and veridical perceptions have different phenomenal characters—i.e., what it is like to be in those states is different (see, among many other places, Martin (2002)). Disjunctivists of this stripe also maintain that when we instrospect it *seems* to us like these states have the same phenomenal character. Hence the 'seemingly' qualification in the text.
[15] See Haddock & Macpherson (2008) and Crane & French (2015) for discussion and extensive citations.

6.4.1 Part I: against the Normative Reasons-First view

The Normative Reasons-First view defies the basic set up of the debate. I introduced the debate by pointing out that it is extremely plausible that there are some cases of acting for motivating reasons that are not cases of acting for normative reasons. In §6.2.1, I offered Taylor's case and Harry's case as cases of acting for motivating reasons that aren't cases of acting for normative reasons. In Taylor's case, he stockpiles AK-47 ammunition. This is because he thinks there is an imminent zombie invasion. In Harry's case, she is extremely inquisitive with Parisians because she falsely believes that they are charmed by stereotypical Americans.

These cases do seem like cases of merely acting for motivating reasons. It is not the case that there is an imminent zombie invasion, nor is it the case that Parisians like stereotypical Americans. Because of this, it's plausible that neither Taylor nor Harry act for normative reasons. This is because normative reasons are provided by the facts.

Indeed, things are more severe with Taylor. This is because he completely lacks evidence that there is an imminent zombie invasion. That belief is irrational. Given this, it is even more implausible that Taylor acts for a normative reason. Yet, he does clearly act for a motivating reason. His action has a rationale. It can be made intelligible.

Despite this pre-theoretical pressure to say that these are cases of acting for motivating reasons even though they are not cases of acting for normative reasons, there are two Normative Reasons-First views worth considering.

The Rationality View

As we saw in chapter 5 (at least in the notes), both Wedgwood (2006b, 2007) and Arpaly (2006), Arpaly & Schroeder (2014) defend similar views to mine about reacting for reasons in a creditworthy way.[16] Wedgwood's interests are only in this. He explicitly sets aside cases where one merely reacts for a motivating reason.[17] Arpaly & Schroeder do explicitly endorse the thought that all acting for reasons is a matter of acting for considerations that rationalize the act performed. Given that they hold that to act for normative reasons is to act for reasons that rationalize, they hold a Normative Reasons-First View. Let me sketch their view more completely before arguing against it.

They are focused only on action and they adopt a Humean view of acting for normative reasons. According to this view, whenever you ϕ for a reason, you have an intrinsic desire for p and a belief that ϕ-ing will bring about p. They maintain that when this is the case, the belief-desire pair has a certain normative property—viz., the

---

[16] I put it this way because neither is strictly speaking committed to their account being an account of reacting for normative reasons, although Arpaly and Arpaly & Schroeder do commit themselves to this. Wedgwood does not and I suspect he would resist it.

[17] He mentions the thought (in n. 5 of Wedgwood (2006b)) that one can understand cases where one merely reacts for a motivating reason in terms of reacting for normative reasons (and cites Grice (2001)). He doesn't pursue the thought in any of his work.

property of rationalizing ϕ-ing. When the belief-desire pair rationalizes ϕ-ing, ϕ-ing is at least partially rational. They hold that when you ϕ for a reason, you ϕ in virtue of the property of rationalizing. This is the same causal in-virtue-of relation I appeal to in my account.

They use this account in their account of morally worthy actions. This is because they hold that for an action to be morally worthy, it has to be performed for moral reasons. And what it is to perform an action for moral reasons is for one to intrinsically desire the right or good, believe ϕ-ing brings about the right or good, and ϕ in virtue of the property of rationalizing that that belief-desire pair has. Thus, on their account, acting for moral reasons is just a special case of acting for reasons. They thus analyze a hypological notion—moral worth—in terms of their account of acting for motivating reasons.

Before moving on to my main arguments against Arpaly & Schroeder, let me remind the reader (a similar point was also made in chapter 4) that their account is only applicable to action. This is because it is not at all plausible that belief-desire pairs play a central role in holding attitudes for normative reasons. When we, for example, believe for a motivating reason, it is not because a desire to have the belief and a instrumental belief causes us to have the belief. So if Arpaly & Schroeder's view is true of anything, it's only true about action. Many, including myself, will find this objectionable since it would be surprising if a theory of acting for normative reasons was radically different from a theory of holding attitudes for normative reasons. With that said, let's move onto my main criticisms of their account.

Arpaly & Schroeder's account makes the radical prediction that all actions done for motivating reasons are rational, at least to some degree. This is a hard prediction to accept given the range of cases. Further, it is hard to fully test Arpaly & Schroeder's view because they do not provide an account of rationality. Their theory selection is constrained by their view. They can only choose theories that allow for the prediction that all actions performed for motivating reasons are rational. That will narrow down their options quite quickly!

Still, there is a natural view that they could adopt that allows for the radical prediction and has some plausibility. According to this view, to be rational to some degree just is to be intelligible. This would certainly accommodate the prediction that all actions performed for motivating reasons are rational to some degree since all actions done for motivating reasons are intelligible. This view also has some plausibility. For these reasons, I think that this is Arpaly & Schroeder's best shot at vindicating a Normative Reasons-First univocal view.

The problem with this view in this context is that the resulting view does not give a plausible account of acting for reasons in a way that is creditworthy (or, to use their preferred terminology, morally worthy). The reason why is that there are too many ways for a belief-desire pair to make an action intelligible. In only some cases where a belief-desire pair makes the right action intelligible will it be plausible that one's action has moral worth.

We can begin to see this by thinking about our grocers from above. Recall that Gary is a virtuous grocer. He gives his customers the correct change out of a sense of fairness. Gerald doesn't care much about fairness, but he does care about profit. Further, he believes that giving the correct change is an important part of maximizing profit.

Now imagine that they each just returned the correct change to a customer. Both desired to give correct change and believed that handing the customer $9.76 was a way to do this. Further, we can stipulate that they both did it in virtue of the fact that that belief-desire pair rationalized returning the change. Importantly, Gary's action is intuitively morally worthy and Gerald's is not. How can Arpaly & Schroeder's account explain this? They think that there is only one rationalizing relation—intelligibility—and it obtains in both cases.

An initially promising suggestion on their behalf is that while Gary and Gerald both act for the same reason, only Gary acts on that reason as a *moral* reason. They might insist on this because they might insist that only Gary *intrinsically* desires to return the change. Gerald only *instrumentally* desires to return the change; he desires to return the correct change as a means to maximizing profit. They might insist that this is the relevant difference between the two and it shows that only Gary acts for that reason *qua* moral reason.

I agree that it's very natural to interpret Gerald's desire as instrumental and Gary's as intrinsic. But that doesn't mean that it's *impossible* for Gerald's desire to be intrinsic. This is because we can have intrinsic desires that are *conditioned* on certain things obtaining without those desires being instrumental.[18] To take a famous example from Kantian ethics, I might intrinsically desire that Tom is happy conditioned on Tom having a good will. To take a more humdrum example, I might intrinsically desire that my team win conditioned on none of the players cheating. These desires are intrinsic but I won't have them come what may. I will give them up if the conditions are not met.

The version of Gerald we should focus on is the version where he intrinsically desires to return the correct change conditioned on giving correct change maximizing profit in the long run. It is possible for Gerald to be like this.[19] But in this version of the case Gerald's act still doesn't seem to be morally worthy. Making his desire intrinsic doesn't seem to make a difference. The problem for Arpaly & Schroeder is that these are all of the resources their account has. It's not as if there is some distinctively moral kind of intrinsic desire.

At this point they might complain about how I've presented their view. This is because I have left out two subtleties of their view. The first is the fact that they hold that in order for an action to be morally worthy, the act has to express a good

---

[18] See Korsgaard (1983), Railton (1984), Dreier (2000), Bradley & McDaniel (2008), Lord (2017a).

[19] Indeed, it's plausible that Gary's desire is conditioned as well on at least some things. For example, he likely wouldn't intrinsically desire to return correct change in this instance if it would lead to his utter ruin. This doesn't make his desire instrumental and I don't think it speaks badly of his character either.

will. The second is the distinction between ideal and partial good will. This allows them some more machinery. It allows them to say that only Gary's action expresses a good will.

It is plausible that Gerald's action does not express an *ideal* good will. This is because in order to have an ideal good will, one must intrinsically desire what is right or what is good using the concepts that figure in the correct moral theory. Thus, if Kantianism is true, you must intrinsically desire that autonomy be respected. To express that good will, our grocers need to form the belief that giving the correct change is a way of respecting autonomy and one's action would need to happen in virtue of the fact that that belief-desire pair rationalizes giving correct change. It's plausible that Gerald's action does not have this etiology.[20]

So far, so good. The first problem for Arpaly & Schroeder is that it's not plausible that Gary's action has this etiology either. This is because we are imagining Gary to be an ordinary grocer. Ordinary grocers are not competent with the concepts that figure in the correct moral theory. Thus, it's not plausible that Gary intrinsically desires respecting autonomy under that description. Gary is sensitive to the normatively relevant facts, but he's not sensitive to them in this way.

This leaves them with partial good will. Their last resource is to insist that Gary's action expresses partial good will and Gerald's doesn't. Their second problem is that this isn't going to work given their view of the partial good will. They hold that to have a partial good will is to (i) intrinsically desire some state of affairs that one has moral reason to bring about and (ii) desire that state of affairs using concepts that would allow one to infer that the act is right (or good) if one were to have the concepts that figure in the correct moral theory.[21] This second condition is, among other things, supposed to rule out Gerald's desire from counting as an instance of partial good will. It doesn't, though. Given what we've been told about Gerald, it is possible that were he to possess the concepts that figure in the correct moral theory, he would be able to infer that (for example) autonomy would be respected by giving back $9.76. Given that it's possible, we can stipulate that Gerald is in fact like this. But this changes nothing. His act is still not creditworthy even though it expresses a partial good will according to Arpaly & Schroeder.[22]

The upshot is that an appeal to the two further subtleties of Arpaly & Schroeder's view is not going to save them. They still cannot distinguish Gary and Gerald. The reason why, I claim, is that they hold a univocal view. This pushes them into a dilemma. Either they beef up their account of acting in a creditworthy way or they don't. If they do, then they won't be able to explain the whole range of cases of acting for motivating reasons. They won't be able to explain the Geralds, Taylors, and Harrys

---

[20] Although, we can imagine a version of the case where Gerald has an intrinsic desire to respect autonomy conditioned on it maximizing profit. Is Gerald expressing an ideal good will in that version of the case? Probably not.

[21] See Arpaly & Schroeder (2014, p. 167). See Lord (2017a) for extensive discussion.

[22] For a more systematic presentation of this argument and further discussion, see Lord (2017a).

of the world. If they don't, then they won't be able to explain acting in a creditworthy way. The right reaction to this is to abandon their univocal view.

The Subjective Normative Reasons-First view

The Subjective Normative Reasons-First view holds that there is a distinction between two different types of normative reasons.[23] The first type are *objective* normative reasons. These are the normative reasons that are provided by the facts. The second type are *subjective* normative reasons. As we've seen in several other chapters, according to several popular theories of subjective reasons, subjective reasons needn't be provided by the facts. On several popular views of subjective reasons, subjective reasons are the contents of presentational mental states—states that represent their contents as true—that would be objective reasons if one's perspective on the world obtained.[24]

The Subjective Normative Reasons view holds that whenever we act for motivating reasons we act for subjective normative reasons. This view can thus resist my claims about Taylor and Harry above. This is because subjective reasons needn't be true. Thus, it is no impediment to Taylor and Harry acting for subjective normative reasons that their beliefs are false. Moreover, there is something to the thought that even Taylor and Harry act for subjective normative reasons. If true, this would provide an interesting explanation of why it is that the motivating reasons for which we act make our acts intelligible given our perspective. The fact that they would be objective normative reasons if our perspective were correct seems to be the kind of thing that could explain why motivating reasons make our actions intelligible.

Despite the initial promise of the Subjective Normative Reasons view, I think that there are two major problems with it. First, it cannot capture the sense in which acting for normative reasons is an achievement. Second, it still has a hard time accounting for cases like Taylor's.

Let's start with the second problem as it will inform the first. Let's fill in Taylor's case a bit more. Suppose that he believes that there will be an imminent zombie invasion because a charismatic TV personality is predicting that there will be one. We can imagine that he has decisive evidence that there will be no zombie invasion. Suppose he heard it from the world's foremost zombie biologist that zombies are biologically impossible. This is decisive evidence to believe that there will be no zombie invasion. Moreover, we can suppose that he has decisive reason to discount the word of the TV personality. He knows, let's say, that the TV personality has made many predictions like this before and they have all been wrong. He also

---

[23] Earlier chapters have argued against other uses of the subjective reasons ideology (especially chapters 3 and 4). To be clear, the view I am considering here is different than the views I considered before. The view considered here is a view about reacting for reasons, not a view about possession. This is why I am discussing subjective reasons again here.

[24] See Schroeder (2009b), Whiting (2014), and Sylvan (2015). I have used a mixture of Schroeder's counterfactual gloss and Whiting's perspective-talk for concreteness. These three authors disagree about the details. Their disagreements won't matter for my purposes.

knows that the TV personality has a financial incentive to convince people that the zombie invasion is coming (he owns lots of stock in ammunition companies). Finally, suppose that he also believes—although this belief is merely dispositional and hard for Taylor to make occurrent—that AK-47s are ineffective at stopping zombies. Despite this belief, he akratically stockpiles ammunition. It soothes his anxiety to buy more ammunition (although this fact doesn't play a role in his deliberations about what to do). Still, Taylor believes that the zombie invasion is imminent on the basis of the TV personality's word. And Taylor stockpiles ammunition because of his belief that the zombie invasion is imminent.

According to the Subjective Normative Reasons view, Taylor acts for a subjective normative reason when he stockpiles ammunition. This is because Taylor acts for a reason when he does this and all actions done for reasons are actions done for subjective normative reasons. However, it is not particularly plausible that the claim that a zombie invasion is imminent is a subjective normative reason. That is, it is not plausible that that claim would be an objective normative reason if Taylor's perspective on the world obtained. This is because Taylor's perspective includes the belief that AK-47s are ineffective at stopping zombies. This fact plausibly *undercuts* the support relation between the zombie invasion and buying AK-47 ammunition. If AK-47s are ineffective at stopping zombies, then the fact that there is an imminent zombie invasion doesn't provide an objective reason to stockpile AK-47 ammunition. Given this, if Taylor's perspective were to obtain, the fact that there is an imminent zombie invasion would not be an objective normative reason to stockpile AK-47 ammunition. Thus, that consideration is not a subjective reason for Taylor.[25]

Still, it is possible that that consideration is Taylor's reason for buying the ammunition. Even if Taylor believes that AK-47s are ineffective, he might akratically buy the ammunition because of his belief that the invasion is imminent. That is, he might feel the pull towards the ammunition despite his beliefs about what is effective. Nevertheless, given what is in his perspective, the claim that the invasion is imminent is not a subjective reason for Taylor to buy the ammunition. If this is right, then the Subjective Normative Reasons view is false.

There are various ways to resist this argument. Rather than rebut these paths of resistance, I will instead argue that it doesn't matter if the argument can be resisted. This is because even if we decide that Taylor acts for a subjective normative reason, the Subjective Normative Reasons-First view is not going to be able to explain all of

---

[25] Some might think that Whiting (2014)'s view of subjective reasons could save the thought here. This is because he rejects the counterfactual formulation in favor an indicative formulation. I've intentionally set the case up to block this, though. I did this in two ways. First, I made Taylor's perspective inconsistent. Second, I made the relevant beliefs irrational. They thus wouldn't be relevant to Whiting's test. In other words, those beliefs would not be part of the relevant version of Taylor's perspective on Whiting's view. They thus could not provide subjective reasons and thus they couldn't be the subjective reasons for which Taylor acts, even though they seem to play an important role when it comes to Taylor's motivating reasons. For a similar discussion, see §4.3.1 of chapter 4.

the data. This is because of the first main problem. The first main problem is that it is unlikely that acting for subjective normative reasons is an achievement. Because of this, it is unlikely that this relation will undergird the connections between acting for normative reasons and the hypological/deontic.

We can see this in Taylor's case. Suppose that what I argued for above is wrong—Taylor really does act for a subjective normative reason. Nevertheless, it is implausible that Taylor's action is thereby an achievement! It is not at all plausible that acting akratically in light of a thoroughly unjustified belief constitutes an achievement.

Other cases further reinforce the point. Consider Billy. Billy owns a lot of Apple stock. He also believes that Apple's stock will crash next week. Because of this he sells off all of his stock. As it happens, Billy lacks good reason to believe that Apple's stock will crash next week. Fortunately for him, his unjustified belief turns out to be correct.

Billy plausibly does act for a subjective normative reason. But Billy's action is not an achievement. This is because he has no legitimate contact with the fact that provides him with the reason. He believes the claim that constitutes the fact. But given that he believes it for no good reason, it is not plausible that acting upon this belief constitutes an achievement.

One might take pause here because it does seem like Billy's action has something going for it.[26] After all, it looks like Billy correctly responds to his perspective *in some sense*. If his beliefs are true, then selling is definitely the thing to do. He does sell; further, his selling is sensitive to the beliefs that make it the case that selling is the thing to do if they are true. This makes it more plausible that Billy's action really is an achievement and thus that he is creditworthy for selling.

It's not clear how to extend this to Taylor's akratic hoarding. For the technical problem remains that the content of Taylor's belief is not an objective reason if it is true. Even if this technical problem can be solved, it isn't true that Taylor's perspective points in favor of hoarding, at least not in the same way that Billy's perspective supports selling. So it's not clear that Taylor's action is an achievement in the way that Billy's is. Yet, it's still plausible that Taylor acts for a motivating reason.

There is a bigger problem for this defense of the Subjective Normative Reasons-First view. This is that even if we decide that Billy's action is some kind of achievement, I do not think it is the same kind of achievement involved in paradigmatic cases of reacting for normative reasons. In paradigmatic cases, it is very important that one is getting things right from top to bottom. Characters in paradigmatic cases are *not* simply reacting to the perspective that is determined by their mere beliefs. Rather, they are in tune with their actual environment. They not only have the right view of the normative upshot of what they believe, they know things about their environment and this knowledge facilitates the manifestation of competences that are sensitive to the actual normative facts. Billy is falling well short of this. For this reason, I think it

---

[26] Thanks to Daniel Whiting for raising this line of objection.

is implausible to maintain that Billy's achievement is the same kind of achievement that is involved in reacting for normative reasons. Thus, it seems possible to react for subjective normative reasons without reacting in a way that is creditworthy. If this is true, then the Subjective Normative Reasons view is false.

The upshot of this is that even if we accept the Subjective Normative Reasons-First view, we still need to appeal to something else to explain why acting for (objective) normative reasons is the kind of achievement it is. Acting for subjective normative reasons needn't be an achievement in the relevant way. So there must be another relation one stands in with objective normative reasons when one acts for them.

The upshot is subtle and it is thus worth harping on the point. It helps to recall the ambitions of the Univocal Theory. The Univocal Theory maintains that there is only one acting-for-reasons relation. The Subjective Normative Reasons-First version of the Normative Reasons-First view holds that the single relation is the acting-for-normative-reasons relation. Further, this view holds that this is the relation that Gary stands in when he acts for a normative reason. It then holds further that what all agents who act for reasons have in common is that they all act for normative reasons. What I've argued is (1) the Subjective Normative Reasons-First view is not a plausible view of acting for motivating reasons and (2) acting for a subjective normative reason is not sufficient for one's act to be an achievement. Thus, the Subjective Normative Reasons-First view cannot explain all of the essential features of acting for motivating reasons on the one hand and all of the essential features of acting for normative reasons on the other. Thus, something else must be going on in cases where one acts for a normative reason. A plausible hypothesis is that one stands in a different relation to the reasons for which one acts in those cases.[27] If this is the case, then the Univocal View fails.

6.4.2 Part II: against the Motivating Reasons-First view

If my arguments in the last section are sound, then the univocal relation is not the acting-for-normative-reasons relation. It might be that we always act for subjective normative reasons when we act for motivating reasons, but not all actions performed for subjective reasons are achievements in the relevant way. Thus, something more is going on when we act for normative reasons. It follows that the Normative Reasons-First version of the Univocal view fails.

The other type of Univocal view takes acting for motivating reasons as more fundamental. This is the Motivating Reasons-First view.[28] It holds that the univocal relation is the acting-for-motivating-reasons relation. Unlike the Normative Reasons-First view, this view fits the set-up of the debate very well. This is because it is very

---

[27] This hypothesis won't be confirmed until I present the arguments in the next section.

[28] As we will see, this is the view that was central to chapter 5. This section is more or less a rehashing of chapter 5. I include it in this much detail for the sake of completeness when it comes to the argument of this chapter.

plausible that all of our characters are acting for motivating reasons. Given that this is what they have in common, it is plausible to suppose that what they are doing when it comes to acting for reasons is acting for motivating reasons. There is some other feature of those who act for normative reasons—e.g., the fact that their motivating reasons are normative reasons—that explains why their actions are achievements. (This is just the Similarity Argument in different words.)

The Motivating Reasons-First version of the Univocal view is very widely held. In fact, it is so natural that its acceptance is usually tacit and it is very rarely argued for. As we saw in chapter 5, there are some explicit mentions of it, though. After defending a view of believing for motivating reasons, Audi (1993, p. 267) writes, 'since believing for a good reason is believing for a reason (one that is good), the account clarifies believing for a good reason.' Similarly, Dancy (2000, pp. 136–7) writes of action that 'it seems, then, that the explanation of action [. . .] can always be achieved by laying out the considerations in light of which the agent saw the action as desirable, sensible, or required. If things were as the agent supposed, there is no bar against the agent's reasons being among the [normative] reasons in favor of doing what he actually did.' Both Audi and Dancy are expressing the thought that reacting for normative reasons is a matter of reacting for motivating reasons plus some other conditions. For Audi, the extra condition is that the motivating reasons are 'good' reasons, by which he means normative reasons. For Dancy, the extra condition is that 'things were as the agent supposed.'

We can use Audi and Dancy's remarks to develop a full blown theory of reacting for normative reasons in terms of reacting for motivating reasons. Since we already have a grip on the view that what it is to act for motivating reasons is to act for subjective reasons, I will take that as a model of what it is to act for motivating reasons.[29]

The easy way to extend this account of reacting for motivating reasons to an univocal account of reacting for normative reasons is to say that when one ϕs for normative reasons, one ϕs for subjective reasons that *are also* objective reasons to ϕ.[30] This gives us the Composite Account, which we first investigated in chapter 5:[31]

Composite Account: What it is for A to ϕ for a normative reason r is for r to be A's motivating reason for ϕ-ing and for r to be an objective normative reason to ϕ.

The Composite Account is the natural view to hold in response to the objections to the Subjective Normative Reasons view above. This is because even though it's not plausible to think that all reactions done for subjective reasons are achievements, it is

---

[29] Thus, I will set aside my objection in the previous section to the claim that whenever one acts for a motivating reason one acts for a subjective reason.

[30] This is a generalization of the view of believing for normative reasons developed in Schroeder (2015c). Schroeder clearly intends believing for normative reasons to be an achievement since he seeks to analyze knowledge partially in terms of believing for normative reasons.

[31] See Lord & Sylvan (FC) for a sustained attack on Composite Accounts of believing for normative reasons. The arguments given below are analogues to some of the arguments given in that paper.

much more plausible to think that all reactions done for subjective reasons that are also objective reasons are always achievements. After all, in some sense you have to get something right in order for the subjective reason you act for to be an objective reason. This is because in order for p to be an objective reason, p has to be true. Thus, you have to have a true belief in order for your subjective reason to be an objective reason. This makes it more plausible that acts done for subjective reasons that are also objective reasons are achievements.

Unfortunately for friends of the Composite Account, not all reactions done for subjective reasons that are also objective reasons are achievements. I showed this in chapter 5 by appealing to El Clasico. In El Clasico, Sam believes that Barcelona won. Her motivating reason is that Real Madrid lost. The fact that Real Madrid lost is also a normative reason to believe that Barcelona won. However, Sam doesn't believe Barcelona won for a normative reason. This is because she forms her belief via the Explosion inference rule, which says to infer that Barcelona won from any p.

In this chapter we've seen another counterexample to Composite. This is Gerald the grocer. He gives his customer \$9.76 in change. His motivating reason for doing this is that \$9.76 is the correct amount of change. This is his subjective reason. It is also an objective reason to give his customer \$9.76. However, Gerald doesn't care about giving correct change because it is the fair thing to do. He only cares about it because it is the best way to maximize profit. Intuitively, Gerald's action is not creditworthy. Indeed, it is often thought to be a *paradigm* case of an act that is not creditworthy. Since it's not creditworthy, it's plausible that it's not an achievement.[32]

Nevertheless, the Composite Account predicts that Gerald acts for a normative reason. This is because his motivating reason for action happens to be a normative reason for action. The problem, though, is that it just seems like an accident that this is true. In worlds where Gerald has different views about what maximizes profit, he doesn't provide correct change. This is so even though in (some of) those worlds giving correct change is still the fair thing to do. Thus, the Composite Account cannot distinguish between cases of genuine achievement and cases of accidental alignment between one's motivating reasons and normative reasons. This is a decisive reason to reject the Composite Account.

As I argued in chapter 5, the best way to respond to the problems of the Composite Account is to appeal to knowledge about how to use facts as reasons. As we saw at the beginning of this chapter, in order to accept that account, we must reject the Univocal View. This is what we should do.

Further, now we are in a position to see that there are much more general reasons to reject univocal views. These reasons mirror the reasons to reject univocal views in

---

[32] As I said in n. 10 above, I am not claiming that the sort of achievement I am interested in is always a moral achievement. It is tempting to think that while Gerald's action is not a moral achievement, it is a prudential achievement—he obviously has some reason to maximize profit. To avoid this possible confound, just imagine that he is wrong about what will maximize profit.

the philosophy of perception. Univocal views about both perception and reacting for reasons fail to explain why the good cases involve achievements. This is because it's not plausible that the relation involved in cases of achievement can be built out of the relation involved in the cases that don't involve achievements. This is what univocal views demand, though. We should thus reject univocal views.

6.5 What it is to React for Motivating Reasons

Once we reject univocal views, we are committed to there being (at least) two relations. We are committed, in other words, to Disjunctivism:

Disjunctivism: We stand in a different relation to normative reasons when we react for normative reasons than we do when we (merely) react for motivating reasons.

I defended a view of the relation involved in reacting for normative reasons in chapter 5. While this is all that I need to defend my view of rationality, one might be suspicious of this view if it is unclear whether there is a plausible account of reacting for motivating reasons that accompanies it. In this section, I will sketch such a view and argue that it can solve the deviant causal chain worries introduced in chapter 5.

6.5.1 Reintroducing deviancy

Let's first remind ourselves of the classic cases of deviant causal chains for causal accounts of reacting for motivating reasons. In chapter 5, I gave three deviancy counterexamples from Chisholm (1966), Davidson (1980), and Pollock & Cruz (1999):

Dead Uncle

Dan has decided to kill his uncle Fred because he is set to inherit a vast amount of money from his uncle. The thought of inheriting the money excites him so much that he loses control of his car and kills a pedestrian. The pedestrian happens to be his uncle. He inherits the fortune.

Dead Climber

Dan and Fred are climbing an arduous mountain together. Dan decides that he will only survive the climb if he rids himself of the burden Fred brings to the project. He thus believes that he must get rid of Fred in order to survive. This thought so terrifies him, though, that it causes him to loosen his grip on the rope that is supporting Fred. Fred falls to his death. Dan survives.

In both of these cases there is some consideration that causes some event even though it doesn't seem like the event caused is an action done for that consideration. The trick, of course, is to explain the difference between these cases and cases where Dan does perform the actions for the relevant reasons.

I gave one case of a deviant causal chain in the case of belief from Pollock & Cruz (1999):

Late for Class

Joe is late for class. This causes him to quicken his pace. This causes him to slip, which causes him to fall on his back and look skyward. This causes him to believe there are birds in the tree.

The structure is the same. There is some consideration that causes Joe's belief that there are birds in the tree, but intuitively that consideration is not a reason for which Joe believes. The trick is to explain the difference between cases like Late for Class and a case where Joe does hold the belief for the relevant consideration.[33]

6.5.2 Conceiving of motivating reasons

It's trickier to see exactly what's going wrong in these cases than in the deviancy cases for causal accounts of ϕ-ing for normative reasons. The main reason for this, I think, is that in the cases of reacting for normative reasons, there is an independent property the facts have—the property of being a normative reason—that one needs to stand in a certain relation to in order to react for it. The normative reason is always going to be there, by hypothesis. This gives us something to work with. Now, of course, there is also some independent entity—the consideration—in cases of merely reacting for motivating reasons. But the analogous move in these cases—to say that one must act in virtue of the fact that the consideration is a consideration—is unilluminating. Something else must be going on.[34]

The key, I think, is that in non-deviant cases the agent is reacting in virtue of the fact that the consideration has a certain status in one's psychology. The status, I claim, is that of *being conceived of as a normative reason for the reaction*.[35,36] We can use this idea to get Motivating:

---

[33] It's harder to imagine the good case with this example. Here's one: Joe's class is held during lunch, when a lot of the university members feed the birds. The birds are thus usually not in the trees during this time because they are on the ground to get the food. Joe notices he's late for class (and lunch is thus over). He infers from this that the birds are back in the trees.

[34] Note that I'm going to start using 'consideration' more than 'reason' so as to not confuse the things for which we act when we merely react for motivating reasons with the things for which we react when we react for normative reasons. I might occasionally use 'reason.' When you see 'reason' unadorned by 'normative,' I am talking about considerations. I am taking considerations to be the objects of thought (whatever those turn out to be).

[35] Many philosophers talk about *treating* things as reasons (including some of my past time-slices (Lord (2014a), Lord & Sylvan (FC))). For example, Schossler (2007, 2012) takes the notion of treating as a reason as central to his account of intentional action. I think that what I am getting at with conceptions is another way to get at what at least most of those philosophers are getting at. However, I think it's best to understand the issue in terms of conceptions because conceptions are something we already need to posit and are better understood. This is welcome news since talk of treating is often quite mysterious. Others who appeal to treating include Milligan (1974), Broome (1997), Velleman (2000), Schroeder (2007), Hornsby (2008). Setiya (2007b) argues against the claim that treating as a normative reason is necessary, but still appeals to treating as a reason.

[36] It should be noted that Elizabeth Camp's notion of an *interpretation* in light of a *perspective* is very similar to conceptions as I will use them. See Camp (2003).

Motivating: What it is for A to ϕ for a motivating reason r is for A to ϕ in virtue of the fact that A conceives of r as a normative reason to ϕ.

The in-virtue-of relation in Motivating is the causal in-virtue-of relation. Motivating has considerable intuitive plausibility. First, it does a good job fleshing out a thought that has been at the heart of many accounts of reacting for motivating reasons.[37] This is the thought that reactions for motivating reasons are intelligible because when we react for motivating reasons, the considerations for which we react shine a positive light on the reaction *from our perspective*. Motivating explains this by appealing to the claim that we always conceive of considerations that are motivating reasons as normative reasons. Further, and this is a second reason to find it intuitively attractive, Motivating also maintains that the fact that one conceives of the consideration as a normative reason must play a causal role in the generation or sustenance of the reaction. So not only do you have to see the consideration as shining a light on the reaction, you have to react in virtue of the consideration having this feature. If Motivating is correct, then it's no wonder that motivating reasons make reactions intelligible.

While it's a virtue that Motivating captures some core thoughts about motivating reasons, a full defense requires some elucidation of the account's central notion, viz., conceiving of some consideration as a normative reason.

We can start by thinking more about the nature of conceptions and conceiving. Following Bengson & Moffett (2007) and Bengson (2015, 2017), we can say that conceptions have at least the following features:

Non-Factivity: A conception of Γ can be correct or incorrect.

Non-Exhaustiveness: A conception of Γ can be incomplete.

Diversity: There can be many different conceptions of Γ.

Fine-Grainedness: Necessarily co-extensive conceptions are not necessarily identical.

Non-Articulatedness: A conception of Γ can be either partially or wholly demonstrative.

Non-Overtness: An individual can have a conception of Γ either explicitly or implicitly.

Publicity: Distinct individuals can share a conception of Γ.

Non-Exclusivity: One can have more than one conception of Γ at the same time.

These properties bestow conceptions with great flexibility. Several of these properties are worth highlighting for present purposes. First, it's obviously important that Non-Factivity is true for our purposes. This is because it is clear that one can react for

---

[37] A far from exhaustive list: Anscombe (1957), Davidson (1963), Dancy (2000), Hornsby (2008), Alvarez (2010).

a motivating reason even though they are wrong about the normative upshot of the consideration for which they act. When this happens, they incorrectly conceive of the consideration as a normative reason. Second, it's important that one can have a non-exhaustive conception. This is because it's clear that we often conceive of a consideration as a normative reason even though we lack a comprehensive conception of the normative upshot of the relevant fact. For example, one might conceive of the fact that one promised to read a friend's paper as a reason to read the paper even though one lacks a complete conception of the normative upshot of promising.

Non-articulatedness and non-overtness are important for avoiding certain forms of overintellectualization. So, for example, I think it would be bad news for Motivating if conceiving of p as a normative reason to ϕ required one to believe that p is a normative reason to ϕ. This would be an overintellectualization. This is because it is plausible that some agents that cannot have beliefs with explicitly normative contents can react for motivating reasons. For example, I think that my dog can conceive of the fact that I called her as a reason to come to me. However, I don't think that my dog can even implicitly believe that the fact that I called her is a normative reason to come to me. I doubt she's conceptually sophisticated enough to have that belief. Similarly for my toddler daughter. I think she conceives of the fact that honey nut cheerios are tasty as a normative reason to eat her breakfast, but I'm confident that she doesn't have the conceptual capacities to have beliefs about reasons. This doesn't mean that she completely lacks the concept of a reason. I think she (and my dog) partially have the concept, just not enough to have beliefs about reasons.

Fortunately, conceptions in general do not require this level of conceptual sophistication. To see this, consider my dog's and daughter's *physical* conception of the world. They both have a Newtonian conception of the physical world. This conception informs how they think about the world. But neither has thoughts that have as their contents propositions about Newtonian mechanics. Non-articulatedness and Non-overtness ensure that this is possible. My daughter's physical conception might only be expressed demonstratively. She might point to the ball in the air and say of it 'if it's like that, then it will be like this' while pointing to its falling trajectory. Similarly, she might express her normative conception by referring to the cereal's tastiness and then showing that this speaks in favor of eating (she might say 'if it's this (pointing to the Cheerios), then that' (referring to her eating)).[38] Furthermore, my dog's and daughter's physical conception might be implicit. They might not have occurrent thoughts about their conception. They might not even have occurrent demonstrative

---

[38] I am not claiming that my daughter fails to have any beliefs in this case. She is expressing *some belief* when she utters the conditional in question. The point is that the belief she expresses is *not* a belief that tokens normative concepts. Still, I think such an assertion can express her normative conception (and her non-normative belief).

thoughts like the ones referred to above. Their conceptions might run offline, as it were.[39]

The upshot is that conceptions in general have attractive features for giving an account of reacting for motivating reasons. We might wonder, though, whether there is anything more one can say about conceiving of a consideration as a normative reason. While I am happy to remain neutral about any further features, I think there are some that should be seen as fairly uncontroversial.

First, our normative conceptions inform our expectations. So, for example, if I conceive of the fact that my son got an A on a test as a (strong) normative reason to be happy, I will expect happiness upon finding out that he got an A. If I conceive of the fact that Real Madrid lost as a reason to believe Barcelona won (at least when they play), then I will expect to believe Barcelona won upon learning that Real Madrid lost.

Second (this is a special case of the previous point), our normative conceptions ground motivational dispositions. When I conceive of the fact that there will be whisky at the party as a reason to go to the party, I tend to gain motivation to go to the party when I learn that there will be whisky there. When I conceive of the fact that it looks like the table is red as a normative reason to believe it is red, I will gain a disposition to believe it is red when the table appears red.

Third, when we conceive of p as a normative reason to ϕ, we are disposed to think p is positively relevant to the question of whether to ϕ when we're reasoning about the merits of ϕ-ing under certain conditions. The conditions are, roughly, what Gibbard (1990) calls *normative discussion*. Normative discussions are unconstrained in certain ways. For example, in normative discussion social pressures against seeing certain things as salient are lifted. Moreover, in normative discussions we are trying to discover *all* of the merits of ϕ-ing. Thus, there are not the usual pragmatic pressures to only reason about the considerations that are especially weighty.[40] When you conceive of p as a normative reason to ϕ, you are disposed to think that p is relevant to the question 'why ϕ?' in normative discussion.

These three features are common when we conceive of considerations as normative reasons. I don't think there are strong reasons to think that they are either necessary or sufficient. I won't give necessary and sufficient conditions for conceiving a consideration as a normative reason. I don't think that is required in the same way I don't think it would be required to provide necessary and sufficient conditions for believing something is a normative reason if I were understanding reacting for motivating reasons in terms of believing that considerations are normative reasons. As long as

---

[39] Again, I am not claiming that they can have the conceptions they have without having *any* beliefs. Perhaps they always have to at least have non-occurrent beliefs (e.g., the demonstrative beliefs). I am merely claiming that no *occurrent* beliefs are required in order to conceive of r as a normative reason.

[40] See Schroeder (2007) for an excellent cataloguing of the effect such pragmatic features have on our normal discourse about reasons.

conceptions/conceiving has the abstract features listed above, the notion can do the work I need it to do.

6.5.3 Reacting in virtue of conceiving and deviancy

I think it's no surprise that normative conceptions play a pivotal role in the correct account of reacting for motivating reasons. Preliminary evidence for this is the fact that the considerations we see as salient when reasoning about what to do and believe are, if things go well, the considerations we believe and act for.

There is a composite way to incorporate conceiving into an analysis of reacting for a motivating reason. According to this view, what it is to ϕ for some reason r is for r to cause one to ϕ and for one to conceive of r as a normative reason to ϕ. Unsurprisingly, this view leads to further deviancy problems, as is shown by the following example.[41]

> **Virus**
>
> Joe likes to dance and thus conceives of the fact that there will be dancing at Liz's party tonight as a reason to go to Liz's house (when he believes that Liz is throwing a party with dancing). However, he also has a bizarre virus that compulsively causes him to go to Liz's house whenever he believes there is a party at Liz's house. He comes to believe that there is a party at Liz's house (and that there will be dancing at said party). The virus causes him to compulsively head to Liz's house. The fact that he conceives of the dancing as a reason to go plays no role in the etiology of his behaviour.

Joe meets the two conditions laid down by the composite account. He is caused to go to Liz's house by a consideration that he happens to conceive of as a normative reason to go to Liz's house. However, he intuitively doesn't act for that consideration—perhaps he doesn't act at all. So the composite version of the view must be false.

No need to worry, though, for there is a prime version of the view that doesn't have this problem. The form of the view is by now familiar. What needs to happen for Joe to act for the reason is that he needs to go to Liz's house in virtue of the fact that he conceives of the dancing as a normative reason to go to Liz's house. This isn't true of Joe in Virus. The fact that he conceives of the consideration as a normative reason is idle.

This further motivates Motivating (which I will repeat to maintain flow).

Motivating: What it is for A to ϕ for a motivating reason r is for A to ϕ in virtue of the fact that A conceives of r as a normative reason to ϕ.

In order for this to be fully satisfying, an account of the *in virtue of* relation must be given. Once again, I think it should be fleshed out dispositionally.

---

[41] This case is inspired by Schroeder (2007, ch. 8). A referee pointed out to me that Setiya (2003, 2007b) discusses a similar case originally in Milligan (1974).

As it was in chapter 5, there are two different causal relations that are relevant: Creation and sustenance. On the one hand, sometimes when you react for a motivating reason, your reaction is created by the motivating reason. On the other hand, sometimes when you react for a motivating reason, the motivating reason sustains your reaction. In the former cases, when you ϕ in virtue of the fact that you conceive of r as a normative reason to ϕ, your reaction is the result of a disposition that manifests when you conceive of r as a normative reason to ϕ. In the latter cases, when you ϕ in virtue of the fact that you conceive of r as a normative reason to ϕ, you are disposed to revise ϕ-ing if you cease conceiving of r as a normative reason to ϕ. This is just to say that Motivating–Sustaining, Motivating–Production, and Motivating–Fleshed Out are true:

> **Motivating–Sustaining:** A ϕs for a consideration r if A is disposed to revise ϕ-ing when A ceases to conceive of r as a normative reason to ϕ.

> **Motivating–Production:** A ϕs for a consideration r if A's ϕ-ing is the manifestation of a disposition to ϕ when A conceives of r as a normative reason to ϕ.

> **Motivating–Fleshed Out:** A ϕs for a consideration r just in case A's ϕ-ing is produced or sustained by r (in the ways specified by Motivating–Sustaining and Motivating–Production).

These accounts solve the deviancy problems. Dan does not hit the pedestrian in virtue of the fact that he conceives of the fact that he will inherit a large sum from his uncle if his uncle dies as a normative reason to kill the pedestrian. Likewise, Dan does not loosen his grip in virtue of the fact that he conceives of the fact that he will survive only if his partner dies as a normative reason to loosen his grip. Joe does not go to Liz's house in virtue of the fact that he conceives of the fact that there will be dancing as a reason to go to Liz's house. Finally, Joe does not believe there are birds in the trees in virtue of the fact that he conceives of the consideration that he is late for class as a normative reason to believe there are birds in the trees. The dispositions that manifest when Dan and Joe react have nothing to do with conceiving of the considerations that cause the reactions as normative reasons. In Dan's cases, it's his excitement and terror, respectively, and in Joe's case it's his disposition to conceive of the contents of visual perceptions as reasons.

I thus think that Motivating has a good bit going for it. It provides a natural way of fleshing out the idea that motivating reasons are considerations that count in favor of reactions given one's perspective. Further, it causally links the feature of considerations that account for this illumination to the reactions themselves. This is what allows it to provide a solution to the problem of deviant causal chains. Finally, it seems flexible enough to account for all of the cases. This is because of the flexibility of conceptions. The range of motivating reasons is only constrained by the range of conceptions of things as normative reasons. Since the latter range is very large, the former range is as well. This is exactly what the phenomena seem to demand.

6.6 How Disjunctivist is This?

So far I have done two main things in this chapter. I first argued against univocal views that hold that there is only one reacting-for-reasons relation. I argued that no univocal view can explain the essential features of both reacting for motivating reasons and reacting for normative reasons. The second main task was to sketch a new view of reacting for motivating reasons. When you combine this view with the view of reacting for normative reasons defended in chapter 5, you have a complete view of reacting for reasons.

The failure of univocal views entails what I called Disjunctivism above, which holds that the relation one stands in with the normative reasons one reacts for is different than the relation one stands in with the motivating reasons one reacts for. In this section, I want to explore two important ways in which a view can be disjunctivist. This will help illuminate the connections between reacting for motivating reasons and reacting for normative reasons.

While it is controversial exactly what disjunctivism about perception is,[42] much of the literature on disjunctivism in the philosophy of perception focuses on what I'll call Negative Disjunctivism:

Negative Disjunctivism: The perceptual state one is in in the good case is fundamentally different from the perceptual state one is in in the bad case.

Negative Disjunctivism is a bold thesis that has generated serious controversy. It is the thesis that the arguments from illusion and hallucination are meant to refute.

So far this chapter has focused on the analogous claim to Negative Disjunctivism about reacting for reasons. This is just what I called Disjunctivism above. I have argued that we should accept the view that there is more than one relation, which is analogous to the claim that there is more than one state.

That said, there is also another thesis that is at stake in the debate about the nature of perception. This is what I will call Positive Disjunctivism:

Positive Disjunctivism: There is some perceptual phenomenon—e.g., it appearing to one as if *p*—that is *essentially disjunctive in nature.*

Positive Disjunctivism holds that it appearing to one as if *p* is a disjunctive phenomenon. This means that it can appear to one as if *p* in two different ways that are fundamentally different from one another. Each way—e.g., veridically perceiving *p* and non-veridically perceiving *p*—can realize the disjunctive phenomenon. To put it another way, the disjunctive phenomenon can consist in either veridically perceiving *p* or non-veridically perceiving *p*.

Positive Disjunctivism is a stronger claim than Negative Disjunctivism. This is because it holds that in both the good case and the bad case there is a common

---

[42] See Soteriou (2014) for a nice overview of this controversy.

phenomenon. Further, it holds that this phenomenon is essentially disjunctive. This is means that its disjunctive nature is part of what it is.

The analogous claim for reacting for reasons is Action-Theoretic Positive Disjunctivism:[43]

> **Action-Theoretic Positive Disjunctivism:** There is some action-theoretic phenomenon—e.g., one reacting for a reason r—that is essentially disjunctive in nature.

Action-Theoretic Positive Disjunctivism posits some disjunctive phenomenon. It holds that reacting for a reason r consists in either reacting for a normative reason r or reacting for a motivating reason r. To put it another way, it holds that reacting for a normative reason r or reacting for a motivating reason r realizes reacting for a reason r. Further, it holds that it is part of the essence of reacting for a reason that it is disjunctive.

While there has been a very large amount of discussion of Negative Disjunctivism in the philosophy of perception, there has, as far as I can tell, been relatively little discussion of Positive Disjunctivism. For this reason, it is not very clear why some have opted for Positive Disjunctivism when it seems like they are really most interested in establishing Negative Disjunctivism.

This raises the question of whether I accept Action-Theoretic Positive Disjunctivism. Once one accepts Disjunctivism (i.e., the negative disjunctivist thesis), the alternative to Action-Theoretic Positive Disjunctivism is to hold that while reacting for normative reasons and reacting for motivating reasons bear similarities to each other, they do not each realize some higher-order kind. I am not sure what the rules are for adjudicating between these two options. In the philosophy of perception, many seem to embrace Positive Disjunctivism on the grounds that Negative Disjunctivism is true *and* that the kinds of perception have something essential in common. If one accepts both of these commitments, then Positive Disjunctivism is very plausible. It's unclear to me why we should accept the second claim.[44]

Lisa Miracchi has suggested (in personal communication) that one way we can test for whether there is a disjunctive kind is to see if we have an explanatory need for the disjunctive phenomenon. This test speaks favorably for the positive disjunctivist theses. After all, we do need to explain what characters in the good cases and the bad cases have in common. We can offer an elegant explanation of this by appealing to the disjunctive kind. The thing that those who react for normative reasons have in common with those who react for motivating reasons is that they *react for reasons*. They do this in fundamentally different ways; nevertheless, each way is a way of realizing the higher-order disjunctive kind.

---

[43] Note that I don't mean to suggest by the name of this view that the only reactions relevant are actions. I'm still thinking the full gamut of reasons are on the table. The trouble is that it's hard to think of a nice name that clearly covers them all, which is why I went with this name.

[44] It seems to me that many people inherit something like the second commitment from Hinton (1967, 1973), who offers his view up as, among other things, a view about the semantics of appearance ascriptions.

This is suggestive but obviously not decisive. I can't hope to fully adjudicate this here. I do, however, tentatively endorse Action-Theoretic Positive Disjunctivism. I note that in closing that this has other benefits for several other bits of this book. For example, it helps me in the debate from chapter 3 about the factivity of reasons explanations. Recall that I hold that there were two different kinds of reasons explanations. One of them—normative achievement explanations—is factive and the other—rationale explanations—is not. This allowed me to grant to my opponents that they are getting at something true when they deny that reasons-explanations are factive. They are getting at rationale explanations. Nevertheless, I argued that they were wrong to think that these explanations are intimately tied to rationality. Instead, normative achievement explanations are tied to rationality. These explanations are factive. So while my opponents are right about something, they aren't right about the right thing.

Negative disjunctivism does vindicate this story to a large extent. This is because it shows that there is independent motivation for thinking that there are two different relations. Further, I think it's plausible that the reacting-for-normative-reasons relation is factive and the reacting-for-motivating-reasons relation is not. This vindicates most of what I wanted to vindicate in that section of chapter 3.

That said, this positive disjunctivist thesis is even more vindicatory. This is because it allows me to say that even though the two relations differ in factivity, they both can realize the disjunctive reacting-for-reasons relation. If this were true, then not only would the disjunct relations have the features I claimed they did, it would also be right that all of the characters were reacting for reasons. This would provide a natural explanation for where my opponents went wrong. They assumed that the nature of reacting-for-reasons relation was univocal across all cases when in fact it is disjunctive.

Relatedly, the positive thesis allows me an easy response to a pressing question. The question is what the relationship is between reacting for normative reasons and reacting for motivating reasons. As we saw from the Similarity Argument, it is very plausible that we do the same thing in both cases of reacting for normative reasons and cases of reacting for motivating reasons. This is why it is so tempting to hold a univocal view, especially a Motivating Reasons-First Univocal view. Given this, there is some pressure for even me to say that in all cases of reacting for reasons one reacts for motivating reasons.[45] The positive disjunctivist thesis allows me to say something else that, it seems to me, is more satisfying. This is because the positive thesis allows me to insist that the characters in the good cases are doing the same kind of thing as those in the bad cases. They are all reacting for reasons. However, the lower-order *ways* in which they do this are different. While one could try to show that whenever one reacts for a normative reason one reacts for a motivating reason, I don't (anymore) see strong reason to do this. Instead, we should hold that everyone reacts for reasons

---

[45] Kurt Sylvan and I give in to this pressure in Lord & Sylvan (FC).

even though many agents who react for normative reasons do not react for motivating reasons. The positive thesis allows me to say these things.

6.7 Conclusion

The main goal of this chapter was to provide an argument for (negative) disjunctivism about reacting for reasons. I did this by arguing that univocal views of reacting for reasons cannot explain the core features of reacting for normative reasons on the one hand and reacting for motivating reasons on the other. Some univocal views do a good job explaining how reacting for normative reasons is an achievement at the expense of being able to explain how reacting for motivating reasons makes reactions intelligible. Other views have the opposite problem. Given this, I think we should inductively infer disjunctivism. Once we embrace disjunctivism, though, my burden is to provide an account of reacting for motivating reasons. I did this in §6.5. According to this account, what is to ϕ for a consideration r is to ϕ in virtue of the fact that one conceives of r as a normative reason to ϕ. I argued that conceptions are the right psychological states to appeal to in giving the account. I also argued that the resulting account can solve the problem of deviant causal chains in much the same way my account of reacting for normative reasons solves various deviancy problems.

Chapters 5 and 6, then, have developed a disjunctivist account of reacting for reasons that provides plausible solutions to various deviancy problems while at the same time explaining the core features of the phenomena.

PART IV

Two Problems Solved

Summary of Part III and Introduction to Part IV

The main result of Part III was my view of what it is to correctly respond to possessed normative reasons. According to this view, what it is to correctly respond to a possessed normative reason r to ϕ is to manifest knowledge about how to use r as the reason it is to ϕ. I also defended a new view about merely reacting for motivating reasons and defended disjunctivism about reacting for reasons. When we combine the results of Part II with the results of Part III, we get a complete view about the central notions invoked by Reasons Responsiveness.

Part IV is dedicated to showing that these views can solve two important problems. The first is the New Evil Demon problem. The New Evil Demon problem is a problem for views (like mine) that hold that what is rational is not solely determined by internal states of the agent. To solve the New Evil Demon problem one has to show that internal state duplicates always share the same rational status. In chapter 7, I argue that my view can solve the New Evil Demon problem. I also argue that it solves a related problem (that is largely ignored) about correctly responding to reasons.

Chapter 8 is about whether we ought to be rational—i.e., whether rationality is deontically significant. Although this is a truism, skepticism about whether we ought to be rational is popular in the wake of very influential work by John Broome and Niko Kolodny. In chapter 8, I argue that Reasons Responsiveness vindicates the deontic significance of rationality. I do this by arguing that it is independently plausible that what one ought to do is determined by the reasons one possesses. If this is right, then what one ought to do and what one is rationally required to do are the same thing. Thus, rationality has ultimate deontic significance.

7

Defeating the Externalist's Demons

7.1 Introduction

Internalist theories about rationality hold that the rational status of a reaction solely depends upon the non-factive internal states of the agent—i.e., the states one can be in even if the content of the state is false.[1] Externalist theories of rationality deny this. They maintain that the rational status of a reaction depends on facts that are external to an agent's non-factive internal states—e.g., facts about *reliability* or what the agent *knows*. At least since Cohen & Lehrer (1983) and Cohen (1984), it has widely been thought that the radically deceived pose a special problem for externalist theories. To see this, compare The Good Case to The Bad Case:

The Good Case

Sam is in a favorable environment and has reliable belief forming capacities. She sees that the table is red, hears the baby crying, and learns interesting truths from her history textbook.

The Bad Case

Pam is Sam's non-factive internal state duplicate. So when Sam perceives the table is red, Pam has a phenomenologically indistiguishable visual perception; when Sam has an auditory perception of a baby crying, Pam has a phenomenologically indistinguishable auditory perception; and when Sam makes a certain inference because of what her history textbook says, Pam makes a phenomenologically indistinguishable inference. The only difference between Sam and Pam is that Pam is radically deceived by an evil demon. Nearly all of her beliefs about the external world are false.

It's very natural to think that both Sam and Pam are fully rational. It's easy for an internalist to explain this. This is because internalists think that Sam and Pam have all

---

[1] Usually internalism/externalism are formulated as supervenience theses. Internalism is formulated as the view that the rational status of a reaction supervenes on non-factive internal states. A corollary of the main upshot of this paper is that this is a bad way of formulating internalism. This is because I will argue that the supervenience thesis is true even though the rational statuses of reactions depend on external stuff. Formulating internalism/externalism in terms of dependence allows us to better map the terrain. This, of course, is an instance of a more general phenomenon that has been well documented in the literature on grounding (see, e.g., Rosen (2010)). I will keep track of the supervenience issue in notes as we go. Thanks to Jonathan Jenkins Ichikawa and his Ichikawa (2018) for leading me to see things in this light (although he still uses supervenience throughout his paper).

the same rationalizers. Since Sam and Pam are non-factive internal state duplicates, they are in identical situations when it comes to rationality. Thus, given that Sam is rational to degree n, Pam is rational to degree n.

It's not easy to see how an externalist can explain the natural thought that Sam and Pam are rational to the same degree. This is because the externalist is committed to saying that Sam and Pam don't have the same rationalizers. They are in radically different situations when it comes to the external factors relevant in externalist theories of rationality. Take the externalist view Cohen (1984) was arguing against—viz., a naïve form of reliabilism. According to this view, a belief that p is justified only if it is produced by a reliable process. By hypothesis, Pam's beliefs are not formed by a reliable process. Thus, the reliabilist is committed to saying that she is not rational. So some externalist views—e.g., naïve reliabilism—clearly cannot vindicate the thought that Sam and Pam are rational to the same degree.[2] This has come to be known as The New Evil Demon problem for externalism.

A trend amongst externalists has been to bite the bullet and then do damage control. The most popular version of this response maintains that two separate properties are conflated when one states the New Evil Demon problem. The externalist view is correct about the more demanding state and the internalist view is correct for the less demanding one. To illustrate, take Goldman (1988)'s reply to the problem. According to Goldman, his reliablist view is correct when it comes to what he calls strong justification. Pam is not strongly justified. However, Pam is weakly justified, or rational. Thus some internalist view is true when it comes to rationality or weak justification. The New Evil Demon problem only seems like a problem because the internalist has conflated strong and weak justification. Or so the response goes.[3]

The view defended in this book is an externalist view. This is because it maintains that the rational status of any particular reaction is determined by *objective* reasons. This means that Sam and Pam do not share all of the same possessed reasons. Thus, I have the New Evil Demon Problem. In this chapter, I aim to solve it.

My solution does not appeal to two different normative notions. Instead, I am going to argue that it's not necessary for the externalist to bite the bullet—or at least not any real bullets. I'll argue that my view can explain why Sam and Pam are both rational and why it's plausible to say that, in some sense, they are both rational to the same degree.

The structure will be as follows. In the next section, I will explicate the particular version of the New Evil Demon problem that plagues my type of view. I will then show how my view can solve the problem. My work won't be done, yet, because there is a related problem—The New New Evil Demon problem—that still plagues my view. I'll

---

[2] That's not to say there aren't reliabilist replies to the problem. See Comesaña (2002) for a nice explication of a popular reliabilist response.

[3] Others who pursue this type of response—although they don't all think the properties being conflated are strong and weak justification—include Bach (1985), Engel (1992), Weatherson (2008), Littlejohn (2009, 2012), Williamson (FC), Lasonen-Aarnio (FCb), Miracchi (FC), Sylvan (MSb). Cohen (2016) argues that this way of proceeding is incoherent.

introduce that problem in §7.4. I'll then offer a solution to The New New Evil Demon Problem. Along the way I'll also show how my solutions to the Evil Demon problems can also solve three related problems. The first is raised by so-called Knowledge from Falsehood cases (see Warfield (2005), Fitelson (2010), Arnold (2011)), the second is a puzzle about non-veridical perception raised by Schroeder (2011b), and the third is a puzzle about rational actions motivated by false beliefs raised by Schroeder (2008) and Comesaña & McGrath (2014).

7.2 Preliminaries and a Statement of the Problem

The New Evil Demon problem is a problem for any view that is committed to Different Rationalizers:

Different Rationalizers: Sam and Pam do not share the same rationalizers.

My view is committed to Different Rationalizers. This is because I hold both that what rationalizes reactions are possessed (objective) normative reasons and that Sam and Pam possess different reasons. That is, I'm committed to both Reasons Rationalize and Different Reasons:

Reasons Rationalize: Possessed normative reasons are the rationalizers of beliefs.

Different Reasons: Sam and Pam don't possess the same reasons.

Again, there are a variety of views that hold Different Reasons. I hold that Different Reasons is true because Reasons Factivity is true:

Reasons Factivity: p can be a reason to ϕ only if p is true.

If Reasons Factivity is true, then Sam possesses many more reasons to believe what she believes than Pam does. This is because Sam is in a position to know a lot of truths that constitute reasons. While Pam believes those claims, they aren't reasons for Pam because they are false.

Cohen (1984)'s original argument against naïve reliabilism shows that the naïve reliabilist can't account for the fact that Sam is rational *at all*. This is because a necessary condition for a belief to be rational is that the belief be formed by a reliable process. Since Sam's belief isn't formed by a reliable process, it isn't rational at all. Thus, the *very first step* one must make in solving The New Evil Demon problem is vindicating Same Status:

Same Status: Sam and Pam are both rational.

Vindicating Same Status is just the first step. This is because many have a stronger intuition. Many think that not only are both Sam and Pam rational, they are *equally* rational. That is to say, one must also account for Same Degree:

Same Degree: Sam and Pam are equally rational.

It's often unclear what it would take for Sam and Pam to be equally rational. Usually it seems that objectors mean that Sam and Pam have the same rationalizers. If this is what people mean by 'equally rational', then obviously those who accept Reasons Factivity (and Reasons Rationalize) will have to deny that that Sam and Pam are equally rational.

The final preliminary is that, at this point, we are only talking about *ex ante* rationality. That is to say, we are only talking about what it takes for a belief to be rationalizable. As we've seen, in order for a particular belief to be *ex post* rational, the belief has to be suitably connected to the rationalizers. Wishful thinkers might sometimes hold beliefs that are rationalizable even though their token beliefs aren't rational because they aren't suitably related to the reasons. I take the New Evil Demon problem to be a problem about *ex ante* rationality. This is because it arises for views that hold that Sam and Pam have different rationalizers. Rationalizers are direct inputs into one's theory of *ex ante* rationality. They will also be highly relevant to one's theory of *ex post* rationality, but only derivatively through one's view of *ex ante* rationality.[4]

The New Evil Demon problem applied to my view looks like this: Same Status is surely true. Yet it's not clear why if Reasons Rationalize and Reasons Factivity are both true. For if they are, then Sam and Pam differ dramatically in the epistemic reasons that they possess. Sam has a lot more reasons to hold her beliefs than Pam does. Indeed, it's not clear that Pam has *any* (objective) reasons to believe what she believes. So it's mysterious how the defender of Reasons Factivity can account for Same Status. Moreover, even if she could, it's especially mysterious how she could vindicate Same Degree. After all, according to her, Sam has a lot more reasons to believe what she does than Pam. Moreover, Sam's reasons seem to be much better than Pam's. So it seems like she must be more rational than Pam, and thus it seems the friend of Reasons Factivity cannot account for Same Degree.

With this in hand, it's interesting to note that three more specific problems for my view are (close to) special cases of The New Evil Demon problem. The first problem is anchored in so-called *knowledge from falsehood* cases. Here's one purported case from Warfield (2005):[5]

Reliable Watch
Fritz has a 7 pm meeting and extreme confidence in the accuracy of his fancy watch. Having lost track of the time and wanting to arrive on time for the meeting, he looks carefully at his watch. He reasons: It is exactly 2:58 pm; therefore I am not late for

---

[4] Some disagree about what the problem's focus is (see especially Silins (2005)). Don't worry, I'll address the *ex post* version below—this is what I call the New New Evil Demon Problem. I think the New New Evil Demon problem is a much bigger problem than the New Evil Demon problem.

[5] I've modified the wording slightly. These cases are also discussed in Fitelson (2010), Arnold (2011).

my 7 pm meeting. He knows the conclusion, but as it happens it's exactly 2:56 pm, not 2:58 pm.

It's very plausible that Fritz knows and thus rationally believes that he's not late for his 7 pm meeting. Moreover, it's intuitive that a false proposition—viz., that it's exactly 2:58 pm—plays an essential rationalizing role in his obtaining the knowledge that he's not late. If this is right, then my view is in trouble. Call this the Knowledge from Falsehood problem.

It's reasonable to expect, I think, that the solution to the Knowledge from Falsehood problem will be just like a solution to the New Evil Demon problem. For in solving both problems one has to pick out some possessed reasons that rationalize the relevant beliefs. In The Bad Case we need to find some facts that constitute reasons that rationalize Pam's beliefs, and in Reliable Watch we need to find some facts that constitute reasons that rationalize Fritz's belief.

The second problem comes from Schroeder (2011b). Schroeder's problem has to do with how it is that non-veridical perceptual beliefs are rationalized. Views like mine have a nice story to tell about veridical perceptions—the perceptual beliefs are rationalized by the contents of the perceptions.[6] This obviously won't do for non-veridical perceptions since the contents of those perceptions are false.

There is an obvious way in which this is an argument against Reasons Factivity. Schroeder also argues—and this is what he's primarily interested in showing—that this is a strong reason to deny High Bar views of the possession relation. Recall from chapter 3 that High Bar views hold that in order to possess a reason, you have to stand in a positive epistemic relation with that reason. Many High Bar views commit one to Reasons Factivity, but not all do. So, for example, the view that in order to possess p you have to know p entails Reasons Factivity, but the view that in order to possess p you have to justifiably believe p does not (at least given plausible assumptions about justification). So Schroeder's argument is more than just an argument against Reasons Factivity.

Again, I think we should expect a solution to the New Evil Demon problem to provide (part of) a solution to Schroeder's problem.[7] The key to a solution is to show that there are some other facts that constitute possessed reasons that rationalize one's beliefs in non-veridical perceptual cases. As we'll see, Schroeder ends up arguing that in the case of non-veridical, basic, perceptual justification, it's not plausible to appeal to other facts to account for beliefs rationalized by non-veridical perceptions. This is a version of the New New Evil Demon problem. This will be discussed at length below. For now the important point is that *at the very least* I need to appeal to other facts to explain why some beliefs are rationalized by non-veridical perceptions.

---

[6] Cf. Williamson (2000), Schellenberg (2013).

[7] It won't solve all of it because Schroeder's problem is an amalgam of the New Evil Demon problem and what I'll call the New New Evil Demon problem. We thus won't have a full solution to Schroeder's problem until we solve the New New Evil Demon problem.

The third and final related problem is anchored in cases of rational actions that are motivated by false beliefs.[8] This is anchored in cases like Happy Bernie and Deceived Bernie:[9]

Happy Bernie

Bernie just got to a friend's birthday party after a grueling day at the office. The birthday party is at a respectable bar. The bartender also makes excellent gin and tonics. Bernie quickly makes his way to the bar and orders a gin and tonic. He receives one, takes a sip, and is happy.

Deceived Bernie

Bernie just got to a friend's birthday party after a grueling day at the office. The birthday party is at a respectable bar. The bartender also makes excellent gin and tonics. Bernie quickly makes his way to the bar and orders a gin and tonic. However, unbeknownst to deceived Bernie, the bartender gives him a petrol and tonic instead of a gin and tonic. He takes a sip and is not happy.

Consider the rational status of taking a sip for each Bernie. It's plausible that each was rational in taking a sip. Similarly to the Bad Case, it's hard to see how my view can accommodate the rational status of deceived Bernie's action. After all, both Bernie's actions seem to be rationalized by the claim that the glass contains gin and tonic. But my view maintains that that claim cannot rationalize deceived Bernie's action, for it is not an objective reason to drink.

Once again, this problem looks to be a special case of the New Evil Demon problem. In order to solve it, I need to appeal to some other reasons that rationalize deceived Bernie.

The upshot is this. The New Evil Demon problem poses a grave risk to my view. Claims like Same Status and Same Degree are very plausible, and I need to account for them if I am going to successfully defend the main thesis of this book. Moreover, there are at least three related problems that seem to be open to the same type of solution as the New Evil Demon problem. If one can solve the New Evil Demon problem, then one can solve the related problems too. So there is a large payoff awaiting the theorist who can provide a compelling solution to the problem. In the rest of the chapter, I aim to collect this payoff.

7.3 A Solution to the New Evil Demon Problem

The core of the New Evil Demon problem is that it's mysterious how the externalist can account for why both Sam and Pam possess sufficient reasons to hold their beliefs.

---

[8] This problem is discussed in Schroeder (2008), Alvarez (2010), Lord (2010), Comesaña & McGrath (2014).

[9] These problems are structurally similar to Normal Colloquium and Unusual Colloquium discussed in chapters 3 and 6.

As we saw above, many also have the intuition that Sam and Pam have equally strong reasons to believe what they do. It's particularly mysterious how the externalist can account for that intuition. In order to solve the version of the problem that plagues my view, I first need to explain what could rationalize the beliefs of the systematically deceived.

At this point we need to be more precise about possession. Ultimately I am most interested in showing that my view of possession can solve the problems. That said, I am also interested in showing that P→K can also solve the problem.[10] As we'll see at the very end of the chapter, there is a reason local to the debate about the New Evil Demon problem to prefer my view. Nevertheless, for much of the chapter I'll assume that the epistemic condition on possession is knowledge. My main motivation for making this assumption is to show that my solution to the New Evil Demon problem is available to defenders of P→K. Further, at some points this assumption will act as a helpful simplifying assumption.

Accounting for Same Status

Let's start with how to account for Same Status—the datum that Sam and Pam are both rational. The trick is to find some facts in the bad case that are sufficient reasons to believe that the relevant agents possess. Timothy Williamson explicitly addresses this challenge.[11] He writes,

> In unfavorable circumstances, one fails to gain perceptual knowledge, perhaps because things are not the way they appear to be. One does not know that things are that way, and E=K [i.e., P→K] excludes the proposition that they are as evidence. Nevertheless, one still has perceptual evidence, even if the propositions it supports are false. True propositions can make a false proposition probable, as when someone is skillfully framed for a crime of which she is innocent. If perceptual evidence in the case of illusions consists of true propositions, what are they? The obvious answer is: the proposition that things appear to be that way.
>
> (Williamson, 2000, p. 198)

Given normal background conditions, the fact that it appears to you as if p is a reason to believe p. One's perceptual faculties wouldn't be very trustworthy if this were false.[12] Williamson thus thinks that the reasons that rationalize the beliefs of the deceived are facts about how the world appears to them.

---

[10] Remember that P→K is the view that the epistemic condition on possession is knowledge.

[11] More recently Williamson has given up the view I will rely on here. See Williamson (FC).

[12] Note that I'm *not* making a claim about reliability. I'm making a claim about epistemic trustworthiness. It might be that perceptions are trustworthy but not reliable (although they won't ever be trustworthy when one knows they're unreliable). The claim in the text thus doesn't conflict with claims made by some internalists about justification (see, e.g., Pryor (2000), Silins (2005)).

Note that if this is going to work for all the cases, it has to be that *nearly every time* we perceive *p*, we *know* that it appears as if *p*. In other words, if this is going to work, Always Knows has to be true:

Always Knows: *Ceteris paribus*, every time *A* perceives *p*, *A* knows that it appears as if *p*.

Always Knows is *prima facie* implausible. After all, in some cases one simply doesn't have time to go on to form the extra belief that it appears that *p*. And sometimes it would simply be a waste of time to go on to form the extra belief that it appears that *p*.

In the sentences immediately following the passage already quoted, Williamson addresses this challenge. He writes

> Of course, unless one has reason to suspect that circumstances are unfavorable, one may not consider the cautious proposition that things appear to be that way; one may consider only the unqualified proposition that they really are that way. But it does not follow that one does not know that things appear to be that way, for one knows many propositions without considering them. When one is walking, one normally knows that one is walking, without considering the proposition. Knowing is a state, not an activity. In that sense, one can know without considering that things appear to be some way. (Williamson, 2000, p. 198)

This passage is a bit opaque, but I think that with a little unpacking we can see how the P→K theorist has a somewhat plausible response to the challenge. I take it that Williamson agrees with the thought that it would be a waste of time to always form a certain kind of belief about how things appear to you upon having a perception. This would require you to *consider* whether things appear to you in a certain way. He argues here, though, that one needn't consider something in order to know it—one usually knows one is walking when one is walking without considering whether one is walking. I'm not entirely sure how Williamson wants to spell this out. The way I think of it is that you have tacit knowledge when you know things you've never considered. This doesn't seem crazy. It does seem like, when I'm walking, I have tacit knowledge that I'm walking.[13]

Even granting that the facts about how things appear to the deceived are possessed reasons, one isn't home free yet. For we need the facts about how things appear to the deceived to be *sufficiently weighty* to make the deceived's beliefs rational. Let's focus on a particular belief of Pam's. Suppose both Sam and Pam have a visual perception that represents what looks to be a red table. Sam sees an actual red table, Pam does not. However, it appears to Pam that there is a red table. It's plausible that this fact is a reason to believe <THE TABLE IS RED>. Moreover, it's not crazy to think that Pam knows that <IT APPEARS THAT THE TABLE IS RED>.

I think it's also quite plausible that this reason is sufficiently strong. This is because what's relevant to whether Pam's belief is rational is the weight of the reasons Pam

---

[13] Unfortunately, not nearly enough work has been done on tacit knowledge. Most work suggests that it will be quite hard to successfully analyze tacit knowledge as a state we're actually in when we have tacit knowledge. See especially Lycan (1988, ch. 3).

possesses. Given the reasons Pam possesses, it's plausible that the reason provided by the appearance fact is sufficiently weighty to rationalize Pam's belief. In order for the reason not to be sufficiently weighty, she would have to possess some defeater. This would have to be some strong evidence against the claim that the table is red or it would have to be some kind of undercutting defeater—some fact that severs the indicatory connection between her appearance and the table being red. Now certainly there are some facts that would be defeaters of either kind *if Pam came to possess them.* The rub, though, is that she doesn't *possess* any of those reasons. The world seems to her the same way the world seems to Sam. Thus, it seems plausible that the reason provided by the fact that the table appears red is sufficiently strong for Pam.

Crucially, I think that it follows from the nature of non-factive internal state duplicates that Sam possesses a sufficient reason to believe p just in case Pam does.[14] This is because if Sam possesses some reason r to believe p, then Pam will have some corresponding non-factive state that allows her to know that it appears that r. And if the reason provided by Pam's appearance gets defeated, then Sam will have some internal state that is also a defeater of r. For example, if it appears to Pam that r' and r' defeats r, then it will also appear to Sam that r'. And this will be true for any r and r'. Thus, it looks like the perspectival similarities between Sam and Pam guarantees that whenever Pam possesses a sufficient reason to ϕ, there will be a corresponding reason that Sam possesses that is also sufficient.

We can use this machinery to solve the other three problems. In the knowledge from falsehood case, there are other possessed sufficient reasons for Fritz to believe he won't be late. For example, Fritz knows that it appears to be 2:58 pm. He also knows that his extremely reliable watch says that it is 2:58 pm. Because of the reasons provided by these pieces of knowledge, he also knows that it's earlier than 4 pm, earlier than 5 pm, earlier than 6 pm etc. Those are all sufficient reasons Fritz possesses to believe that he won't be late.[15]

When we turn to Schroeder's problem, we needn't go past the first Williamson quote to have a (partial) solution to Schroeder's problem. The sufficient possessed reason for one to believe as one does in paradigm cases of non-veridical perception is the fact that things appear to be thus and so. The appearance fact is what is doing the rationalizing.

Finally, when it comes to Deceived Bernie, it seems as if there are several nearby reasons that count in favor of taking a sip. These are just the reasons that rationalize his belief that the drink is a gin and tonic. For example, the fact that he's at a respectable bar, the fact that he just ordered a gin and tonic from a bartender that makes good gin and tonics, the fact that it appears that many other people are in the room enjoying drinks that were served by the bartender, etc.[16]

---

[14] Kiesewetter (2017, ch. 7) briefly defends a very similar solution the New Evil Demon problem to mine. See pp. 172–3 for his version of the following argument. He doesn't discuss the New New Evil Demon problem (nor does he discuss what it is to correctly respond at all).

[15] Perhaps not surprisingly, this is the most popular solution offered in the literature on knowledge from falsehood (see Coffman (2008), Fitelson (2010), Arnold (2011)).

[16] I initially made this response to this problem in Lord (2010). I didn't tackle the New New Evil Demon problem in that paper, though.

My explanation of Same Status is thus quite simple. There are nearby truths that are sufficient reasons to believe the relevant propositions. Moreover, those in the bad cases do possess those reasons. Thus, their beliefs are *ex ante* rational—supported by possessed sufficient reasons.[17]

Accounting for Same Degree

If what I said in the last subsection is true, then both Sam and Pam are in a position to have rational beliefs. Both of their beliefs are well supported by the reasons they possess. As we saw above, this is weaker than the conclusion many want to draw about characters like Sam and Pam. Many want to say that not only are Sam and Pam both rational, they are *equally rational*.

Before we start, let me say that I am not interested in showing that all of Sam and Pam's beliefs are *necessarily* rational to the same degree.[18] I don't think that's true. But this is just part and parcel of being the type of externalist I am.[19] What I aim to show is that, given a very natural way of understanding the cases, there is an important sense in which Sam and Pam are rational to the same degree. Moreover, I am going to argue that the ways in which my view predicts they are not rational to the same degree are virtues of my theory, not bugs.

With that said, it's not always clear what is meant by 'equally rational.' Often, it seems to me, this is synonymous with 'don't have the same rationalizers.' If that is what is meant by 'equally rational,' then of course the externalist has to deny that Sam and Pam are equally rational! One might find externalism implausible on its face, but mounting an objection to the view in this way is dialectically unhelpful.

I think the best way of thinking of a set of reasons making a belief more rational is by thinking that a belief, b_1, is more rational than a belief, b_2, just in case the set of possessed reasons supporting b_1 is *weightier* than the set of possessed reasons supporting b_2. At the very least, this is a natural starting point. The weight of reasons comes in degrees. The phenomenon we're investigating—the relative rationality of beliefs—also comes in degrees. It's thus natural to think that the relative rationality of beliefs tracks the weight of the possessed reasons supporting those beliefs.

One might be surprised that I've initially committed myself to this view of what it is for one belief to be more rational than another. After all, at first blush it seems very plausible to think that Sam must be more rational than Pam if externalism is correct because the reasons Sam possesses are, in an obvious way, better than the reasons Pam possesses. After all, Sam possesses the reason constituted by the fact that the table is

---

[17] I imagine some readers are jumping up and down about the fact that I've said nothing about how those in the bad cases are suitably connected to the nearby truths to count as *ex post* rational. Fear not, I will deal with that issue in a bit.

[18] Kiesewetter (2017) does argue that they are necessarily rational to the same degree.

[19] Indeed, I think it's very plausible that this is part and parcel of being an externalist about rationality at all. Some externalists about justification try to maintain that it's necessarily true that Sam and Pam are *rational* to the same degree by pursuing the disambiguation strategy mentioned in the introduction.

red, whereas Pam only possesses the reason constituted by the fact that it appears as if the table is red. A natural way to spell out the way in which Sam's reason is better than Pam's is in terms of weight—it's better because it's weightier.

While I agree that this is a natural thought, I think that it is mostly irrelevant to the question at hand. This is because it confuses what we can call a reason's *atomic* weight with a set of reasons' *relative* weight. Atomic weight—if it exists—is the weight that a reason has independently of how it interacts with the other reasons in a particular situation.[20] Relative weight is the weight that sets of reasons have after they are weighed against reasons for alternatives in any given situation. Sam's reason is *necessarily* weightier only in the atomic sense. We can't know what a set of reasons' relative weight is until we know what the other reasons are.

The rub, though, is that the relevant weighing for assessing how rational a particular belief is the relative weighing. So we aren't going to learn that Sam's belief is more rational than Pam's just by learning that her reason has greater atomic weight. We need to know what other reasons there are.

Notice that the natural way to fill in the details of The Good Case and The Bad Case is to assume that not only does Sam have better reasons for the beliefs she holds, she also has better reasons not to hold the beliefs she holds. So while Sam *knows* that she sometimes makes perceptual errors, Pam only knows that it appears to her that she sometimes makes perceptual errors. Sam might know that Tom said the store was to the left (even though she believes it to be to the right; she knows Tom is terrible at directions and has other reasons to believe it to be to the right), but it only appears to Pam that Tom said the store was to the left, etc.

If this is how we fill in the case, then the reasons Sam has for not believing what she does will have greater atomic weight than the reasons Pam has for not believing what she does. Indeed, I boldly conjecture that the difference in relative weight between Sam's and Pam's reasons for believing what they do is *identical* to the difference in relative weight between Sam's and Pam's reasons for not believing what they do in fact believe. If this is right, then the so-called gap between the reasons for believing and reasons against believing will be the same. This just is a way of measuring relative weight. If this is right, then there is a natural sense in which the relative weight of Sam's reasons is the same as the relative weight of Pam's—the ratio between the reasons for and reasons against will be the same for both Sam and Pam.[21]

Of course, we're not forced to fill in the cases this way. It's possible for Sam to just have the reasons Pam does against what she believes even though she has more reasons to believe what she does believe. In that filling out of the case, the relative weight of Sam's reasons for believing what she does will be greater than the relative weight of Pam's reasons for believing what she does. Two things to note about this. First, it's not damning because it's so obviously true. That is, in this version of the case,

---

[20] I am going to assume for now that there are atomic weights. I will question this below.
[21] I thank Gideon Rosen for this formulation of the idea.

I don't think it's plausible that Same Degree is true. Second, this is *not* the most natural way of filling out the case. The most natural way of filling out the case is that where Sam is well-informed about the external world, Pam is misinformed. This goes for reasons against as much as it goes for reasons for. Thus, I think those who endorse Same Degree are thinking of the case in a way that suggests that the relative weight of Sam's reasons is the same as the relative weight of Pam's.

Thus, there is a true reading of Same Degree. Sam and Pam are equally rational because the relative weights of the sets of reasons they possess for the beliefs they hold are the same. Moreover, I think that this is the most important reading of Same Degree. This is because what we should be interested in determining the comparative rationality of a group of agents is the relative weights of the sets of reasons they possess.

I've run the explanation by appealing to atomic weights. It is important to note that this isn't necessary. As long as there is some way to measure the strength of all the reasons together—i.e., as long as there's a way to measure the strength of the reasons all things considered—then we will have what my explanation needs. And anyone who thinks that we can build up strict notions like obligation, justification, and rationality out of reasons and their weight is committed to thinking that there is some relative notion.

On the other hand, not everyone is committed to thinking that there is some atomic notion. Indeed, in the epistemic case it is a bit mysterious what the atomic weights could be. This is because the orthodox way of measuring the strength of some evidence is by using conditional probability. We can measure the strength of a reason r to believe p by measuring how likely p is given r *and* some background information. Usually, the background information will just be the rest of one's evidence. So on this view, there really isn't anything like atomic weights. This is because in order to measure the strength of any particular reason r, you have to use the other evidence. So each measure is relative in an important way.[22]

There are two important conclusions to draw from this. First, it seems like the internalist thought we started out with—viz., the thought that Sam's reasons must be weightier because her reason is weightier—tacitly assumes a notion of atomic weight that is mysterious. Second, my explanation doesn't need to assume that there are mysterious atomic weights.

There is another objection to my idea in the ballpark. According to this line, Sam's reasons must be weightier because Sam has more reasons to believe what she believes than Pam does. It appears to Sam that the table is red just like it appears to Pam that the table is red. So Sam not only has <THE TABLE IS RED> as a reason to believe it's red,

---

[22] Of course, once you have the partial ordering of relative weights, it's trivial to assign atomic weights to the individual reasons. But these atomic weights will be parasitic on the relative weights. Further, and most importantly, the reasons will not take those atomic weights with them to other contexts where the other reasons have changed in a way that affects the relative weighing. For more discussion of these general issues, see Lord & Maguire (2016).

she also has the appearance fact as a reason to believe it's red. So she has two reasons to Pam's one. It is natural to think that if A has reasons r_1 and r_2 to ϕ and B just has r_1, then A is guaranteed to have weightier reasons to ϕ than B.

This is natural, but also resistable. To see this, consider my belief that $2 + 2 = 4$. My belief that $2 + 2 = 4$ is maximally rational. Moreover, my maximal rationality is *overdetermined* in an important way. That is to say, there are several proper subsets of my set of possessed reasons to believe that $2 + 2 = 4$ that are all strong enough on their own to make me maximally rational in believing $2 + 2 = 4$. Consider two of the subsets, S_1 and S_2. By hypothesis, each is weighty enough to maximally rationalize— so each is as weighty as they get. Now consider the union of S_1 and S_2. Imagine I came to possess the set comprised of the union, call it S_3. Plausibly, possessing S_3 is in some way *better* than merely possessing S_1 or S_2. But it can't be that my belief that $2 + 2 = 4$ is more rational given S_3 than it is given merely S_1 or S_2. My belief is maximally rational no matter which set I possess. So what's better about possessing S_3?

I think the answer is that the rational status of my belief is more robust when I possess S_3. This is because there are multiple proper subsets of S_3 that have sufficient weight. It's *not* that S_3 is weightier than S_1 or S_2 in any helpful sense of the word. Rather, it's just as weighty as S_1 and S_2. It's rather that its weight is overdetermined.

I think that something similar is happening with Sam and Pam (although I also think there is a feature of the $2 + 2 = 4$ case that isn't present in the Sam and Pam cases). It's not that the set of reasons Sam has is weightier in any helpful sense of the word. It's rather that her rationality is overdetermined. Multiple proper subsets of her set of reasons are sufficient all on their own.

A promising objection to this application of the overdetermination thought is that it might seem to commit me to the idea that Pam's (and Sam's) belief that the table is red is maximally rational. After all, the fact that there are multiple proper subsets of my evidence for $2 + 2 = 4$ that maximally rationalize is what started us down the overdetermination path to begin with. Because of this, it's plausible to think, at this point, that the proper application of the overdetermination lesson is only in cases where one's reasons maximally rationalize.

This isn't right. It's just that the cases of maximal rationalization are the easiest to cotton onto. I think what is overdetermined in these cases is the *sufficiency* of the (relative) weight of reasons to believe $2 + 2 = 4$. When I possess S_3, the sufficiency of my reasons to believe $2 + 2 = 4$ is more overdetermined than when I possess just S_1 or S_2. Similarly for Sam. The sufficiency of the set of her reasons to believe the table is red is more overdetermined than the set of Pam's reasons to believe the table is red.[23]

---

[23] The difference between Sam and me, I think, is that S_3 overdetermines the sufficiency much more than Sam's reasons do.

The important point is that it doesn't follow that the relative weight of Sam's reasons is greater than the relative weight of Pam's just because Sam has two reasons to Pam's one. Sam's reasons are more overdetermined than Pam's, but the relative weight is the same.

If something like this is correct, then the externalist has a ready answer to a seemingly forceful complaint made by Silins (2005). Silins writes,

As far as propositional [i.e., *ex ante*] justification is concerned, the evidential externalist should allow that internal twins can have different degrees of justification for their beliefs. Suppose an externalist said that, even though internal twins have different evidence, they are equally justified in their beliefs... On this sort of externalist position, however, evidential differences between internal twins are epistemically idle. Evidential differences here would not even explain differences in knowledge—it seems that one can have knowledge in the good case even if one has the same evidence in the bad case. However, I take it that evidential differences between internal twins are interesting and important only if those differences can generate differences in propositional [i.e., *ex ante*] justification between twins. So I take it that, if Evidential Externalism is true, then internal twins can fail to have the same degree of propositional [i.e., *ex ante*] justification. (Silins, 2005, p. 386)

Silins seems to think that if Sam's reasons for believing the table is red are better that Pam's, then it must be because they are weightier. Moreover, he thinks that if the externalist denies that Sam's reasons are weightier, then the difference between Sam and Pam is epistemically idle. I think neither of these claims are true. Sam's reasons might be more robust than Pam's even though Pam's reasons are just as weighty as Sam's. Moreover, the robustness of Sam's reasons is not epistemically idle. She is in a better position than Pam precisely because the weight of her reasons is overdetermined.

There are thus two parts to my accounting for Same Degree. Most importantly, I think that there is a natural way in which Sam and Pam are equally rational—i.e., there is a reading of Same Degree that is true. Sam and Pam are equally rational because the relative weight of the set of reasons Sam has for believing what she believes is equal to the relative weight of the set of reasons Pam has for believing what she does. If you posit atomic weights, then there is at least one sense in which Sam's reasons are weightier than Pam's. The reasons Sam has for believing as she does have greater atomic weight than the reasons Pam has for believing what she does—but, then again, the reasons Sam has for not believing as she does also have greater atomic weight than the reasons Pam has for not believing as she does. Despite these (purported) facts about the atomic weights, atomic weights are not the weights we should be most interested in. We should be most interested in the relative weighing. This is because a belief that p is (*ex ante*) rational only if the weight of the reasons possessed to believe p is at least as weighty as the set of reasons to disbelieve p and the set of reasons to withhold belief in p. This is a relative weighing. Moreover, it's quite plausible that the reasons Sam has to believe as she does have the same relative weight as the relative weight of the set of reasons Pam has to believe as she does.

The second part of my story is about what it is that makes Sam's position better than Pam's. Some have argued that to concede that there is something better about Sam's situation is to concede Same Degree. This is true in one sense. If you think *what it is* for Sam to be more rational than Pam is for Sam to be in a better position than Pam, then obviously I deny Same Degree. But I don't think this is the right way to see things. For I think the best way of thinking of Same Degree is in terms of the relative weights of Sam and Pam's reasons. Those are the same, and thus I think we should think of them as equally rational. On the other hand, Sam is in a better position. This is because the sufficiency of the reasons she possesses is overdetermined in virtue of there being two proper subsets of her set of reasons that are each sufficiently weighty. This is why Sam is in a better position. This is compatible with thinking Same Degree is true.

To close this section, let's return to our three related problems. Whereas with Same Status I could easily extend the story to the three problems, Same Degree is more complicated. This is because it seems that at least for some of the cases involved in the problems, my view does not predict that the pairs of characters are equally rational. Take Deceived Bernie and Happy Bernie. Unlike Pam and Sam, Deceived Bernie shares a lot of knowledge with Happy Bernie. In fact, we can stipulate that Deceived Bernie possesses all of the reasons Happy Bernie possesses to *not* take a sip. Thus, the weight of the reasons not to take a sip will be the same. And since Happy Bernie possesses the reason provided by the fact that the glass contains gin and tonic and Deceived Bernie doesn't, it's natural to suppose that my view predicts that Happy Bernie has stronger reasons to take a sip than Deceived Bernie. It follows that Happy Bernie is more rational to take a sip than Deceived Bernie.

Similar things can be said about non-veridical perceptions in normal worlds. Suppose Sai sees a red table and Harsha has a hallucinatory experience as of a red table. On my view, Harsha possesses a reason to believe the table is red that is provided by the fact that it appears to her as of a red table. Sai possesses this reason and one other reason, which is provided by the fact that the table is red. We can imagine that they have all the same background knowledge. Thus, it looks like the reasons they possess to not believe there is a red table will be equally weighty. And since Sai possesses the reason provided by the fact that the table is red and Harsha doesn't, it looks like it follows like Sai's reasons to believe the table is red are weightier. (I'll return to knowledge from falsehood in a moment.)

While internalists won't be happy with my reaction, my reaction to these cases is that my view makes the correct predictions. Think of it this way: Happy Bernie's action is more *defensible* than Deceived Bernie's. Similarly, Sai's belief is more defensible than Harsha's. Sai and Happy Bernie have resources that Harsha and Deceived Bernie lack. This is not to say, of course, that Harsha and Deceived Bernie cannot make an adequate case for their reactions. They can in virtue of the fact that the reasons they possess for their reactions are sufficient. They can thus defend their reactions against the charge of irrationality. But it seems to me that they cannot defend their reactions as well as Happy Bernie and Sai.

The internalist will likely point out at this point that this means that my view makes a somewhat puzzling pair of predictions. On the one hand, it holds that in many evil demon scenarios, the duplicates are equally rational even though in cases with less deception the duplicates are not. This means that one can, in some sense, be made better off rationally by being more systematically deceived. How can that be?

This is initially puzzling. Upon reflection, though, I don't think that it is. This is because reflection teaches us that the systematically deceived are made worse off when it comes to *all* of their reasons. Further, what matters to rationality is how the possessed reasons line up *against one another*. Given this, it's not puzzling to think that the systematically deceived would be, in one sense, just as well off as their well-informed counterparts. Things are not like this with the locally deceived. They are doing well when it comes to the reasons to not have particular reactions. The reasons to not have reactions will exert more force in the locally deceived cases than they do in the systematically deceived cases.

Notice also that while this means that there is a sense in which the locally deceived are doing worse rationally than the systematically deceived, there is also a way in which they are doing much better. This is because they possess many more reasons provided by facts about the external world than the systematically deceived. In fact, *this* is what makes it the case that their particular reactions are less rational. It is because they are doing better when it comes to the reasons against that they do worse when it comes to the reaction they have. For these reasons, I don't find these predictions troubling.

Now let's return to the knowledge from falsehood cases. I don't think that it's obvious that a completely well-informed counterpart to Fritz is more rational than Fritz. This is because Fritz knows things that *entail* that he's not late—e.g., that it's before 5 pm. Reasons that entail the claims they are reasons for are as good of reasons as one can get. For this reason, I do not think it's plausible to think that Fritz's counterpart who knows it is exactly 2:58 has stronger reasons than Fritz. It is true that the relative weight of Fritz's counterpart's reasons to believe he is not late is overdetermined in the way that Sam's reasons are. This is because the fact that it is exactly 2:58 also entails that Fritz is not late for his meeting. Thus, Fritz's counterpart has more reasons that are as good as reasons get than Fritz. As we've seen, this does not guarantee that Fritz's counterpart has stronger reasons.

7.4 But Wait, There's More: The New New Evil Demon Problem

The new evil demon problem, as I've characterized it, is about *ex ante* rationality. It is thus primarily a search for suitable rationalizers of the beliefs of those in the bad cases. Moreover, as we saw, the Knowledge from Falsehood problem, Schroeder's non-veridical perception problem, and rational action motivated by false beliefs problem were also largely about what rationalizes subjects in less than ideal circumstances. I argued above that there are plausible solutions to these problems.

Unfortunately for me, the New Evil Demon problem is not the only, nor is it the hardest, problem for externalists posed by the deceived. This is because we are not only interested in *ex ante* rationality, we are also interested in *ex post* rationality. It's not just that Pam is *ex ante* rational—i.e., it's not just that the things she believes are sufficiently supported by possessed reasons; her beliefs themselves are rational, at least if Sam's are.

As we saw in chapter 5, what fills the gap between *ex ante* rationality and *ex post* rationality is *reacting for normative reasons*. In order for a token belief to be *ex post* rational, there must be the right connection between the belief and the rationalizers of the belief—on my view, the reasons that sufficiently support the belief. Thus, if Pam is *ex post* rational, it must be that her beliefs are held for the reasons that sufficiently support her belief. The same goes for the likes of Fritz and for those who have rational non-veridical perceptual beliefs.

This problem is much harder than the original problem. This is because it's completely mysterious how to account for the full range of cases, at least given the orthodox understanding of how large the range of cases is (foreshadowing!). On the orthodox understanding, there are two interesting types of cases of basing reactions on reasons. The first type of basing relationship is the *inferential* relationship. Many of Sam's and Pam's beliefs will be inferential in their origins. For example, both Sam and Pam might infer certain historical beliefs from other beliefs they have about what their history textbooks say (or, in Pam's case, what appears to be a history textbook). Focus on a particular belief: the belief that Fermat's last theorem was proved by Andrew Wiles.

Sam infers that Fermat's last theorem was proved by Andrew Wiles from her knowledge that her textbook says that he proved Fermat's last theorem. Since her textbook is reputable, this seems like a sufficient reason to believe that Wiles proved Fermat's last theorem. Moreover, provided that her inference was normal, it's very plausible that her belief is *ex post* rational partially because of the inference. By inferring the belief from a rational belief in a sufficient reason, she comes to base her belief on the sufficient reason.

The etiology of Pam's belief is very similar to the etiology of Sam's. She also infers that Wiles proved Fermat's last theorem from a belief that her history textbook says so. However, there is no history textbook in front of Pam and in her world Wiles didn't prove Fermat's theorem. Thus, given Reasons Factivity, Pam's belief cannot be rationalized by the reasons that rationalize Sam's beliefs since those aren't reasons for Pam. This means that Pam's inference can't be doing the epistemic work that Sam's inference is. Sam's inference is what's connecting her to the reasons in the right kind of way to make her belief *ex post* rational. Pam's inference must not be doing this since the content of the belief is not a reason to have the belief. Above I argued that the reason that sufficiently supports Pam's belief is something like <IT APPEARS

THAT A REPUTABLE HISTORY TEXTBOOK IS REPORTING THAT ANDREW WILES PROVED FERMAT'S LAST THEOREM>. It's very implausible that Pam *infers* her belief from *that* claim. Thus, if she is going to be suitably connected to the sufficiently strong possessed reason, it looks like the connection can't be inferential.

Note that this problem also crops up in Fritz's knowledge from falsehood case. Fritz infers that he won't be late to his 7 pm meeting from his belief that it is exactly 2:58 pm. Given Reasons Factivity, <IT'S EXACTLY 2:58 PM> cannot be the sufficiently strong possessed reason that rationalizes Fritz's belief. Thus, Fritz's inference must not be what's putting Fritz in suitable contact with the rationalizer of his belief. So, if he is *ex post* rational—which he must be if he has knowledge—then the process by which he becomes suitably related to his sufficient reasons must not be inferential.[24]

Finally, something analogous seems to be going on with the Bernies. It looks like both of them move from a belief that the glass contains gin and tonic to the act of taking a sip. It seems like this transition is what connects Happy Bernie to the reasons that rationalize his action. However, on my view, it doesn't look like this transition can be what connects Deceived Bernie to the reasons that rationalize his act. This is because <THAT THE GLASS CONTAINS GIN AND TONIC> is not what rationalizes his act (according to my view). But it seems like this transition is the motivational transition relevant to the rational etiology of the actions of both Bernies. Thus, it's mysterious how Deceived Bernie's act is connected in the right way to the reasons that rationalize it. Without that connection, I'm committed to thinking his act is not *ex post* rational.[25]

The second type of case is the *non-inferential* case. It's very plausible that some of Sam's and Pam's beliefs have non-inferential origins. The paradigm non-inferential beliefs are perceptual beliefs. Let's take a particular perceptual belief of Sam's: the belief that the table in front of her is red. Given that this is a normal perceptual belief, it's plausible that Sam and Pam don't infer this belief from some other beliefs. The etiology is rather different. The belief is rather caused by their perceptual systems themselves—the etiology is sub-inferential in some sense. In Sam's case, this perceptual system puts her into appropriate contact with a sufficient reason to believe that the table is red. It's controversial which reason that is; for simplicity's sake, I'll stick to the simplest proposal and the proposal I like best: the reason is the fact that the table is red.[26] Even though Sam doesn't infer the table is red from another belief, she is still suitably connected to her reason because of the etiology.

The etiology of Pam's belief is very similar to the etiology of Sam's. Pam's belief, just like Sam's, is caused by her perceptual system—it's sub-inferential in the same way. The only difference is that Sam's belief is in some sense caused by the redness of the table, whereas Pam's isn't. This is a crucial difference, according to those who believe

---

[24] This is pressed forcefully in the knowledge from falsehood literature by Fitelson (2010), Arnold (2011).

[25] This challenge is raised by Comesaña & McGrath (2014).

[26] Another externalist candidate is the fact that Sam sees a red table (see, e.g., McDowell (1994), Neta & Pritchard (2007), Pritchard (2012)).

Reasons Factivity. For it means that only Sam's belief can be rationalized by *the table is red*, despite the similar etiologies. Above I argued that the sufficient reason Pam possesses to believe the table is red is rather the fact that it appears to her that there is a red table. But it's plausible that her belief isn't connected to *that* reason in the way Sam's belief is connected to the fact that the table is red—it's not paradigmatically non-inferential. But, again, it's not inferential either. So Pam's belief, if it is going to be *ex post* rational, has to be connected to her sufficient possessed reasons in some other, mysterious, way.

The problem is magnified if we make a widely held assumption about the nature of non-inferentially rational beliefs. They are often thought to be *foundational*. Foundational beliefs are rational beliefs whose rational status doesn't depend on one having any other rational beliefs. One doesn't need other rational beliefs in order to have rational non-inferential beliefs. This is what makes non-inferential beliefs foundational beliefs.

It's natural to think that both Sam's and Pam's beliefs about the table are foundational. Sam's certainly seems foundational. She doesn't need to rationally believe anything else in order to rationally believe that the table is red. After all, her perceptual system puts her into contact with the fact that the table is red. This is enough to rationalize her belief. But this can't be what's going on with Pam if Reasons Factivity is true and my story in the last section is correct. For according to that story, in order for Pam to be rational, she must know that the table appears red to her. Thus, Pam does need to have another rational belief—the belief that it appears that the table is red—in order to be rational. Thus, her belief isn't foundational. On the other hand, it's not inferential either, which is the paradigm type of non-foundational rational belief.

It's interesting to note that Schroeder presents a more nebulous version of this very problem. He writes,

That means that this view predicts that internal duplicates with duplicate pasts in very similar environments can nevertheless differ not just in whether they know, but in whether their belief is justified [i.e., rational], if for the very first time one sees something green in front of her while the other experiences a vivid hallucination as of something green in front of her, and both form the perceptual belief that there is something green in front of them . . . So unfortunately the high bar on having evidence is not a bar that can be met in the full range of foundational perceptual cases. At most it can be met in the case of veridical perceptual experiences, but it would be best to avoid needing to distinguish between the justification provided by veridical and by non-veridical perceptual experiences. (Schroeder, 2011b, p. 217)

The reason why I think this is nebulous is that it runs together the New Evil Demon problem and the New New Evil Demon problem. I don't think Schroeder ever shows that, according to externalists of a certain kind, internal duplicates will differ when it comes to *ex ante* rationality (or justification). But it's plausible that he shows that externalists of a certain kind can't think that those in the bad cases will have rational beliefs that are *foundational*. If you think that all the foundational beliefs are non-inferential, you think that there are only inferentially or non-inferentially based rational beliefs, and you think that those in the bad case don't have inferentially rational perceptual beliefs, then it follows that internal duplicates will differ when it comes to *ex post* rationality.

The New New Evil Demon problem, then, is a puzzle about reacting for normative reasons. On the one hand, those committed to Reasons Factivity have trouble accounting for some seemingly inferentially rational beliefs that are based on falsehoods. If Reasons Factivity is true, then it can't be that one's beliefs are rationalized by falsehoods. So they can't be rationalized by the propositions they are inferred from. But then one must tell some story about how it is that there is a suitable connection between one's beliefs and actual possessed reasons. It doesn't seem like the connection can be inferential. Moreover, it doesn't seem like it can be non-inferential in the usual sense of non-inferential. This is because it's clear that the beliefs aren't foundational beliefs. Indeed, according to the story I told above, in order for Pam to have an *ex post* rational belief that Andrew Wiles proved Fermat's last theorem, she has to have an *ex post* rational belief that it appears to her that a reputable history textbook says Andrew Wiles proved Fermat's last theorem. So it can't be a foundational belief and thus it doesn't seem like it can be non-inferential. Thus, it can't be inferential or non-inferential.

On the other hand, those committed to Reasons Factivity have trouble accounting for perceptual beliefs caused by non-veridical perceptions. While there is a nice story to tell about The Good Case—perceptual beliefs in The Good Case are based on their contents—this story doesn't carry over to The Bad Case. Pam's belief that the table is red can't be based on <THE TABLE IS RED> because that isn't a reason for Pam. However, Pam's belief clearly isn't inferential. Moreover, according to the story above, her belief can't be foundational either. This is because in order for her belief that the table is red to be rational, she has to rationally believe that it appears to her that there is a red table. If it's not foundational, then it doesn't seem like it can be non-inferential. So it's not inferential or non-inferential.

7.5 Solving the New New Evil Demon Problem

The main idea behind my solution to the New New Evil Demon problem is that there is another way to react for normative reasons besides paradigmatic inferential basing and paradigmatic non-inferential basing. I'll call this type of basing *uninferential basing*.[27] Here are some examples of uninferential basing:

---

[27] This type of basing has been bumped up against at points in the literature, although no one has picked it out as relevantly different than inferential and non-inferential basing. See especially Harman (1973), Kelly (2002), Evans (2013).

Lottery

Max learns that Richard won the lottery. He then infers from this knowledge that Richard is rich. Suppose, though, that Max later comes to learn that when Richard won the lottery he was in deep debt. He had so much debt, in fact, that winning the lottery didn't make him rich; it only allowed him to get out of debt. Max also learns, however, that he has subsequently become rich because of some good investment decisions. This knowledge becomes the basis of Max's belief that he is rich *and* Max's knowledge that he won the lottery ceases to be the basis of Max's belief that he is rich.

Red Widgets[28]

Max is touring a widget factory. He visually perceives a red widget and comes to believe that it's a red widget. The factory owner comes up to him and says 'That's a fine red widget, isn't it? I just finished painting it.' He then goes on to tell Max that one has to be careful about which widgets are red because they light the place with red lights. Max looks up and, sure enough, the factory floor is lit by red lights. The fact that the widget looks red ceases to be the basis of Max's belief but he still believes the widget is red because of the owner's testimony—that becomes the basis for his belief.

In both of these cases, it's very plausible that the bases of Max's beliefs change over time even though he never drops the beliefs. In Lottery, Max continuously believes that Richard is rich even though the basis of that belief changes over time. For a while Max believes this because Richard won the lottery. He later comes to find out that reason wasn't sufficient to rationalize believing that he was rich because of his debt. However, he doesn't drop the belief because he also finds out that Richard is rich through smart investments. This fact becomes the basis of Max's belief. Something similar happens in Red Widgets. Max continuously believes the widget is red despite the fact that the basis for this belief changes. At first he believes it because it looks red. However, the factory owner alerts him to a defeater of this reason—the red lights. Before defeating the original reason, though, the factory owner provides another sufficient reason through his testimony. This testimonial reason becomes Max's belief's new basis.

Despite the fact that these are clear cases of believing for normative reasons, I don't think they have the hallmarks of either inferential or non-inferential basing. They are obviously not non-inferential in the way we've been understanding non-inferential reactions. This is because the beliefs in question are obviously not foundational. Max only rationally believes Richard is rich because he rationally believes he got rich through smart investments and Max rationally believes it's a red widget only because he rationally believes the owner confirmed it was red. Since the output beliefs aren't foundational, the basing isn't non-inferential.

---

[28] This comes from Evans (2013) and is a variation of a case from Pollock (1974).

On the other hand, the beliefs are not obviously inferential, either. This is because paradigm cases of inference are *creative*. New beliefs come into existence because of the inference. Inference is a deliberative activity that results in new beliefs. This is not happening in these cases. In both cases Max's output belief stays the same. What changes is how those beliefs relate to other reasons he possesses.[29] In this way, the basing isn't paradigmatically inferential.

At this point in the book we should not be surprised that there are cases of this kind. This is because my view of reacting for normative reasons predicts that these cases are possible. This is because my view of reacting for normative reasons maintains that normative reasons *sustaining* a reaction is sufficient for reacting for those normative reasons. This straightforwardly predicts that not all cases of believing for normative reasons will generate new beliefs. In other words, it predicts that there will be cases where the normative reasons for which one believes have nothing to do with the creation of the belief.

My view also provides a nice explanation of what is going on in these cases. What changes is the relationship between the old belief and the new reasons. In Lottery, the fact that Richard became rich through investments comes to sustain Max's belief that Richard is rich. It does this, on my view, because Max gains a disposition to revise his belief that Richard is rich when the reason is defeated. Similarly, in Red Widgets the fact that the supervisor said the widget was red comes to sustain Max's belief that the widget is red. It does this, on my view, because Max becomes disposed to revise his belief that the widget is red if the reason is defeated.

We can use this third type of basing to solve the New New Evil Demon problem. We'll take the two types of cases one at a time, starting with the inferential case.

7.5.1 The inferential case

We discussed two inferential cases. The primary case has to do with Sam and Pam's belief that Andrew Wiles proved Fermat's last theorem. The problem for Reasons Factivity is that the only reason that Pam plausibly possesses to rationalize her belief is constituted by the fact that it appears to Pam that a reputable history book says that Andrew Wiles proved Fermat's last theorem. But this isn't what Pam infers her belief from—she infers it from the claim that a reputable history book says AW proved Fermat's last theorem. So it doesn't seem like her basing is inferential. But it also isn't non-inferential since her belief that AW proved Fermat's last theorem isn't foundational—it depends on her rationally believing that it appears to her that a reputable history book says that AW proved Fermat's last theorem. Thus, it's not clear how her belief could be based on the reason provided by the appearance fact.

---

[29] On some conceptions of inference, these cases might be inferential. Wedgwood (2012), for example, holds that as long as you 'reaffirm' a belief in a certain type of way, you count as inferring the belief. I would be fine if this turned out to be inferential. My point here is just that it isn't paradigmatically inferential.

My answer is that her belief is uninferentially based on the reason provided by the appearance fact. It's plausible that her belief that AW proved Fermat's theorem is sensitive to her belief that it appears that a reputable history textbook says that he did. She is disposed to give up the former belief if she loses the reason provided by the appearance. For example, if she found out that a demon was tricking her in this case, she would likely drop her belief that AW proved Fermat's last theorem because her reason would then be defeated. Or if she gained a reason to believe the particular history book wasn't reputable, then she would drop her belief about who proved Fermat's last theorem. More extremely, it seems like she would drop the belief that AW proved Fermat's last theorem if she stopped believing that it appeared to her that the book says he did. Since the appearance facts provide sufficient reason to believe that AW proved Fermat's last theorem and Pam bases her belief on that reason, her belief is *ex post* rational.

Not only is all of this plausibly true for Pam, but it also is for Sam. It's plausible that Sam's belief is also sensitive to the appearances. It's very plausible that she is disposed to drop her belief if she loses confidence in the trustworthiness of the appearances. Of course, it's also plausible that she is sensitive in the right kind of way to the way things actually are, unlike Pam. But this is just to say that not only is her *ex ante* rationality overdetermined, so is her *ex post* rationality. She bases her belief on more than one sufficiently strong reason. This seems like the right result, and it's a virtue of a view that embraces uninferential basing that it can explain how it is that Sam bases her belief on the reason provided by the appearance fact.[30]

None of this is to deny that one of Pam's motivating reasons for believing AW proved Fermat's last theorem is the claim that her history textbook says so. I think this is one of her motivating reasons. This is because her belief is sustained by the fact that Pam conceives of the claim that her history textbook says AW proved Fermat's last theorem as a normative reason to believe AW proved Fermat's last theorem. This does not mean that that claim rationalizes her belief. It is part of what makes it intelligible, but it does not rationalize it.

The same thing is going on, I conjecture, in Fritz's knowledge from falsehood case. His belief that he won't be late for the 7 pm meeting is sensitive to the reasons that actually rationalize his belief—e.g., the fact that his extremely reliable watch says it's 2:58 pm. It's plausible that he's disposed to drop his belief if he either stopped believing that or if that was defeated in some way. Of course, this doesn't change the

---

[30] Objection: If Sam is sensitive to the appearances, then it is less likely that she is sensitive to the facts. After all, if she is sensitive to the appearances, then in a case where the facts are different but the appearances are the same (e.g., a case like Pam's), she would continue to have the belief. This looks incompatible with her being sensitive to the facts. Reply: This looks incompatible, but it is not. Sam still might be *disposed* to revise if the facts change even if she wouldn't revise were she in Pam's position. If she were in Pam's position, her disposition to revise would be masked. Further, it is not plausible that the nearest world where the facts change but the appearances stay the same are worlds like Pam's. The nearest worlds are worlds where both the reason provided by the appearance are defeated and thus Sam does revise. Thanks to an anonymous referee for raising this objection.

fact that one of Fritz's motivating reasons for believing he's not late is the claim that it's exactly 2:58 pm. But part of what explains (at least partially) why he doesn't drop the belief is the fact that his belief is sensitive to the nearby reasons. Since the nearby reasons rationalize his belief and his belief is based on those reasons, his belief is *ex post* rational.

What about Deceived Bernie? His case seems to be a practical analogue to the epistemic cases involving inference. This is because it's clear that one of his motivating reasons is the claim that his glass contains gin and tonic. Further, it seems like his intention to drink and his drinking is produced by that consideration. Nevertheless, just as it is in the epistemic cases, I think his intention and action are sustained by the nearby reasons—e.g., the reason provided by the fact that he's at a reputable bar, the reason provided by the fact that he just ordered a gin and tonic, the reason provided by the fact that the bartender makes good gin and tonics etc. That is, he's disposed to stop drinking if he loses those reasons or they are defeated. Indeed, it's very plausible that those dispositions will manifest as soon as he tastes what's in the glass. He will not drink the contents of the glass like he does actual gin and tonics! Given the view of intending and acting for normative reasons defended in chapter 5, having those dispositions is sufficient for intending and acting for those normative reasons. Further, they are sufficiently strong to make the intention and action *ex ante* rational. Thus, Deceived Bernie's intention and action are *ex post* rational.

7.5.2 The non-inferential case

The non-inferential cases we focused on are all perceptual cases. Sam sees a red table; Pam has a phenomenologically indistinguishable perception and comes to believe that the table is red. The problem for Reasons Factivity is that while it's possible for Sam to base her belief on the fact that the table is red, it's not possible for Pam to base her belief on that reason since it's not a reason for Pam. My story about Pam's *ex ante* rationality is that her belief is *ex ante* rational because the fact that it appears as if there is a red table provides a sufficiently strong possessed reason to believe the table is red. The problem is that Pam's belief isn't inferred from that reason, nor is it non-inferentially based on that reason. Thus, it's not clear how Pam's belief can be based on the possessed sufficient reason.

Once again, my answer is that her belief is uninferentially based on the reason provided by the appearance fact. That is, her belief that the table is red is sensitive to whether the content of her belief that it appears as if there is a red table is a sufficient reason to believe that it is a red table. Other things equal, if she stopped believing it appeared as if there is a red table, she would stop believing there is a red table. Moreover, other things equal, if the reason provided by the appearance fact were defeated, she would stop believing there is a red table. If this is right, then her belief is suitably connected to the sufficient possessed reason. Thus, she is *ex post* rational.

Recall that Schroeder claimed that 'it would be best to avoid needing to distin-guish between the justification provided by veridical and by non-veridical perceptual experiences' (16). Given the contours of the present discussion, this is multiply ambiguous. Schroeder might just mean that it would be best to not have to posit that Sam and Pam have different rationalizers. I take it he doesn't mean this, though, since it's obvious that externalists have to claim that Pam's belief, if rationalized at all, will be rationalized by different rationalizers than Sam's. More importantly, externalists think of this part of their view as a *virtue*. Williamson (2000), for example, thinks that making this move is a key component of responding to a certain type of skeptic.

A more plausible interpretation is that Schroeder thinks we shouldn't distinguish between the way in which Sam's and Pam's beliefs are based. If we think that the only types of basing are inferential and non-inferential, then the problem is acute. It's very implausible in the perceptual cases (and the inferential cases, for that matter) that Pam either inferentially bases her belief *or* non-inferentially bases her belief on the appearance fact. Nevertheless, I've argued, she is still sufficiently sensitive to those facts to count as basing her belief on those facts. This sensitivity doesn't arise because her beliefs about the appearances play a direct causal role in the *formation* of the belief. The perceptual process is what directly causes the production of the belief. Nonetheless, the belief itself is sensitive to the appearance facts in the right kind of way.

Of course, we've already noted that Pam's perceptual beliefs won't be foundational. They are only rational because she holds rational beliefs about the appearances. Schroeder thinks that this is a cost. I think the externalist should be happy to embrace this result. This is because the externalist should think that, at least for those of us in favorable epistemic environments, our foundational beliefs about the external world are rationalized by the external facts themselves. This is one side of the coin that gives us an advantage over the skeptic. Moreover, despite the fact that Pam's belief about the color of the table isn't foundational, it's plausible that her belief about the appearances is foundational. It is a type of foundational self-knowledge. Thus, at least in this case, the chain of non-foundational beliefs only goes back one link before getting to a foundational belief.[31]

7.6 Conclusion (with a Reason to Reject P→K)

The discussion so far has assumed that the epistemic condition on possession is knowledge. This was mostly a simplifying assumption. P→PTK is compatible with everything I've said. This is because one is automatically in a position to know what one knows. Thus, if P→PTK is true, then one has all the reasons P→K predicts one has. Moreover, nothing about P→PTK prevents the possibility that Pam's beliefs are uninferentially based on the reason she has in virtue of knowing that it appears that *p*.

---

[31] Surely things are a bit more complicated in some of the inferential cases, but I think a foundational belief won't ever be too far from the non-foundational belief in question.

It is not my aim in this chapter to fully adjudicate between these two views—see chapter 3 for my reasons for rejecting P→K. However, it is worth pointing out that P→PTK has an easier time solving the New Evil Demon problem.

P→PTK has an easier time solving the New Evil Demon problem because it can do so using weaker assumptions than P→K. Most importantly, the P→PTK theorist needn't be committed to Always Knows:

Always Knows: *Ceteris paribus*, every time A perceives p, A knows that it appears as if p.

The P→K theorist needs Always Knows in order to secure the claim that in normal cases one possesses the reason provided by the fact that it appears that p when one has the perceptual experience that p. However, according to the P→PTK theorist, one needn't actually know p in order to possess it. One merely needs to be in a position to know p. Thus, in order to solve the New Evil Demon problem the P→PTK theorist just needs Always PTK:

Always PTK: *Ceteris paribus*, every time A perceives p, A is in a position to know that it appears as if p.

Always PTK is much more intuitively plausible than Always Knows. It is not at all obvious that every time one perceives p, one knows that it appears that p. However, it is very plausible that every time one perceives p, one is in a position to know that it appears that p. Thus, P→PTK has this advantage over P→K.

My main aim in this chapter was to give an existence proof of a plausible externalist view of rationality that solves two problems posed by those in less than ideal environments. I've argued that there are at least two plausible externalist views that predict that the deceived can not only be rational, but can also be rational to the same degree as their undeceived counterparts. This doesn't mean, however, that those of us in favorable environments don't have epistemic advantages, but it does show that one can be externalist and respect the rationality of the radically deceived. I've also argued that my story about the radically deceived can be extended to three other problems. The first is the problem of knowledge from falsehood, the second is Schroeder's non-veridical perception problem, and the third is the problem of rational action motivated by false beliefs. All of these problems can be solved by appealing to the machinery I use to solve the Evil Demon problems. A nice payoff indeed.

8

What You're Rationally Required to Do and What You Ought to Do (Are the Same Thing!)

8.1 Introduction

It has been notoriously difficult to vindicate the natural thought that moral considerations necessarily bear on what one ought to do. That is to say, it has been difficult to explain why it is that the facts that determine what one is morally required to do necessarily affect what one ought to do, full stop. The requirements of morality thus face a sort of skeptical challenge. The challenge is to explain the *deontic significance* of morality. In order to meet the challenge, one must explain why we always have most reason (or any reason) to do what morality requires.

Despite this skepticism about morality, other types of requirements have traditionally been seen to be on steadier deontic footing. A paradigm case is *rationality*. Rationality, it is often thought, is clearly deontically significant. The considerations that bear on what's rational seem to necessarily affect what one ought to do, full stop. In fact, something stronger seems to be true. Namely, that you always ought to be rational. It does not seem like much of a challenge at all to explain why we always have most reason (and thus some reason) to do what rationality requires. It is a striking fact that many of the classic positions—both skeptical and non-skeptical—concerning the deontic significance of morality assume the deontic significance of rationality.[1] This is evidence enough that rationality is usually seen to be on steady deontic ground.

Despite this (or perhaps because of it), it has become increasingly popular in the literature on practical reason to deny that you should be rational.[2] And given some assumptions about rationality and about what determines what you should do, this actually seems plausible. Moreover, those assumptions about rationality and about what determines what you should do are thought to be supported by powerful

---

[1] This breaks down roughly into Humean skeptics and Kantian rationalists. On the skeptical side, see (just to name two) Foot (1972), Harman (2000). On the rationalist side, see Smith (1994), Korsgaard (1996).

[2] I will follow the standard practice of treating 'should' as a synonym for 'ought.'

arguments. Because of these rather surprising facts, skepticism about the deontic significance of rationality is alive and kicking.[3] Back to this in a moment.

Another corner of normative philosophy is concerned with what determines what one ought to do, full stop. This debate is about what the best theory is of what we might call the *ought of deliberation*. This is the 'ought' that figures in the central deliberative question: What ought I do?[4] It's commonly assumed that the answer to the central deliberative question is the thing that you ought to do, full stop—it *settles (correct) deliberation*. What you ought to do and believe full stop is, we'll say, what you ought to do and believe. The debate I'm interested in here is about which facts *determine* what you ought to do (and believe). The relevant question is this: Do all the facts determine what you ought to do or do only some of them?

Consider an example. Jack's mother is in the hospital. She needs an operation in order to survive past this week. Her insurance won't pay. Jack, being a fledgling Art Historian/dealer, doesn't have the money. It looks like his mother is going to die. She will, however, be extremely comforted by Jack's presence in her final days. She lives in California; Jack lives in New York. Jack needs to decide whether to go see her. As it happens, a pawn shop owner in Queens has just unknowingly (and legitimately) bought a rare Picasso. He's selling it at a fraction of the price it's worth. If Jack were to buy it, he would be able to use it as collateral for a loan that would pay for his mother's surgery. The rub, of course, is that he has no idea that this pawn shop even exists, much less that such a deal is to be had there. Interesting question: What ought Jack do with his day? Go to California or go to Queens?[5]

If you think that what you ought to do is determined by all the facts, then you are committed to thinking that the place for Jack to go is Queens. If you don't like that answer, then you should think that what you ought to do is determined by only some of the facts.[6] The trick is to explain which facts are relevant.

There is a tight connection between the correct resolutions to these two debates—i.e., the debate about whether you ought to be rational and the debate about

---

[3] This skepticism is usually described as skepticism about the 'normativity' of rationality. I think this is unfortunate terminology because it is not specific enough. I know of no one that denies that rationality is *evaluatively* relevant—e.g., it's relevant to whether one is a bad agent or reasoner. Indeed, Kolodny (2005)—the *locus classicus* of skepticism about the 'normativity' of rationality—explicitly considers whether rationality is merely evaluative rather than 'normative.' This is confusing, I think. This is because evaluative properties are presumably normative. What Kolodny and others have worried about is the more specific property of being deontically significant. Thanks to Kurt Sylvan for discussion about this.

[4] In setting things up this way I'm following (among others) Kolodny & MacFarlane (2010), Kiesewetter (2011), Ross (2012), Broome (2013). The term 'deliberative ought' comes from Williams (1965).

[5] Some think that there isn't really any good question here. This is because, claim these theorists, all we need to do is distinguish between a subjective and objective sense of 'ought.' Once we do this, we can see that Jack objectively ought to go to Queens and subjectively ought to go to California. I disagree that this is enough to solve the problem, as do many others. I spell out why I disagree in §8.4.1.

[6] Of course, the last two sentences are shorthand. There are all sorts of ways all the facts could determine what one ought to do. According to some of those ways, it might not be true that you ought to go to Queens. But on all the most plausible accounts that take into consideration all of the facts, you ought to go to Queens.

what determines what you ought to do. In this chapter, I will argue that Reasons Responsiveness can vindicate the deontic significance of rationality.[7] If Reasons Responsiveness is correct, I will argue, then what you ought to do *just is* what you are rationally required to do. In order to show this, I will argue for a view about what determines what you ought to do. I will argue that there are independent reasons to think that what determines what you ought to do are the reasons you possess. The basic idea behind my main argument for this is that the reasons that obligate have to be potentially action guiding in a certain sense—we have to be able to act *for* the normative reasons that obligate. I will argue that in order to be able to act for a normative reason in the appropriate way, one has to possess the reason. It is a few short steps from here to the claim that the reasons one possesses determine what one ought to do.

The chapter has the following structure. I begin by canvassing the recent literature in metaethics about rationality and its deontic significance. The upshot will be that the two most discussed views have serious problems vindicating the deontic significance of rationality. This will initially motivate Reasons Responsiveness, which immediately entails that we always possess reasons to be rational. Unfortunately, it doesn't immediately follow from Reasons Responsiveness that one always ought to be rational. In order to settle this question, we must investigate the second debate. So in the second half of the chapter we will focus on this. I will argue that it is independently very plausible that what you ought to do is determined by the reasons you possess. Given that Reasons Responsiveness maintains that the reasons you possess determine what you are rationally required to do the view vindicates the full deontic significance of rationality. This is a powerful reason to accept the view.

8.2 Why Be Rational?

In the middle of the last decade, a wave of philosophers started to question the deontic significance of rationality.[8] Unfortunately, what exactly is being questioned is itself a matter of debate. Because of this, I'll start by explicating what I take to be the core of the challenge. I will then introduce the main views discussed in the literature and show how they have a hard time meeting the challenge.

8.2.1 Preliminaries

The easiest way into the question being asked is to think about the most obvious way in which rationality could turn out to be deontically significant. Rationality would obviously be deontically significant if you *should* be rational. This, of course, is not

---

[7] Kiesewetter (2017) argues for a similar view. His view differs from mine because he holds that there is no distinction between possessed and unpossessed reasons. The only reasons, on his view, are the reasons inside one's perspective. For my dissatisfaction with this, see n. 17 in chapter 1.

[8] See Kolodny (2005, 2007a, 2008a,b), Broome (2005a,b, 2008a, 2013), Raz (2005a,b), Southwood (2008), Way (2010a,b).

simply to say that you *rationally should* be rational—i.e., that you are required by rationality to do the things rationality requires of you. It's certainly not open to dispute whether you rationally should be rational. Rather, the question is whether you should, full stop, be rational.

One way to think about the question is to imagine that there are different systems of requirements—e.g., morality, prudence, etiquette, and rationality.[9] Some of these requirements are deontically significant in particular kinds of ways. Some of them, for example, might be such that if you are required by that system to ϕ, you thereby ought full stop to ϕ. Some of them might not be this strict. Some of them might just be such that if you are required by that system to ϕ, there is thereby a reason for you to ϕ. The question has been whether rationality is a system that is either such that if it requires you to ϕ, then you thereby ought to ϕ or such that if it requires you to ϕ, then you thereby have a reason to ϕ.

Despite the fact that the literature has focused on these rather narrow questions, I don't think this is the best way to see things. These questions are *too narrow*. This is because they assume that rationality is deontically significant only if *the fact that rationality requires ϕ-ing* grounds either a full stop requirement to ϕ or a reason to ϕ. I agree that these are two ways that rationality could turn out to be deontically significant. But we can also ask the broader questions of whether it's true that we always ought to do what rationality requires or whether it's true that we always have a reason to do what rationality requires. It might be true that we always ought to do what rationality requires or have reason to do what rationality requires *even if* those facts aren't grounded in the fact that rationality requires one to do the thing in question. Let's focus, then, on the broader questions. To ease discussion, let's say that rationality is *Strongly (Deontically) Significant* if it turns out that we always ought to do what rationality requires. And let's say that rationality is *Weakly (Deontically) Significant* if it turns out that we always have reason to do what rationality requires.

8.2.2 Coherence, rationality, deontic significance

Now that we have some understanding of what the relevant questions are, we can evaluate how well various theories of rationality do answering them. In the next section, I will argue that the view defended in this book does very well. In this section, I will lay out why it's become popular to think that rationality is not deontically significant in recent literature.[10] As we saw in chapter 2, the literature has focused on two different views of rationality. Both views are motivated by the thought that rationality has a tight connection with being coherent in certain ways. Common examples are means-end coherence, belief consistency, and following your conscience. Both

---

[9] This is how the question is normally asked in the literature. This is largely because this is the way John Broome thinks of the issues. See, for example, Broome (2007b, 2013). Ultimately, I think that this way of thinking of things is misleading, but it is a good way to initially glom onto what's going on.

[10] This section covers the same ground as §2.2. I repeat the set-up given how far chapter 2 is from here.

WHAT YOU'RE RATIONALLY REQUIRED TO DO 213

views think that you are rational when you are means-end coherent, and that you are irrational when you are means-end incoherent.

The views diverge when it comes to *why* you are rational when you are means-end coherent and irrational when you are means-end incoherent. That is to say, the views diverge when it comes to which requirement you comply with when you are means-end coherent and which requirement you violate when you are means-end incoherent. According to the narrow-scope view, you are irrational when you fail to intend to ψ when you intend to ϕ and believe that in order to ϕ you must intend to ψ because Means-End N is true:

Means-End N: If you intend to ϕ and believe that in order to ϕ you must intend to ψ, then you are rationally required to intend to ψ.

Narrow-scopers think that you are irrational when means-end incoherent because you lack an intention rationality requires you to have.

Usually the narrow-scope view is introduced merely as a foil for what has come to be the dominant view (more on why it has become the foil below). This view—the wide-scope view—holds that you are irrational when you are means-end incoherent because you violate Means-End W:

Means-End W: You are rationally required to [intend to ψ if you intend to ϕ and believe that you must intend to ψ in order to ϕ.]

Wide-scopers think you are irrational when means-end incoherent because a conditional you are required to make true is false.

The literature has assumed that we can discover what the requirements of rationality are in a way that's independent from asking whether they are deontically significant. This is because it has been assumed that rationality is paradigmatically a matter of coherence, and that we can home in on questions about coherence without having to talk about the deontic significance of the resulting requirements.

The wide-scope view, being the dominant view, has been the main target of the skeptical arguments. Its failure to account for the deontic significance of rationality is all the more surprising because it is largely motivated by the thought that only it can account for why you should be rational.[11] The argument that motivates the wide-scope view goes something like this:[12]

(1) Either the wide-scope view is true or the narrow-scope view is true.
(2) If the narrow-scope view is true, then it's not the case that you always should be rational.
(3) You always should be rational.

---

[11] The thought goes back at least until the 1970's / early 1980s (see, e.g., Hill (1973), Greenspan (1975), Darwall (1983)). It became widely thought about and accepted because of the work of John Broome, especially Broome (1999).

[12] Cf. Schroeder (2004, 2005a).

(4) Thus, the narrow-scope view is false.

(C) Therefore, the wide-scope view is true.

Let's start with (2). If the narrow-scope view were true and rationality were deontically significant, then rationality would give rise to objectionable bootstrapping. To see this, suppose John intends to eat a planet made of Stilton cheese and believes that in order to do that he needs to intend to build a space ship. If Means-End N is true, then it thereby follows that rationality requires John to intend to build a space ship. This is in itself implausible. But it gets even worse if you think that rationality is deontically significant. If it's strongly significant, then it would follow that John ought full stop to intend to build a space ship. This is certainly false. If it's weakly significant, then it would follow that John has a reason to intend to build a space ship. This isn't as obviously false as the last claim, but it still strikes nearly everyone as very implausible.[13]

Means-End W doesn't have these problems. This is because John can comply with Means-End W without intending to build a space ship. He can comply by giving up his end or his means-end belief. Thus, it doesn't follow from Means-End W that John is rationally required to intend to build a space ship when he intends to eat a planet made of Stilton cheese and believes that he must intend to build a space ship in order to eat a planet made of Stilton. Thus, there is no bootstrapping even if rationality is strongly or weakly significant.[14]

Despite the wide-scopers' (apparent) ability to avoid bootstrapping, it has become increasingly unclear whether the wide-scope requirements are deontically significant in either the strong or the weak senses. Before seeing why, it's very important to add one more clarification about the question being asked.[15,16]

Suppose I believe I am writing and disbelieve I am writing. It's plausible that I'm irrational. The wide-scoper thinks I'm irrational because I'm rationally required to [not disbelieve I am writing if I believe I am writing]. When asking whether this requirement is strongly significant, we are asking whether I ought to not-disbelieve-I'm-writing-or-not-believe-I'm-writing. We are not merely asking whether I ought to be in some state other than the incoherent one. It's plausible that it's never permissible

---

[13]   Schroeder (2004, 2005b) argued that the narrow-scope requirements are weakly deontically significant. He has since given this up (see Schroeder (2009b) for his retraction of the earlier view). More recently, Smith (2016) has argued that intentions provide reasons to take the means.

[14]   Some argue that the wide-scope view does have a bootstrapping problem in cases where it's impossible in some way to comply in certain ways. See, for example, Greenspan (1975), Setiya (2007a), Schroeder (2009b).

[15]   The following clarification only applies to the wide-scope view. The narrow-scope view doesn't maintain you are required to be coherent in the way that the wide-scope view does. That is, the narrow-scope view doesn't hold that the thing you are required to do is be coherent. The narrow-scope view holds that given that you hold certain attitudes, you are required to hold some other attitudes. It turns out—by design—that whenever you hold the attitudes you are required to hold, you will be coherent in the right ways. This allows the narrow-scoper to avoid this type of objection, but it also seems to lead directly to the argument against the narrow-scope view sketched above.

[16]   The following discussion assumes that the inheritance princple discussed in chapter 2 is false.

to hold contradictory beliefs. In this case, either my evidence will sufficiently support the claim that I'm writing or it will sufficiently support the claim that I'm not or neither claim will be sufficiently supported. My evidence will never sufficiently support both claims at the same time. So whenever I both believe and disbelieve I'm writing right now, it will be the case that I ought not have (at least) one of those beliefs. In this case, it's the belief that I am not writing right now.

So we can stipulate that I ought not disbelieve that I'm writing right now. And it's true that if I comply with that requirement, I will be coherent. It is very important to note that the literature in question assumes that *this is not to say* that I ought to comply with the wide-scope requirement.[17] In other words, we are assuming there is a gap between being required to do something that guarantees I'll be coherent and being required to be coherent. It should be noted that it's quite plausible that it doesn't immediately follow from the fact that you are required to do something that guarantees that *p* obtains that you are required to see to it that *p* obtains. To take a famous example, if I comply with my requirement to post the letter, I will guarantee it is true that *I post the letter or I burn the letter*. It is counterintuitive that it *follows* that I'm required to post the letter or burn the letter.[18] So it goes for the coherence requirements as well. It doesn't follow from the fact that I ought to have some attitude that will guarantee coherence that I ought to be coherent.[19]

Similar points apply to vindicating the weak significance of the wide-scope requirements. We can stipulate that I have reason to not disbelieve that I'm writing right now. And thus I have reason to do something that guarantees I'll be coherent. This is not yet to say that I have reason to be coherent. I have a reason to not disbelieve I'm writing. This is not necessarily a reason to not-disbelieve-I'm-writing-or-not-believe-I'm-writing. When we're asking whether the wide-scope requirements are weakly significant, we are asking whether there is always reasons to be like that, not merely whether there are always reasons to be in states that guarantee that you'll be like that.[20]

Once this is made clear, I think the problem becomes acute. What would make it the case that we ought to always comply with the wide-scope requirements? Remember it *can't* merely be that we are always required to do things that guarantee we'll be

---

[17] Unfortunately participants in the literature have been very bad at making this clear. In fact, in many cases it appears as if participants don't even notice that there needs to be a gap between being required to do something that guarantees you'll be coherent and being required to be coherent in order for the question to be interesting at all. The only two places I know of where this is explicitly mentioned (besides Lord (2018b) and §2.5.1 of chapter 2) is (Kolodny, 2007a, n. 15), Way (2013), and Schroeder (2015a).

[18] This, of course, is Ross's Paradox. See Ross (1944). For a nice discussion in this context, see Broome (2007b).

[19] Another way to make the point is to stipulate that not-disbelieving-I'm-writing-or-not-believing-I'm-writing is a disjunctive action. If you thought this, then the wide-scope requirements require you to perform that disjunctive action. They are strongly significant if you ought to perform that action and weakly significant if you have reason to perform that action. But that action is different than the actions that are the disjuncts of the disjunctive action. Thus, it doesn't follow you ought to perform the disjunctive action just because you always ought to perform one of the actions that are the disjuncts.

[20] Again, it's important to note that it's very plausible that there is such a gap. If there wasn't, then my reason to post the letter would thereby be a reason to post the letter or burn it.

coherent. In order to show that the wide-scope requirements are strongly significant, we'd have to show that there are reasons over and above the reasons we have for individual attitudes that make it the case that we ought to be coherent. But it's completely mysterious what reasons there could be to always make it the case that I ought to be coherent.

To bring out the mystery, let's look at the three strategies most often pursued in the literature.[21] The first strategy is that you always instrumentally ought to be coherent. According to this strategy, it's always the case that by being coherent you are doing something else that you ought to do. Although it's very plausible that you are always doing something else you ought to do when you are coherent *in certain ways*, it's not plausible that you are always doing something else you ought to do by being coherent in any way. To use our earlier example, it's stipulated that I am doing something else I ought to do when I fail to disbelieve I am writing right now. But it seems very implausible that I am doing something else I ought to be doing if I instead drop my belief I am writing right now and continue to disbelieve I am writing right now. This is a way to do what the wide-scope requirement requires. Thus, it's not generally true that I do something else I ought to do by complying with the wide-scope requirement.

The second strategy claims that you ought to comply with the wide-scope requirements because doing so is constitutive of some activity you're engaged in. Candidate activities include believing, intending, and reasoning.[22] The underlying idea is that if you are a creature whose attitudes never cohere in the ways mandated by the wide-scope requirements, then you are not a creature with beliefs/intentions or a creature who reasons. While this might be true, it simply does not follow from this that you always ought to comply with the wide-scope requirements. This is because, *inter alia*, it doesn't follow from this that you cease being a creature with beliefs, intentions or a creature who reasons *every time* you are incoherent. Perhaps a requirement to *sometimes* be coherent follows from these supposed agential facts, but this is a far cry from a full vindication of the wide-scope requirements.[23]

The final strategy holds that coherence is intrinsically very good. So good that you always ought to be coherent. This is very implausible. It is not that implausible to think that coherence is an intrinsic good. But it does seem very implausible that it is so good that its goodness always makes it the case that you ought to be coherent. This is what would need to obtain for coherence's intrinsic goodness to vindicate the strong significance of the wide-scope requirements.

None of the three strategies seem promising when it comes to vindicating the strong significance of the wide-scope requirements. Do any of them hold promise for vindicating rationality's weak deontic significance? I think the same type of arguments

---

[21] Both Broome and Kolodny discuss all of these strategies at length in the work cited in n. 8. What follows is mostly just a rehashing of what they say. See also Way (2010a,b).

[22] See Bratman (2009a,b), Buss (MS) for a defense of the first two, and see Hussain (MS) for a defense of the reasoning account.

[23] Even this weaker claim is open to a form of the agency, shmagency objection a la Enoch (2006).

can be given against the analogous strategies for vindicating the weak significance of the wide-scope requirements. The instrumental strategy holds that you have a reason to be coherent because by being coherent you will always be doing something else you have reason to do. But it seems possible that you can comply with the wide-scope requirements in ways that are such that you aren't doing something else you have reason to do by complying in those ways. The constitutivist strategy holds that some agential facts ground a reason to be coherent. Again, it's not clear which agential facts could do this. Some agential facts might ground reasons to sometimes be coherent, but this is a far cry from always grounding reasons to be coherent. And the intrinsic goodness strategy holds that the intrinsic goodness of coherence grounds a reason to be coherent.

While the intrinsic goodness strategy is the most plausible of the three when it comes to weak significance, it is still not obvious that coherence is intrinsically good. What is *intrinsically* good about it, exactly? Moreover, even if coherence did turn out to be intrinsically good, it's not plausible that the reason grounded by such goodness would be very strong, very often. It's cold comfort for those of us who think rationality is very important to find out that we have weak reasons to be rational because coherence is an intrinsic good! These three strategies seem the most *prima facie* plausible. Since none of them seem promising, it's plausible to think that the wide-scope requirements are neither weakly nor strongly deontically significant.

A recap is in order. We started off by clarifying two ways in which rationality could be deontically significant. It is *strongly significant* if it is such that we always ought to do what rationality requires. It is *weakly significant* if it is such that we always have reason to do what rationality requires. The next step was to investigate what rationality requires. Those in the literature start with the assumption that there is a tight connection between rationality and coherence. There are two main views about what the connection is. The narrow-scope view was rejected because if it were true then it's very plausible that rationality is not deontically significant in either the strong or the weak ways. This left the wide-scope view. Although the wide-scope view is traditionally motivated by the thought that it alone can account for the deontic significance of rationality, it turns out to be mysterious how the wide-scope view can account for the deontic significance of rationality. What we're left with is skepticism about the deontic significance of rationality.

8.3 A Better Way: Reasons Responsiveness

8.3.1 Initial motivations

A shared assumption of the views discussed above is that there is a tight connection between rationality and coherence. This leads us to the narrow- and wide-scope views, which leads us to skepticism about the deontic significance of rationality. That is not a good place to be. This provides motivation for exploring the hypothesis that rationality is directly analyzable in terms of reasons. Unsurprisingly, I will do this by exploring how well Reasons Responsiveness does when it comes to the deontic significance of rationality. Recall Reasons Responsiveness:

> **Reasons Responsiveness:** Rationality consists in correctly responding to the objective reasons one possesses.

I should be explicit (and reiterate a point important for the last chapter) from the outset that I think that reasons are easy to come by. This is in tension with the views of many ethicists. To take two stark examples, I think that testimonial facts can be objective reasons and I think that existential facts about what there is reason to do and what one ought to do can also be objective reasons. So, if a reliable advisor tells you that you really shouldn't go into the next room but doesn't tell you why, he still gives you a reason not to go into the next room. In the simplest case, this will just be the fact that you shouldn't go into the next room. When the reliable advisor happens to say something false, it will be the fact that a reliable advisor said you shouldn't go into the next room. Many deny that these types of facts can be objective normative reasons.[24]

Why do I think these facts can be objective reasons? To echo the book's introduction, it is because they bear the earmarks of objective reasons. First, they intuitively count in favor of some actions and attitudes. You should treat what the advisor says as a reason in deliberation. Indeed, you should treat it as a very strong reason. Because of this, it's plausible they can justify actions and attitudes. Moreover, they can also be the reasons *for which* we act or hold attitudes.[25]

It will be important for the overall plausibility of my view that objective reasons come cheap. For one thing, this allows me to account for the rationality of those who have false but rational beliefs. The most extreme version of this is the radically deceived characters that were the subject of chapter 7. I won't rehash those details here. It's worth keeping in mind in this chapter, however, that I think reasons come cheap.

It's also important to recall a main lesson from chapter 2. Namely, that Reasons Responsiveness has the resources to explain why irrational incoherence is irrational. Other things equal, when you are incoherent, you aren't correctly responding to all the reasons you possess. To use our earlier example, it's plausible that there will never be a single time where I possess sufficient reasons to believe that I am writing and

---

[24] See, for example, Broome (2008b), McNaughton & Rawling (2011), McKeever & Ridge (2012).

[25] Furthermore, I think that stock objections to the idea that they can be objective reasons are misguided. Some objections involve misguided worries about doublecounting (see Schroeder (2009a) and Väyrynen (2006) for reasons why these objections are misguided). Others appeal to intuitions about right-making, holding that these facts can't intuitively be right-makers (see, e.g., Broome (2008b), McNaughton & Rawling (2011), McKeever & Ridge (2012)). This thought cuts both ways, however, for it does seem like these facts can justify actions and attitudes. Given this, it's unclear why we shouldn't think that these reasons are counterexamples to whatever theory of right-making objectors have in mind. Because of this, it is very unlikely these intuitions will adjudicate the dispute.

possess sufficient reasons to disbelieve that I am writing. I will always possess decisive reasons to not have at least one of those beliefs. In our example, it's disbelieving that I am writing. I possess decisive reasons to not have that belief. Thus, when I hold it, I am irrational.

Before moving back to deontic significance, it is important to consider a dialectical complication.[26] The complication arises out of the way in which Kolodny (2005) initially sets up the debate. One might think that Kolodny is not exploring the deontic significance of rationality *per se*, but rather just the deontic significance of coherence requirements like Means-End N and Means-End W. He lends this impression at the very beginning of Kolodny (2005) when he discusses two different ways of talking about rationality. According to one way of talking, what rationality requires is determined by (objective) normative reasons—he calls this objective rationality. According to a different way of talking, what rationality requires is determined by considerations about coherence—he calls this subjective rationality. He then makes it clear that he is only interested in discussing subjective rationality. It is plausible to conclude that Kolodny and I aren't even talking about the same concept. He is talking about a stipulative concept that is constitutively tied to coherence. Further, if this is right, then the only way to refute Kolodny's arguments is by showing that the coherence requirements are deontically significant. This is obviously not the tack I will take. As we saw in §8.2.2, I agree with Kolodny that the coherence requirements are not deontically significant. The tack I take is to argue that the requirements that are determined by the reasons one possesses are deontically significant. Thus, if this interpretation of Kolodny is right, my arguments appear to not be responsive to his.

The first point to make is that Kolodny's discussion is simplistic in an important way.[27] As he is thinking of it, the contrast is between a fully objective notion of rationality—one that is tied to all of the facts—and a fully subjective notion of rationality—one that is tied solely to one's non-factive internal states. This contrast neglects my kind of view, which places importance both on the mind-independent reasons and on the agent's perspective. Thus, I don't think we can conclude that Kolodny is not interested in my notion of rationality simply because he denies interest in his objective notion of rationality.

Still, this first point doesn't show that Kolodny and I are talking about the same concept. My second point is that I think Kolodny and I are using the same concept because we both agree on some basic roles that the relevant concept of rationality is supposed to play. While this might not be a deductive proof that we are using the same concept, it is good evidence. What roles do we agree the concept plays?

First (and perhaps foremost), we agree that the relevant concept of rationality provides a distinctive kind of explanation of why there is something amiss with

---

[26] I thank an anonymous referee for pressing me to say something about this.

[27] I am not suggesting that this simplicity is objectionable given Kolodny's aims in that paper. But as I've been stressing throughout the book, I think it is important to be more sophisticated on this score.

(at least some forms of) incoherence.[28] Kolodny maintains that certain narrow-scope coherence requirements are the materials that the correct theory of this concept use to explain what is amiss with incoherence.[29] I deny this. Nevertheless, as we saw in chapter 2, I think that we can explain why there is something amiss by appealing to my theory's requirements.

A second role for the concept is its connection to a certain sort of criticism.[30] When one is irrational, they are open to a particular kind of criticism. This is because there is some part of their perspective that severely clashes with some reaction of theirs. This doesn't necessarily mean that *every* time someone is irrational they should be condemned; it just means that a certain kind of criticism is apt in paradigm cases of irrationality. This is a role that I think my concept of rationality plays. I think the concept Kolodny is picking out is also supposed to play this role.[31]

As I said above, while this is good evidence we are using the same concept, it doesn't provide a deductive proof. My third point is that even if Kolodny is stipulating that the concept of rationality he is interested in is necessarily tied to the coherence requirements, my argument is important for the debate he is engaging in. This is because if he is so stipulating, the debate should be seen as a debate about what David Plunkett, Alexis Burgess, and Timothy Sundell call *conceptual ethics*.[32] In other words, the debate is not about the nature of some concept, but rather about which concepts we should use. If it is a debate about this and my arguments below are sound, then I think my concept has a huge advantage over Kolodny's. This is because my concept is intimately connected to the concept of deliberative obligation. Given this connection, my concept can vindicate many more of the platitudes about rationality than Kolodny's concept can—viz., all of the platitudes associated with deontic significance. Thus, even if Kolodny and I are using different concepts, there is a debate to be had between my view and Kolodny's. Further, there are strong reasons to think my view is winning that debate. With that said, let's return to deontic significance.

---

[28] See, e.g., Kolodny (2007a, §4.2).

[29] The content of the requirements Kolodny endorses changes slightly between papers, but the basic idea is that you are rationally required to ϕ if you believe you have decisive reason to ϕ.

[30] A further consideration in favor of the hypothesis that Kolodny and I are talking about the same concept is that we are both hypothesizing about Broome's concept, which is centrally tied to the requirements of rationality being *strict* (see especially Broome (1999)). The strictness of the requirements explain why one is open to criticism and explain why there is something distinctively amiss when one is incoherence. Further, Broome clearly thinks that *it's possible* that his concept is analyzed in terms of reasons. After all, he has written several papers about whether rationality can be understood in terms of reasons (see Broome (2007a, 2013) and chapter 2 for an antidote). Although he argues against the view, it's not on the grounds that it invokes a separate concept.

[31] It is uncontroversial that Kolodny's notion of objective rationality does *not* play this role. So this is a further way of distinguishing my notion from that one.

[32] See Burgess & Plunkett (2013a,b), Plunkett & Sundell (2013), Plunkett (2015).

8.3.2 Reasons responsiveness and deontic significance

Note that it follows immediately from Reasons Responsiveness that rationality is weakly deontically significant. This is because in order to be rationally required to ϕ, I must possess objective reasons to ϕ. Thus, there will always be objective reasons to ϕ when rationality requires me to ϕ. Securing the weak deontic significance of rationality is thus very easy for Reasons Responsiveness.

Nevertheless, it's far from clear that this view can vindicate the strong deontic significance of rationality. Even though the view entails that there will always be reasons to do what rationality requires, it's far from clear that these reasons will always be weighty enough to ground an obligation. Moreover, according to a very popular view about what one ought to do, it's obvious that sometimes the reasons one possesses won't be sufficiently strong to make it the case that one ought to do what's rationally required.

According to this view, which we'll call *objectivism*, what you ought to do is determined by all the objective reasons. You ought to ϕ, according to the objectivist, only if the balance of all the reasons decisively supports ϕ-ing. If objectivism is true, then Reasons Responsiveness cannot vindicate the strong deontic significance of rationality. This is clear by reflecting on cases. Here's the case from §8.1:

Sick Mother

Jack's mother is in the hospital. She needs an operation in order to survive past this week. Her insurance won't pay. Jack, being a fledgling Art Historian/dealer, doesn't have the money. It looks like his mother is going to die. She will, however, be extremely comforted by Jack's presence in her final days. She lives in California; Jack lives in New York. Jack needs to decide whether to go see her. As it happens, a pawn shop owner in Queens has just unknowingly (and legitimately) bought a rare Picasso. He's selling it at a fraction of the price it's worth. If Jack were to buy it, he would be able to use it as collateral for a loan that would pay for his mother's surgery. The rub, of course, is that he has no idea that this pawn shop even exists, much less that such a deal is to be had there.

In Sick Mother, Jack possesses good reasons to go to California—his mother will be greatly comforted by his presence. However, there is also a very good reason for him to go to Queens—viz., the fact there is a cheap Picasso to be had. The objectivist says that, in this case, Jack ought to go to Queens even though it seems like it would be irrational for him to go to Queens. It would be irrational because the reasons he possesses decisively support going to California.

This is a serious challenge. In order to see if it can be met, we must look at what the best theory is of what we ought to do. If objectivism is the best theory, then Reasons Responsiveness cannot vindicate the strong deontic significance of rationality. This would be a big blow to those of us who think rationality is deontically significant. In fact, I don't much care about a mere vindication of the weak significance of rationality. I will only be fully satisfied if rationality turns out to be strongly deontically significant.

The rest of this chapter will aim to meet the challenge. I don't think that objectivism is the best theory of what we ought to do. Instead, I think that the best theory holds that what we ought to do is what is decisively supported by the reasons we possess. I think this view can be well motivated independently of any debate about rationality. This, I think, is as it should be if rationality is really strongly significant.

8.4 Ignorance and Obligation

In this section, I will argue for Possessed Reasons:

Possessed Reasons: What you ought to do is determined by the reasons you possess.[33]

I will first discuss purported counterexamples to objectivism. I will argue that these cases are in fact counterexamples. Moreover, I will argue that Possessed Reasons provides a very plausible explanation of what's going on in these cases. The second argument runs through the claim that if the members of some set of reasons S make it the case that you ought to ϕ, then you can ϕ because of the members of S. I'll argue that you can only ϕ because of the members of S if you possess them. If sound, this argument will establish that a necessary condition for some set of reasons S making it the case that you ought to ϕ is that you possess the members of S. I will end this section by arguing that once you accept this necessity claim, the relevant sufficiency claim will follow from very plausible assumptions.

---

[33] One of the major objections to anti-objectivist views appeals to bystanders with more information. It seems as if those with more information can have true thoughts about what one ought to do that isn't what one ought to do relative to what one knows. My goals in this chapter do not include answering this objection (I do this in Lord (2015)). My main goal is to provide a new argument for Possessed Reasons. However, I think that this problem can be solved. My solution has two parts. The first part is to show that Possessed Reasons is compatible with the thought that deliberation aims at what's best (or what's supported by all the reasons). Possessed Reasons is compatible with this claim because correct pursuit of one's aims might be constrained in certain ways. Here are two examples. Our obligations might be constrained by our physiological abilities even though we aim to do what's best. Our epistemic obligations might be constrained by, for example, the evidence, even though the aim of epistemic deliberation is to believe the truth. In other words, it doesn't follow from the claim that the aim of epistemic deliberation is to believe the truth that we always ought to believe the truth. The second part of the solution appeals to the semantics of 'ought' in English. 'Ought' is a flexible word insofar as we can relativize our 'ought' claims to different bodies of information. This means that advisors with more information can have 'ought' thoughts about our obligations that are relativized to their information. This is what they're doing, I claim. It's right that this means they aren't having thoughts about our obligations *per se*. This is unsurprising, though, given that the aim is to do what's best. So even though they aren't thinking about our deliberative obligations, they are having thoughts that are relevant to the deliberative project. See Lord (2015) for a full defense of this response.

8.4.1 Ignorance and envelopes

It is obviously true that we are almost always ignorant of the full effects our actions will have. Take this example discussed by Thomson (1990) and Scanlon (2001, 2008).

Day's End

Jack always comes home at 9:00 P.M., and the first thing he does is flip the light switch in his hallway. He did so this evening. His flipping the switch caused a circuit to close. By virtue of an extraordinary series of coincidences, unpredictable in advance by anybody, the circuits being closed caused a release of electricity (a small lightning flash) in his neighbor's house next door. Unluckily, his neighbor was in its path and was therefore badly burned.[34]

Many have thought, and I am one of these people, that cases like Day's End strongly support the rejection of objectivism. After all, the objectivist thinks that Jack ought not flip the switch in his hallway. This is because the fact that it will lead to his neighbor being badly burned is an objective reason not to. Relative to all the reasons there are, this reason is decisive. But since flipping the switch will lead to his neighbor being burned only because of 'an extraordinary series of coincidences' that he has no way of knowing about, it seems quite plausible that, to use Scanlon's words,

If it is true that [Jack] ought not to have flipped the switch, this is true only in a sense of ought not that seems to me to lack the moral content that the idea of permissibility has. Both [Jack] and [his neighbor] may wish, after the fact, that [Jack] had not flipped the switch, but in doing so [Jack] did not act impermissibly. (Scanlon, 2008, p. 48)

Unfortunately for foes of objectivism, there is a standard objectivist reply to this line of reasoning.[35] The core insight is that we must cleave apart the deontic facts—facts about what ought to be done—from the hypological facts—facts about blame and praise. Once we do this, the response goes, we can see that arguments against objectivism like Scanlon's try to draw conclusions about the deontic from conclusions about the hypological. They get their bite only if we assume that the fact that Jack is not blameworthy for flipping the switch entails that he acted permissibly. Once we give up the idea that permissibility lines up with blamelessness, the argument falls apart. Jack might be blameless, but he still does what he ought not do. Indeed, it seems like there is a good explanation of why Jack is blameless despite doing wrong in this case. Jack is blameless because it is rational for him to believe that flipping the switch is permitted by all the reasons. But his belief is *false*. This is what explains why he still is doing something wrong.

---

[34] This is almost exactly how Scanlon (2008) presents this case, following Thomson (1990, p. 229). I've changed the pronouns.
[35] This move goes back to Moore (1912). Thomson herself replies this way in Thomson (1986, 1990, 2008). See also Graham (2010), Sylvan (2014).

I agree that we must separate the deontic facts from the hypological facts.[36] Moreover, I agree that cases like Day's End lose their initial dialectical bite once this standard move is made.[37] Luckily, though, there are other well known cases where the standard move is less than effective. Three Envelopes is a case with this structure:[38]

Three Envelopes

Suppose Margaret is given the choice to pick one of three envelopes placed in front of her. Margaret is informed that the third envelope contains $900. She is also informed that either the first envelope or the second envelope contains $1000, and that whichever envelope doesn't have the $1000 in it is empty. So, given her evidence, there is a .5 chance that the first envelope contains $1000 and a .5 chance that the second envelope contains $1000.

Intuitively, Margaret ought to choose the third envelope—i.e., the one she knows has $900 in it. Moreover, there is an important difference between Three Envelopes and Day's End. Namely, in Three Envelopes Margaret *knows* that choosing envelope three is not the best option. That is, she knows that it is not the option decisively supported by all the reasons. The option best supported by all the reasons is choosing the envelope with $1000 in it. Despite the fact that Margaret knows that choosing envelope three is the second best option, it still seems like she ought to choose it.

This difference between Day's End and Three Envelopes makes the standard objectivist move much less plausible when it comes to Three Envelopes. For in Day's End, it's rational for you to think that flipping the switch is permitted by the balance of all the reasons. It's not rational to think that choosing envelope three is permitted by the balance of all the reasons in Three Envelopes. In fact, Margaret *knows* that it's not. Still, it seems like Margaret ought to choose envelope three. This is important because the standard move seems plausible in Day's End only because you have a rational yet false belief about what the balance of all the reasons supports. The rationality of this belief helps explain why you are blameless, and the falsity explains why what you did was actually impermissible. Three Envelopes doesn't have this structure. Margaret seems blameless all right, but she lacks the false belief. The fact that it still seems like

---

[36] Many other anti-objectivists do this as well. See especially Scanlon (2008) and Zimmerman (2008).

[37] This is not to say that I think the objectivist is right about these cases, nor do I think that these cases lack bite. In the next subsection, I will provide an argument that, I think, provides an elegant explanation for why cases like Day's End actually do have bite against the objectivist. My claim here is just that making the standard move robs these cases of unprincipled intuitive bite. The trick for the anti-objectivist is to give a principled explanation for why objectivism is wrong in these cases. I will try to do that in the next subsection.

[38] This particular case initially comes from Ross (2006). It is discussed further in Schroeder (2009b), Ross (2012), Ross & Schroeder (2013). Ross's case was inspired by a case given by John Broome (Broome's discussion ends up Broome (2013), which was inspired by a case given by Parfit (which eventually ended up in Parfit (2011)), which was inspired by a case in Regan (1980). This case and/or cases with the same structure are discussed, among other places, in Jackson (1991), Wedgwood (2007), Zimmerman (2008), Kearns & Star (2009), Schroeder (2009b), Graham (2010), Kolodny & MacFarlane (2010), Kiesewetter (2011).

she should choose the second best option despite the lack of the false belief strongly suggests that she is blameless because choosing the third envelope is what she ought to do.

Before moving on, let me mention a common reaction to Three Envelopes in order to set it aside. Many ethicists' first reaction is to draw a distinction between what you objectively ought to do and what you subjectively ought to do.[39] They then use this distinction to explain intuitions. First, you have the intuition that what you ought to do is choose the envelope with $1000 in it because that's what you objectively ought to do. Second, you have the intuition that what you ought to do is choose envelope three because that's what you subjectively ought to do. This is supposed to resolve the puzzle.

The problem is that it doesn't resolve the puzzle.[40] At best it changes the subject. That is, at best we find out that there is some sense in which Margaret ought to choose envelope three. It turns out that there are independent reasons to believe in such a sense, and the explanation it gives for why, in some sense, Margaret ought to choose envelope three is a principled one. But this is not the question we were asking. We were asking whether Margaret ought to choose envelope three. We were asking whether Yes would be the correct answer to a question Margaret might ask herself, viz., Ought I choose envelope three?

Here's an objectivist nicely putting the point:

Even if there are two types of moral obligation, the question remains: in which are we interested when doing moral theory about action? That is, in which sense of moral obligation are we interested when we debate whether consequentialism or some other theory provides the correct account of our moral obligations with respect to action? Even if there are multiple senses of moral obligation we still need an answer to this question. (Graham, 2010, p. 95)[41]

And here's an anti-objectivist nicely putting the point.

Others again try to solve the puzzle by distinguishing different senses of ought. . . . I am willing to concede that it might be useful to speak of what an agent ought to do relative to certain considerations, and that different qualified notions of ought might be important in their own right. Nevertheless, I believe that there is a substantial question at issue between objectivists and perspectivists [anti-objectivists] when it comes to what might be called the overall ought of practical deliberation. This is the concept involved in the deliberative question, What ought I to do? (or What should I do?) and deliberative conclusions of the form, I ought to ϕ. Practical

---

[39] Sepielli (2018) calls these theorists Dividers because they want to divide the terrain with the objective and subjective notions and call it a day. Dividers include Ross (2006), Smith (2008), Schroeder (2009b), Sepielli (2018).

[40] Many—both objectivists and anti-objectivists—have pointed this out. See, for example, Jackson (1991), Bjornsson & Finlay (2010), Graham (2010), Kolodny & MacFarlane (2010), Kiesewetter (2011).

[41] It's worth pointing out that Graham is only concerned with moral requirements and explicitly tries to distance himself from the heart of the debate we're interested in. Nevertheless, I think the debate he's interested in is very close to the one I'm interested in, certainly close enough for the passage quoted to be relevant.

conclusions of this sort are supposed to guide rational decision-making and action directly. In other words, the ought at issue is the one that is appealed to in the common idea that it is irrational, or akratic, not to intend what one believes one ought to do. Now, in order to make a rational decision guided by a belief that one ought to do something, one needs a univocal concept of ought that figures in such beliefs. It is perfectly consistent to believe, I ought to ϕ, relative to X, and, I ought not to ϕ, relative to Y, but one cannot rationally intend both to ϕ and not to ϕ. There must be one sense of ought, the belief in which is the relevant one for decision-making. We need to be able to judge, I ought to ϕ, full stop. (Kiesewetter, 2011, p. 2)

The important point is that mere appeal to the distinction between subjective and objective oughts doesn't answer our question because it doesn't specify which obligation provides an answer to the central deliberative question. If Margaret is conceptually sophisticated enough, she is in a position to know that she subjectively ought to choose envelope three and that she objectively ought to choose envelope one or envelope two. But even if she did know those facts, she could meaningfully wonder which requirement she ought to satisfy. She thus doesn't seem to learn what she ought to do, full stop, by learning what she subjectively and objectively ought to do. There is another question that hasn't been answered yet—viz., What ought Margaret do?

Sepielli (2018) questions this type of open question argument. According to Sepielli, when we reason about what to do under certainty—i.e., when we reason about what to do with outright beliefs—we reason about what we objectively ought to do. When we reason about what we ought to do under uncertainty—i.e., when we reason about what to do with credal states—we reason about what we subjectively ought to do. According to his view, then, once Margaret decides she doesn't know exactly what she objectively ought to do, she starts to reason about what she subjectively ought to do. Once she settles on choosing envelope A, she settles deliberation.

Sepielli replies to the open question argument by insisting that his phenomenology does not demand that there be a third concept. His phenomenology suggests to him that in these sorts of cases he does employ two different concepts. He deploys the objective concept when he asks whether he knows what he ought to do. When he realizes he doesn't, he then figures out what the thing to do is given that he doesn't know what he objectively ought to do. When he does this he deploys the subjective concepts. Once he settles what he subjectively ought to do, he's done. He writes[42]

There is simply no need for any further arbitration. If called upon to justify why I stop there and act, I would say something like this: Subjective normative questions are about how best to take into account the various ways the world might be vis a vis what is objectively significant in this case, [maximizing profit]. In saying that I subjectively ought to [choose envelope 3], I've already taken into account that it's certainly not the best for [maximizing profit], but have judged that, from the point of view of [maximizing profit], that fact is not dispositive. There is no serious question whether to go with subjective or objective normativity, even in [cases like Margaret's],

[42] This is on p. 6 of Sepielli's draft version of the final draft.

for to make a judgment about what I subjectively ought to do is to have already implicitly stripped any contrary objective normative judgments of anything more than pro tanto force from my perspective.

Sepielli, then, has a split phenomenology of obligation. He explicitly sees obligation as splitting into two directions. Further, in some cases his recognition that one course of action definitely does not get him what he most wants is not 'dispositive.' The first thing to say is that I invite the reader to consider her own phenomenology. My phenomenology is not split. It seems to me that I am always after the answer to one question—what ought I to do?—and that the concept I deploy when I ask that question is *not* the objective or subjective *concept*. I can't dictate your phenomenology (alas).

The second thing to say is that there is a need for the deliberative ought independent of cases like Margaret's. This is because of cases like Day's End and Sick Mother. The characters in those cases are not reasoning about what to do under uncertainty, in Sepielli's sense. They are reasoning with full beliefs. They are just ignorant of some of the reasons. Given this, they don't do what they objectively ought to do. But still, one might insist that they *know* what they ought to do when they believe they ought to flip the switch and that they ought to go to California. It's hard to see how Sepielli's view can get this result, given that it seems as if he thinks they are using the objective concept. Of course, this argument relies on perspectivalism about the deliberative ought being true. Objectivists will not be moved by the claim that they know what they ought to do. Still, intuition is hardly on the objectivist's side here. So this argument is not completely question begging. Given this, I am not moved by Sepielli's rejection of the open question argument.[43]

I hasten to add that there are at least two ways to use the objective/subjective distinction to answer our question. The first way is to insist that what you ought to do is just what you subjectively ought to do. The second way is to insist that what you ought to do is what you objectively ought to do. I obviously don't think that what you ought to do is what you objectively ought to do. But for all I've said, it might be that what you ought to do is what you subjectively ought to do. In fact, it might be that the theory I give about what you ought to do is the correct theory about what you subjectively ought to do.[44] Because of this, that view is somewhat orthogonal to the current dialectic, whereas the view that what you ought to do is what you objectively ought to do is central to the current dialectic.

Many think that cases like Three Envelopes are counterexamples to objectivism. I agree. Surprisingly, though, hardly anyone has fleshed out anti-objectivist views in

---

[43] This is not to say the issue is settled. A whole paper could (and should!) be dedicated to this. I don't have the space to fully adjudicate the issue here.

[44] It's not always clear what role the subjective ought is supposed to play, but it's commonly thought that it's supposed to have a very tight connection with blame—sometimes it's suggested that you subjectively ought to ϕ only if you'd be blameworthy for not ϕ-ing. If this is true of the subjective ought, then I doubt the view I'm arguing for is the best view of the subjective ought. Indeed, I doubt there is any *deontic* concept that has that tight of a connection to blame.

any detail.[45] Usually theorists are happy to appeal to 'the evidence' and leave it at that. Given the huge variety of views about evidence found in epistemology, the range of evidential views is huge. Blanket appeals to claims with such a large variety of potential interpretations is generally unfortunate. Moreover, I think that it makes it quite a bit easier for objectivists to respond to the cases.

The question, then, is this: Why is it that Margaret ought to choose envelope three? My answer is that it is because that is what the reasons she possesses decisively support. Which reasons does she possess and which ones does she lack? She obviously possesses the reason constituted by the fact that there is $900 in envelope three, and she obviously lacks the reason provided by the fact that there is $1000 in whichever envelope the $1000 is in. This isn't enough, though, because it's very intuitive that she possesses some reason to choose envelope one and some reason to choose envelope two. I think the reason to take envelope one is the fact that there is a .5 chance that there is $1000 in envelope one and the reason there is to choose envelope two is a .5 chance that there is $1000 in envelope two.[46] Those facts are objective reasons to choose envelopes one and two respectively. Moreover, they are reasons Margaret possesses. Nevertheless, neither is weighty enough to make choosing those envelopes sufficiently supported by the reasons that are possessed. Thus, the reason to choose envelope three is the only reason possessed that is sufficient, and it is thus decisive.[47]

Day's End is slightly different. In that case, it's just that you fail to possess a strong reason to not flip the switch—viz., the fact that doing so will lead to your neighbor being badly burned. You possess all of the normal reasons one has to flip on the switch—it allows you to see what you're doing, it makes it easier to navigate etc. Possessed Reasons holds that the fact that by flipping the switch you will badly burn your neighbor doesn't affect what you ought to do because you don't possess that reason. You don't possess that reason because you don't stand in the appropriate epistemic relation with it. Since the reasons you do possess sufficiently support

---

[45] An admirable exception is Zimmerman (2008, 2014). My main problem with Zimmerman is methodological. I think that we should try to fit the view within a reasons framework. I think this is so for two reasons. First, it's plausible that reasons are normatively fundamental. Second, my view is pitched at a higher level of abstraction than Zimmerman's. This allows me to be neutral about the consequentialism/deontology debate. This is because we can see that debate as one about the structure of reasons and their weights. So both sides can accept my claims because they are at a higher level of abstraction. Zimmerman's view, on the other hand, is committed to denying non-consequentialist views.

[46] A note about what the chances are here. I am thinking that they are conditional probabilities. They are the probabilities that the $1000 is in the respective envelopes given what Margaret knows (this is what Williamson (2000) calls evidential probability). I want to be neutral about whether objective chances provide objective reasons (I suspect they do if they exist) or whether subjective chances provide objective reasons (I suspect they don't, at least not always).

[47] Schroeder (2009b) gives a similar explanation. My explanation differs from Schroeder's in key ways. For example, Schroeder thinks that, at least in the relevant sense, Margaret ought to pick envelope three *just so long* as she believes as she does in the original case. Thus, even if she was in a position to know that her beliefs were false it would be the case that she ought to choose envelope three. My explanation doesn't have this result because the relevant facts have to actually be facts (i.e., objective reasons) in order to make it the case that she ought to choose envelope three.

flipping the switch, it's permissible to flip the switch. This is a very natural explanation of both why the fact that flipping will lead to your neighbor being burned doesn't affect what you ought to do and why it's permissible to flip the switch.

There are a few things to notice about the explanations given by Possessed Reasons. First, only objective reasons determine what you are permitted and forbidden from doing. This is a virtue because it allows easy assimilation into the Reasons Program (see chapter 1 for discussion). Since Possessed Reasons analyzes the property of being what you ought to do in terms of objective reasons, it meshes well with the Reasons Program.[48]

The second thing to notice is just how natural and illuminating these explanations are. Appealing to possessed reasons gives one a very plausible explanation for why (at least non-culpably) unknown reasons don't affect what you ought to do. It's intuitively plausible that the possessed/unpossessed reasons distinction is poised to do the kind of work needed in these cases.

8.4.2 Ignorance and acting for the right reasons

I take the last subsection to have demonstrated that Possessed Reasons does a nice job explaining some of the facts on the ground. In this subsection, I'll offer a more abstract argument for Possessed Reasons. I will start by arguing that a necessary condition for some set of reasons S to make it the case that you ought to ϕ is that you possess the members of S. This is not enough to establish Possessed Reasons. However, if it is true, then objectivism is false. Moreover, once you accept this necessity condition, it follows from plausible assumptions that a sufficient condition for being obligated to ϕ is that one possesses a set of decisive reasons to ϕ. Once we have both the necessity and sufficiency claims, we'll be much closer to establishing Possessed Reasons.

We'll start with an argument for the following claim: If the members of some set of reasons S make it the case that you ought to ϕ, then you possess the members of S. The argument's plausibility will be enhanced by some build up.

Upon reflection, it seems very plausible that we aren't always required to bring about the best state of affairs. For example, consider Dunk for Money:

Dunk for Money

Mark Cuban, being the eccentric billionaire that he is, decides to have a raffle. The person whose name is chosen gets a shot at a $10 million prize. In order to win the prize, one has to do a 360° dunk on an NBA regulation sized hoop. Just for fun, Sam enters the raffle. She is the lucky winner. Unfortunately for Sam, she is only 4'11" tall. Because of this, she lacks the ability to dunk on an NBA regulation sized hoop.

---

[48] It's worth mentioning that it also does this without having to appeal to any type of modal analysis. Schroeder (2009b), for example, tries to explain cases like Three Envelopes in a framework compatible with the thought that reasons are basic by appealing to the notion of a subjective reason. Subjective reasons are analyzed in terms of objective reasons, but modally—some proposition p is a subjective reason to ϕ just in case p is an objective reason to ϕ if true. I think this will inevitably lead to intractable conditional fallacy worries. It's a big virtue that my view doesn't have those problems.

Question: Ought Sam dunk the ball? Pretty clearly not, I think. Why is that? It would, after all, be much better for Sam to dunk rather than not. Despite this, the answer is obvious. Sam *can't* dunk. She lacks the ability to *perform the relevant action*. Of course she can try to dunk, and presumably she ought to try to dunk. But that's not to say that she ought to dunk. It's not true that she ought to dunk because she lacks the ability to dunk.

Of course, I don't think Dunk for Money is a counterexample to objectivism. Objectivists can get out of the problem by invoking some version of 'ought' implies 'can.' I think a deeper explanation is that the fact that Mark Cuban will give Sam $10 million if she dunks is not a reason *for Sam* to dunk. Thus, that fact won't be relevant to the objectivist theory that holds that what Sam ought to do is a function of all of the reasons (for Sam).

Although Dunk for Money is not a counterexample to objectivism, it's helpful build up to my argument. Consider Day's End again. In Day's End you face the choice between flipping on the hall light or not. There are good reasons for you to switch it on and a good reason for you to not switch it on. Moreover, in Day's End, unlike in Dunk for Money, it seems like you can perform the relevant action—i.e., you have the ability to refrain from flipping on the switch.[49] Not flipping the switch can be an action of yours. So there both is a reason for you not to flip it on and you can perform that action. Thus, the objectivist thinks that you ought to refrain from flipping the switch. The reason why is that it will badly burn your neighbor. That fact is a decisive reason not to flip, according to the objectivist.

There's a catch, though. Although you can refrain from flipping the switch, it *doesn't* seem like you can do so *because* flipping the switch will badly burn your neighbor. It doesn't seem like you can act for the normative reason provided by the fact that flipping the switch will badly burn your neighbor. This is predicted by my account of acting for a normative reason. You are *not* in a position to manifest knowledge about how to use the fact that flipping the switch will burn your neighbor as a reason not to flip the switch. This is because, at the very least, you are not in a position to know that flipping the switch will badly burn your neighbor.

An advocate of a univocal view of acting for normative reasons might reply by insisting that you can in the relevant sense refrain for the right reason because you can believe that flipping the switch would badly burn your neighbor and be motivated to refrain for that consideration. As we saw repeatedly in chapters 5 and 6, though, these sorts of cases are the univocal view's downfall. In this case, if you were so motivated, you'd be acting like an idiot if you didn't turn on the light. It would be true that your motivating reason would be the consideration that turning on the light would badly burn your neighbor, but it wouldn't be true that you did it because flipping the switch

---

[49] As Schwan (FC) rightfully points out, there are many different kinds of ability. He argues that this causes trouble for the sort of argument I am going to give for Possessed Reasons. I will respond to those criticisms below.

would badly burn your neighbor. This is because you have no idea that flipping the switch will burn your neighbor.

To make this more plausible, compare Delusional Andy to Surprised Andy:

Delusional Andy

Andy knows that his wife has always been an extremely loyal person. He also knows that he has no reason to think that she is cheating on him. Despite this knowledge, he does believe that she is cheating on him. He thus moves out and files for divorce. In fact, his wife is cheating on him.

Surprised Andy

Andy knows that his wife has always been an extremely loyal person. However, much to his surprise, he learns that she is cheating on him—her best friend tells him, he finds some love letters, and he catches his wife with her lover. He thus moves out and files for divorce.

In both Delusional Andy and Surprised Andy, Andy reasons from a belief that his wife is cheating on him to an intention (and subsequent action) to move out and file for divorce. Despite this similarity, it's plausible that only Surprised Andy moves out and files for divorce because his wife is cheating on him. Delusional Andy is, well, delusional. He has no reason to think that she is cheating on him. He gets completely lucky. Because of this, it doesn't seem like he files for divorce because she's cheating on him.[50]

Notice that you are a lot like Delusional Andy when you more or less arbitrarily believe that flipping the switch will badly burn your neighbor. It turns out that you are right, but you are just lucky. It's not like that reason is *guiding you*. You have about as little contact with that reason as one can have while believing the proposition that constitutes it. (We'll return to Delusional Andy and Surprised Andy momentarily.)

I think the fact that you can't refrain from flipping the switch because it will badly burn your neighbor *explains* why it's not the case that you ought to refrain. In other words, I think that Acting On is plausible:

Acting On: If the reasons in some set S make it the case you ought to ϕ, then you can ϕ because of the members of S.

What's the difference between the cases where you can ϕ because of some reason r and cases where you can't? Chapters 4 and 5 provide an answer. The answer is that the cases where you can ϕ because of r are always cases where you *possess* r. This is because to possess a reason is to be in a position to react for it. Thus, when you do act

---

[50] For similar arguments for a similar conclusion, see Gibbons (2001), Hyman (2006), Hornsby (2008), Marcus (2012). The most visible detractor is Jonathan Dancy (see, e.g., Dancy (2000)). I think that Dancy is really talking about what it is to act for motivating reasons, not what it is to act for normative reasons. We are interested in the latter here. He's right about acting for motivating reasons, but not about acting for normative reasons. See chapters 5 and 6 for more on this.

for a normative reason, you possess that reason. On the other hand, you don't possess *r* when you are (non-culpably) ignorant of *r*, and thus you can't φ because of *r* when you are (non-culpably) ignorant of *r*.[51] When you combine this with Acting On, you get an argument for the claim that possessing the members of a set of reasons *S* is a necessary condition for those reasons making it the case that you ought to φ.

(1) If the reasons in some set *S* make it the case you ought to φ, then you can φ because of the members of *S* (Acting On).
(2) If you can φ because of the members of *S*, then you possess the members of *S*.
(C) If the reasons in some set *S* make it the case you ought to φ, then you possess the members of *S*.

If this argument is sound, then objectivism is false—Day's End is a counterexample. So objectivists need to deny one of the premises. In fact, objectivists need to resist what I said about (1). Objectivists have two choices when faced with (1). They can either deny it or they can argue, *pace* what I argued above, that you can act for the reasons that require you to φ when you're ignorant of those reasons. I think both options are implausible. In order to see this, it's important to consider (again) the connection between φ-ing for normative reasons and actions being creditworthy.

Suppose I am required to buy Anne a hat for her birthday because it would make her happy. And suppose I do buy her a hat. As we saw in chapter 5, meeting these conditions is not sufficient for my action to be creditworthy. In order for my action to be creditworthy, there must be the right kind of connection between the reasons that obligate the action and my performance of the action. My act would be creditworthy if I were to buy her a hat because it would make her happy. On the other hand, if I bought her the hat only because it would make *me* happy (it would cover up her hair, which I find distasteful), it doesn't seem like my act would be creditworthy. It would only be an accident that the following conjunction is true: I bought the hat and the hat makes Anne happy. If it's merely an accident that the act I actually perform is the particular act I ought to perform, then it doesn't seem like I deserve credit for it.

These facts are explained by the fact that when it's an accident that the act one performs is the act one ought to perform, one doesn't act for the right reasons—i.e., the reasons that make it the case you ought to do that thing. It's thus plausible that there is some tight connection between acting for the right reasons and being creditworthy. One way to flesh this out is Link:

[51] Not all ignorance is created equal. If we hold that *A* is ignorant about *p* just in case *A* fails to believe *p*, then I think it's implausible that you always fail to possess the reasons you are ignorant of. This is why, in chapter 3, I argue for a *non-holding* account of the epistemic condition on possession. Recall that non-holding accounts claim that you can possess reasons you don't believe. However, I think you are culpable for the reasons you possess that you are ignorant of. Hence the qualification in the text.

Link: When A is required to ϕ by the members of some set of reasons S, A is creditworthy for ϕ-ing just in case A ϕs because of the members of some subset of S that are sufficiently strong to require A to ϕ.[52,53]

When you combine Link with the claim that I don't act for the right reasons when I buy Anne the hat because it will make me happy, you get a principled explanation of the fact that I'm not creditworthy.

With Link in hand, let's return to the objectivist. To repeat, the first premise isn't a problem for the objectivist if it is either false or if, my arguments before notwithstanding, it's possible to act for the right reasons when you are ignorant of them. Let's examine each possibility in turn, starting with the latter.

One type of objectivist will insist that when you are required to ϕ because of some set of reasons S, you can always ϕ because of the members of S. There are two different kinds of cases that are relevant. Day's End is an instance of the first type of case. In that type of case, you not only are not in a position to know the relevant fact, you don't even believe it. I take it that it's extremely plausible that, in this type of case, you can't ϕ because of the reason. You can't refrain from flipping the switch because it will badly burn your neighbor if you don't even believe that your neighbor will be badly burned if you flip the switch. For reasons that will become clear, I don't think this yet decisively tells against this first strategy.

The second kind of case is like Delusional Andy (and the extension of Day's End where you irrationally believe flipping the switch will burn your neighbor). In that case, you do believe the relevant things, though irrationally. This first objectivist reply has serious hope of sticking if it's possible to do the right thing for the right reason in these cases. This is because it's always possible in the relevant sense of possibility to go from the first type of case to the second. This is because it's plausible that something is possible in the relevant sense only if nothing about your epistemic position bars you from doing that thing. Although one's epistemic position does bar one from knowing the relevant fact in both kinds of case, nothing about one's epistemic position in either type of case bars one from believing the relevant proposition.

Unfortunately for the objectivist, it's simply not plausible that you can do the right thing for the right reason in the second type of case. We can see this by reflecting on Link. It's very plausible that Delusional Andy is *not* creditworthy for his moving out and filing for divorce, whereas Surprised Andy is. Similarly, it seems like you are not creditworthy in the extension of Day's End where you refrain from flipping the switch because you irrationally believe that flipping the switch will badly burn your neighbor.

---

[52] See Lord (2017a) for a defense of a view of credit that meshes well with Link. Markovits (2010, 2012) defends a very similar view to this about moral worth. If you replace 'credit worthy' with 'moral worth,' then you get something very close to Markovits's view. The idea is by now familiar from chapters 5 and 6.

[53] The bit about subsets of S is necessary because some obligations are overdetermined. That is to say, in some cases there are multiple proper subsets of the set of all the reasons to ϕ that require one to ϕ. At least in some of these cases, it seems one can be creditworthy in ϕ-ing just so long as they act for the reasons in one of those subsets.

It might be that you end up doing what's best. But you just got lucky, and hence are not creditworthy. It follows from Link that Delusional Andy doesn't move out for the right reason, nor do you refrain from flipping the switch for the right reason. If this is right, then believing the relevant fact (and acting in light of that belief) is not sufficient for acting for the right reason. Thus this first strategy fails.

The second route the objectivist can take is to deny (1). I think Link sheds light on the plausibility of this, as well. If you deny (1), then you are committed to thinking that there are cases where (i) the members of some set of reasons S make it the case that you ought to ϕ and (ii) it's impossible to ϕ because of the members of S. It follows from Link that there are cases where the members of S make it the case that you ought to ϕ and it's impossible for you to ϕ and be creditworthy for ϕ-ing. I think this is deeply implausible.

It's implausible because it robs our full stop obligations of a certain kind of *action guidingness*. If we cannot perform the actions we are obligated to perform in a way that deserves credit, then those obligations are not action guiding. To put it another way, if our full stop obligations are action guiding, then our actions can be guided by the facts that determine our full stop obligations. The paradigm of being guided by some fact is acting because of that fact. But we've just seen that in denying (1), the objectivist is denying that we can always act because of the right-makers of the acts that we are obligated to perform. Thus, there is an obvious way in which the objectivist has to deny that our obligations are always action guiding. This seems very implausible.

The point can be put less abstractly. Consider Day's End again. If objectivism is true and (1) is false, then there is simply no way you can do what you ought for the right reason. In other words, the only way you can do what you ought to do is by doing something idiotic. There's no way for the right-makers of your act to get any legitimate grip on you. But, we're supposed to believe, they require you stumble around in the dark all the same. This is dubious.

Thus, it looks like (1) is enough to topple the objectivist. This isn't enough for me, however. This is because I not only want to defeat the objectivist, I want to establish Possessed Reasons. So we need to consider (2), as well. (2) holds that possessing r is a necessary condition for ϕ-ing because of r.

I think the most plausible route for denying (2) is to hold that in order to possess r, you have to stand in some positive epistemic relationship to r—e.g., you have to know r—but one needn't stand in this relation to r to ϕ because of r. The most natural version of this view holds that you merely have to believe r in order to ϕ because of r.[54] Fortunately for us, we needn't dwell too much on this proposal, for we have already seen that it is implausible. It's implausible because it's implausible that merely believing r (and acting in light of this belief) is sufficient for ϕ-ing because of r. If this

---

[54] It's possible to hold that in order to possess r you have to know r, but in order to ϕ because of r you just have to justifiably believe r. I can't see any motivation for this, though. It's more plausible to think that there is a high bar on possession but a low one on acting for a reason.

were true, then it would follow from Link that Delusional Andy is creditworthy for moving out. But he's not.[55] Thus, it seems like you have to stand in some positive justificatory relationship to r in order to ϕ because of r. If you also have to stand in some positive justificatory relationship to r to possess r, it's plausible that in order to ϕ because of r, you must possess r.

Before moving on, I should consider two related objections to the preceding arguments. The first is raised by Schwan (FC). Schwan contends that the argument just given fails because it equivocates on different senses of ability. As he notes, ability talk is highly flexible because it can be relativized to many different sets of conditions.[56] In one sense I am able to speak German—given my overall intellectual abilities, there is some world where I speak German. In another sense I am unable to speak German—given my current linguistic knowledge, there is no world where I speak German. Schwan (rightly) claims that the objectivist can use this flexibility to accept (1) while denying (2). They can accept (1) by adopting a liberal sense of ability. Schwan suggests O-ability:

O-Ability: An agent is O-able to ϕ [for the right reasons] just in case there is some possible world in which the agent's physical traits and external circumstances are (more or less) the same, and that agent intentionally ϕs [for the right reasons].

Delusional Andy has the O-ability to act for the right reasons. Thus, O-ability does not require possession. So if O-ability is the sense of ability involved in (1), (2) is false. Schwan points out further that the objectivist can accept that there is another sense of ability that makes (2) true. Schwan suggests P-ability:[57]

P-Ability: An agent is P-able to ϕ [for the right reasons] just in case there is some possible world in which the agent's physical traits and external and epistemic circumstances are (more or less) the same, and that agent intentionally ϕs [for the right reasons].

Objectivists can grant that in order to be P-able to act for the right reasons, one must possess those reasons. They just deny that that sense is, to use Schwan's phrase, the *normatively relevant* one. Schwan's objectivist holds that obligation is only constrained by O-abilities.

I think Schwan's underlying framework is a good starting point, and I agree that this is a helpful way of describing a move that the objectivist can make. That said, I don't think that O-ability is the sense of ability relevant to (1).[58] We can see this by

---

[55] This argument works just as well against views that accept (2) but hold that there is a low bar on having (e.g., Schroeder (2008, 2011b)). Thus, this argument supplements my arguments against those views in chapter 3.

[56] Cf. Kratzer (2012).

[57] It's not clear to me that P-ability is true, but I will grant it for the sake of argument. What is important is that there is a more conservative sense of ability that is connected to possession.

[58] Schwan agrees. See §5 of his paper for interesting arguments for this conclusion.

thinking about the *manifestation* conditions of the ability. Schwan's objectivist agrees that delusional Andy does not *in fact* act for the right reasons. This is important because it allows them to agree with my diagnosis of the two Andys. Given that delusional Andy doesn't act for the right reasons, he doesn't manifest his O-ability to act for the right reasons.

What would it take to manifest such an ability? It seems plausible that one is in a position to manifest such an ability only if one is P-able to act for the right reasons. After all, when one manifests the ability, one acts for the right reasons. And Schwan's objectivist agrees that this happens only when one is like surprised Andy. So it looks like being P-able is necessary for being in a position to manifest. If that is right, then O-abilities are very uninteresting on their own. They are uninteresting because they cannot be manifested without obtaining a different sort of ability. It's unclear why we should think that obligation is constrained by such uninteresting abilities.

This opens the door to a revised version of the argument that avoids Schwan's response. We can call this the manifestation version of the argument.

(1_{MV}) If the reasons in some set S make it the case you ought to ϕ, then you are in a position to manifest an ability to ϕ because of the members of S.

(2_{MV}) If you are in a position to manifest an ability to ϕ because of the members of S, then you possess the members of S.

(C_{MV}) If the reasons in some set S make it the case you ought to ϕ, then you possess the members of S.

O-ability is not relevant to (1_{MV}). Further, I think that the arguments I gave above in favor of (1) apply equally to (1_{MV}). Thus, I don't think it is plausible to accept (1) and deny (2) by appealing to O-abilities. The objectivist cannot have her cake and eat it too.[59]

Like Schwan, Way & Whiting (2017) contend that my argument is hampered by the fact that there are many different senses of ability. They focus on *general* and *specific* abilities. Right now I have the general ability to kick a soccer ball 30 yards. I lack the specific ability to because I am seated, indoors, and do not have a soccer ball. As they rightfully point out, (2) is certainly false if we are talking about general abilities. Possession is only linked to specific abilities. Thus, we need to read (1) as also talking about specific abilities.

Way and Whiting focus on my argument for (1) that appeals to credit. The key claim is what they call Credit ((Way & Whiting, 2017, p. 367); I have changed the wording slightly):

Credit: If you ought to ϕ then you have the specific ability to ϕ in a way that is creditworthy.

---

[59] The underlying culprit here, I think, is the purely modal account of abilities that Schwan is assuming. Such a thin view of abilities makes it easy to posit all sorts of uninteresting types of ability. It might be that a thin account like this is what is needed to do the semantics of ability talk in English (which is what Kratzer is doing), but relying on too much in normative debates is likely to cause trouble. See Jenkins & Nolan (2012) and Spencer (2017) for further problems for modal accounts of abilities.

I am committed to Credit because I am committed to (1) and (†):

(1) If the reasons in some set S make it the case you ought to ϕ, then you can ϕ because of the members of S (Acting On).

(†) If you can ϕ because of the members of S, then you have the specific ability to ϕ in a way that is creditworthy.

Credit If the reasons in some set S make it the case you ought to ϕ, then you have the specific ability to ϕ in a way that is creditworthy.

They argue that Credit is false because of the following case (ibid.):

Doctor

A doctor is deciding whether to give drug A or drug B to a patient who has a painful and fatal disease. She knows that A will completely cure the patient, relieving all the patient's suffering and saving her life, and that B will not save the life of her patient but will relieve the patient's suffering. The doctor also knows that, if she tries to give one drug, she will be unable to give the other. However, though she is in no position to know this, and despite evidence to the contrary, the doctor is unable (in the specific sense) to give A. As it happens, the doctor gives B to the patient for the reason that it will relieve her suffering.

Way and Whiting argue that in this case the doctor ought to give drug B even though she cannot give drug B in a creditworthy way. If this is right, then Credit is false.

I agree that the doctor ought to give drug B. However, I disagree that she cannot give drug B in a creditworthy way. In fact, I think that she actually gives drug B in a creditworthy way. After all, the fact that drug B will relieve the patient's suffering is a normative reason to give drug B. And we can suppose that the doctor manifests knowledge about how to use that reason (Way and Whiting are willing to grant this). So she acts in a way that is deserving of credit.

That said, I do think it is right that she only deserves partial credit for what she has done. To put it in terms of quality of will, while the act she performs expresses some good will in virtue of the fact that it shows concern for the patient's suffering, she also expresses a lack of good will in virtue of showing indifference towards the patient's life. This expression of a lack of good will attenuates the credit she deserves.

Way and Whiting consider a response like this and argue that it won't do. They think that to accept this response you must accept Credit*:

Credit*: If you ought to ϕ then you have the specific ability to ϕ in a way that is partially creditworthy.

Credit* does not support (1). We can see this by noticing that Credit* is compatible with a view that holds that reasons outside of one's perspective can make a difference to what one is obligated to do just so long as *some* of the reasons that speak in favor of what one ought to do are within one's perspective. If this view is true, then Credit* would be true because it would always be the case that one has the specific ability to act for at least one normative reason that speaks in favor of what one ought to do and thus always have the specific ability to do what one ought to do in a way that is deserving of partial credit.

I agree that Credit* is too weak. However, it is not forced upon me by my response to Way and Whiting's argument. Instead, I think we should hold (‡):

(‡):   If a set of reasons S obligates one to ϕ, then one has a specific ability to act for those reasons in a way that is at least partially creditworthy.

The doctor meets the condition set down by (‡). There is only one relevant reason in play—the reason provided by the fact that drug B will relieve the patient's suffering. The doctor does respond to this reason in a way that is partially creditworthy. However, (‡) is stronger than Credit*. This is because it holds that in order to be obligated to ϕ, one must have the specific ability to act for *the set* of reasons that obligate. This rules out the sort of view that shows that Credit* is too weak.

The upshot is that while I think that cases like Doctor complicate matters, they don't sink the basic idea behind the argument. There is still an intimate link between obligation and having the (specific) ability to react in a creditworthy way.

***

Even if the preceding arguments are sound, I've only established that a necessary condition for a set of reasons S to make it the case that you ought to ϕ is that you possess the members of S. This is significant in the dialectic with the objectivist, for it entails that objectivism is false. But it's not a full vindication of Possessed Reasons. In the rest of the section, I'll argue for two claims that get us closer to a vindication of Possessed Reasons.

The first claim is a strengthening of the necessity condition. It has to be not only that you possess the members of S, it has to be that the members of S are *decisive reasons* to ϕ. If they are decisive, then they (i) aren't defeated by other reasons you possess—i.e., the members of S will be weightier than the reasons you possess not to ϕ—and (ii) they are much weightier than the reasons you possess for any alternative action. Thus, I think we should replace the conclusion of the above argument with Necessary:

Necessary: If the members of some set of reasons S make it the case that you ought to ϕ, then the members of S are decisive reasons to ϕ that you possess.

I don't think this strengthened necessity condition needs much more defense. It's very plausible that a set of reasons needs to decisively support ϕ-ing in order to make it the case you ought to ϕ. If the members of S are defeated or are not much weightier than the alternatives, then it's independently plausible that they don't make it the case that you ought to ϕ.[60]

---

[60] Things are complicated when the reasons you possess in favor of one option are slightly weightier than the reasons you possess for the other options. In some cases, it will seem like you ought to take the option that is most supported. For example, if you have the choice between taking a $1000 prize or a $1002 prize

We'd be much closer to a vindication of Possessed Reasons if we were to show that Sufficient is true:

Sufficient: If the members of S are decisive reasons to ϕ that you possess, then the members of S make it the case that you ought to ϕ.

If Necessary is true and Sufficient is false, then there is some condition over and above possessing decisive reasons to ϕ that must be met in order for it to be the case that you ought to ϕ. Obviously there are a lot of possible conditions that one could propose. I don't have a good enough imagination to think of all of them (nor do I have the space to consider them all). But it's worth considering two of them.

The first might be some kind of ability condition. It might be that 'ought' implies 'can' but that 'possessing decisive reasons' doesn't imply 'can.' I agree (obviously!) that there is some ability condition. Not only do I think that you must be able to ϕ in order to be required to ϕ, I think you must be able to ϕ because of the right-makers in order to be required to ϕ. But whatever plausibility these claims have when it comes to what you ought to do seems to apply equally well to what you possess decisive reasons to do. We can see this by considering examples. Take the basketball example discussed earlier. It's true that it's not the case that Sam ought to dunk the basketball, but it's equally plausible that she doesn't possess reasons to do that. A plausible generic claim in the vicinity is something like: If r is a reason for A to ϕ, then it's (metaphysically) possible for A to ϕ because of r.

A second proposal is some type of hypological condition. For example, perhaps it's true that if you ought to ϕ, then you are blameworthy for not ϕ-ing, but it's not the case that you are always blameworthy for not doing what you possess decisive reasons to do. If this were true, then there would be cases where you possess decisive reasons to ϕ but wouldn't be blameworthy if you didn't ϕ and thus it wouldn't be the case that you ought to ϕ. One problem with this proposal is that the hypological condition on 'ought' is false. It's just not true that you are always blameworthy for not doing what you ought. There are simple recipes for counterexamples. One is to take a case where your pet theory of obligation says you ought to ϕ at time t. At t_1, bombard your attention with useless data. You can set the case up so that it is very hard to do what you ought (and thus most of the time you won't), but nevertheless the conditions that obligate you to ϕ are still in place. In this type of case, you will seem blameless for not ϕ-ing because of how hard ϕ-ing becomes, even though you will still be obligated to ϕ.

---

and everything else is equal, you ought to take the $1002 prize. However, it doesn't seem like you are obliged to take the option most supported in every case. For example, in some cases of mere permissibility—cases where one has sufficient reasons to perform several actions and is not required to perform any particular action—it seems like adding some lightweight reasons doesn't oblige you to take the option that you add the reasons to. So, if it's merely permissible for me to take job A and merely permissible to take job B, I won't come to be obliged to take job A simply because job A offers me an extra $50 per year. But surely the $50 provides a reason to take job A.

Furthermore, even if you think that you are always blameworthy for not doing what you ought, it's hard to see why you would want to deny that you are always blameworthy for not doing what you possess decisive reasons to do. The most plausible reason I can think of is that what you ought to do is transparent in some way but what you possess decisive reason to do isn't (perhaps because being decisive isn't transparent). You could think this, but I'm not sure why you would. If what you ought to do is transparent, then it seems like it will always be transparent what the facts support, but this is just another way of saying that it will be transparent what the reasons you possess decisively support.

It doesn't seem like these two proposals are plausible, and thus it seems reasonable to think that having decisive reasons to ϕ is sufficient for it being the case that you ought to ϕ. This gives us Necessary & Sufficient:

Necessary & Sufficient: The members of S are decisive reasons to ϕ that you possess iff the members of S make it the case you ought to ϕ.

Necessary & Sufficient is, I think, just a precisification of Possessed Reasons. It tells you how your obligations are a function of the reasons you possess.

8.5 Summary of Results (Or: Why You Ought to Be Rational)

As we saw at the beginning of this chapter, rationality has traditionally been seen to be on steady deontic footing. Finding out you would be irrational for ϕ-ing has struck most philosophers and laypeople alike as bearing very directly on what ought to be done. Despite this, recent work in metaethics makes it surprisingly plausible that rationality has no direct effect on what ought to be done.

As we saw in §8.2.2, this is largely because it has become popular to think that rationality is constitutively tied to coherence. This connection has been spelled out in two different ways in the literature. According to the narrow-scope view, you are required by rationality to have certain attitudes when you have certain other attitudes. For example, you are required to intend to ψ when you intend to ϕ and believe that in order to ϕ you must ψ. According to the wide-scope view, you are never required to have particular attitudes. Rather, you are directly required to be coherent—you are required to [intend to ψ if you intend to ϕ and believe that in order to ϕ you must ψ].

The problem is that it is very hard to show that the requirements posited by these two views have deontic significance. The narrow-scope view seems hopeless because it allows for a pernicious kind of bootstrapping. It is very implausible that one ought to or has reason to intend to ψ *simply because* one intends to ϕ and believes that in order to ϕ one must intend to ψ. On the other hand, it is mysterious how it could be the case that the wide-scope requirements are deontically significant. This is because it is mysterious what reasons there could be to directly be coherent. We might have reasons to have particular attitudes, and they might weigh up such that we always have sufficient reason to have attitudes that cohere. But this is not enough to vindicate the deontic significance of the wide-scope requirements.

These results have led many to a skepticism about the deontic significance of rationality. This, I think, is a mistake. As we have throughout the book, we should question one of the starting points—viz., that rationality is constitutively tied to coherence. Instead, I think we should think that rationality consists in correctly responding to the objective reasons one possesses—i.e., we should hold Reasons Responsiveness.

It was established in §8.3.2 that if Reasons Responsiveness is true, then rationality is weakly deontically significant. This is because there is always reason to do what you possess reason to do. So if you always possess reasons to do what rationality requires, then there will always be reasons to do what rationality requires. This only goes so far, though. It would still be a considerable win for skeptics about the deontic significance of rationality if rationality turns out to only be weakly deontically significant. In order to fully vindicate the deontic significance of rationality, one needs to show that it's strongly significant—i.e., that you ought to be rational.

The last section aimed to show this indirectly. The main claim of the last section was that what you ought to do is determined by the reasons that you possess. The plausibility of this claim is independent of any considerations having to do with rationality—this is why it was indirect.

When you combine §8.3 with the results of §8.4, you see that Reasons Responsiveness can vindicate the strong deontic significance of rationality. If what you are rationally required to do is what you possess decisive reasons to do and what you ought to do is what you possess decisive reasons to do, then the requirements of rationality *just are* the requirements you ought to comply with. Indeed, on my picture, there is no space between what the (possessed) reasons require, what rationality requires, and what you ought to do. For this reason, I think we should drop the Broomean idea that rationality has a *source* that is independent of normative reasons.[61] It is not the case that reasons and rationality are independent of each other in the way Broome envisions. If they were, then the best we could hope for is a correlation between what rationality requires and what we ought to do. I believe this chapter vindicates something stronger: What you are rationally required to do just is what you ought to do.

It is a serious virtue of my view that it can give such a plausible account of why rationality is strongly deontically significant. This is especially weighty since it's completely mysterious how rival views can even account for the weak deontic significance of rationality, let alone the strong deontic significance. Given that it is a truism that we should be rational, the fact that only my view can vindicate the strong

---

[61] As a referee pointed out to me, this makes it seem as if rationality is a source of normative reasons that competes with the other sources. This is not a natural view. Fortunately my view allows us to avoid it.

deontic significance of rationality is a strong reason to accept my view—one which you now possess.

*****

This concludes my defense of Reasons Responsiveness. The conclusion of this chapter justifies the book's title. As I've argued in this chapter, rationality is very important. This is because it is the central deontic notion. This makes it central to our agential lives, for it follows that rationality is at the heart of what we are after when we exercise the capacities that are distinctive of the kind of intelligent creatures we are; i.e., when we exercise our capacities to figure out how to react to the world.

Bibliography

Alston, W. (1988). An internalist externalism. *Synthese*, 74, 265–283.

Alvarez, M. (2010). *Kinds of Reasons*. Oxford University Press.

Anscombe, G. E. M. (1957). *Intention*. Harvard University Press.

Armstrong, D. (1973). *Belief, Truth, and Knowledge*. Cambridge University Press.

Arnold, A. (2011). Some evidence is false. *Australasian Journal of Philosophy*, 91(1), 165–172.

Arpaly, N. (2003). *Unprincipled Virtue*. Oxford University Press.

Arpaly, N. (2006). *Meaning, Merit, and Human Bondage*. Princeton University Press.

Arpaly, N. & Schroeder, T. (2014). *In Praise of Desire*. Oxford University Press.

Audi, R. (1993). *The Structure of Justification*. Cambridge University Press.

Bach, K. (1985). A rationale for reliablism. *The Monist*, 68(2), 246–263.

Bader, R. (2016). Reasons, conditions, and modifiers. In E. Lord & B. Maguire (Eds.), *Weighing Reasons*. Oxford University Press.

Ballantyne, N. & Coffman, E. (2011). Uniqueness, evidence, and rationality. *Philosophers' Imprint*, 11(18), 1–13.

Beddor, B. (2015). Evidentialism, circularity, and grounding. *Philosophical Studies*, 172(7), 1847–1868.

Bengson, J. (2015). A noetic theory of understanding and intuition as sense-maker. *Inquiry*, 58(7–8), 633–668.

Bengson, J. (2017). The unity of understanding. In S. R. Grimm (Ed.), *Making Sense of the World*. Oxford University Press.

Bengson, J. & Moffett, M. A. (2007). Know-how and concept possession. *Philosophical Studies*, 136(1), 31–57.

Bengson, J. & Moffett, M. A. (2011). Nonpropositional intellectualism. In J. Bengson & M. A. Moffett (Eds.), *Knowing How* (pp. 161–195). Oxford University Press.

Berker, S. (FC). The unity of grounding. *Mind*.

Besson, C. (2009). Understanding the logical constants and dispositions. *The Baltic International Yearbook of Cognition, Logic and Communication*, 5(1), 1–24.

Bjornsson, G. & Finlay, S. (2010). Metaethical Contextualism Defended. *Ethics*, 121(1), 7–36.

Boghossian, P. (2003). Blind reasoning. *Aristotelian Society Supplementary Volume*, 77(1), 225–248.

Boghossian, P. (2014). What is Inference? *Philosophical Studies*, 169(1), 1–18.

BonJour, L. (1980). Externalist theories of empirical knowledge. *Midwest Studies in Philosophy*, 5, 53–73.

Bradford, G. (2015). *Achievement*. Oxford University Press.

Bradley, B. & McDaniel, K. (2008). Desires. *Mind*, 117(466), 267–302.

Bratman, M. (1987). *Intention, Plans, and Practical Reason*. Harvard University Press.

Bratman, M. (2009a). Intention, Belief, Practical, Theoretical. In S. Robertson (Ed.), *Spheres of Reason*. Oxford University Press.

Bratman, M. (2009b). Intention, Practical Rationality, and Self-Governance. *Ethics*, 119(3), 411–443.

Bratman, M. (2013). The fecundity of planning agency. In D. Shoemaker (Ed.), *Oxford Sutdies in Agency and Responsibility*, volume 1. Oxford University Press.

Broome, J. (1997). Reasons and motivation. *Proceedings of the Aristotelian Society*, 71(1), 131–146.

Broome, J. (1999). Normative Requirements. *Ratio*, 12, 389–419.

Broome, J. (2001). Are intentions reasons? and how should we cope with incommensurable values? In C. Morris & A. Ripstein (Eds.), *Practical Rationality and Preference: Essays for David Gauthier*. Cambridge University Press.

Broome, J. (2005a). Does rationality give us reasons? *Philosophical Issues*, 15, 321–337.

Broome, J. (2005b). Have we reason to do as rationality requires? A comment on Raz. *Journal of Ethics & Social Philosophy*, 1.

Broome, J. (2007a). Does rationality consist in responding correctly to reasons? *Journal of Moral Philosophy*, 4, 349–374.

Broome, J. (2007b). Requirements. In J. J. Toni Rønnow-Rasmussen, Björn Petersson, & D. Egonsson (Eds.), Homage à Wlodek: philosophical papers dedicated to Wlodek Rabinowicz. Online Tribute (url: http://www.fil.lu.se/hommageawlodek/).

Broome, J. (2007c). Wide or narrow scope? *Mind*, 116(462), 359–370.

Broome, J. (2008a). Is rationality normative? *Disputatio*, 11.

Broome, J. (2008b). Reply to Southwood, Kearns and Star, and Cullity. *Ethics*, 119(1), 96–108.

Broome, J. (2013). *Rationality Through Reasoning*. Blackwell.

Broome, J. (2014). Comments on Boghossian. *Philosophical Studies*, 169(1).

Brueckner, A. (2002). Williamson on the primeness of knowing. *Analysis*, 62(3), 197–202.

Brunero, J. (2007). Are intentions reasons? *Pacific Philosophical Quarterly*, 88(4), 424–444.

Brunero, J. (2010). The scope of rational requirements. *The Philosophical Quarterly*, 60(238), 28–49.

Burgess, A. & Plunkett, D. (2013a). Conceptual ethics I. *Philosophy Compass*, 8(12), 1091–1101.

Burgess, A. & Plunkett, D. (2013b). Conceptual ethics II. *Philosophy Compass*, 8(12), 1102–1110.

Buss, S. (MS). Norms of rationality and the superficial unity of the mind. Manuscript, University of Michigan.

Camp, E. (2003). Saying and seeing-as: the linguistic uses and cognitive effects of metaphor. PhD thesis, University of California, Berkeley.

Carroll, L. (1895). What the tortoise said to Achilles. *Mind*, 4(14), 278–280.

Chang, R. (1997). Introduction. In R. Chang (Ed.), *Incommensurability, Incomparability, and Practical Reason*. Harvard University Press.

Chisholm, R. (1966). Freedom and action. In K. Lehrer (Ed.), *Freedom and Determinism*. Random House.

Christensen, D. (2007). Does Murphy's law apply in epistemology? Self-doubt and rational ideals. *Oxford Studies in Epistemology*, 2, 3–31.

Christensen, D. (2010). Higher-order evidence. *Philosophy and Phenomenological Research*, 81(1), 185–215.

Christensen, D. (2013). Epistemic modesty defended. In D. Christensen & J. Lackey (Eds.), *The Epistemology of Disagreement: New Essays*. Oxford University Press.

Coates, A. (2012). Rational epistemic akrasia. *American Philosophical Quarterly*, 49(2), 113–124.

Coffman, E. (2008). Warrant without truth? *Synthese*, 162(2), 173–194.

Cohen, S. (1984). Justification and truth. *Philosophical Studies*, 46(3), 279–295.

Cohen, S. (2016). Theorizing about the epistemic. *Inquiry*, 59(7–8), 839–857.

Cohen, S. & Lehrer, K. (1983). Justification, truth, and knowledge. *Synthese*, 55(2), 191–207.

Comesaña, J. (2002). The diagonal and the demon. *Philosophical Studies*, 110, 249–266.

Comesaña, J. & McGrath, M. (2014). Having false reasons. In C. Littlejohn & J. Turri (Eds.), *Epistemic Norms*. Oxford University Press.

Crane, T. & French, C. (2015). The problem of perception. In E. N. Zalta (Ed.), *Stanford Encyclopedia of Philosophy*.

Dancy, J. (2000). *Practical Reality*. Oxford University Press.

Dancy, J. (2004a). *Ethics without Principles*. Oxford University Press.

Dancy, J. (2004b). Two ways of explaining actions. *Royal Institute of Philosophy Supplement*.

Dancy, J. (2006). Acting in the light of the appearances. In C. MacDonald & G. MacDonald (Eds.), *McDowell and His Critics*. Wiley-Blackwell.

D'Arms, J. & Jacobson, D. (2000). The moralistic fallacy: on the 'appropriateness' of emotions. *Philosophy and Phenomenological Research*, 61(1), 65–90.

Darwall, S. (1983). *Impartial Reason*. Cornell University Press.

Davidson, D. (1963). Actions, reasons, and causes. *Journal of Philosophy*, 60(23), 685–700.

Davidson, D. (1980). *Essays on Actions and Events*. Oxford University Press.

Dogramaci, S. (2016). Reasoning without blinders: a reply to valaris. *Mind*, 125(499), 889–893.

Dreier, J. (2000). Dispositions and fetishes: externalist models of moral motivation. *Philosophy and Phenomenological Research*, 61(3), 619–638.

Dretske, F. (1981). *Knowledge and the Flow of Information*. MIT Press.

Elga, A. (MS). Lucky to be rational. Manuscript, Princeton University.

Engel, M. (1992). Personal and doxastic justification in epistemology. *Philosophical Studies*, 67(2), 133–150.

Enoch, D. (2006). Agency, shmagency: why normativity won't come from what is constitutive of agency. *The Philosophical Review*, 115(2), 169–198.

Evans, I. (2013). The problem of the basing relation. *Synthese*, 190(14), 2943–2957.

Ewing, A. (1959). *Second Thoughts in Moral Philosophy*. New York: Routledge.

Fantl, J. (2015). What is it to be happy that p? *Ergo, an Open Access Journal of Philosophy*, 2.

Feldman, R. (1988). Having evidence. In *Philosophical Analysis*. Kluwer Publishing Co.

Feldman, R. (2003). *Epistemology*. Prentice-Hall.

Feldman, R. (2007). Reasonable religious disagreement. In L. Antony (Ed.), *Philosophers without Gods*. Oxford University Press.

Feldman, R. & Conee, E. (1985). Evidentialism. *Philosophical Studies*, 48(1), 15–34.

Fischer, J. M. & Ravizza, M. (1998). *Responsibility and Control: A Theory of Moral Responsibility*. Cambridge University Press.

Fitelson, B. (2010). Strengthing the case for knowledge from falsehood. *Analysis*, 70(4), 666–669.

Foot, P. (1972). Morality as a system of hypothetical imperatives. *The Philosophical Review*, 81(3), 305–316.

Friedman, J. (2013). Suspended judgment. *Philosophical Studies*, 162(2), 165–181.

Friedman, J. (2015). Why suspend judging? *Noûs*, 50(4).

Fumerton, R. (1995). *Metaepistemology and Skepticism*. Rowman & Littlefield.

Gibbard, A. (1990). *Wise Choices, Apt Feelings*. Oxford University Press.

Gibbons, J. (2001). Knowledge in action. *Philosophy and Phenomenological Research*, 62(3), 579–600.

Gibbons, J. (2006). Access externalism. *Mind*, 115(457), 19–39.

Gibbons, J. (2010). Things that make things reasonable. *Philosophy and Phenomenological Research*, 81(2), 335–361.

Gibbons, J. (2013). *The Norm of Belief*. New York: Oxford University Press.

Ginet, C. (1990). Justification. *Journal of Philosophical Research*, 15(93), 93–107.

Ginet, C. (2008). In defense of a non-causal account of reasons explanations. *Journal of Ethics*, 12(3/4), 229–237.

Glick, E. (2015). Practical modes of presentation. *Noûs*, 49(3), 538–559.

Goldman, A. (1979). What is justified belief? In G. Pappas (Ed.), *Justification and Knowledge*. D. Reidel.

Goldman, A. (1988). Strong and weak justification. *Philosophical Perspectives*, 2, 51–69.

Goldman, A. (2009). Williamson on knowledge and evidence. In D. Pritchard (Ed.), *Williamson on Knowledge*. Oxford University Press.

Goldman, A. (2012). *Reliabilism and Contemporary Epistemology*. Oxford University Press.

Graham, P. A. (2010). In defense of objectivism about moral obligation. *Ethics*, 121(1), 88–115.

Greco, D. (2014). A puzzle about epistemic akrasia. *Philosophical Studies*, 167(2), 201–219.

Greenspan, P. (1975). Conditional oughts and hypothetical imperatives. *The Journal of Philosophy*, 72(10), 259–276.

Grice, H. P. (2001). *Aspects of Reason*. Oxford University Press.

Haddock, A. & Macpherson, F. (2008). Introduction: varieties of disjunctivism. In A. Haddock & F. Macpherson (Eds.), *Disjunctivism: Perception, Action, Knowledge*. Oxford University Press.

Hale, B. & Wright, C. (2000). Implicit definition and the a priori. In P. Boghossian & C. Peacocke (Eds.), *New Essays on the a Priori* (pp. 286–319). Oxford University Press.

Hare, C. (2009). Perfectly balanced interests. *Philosophical Perspectives*, 23(1), 165–176.

Hare, C. (2010). Take the sugar. *Analysis*, 70(2), 237–247.

Harman, G. (1973). *Thought*. Princeton University Press.

Harman, G. (1976). Practical reasoning. *The Review of Metaphysics*, 29, 431–463.

Harman, G. (1984). Logic and reasoning. *Synthese*, 60(1), 107–127.

Harman, G. (1986). *Change in View*. MIT Press.

Harman, G. (2000). Is there a single true morality? In *Explaining Value and Other Essays in Moral Philosophy*. Oxford University Press.

Hill, T. (1973). The hypothetical imperative. *The Philosophical Review*, 82(4), 429–450.

Hinton, J. M. (1967). Visual experiences. *Mind*, 76(302), 217–227.

Hinton, J. M. (1973). *Experiences: An Inquiry into some Ambiguities*. Oxford: Clarendon Press.

Hornsby, J. (2007). Knowledge in action. In A. Lesit (Ed.), *Action in Context*. De Gruyter.

Hornsby, J. (2008). A disjunctive conception of acting for reasons. In A. Haddock & F. Macpherson (Eds.), *Disjunctivism: Perception, Action, Knowledge*. Oxford University Press.

Horowitz, S. (2014). Epistemic akrasia. *Noûs*, 48(4), 718–744.

Horty, J. (2007). Reasons as defaults. *Philosophers' Imprint*, 7(3), 1–28.

Horty, J. (2012). *Reasons as Defaults*. Oxford University Press.

Horwich, P. (2005). *Reflections on Meaning*. Oxford University Press, Clarendon Press.

Hussain, N. (MS). The requirements of rationality. Manuscript, Stanford University.

Hyman, J. (2006). Knowledge and evidence. *Mind*, 115(460), 891–916.

Hyman, J. (2015). *Action, Knowledge, and Will*. Oxford University Press.

Ichikawa, J. J. (2018). Internalism, factivity, and sufficient reason. In V. Mitova (Ed.), The factive turn in epistemology. Cambridge University Press.

Ichikawa, J. J. & Jarvis, B. W. (2013). *The Rules of Thought*. Oxford University Press.

Ichikawa, J. J. & Jenkins, C. (2017). On putting knowledge 'first.' In J. A. Carter, E. C. Gordon, & B. Jarvis (Eds.), Knowledge first: approaches to epistemology and mind. Oxford University Press.

Jackson, F. (1991). Decision-theoretic consequentialism and the nearest-dearest objection. *Ethics*, 101(3), 461–482.

Jenkins, C. & Nolan, D. (2012). Disposition impossible. *Noûs*, 46(4), 732–753.

Kearns, S. & Star, D. (2009). Reasons as evidence. In R. Shafer-Landau (Ed.), *Oxford Studies in Metaethics*, vol. 4. Oxford University Press.

Kelly, T. (2002). The rationality of belief and other propositional attitudes. *Philosophical Studies*, 110(2), 163–196.

Kelly, T. (2010). Peer disagreement and higher-order evidence. In R. Feldman & T. Warfield (Eds.), *Disagreement*. Oxford University Press.

Kiesewetter, B. (2011). 'Ought' and the Perspective of the Agent. *Journal of Ethics & Social Philosophy*, 5(3).

Kiesewetter, B. (2015). Instrumental normativity: in defense of the transmission principle. *Ethics*, 125(4), 921–946.

Kiesewetter, B. (2016). You ought to Φ only if you may believe that you ought to Φ. *Philosophical Quarterly*, 66(265), 760–782.

Kiesewetter, B. (2017). *The Normativity of Rationality*. Oxford University Press.

Kiesewetter, B. (2018). How reasons are sensitive to available evidence. In C. McHugh, J. Way, & D. Whiting (Eds.), *Normativity: Epistemic and Practical*. Oxford University Press.

Kolodny, N. (2005). Why be rational? *Mind*, 114(455), 509–563.

Kolodny, N. (2007a). How does coherence matter? *Proceedings of the Aristotelian Society*, 107, 229–263.

Kolodny, N. (2007b). State or process requirements? *Mind*, 116(462), 371–385.

Kolodny, N. (2008a). The myth of practical consistency. *European Journal of Philosophy*, 16(3), 366–402.

Kolodny, N. (2008b). Why be disposed to be coherent? *Ethics*, 118(3), 437–463.

Kolodny, N. (2018). Instrumental transmission. In D. Star (Ed.), *Oxford handbook of reasons and normativity*. Oxford University Press.

Kolodny, N. & MacFarlane, J. (2010). Ifs and oughts. *The Journal of Philosophy*, 107(3), 115–143.

Korsgaard, C. (1996). *The Sources of Normativity*. Harvard University Press.

Korsgaard, C. M. (1983). Two distinctions in goodness. *Philosophical Review*, 92(2), 169–195.

Kratzer, A. (2012). *Modals and Conditionals: New and Revised Perspectives*. Oxford University Press.

Lasonen-Aarnio, M. (2010). Unreasonable knowledge. *Philosophical Perspectives*.

Lasonen-Aarnio, M. (FCa). Enkrasia or evidentialism? Learning to love mismatch. *Philosophical Studies*.

Lasonen-Aarnio, M. (FCb). The new evil demon and the disposition to know. In F. Dorsch & J. Dutant (Eds.), *The New Evil Demon: New Essays on Knowledge, Justification, and Rationality*. Oxford University Press.

Lehrer, K. & Paxson, T. (1969). Knowledge: undefeated justified true belief. *The Journal of Philosophy*, 66(8), 225–237.

Lewis, D. (1996). Elusive knowledge. *Australasian Journal of Philosophy*, 74, 549–567.

Littlejohn, C. (2009). The externalist's demon. *Canadian Journal of Philosophy*, 39(3), 399–434.

Littlejohn, C. (2012). *Justification and the Truth-Connection*. Cambridge University Press.

Lord, E. (2008). Dancy on acting for the right reason. *Journal of Ethics & Social Philosophy*, (3), 1–7.

Lord, E. (2010). Having reasons and the factoring account. *Philosophical Studies*, 149(3), 283–296.

Lord, E. (2013). *The importance of being rational*. Princeton University.

Lord, E. (2014a). The coherent and the rational. *Analytic Philosophy*, 55(2), 151–175.

Lord, E. (2014b). The real symmetry problem(s) for wide-scope accounts of rationality. *Philosophical Studies*, 170(3), 443–464.

Lord, E. (2015). Acting for the right reasons, abilities, and obligation. In R. Shafer-Landau (Ed.), *Oxford Studies in Metaethics*, vol. 10. Oxford University Press.

Lord, E. (2016a). Justifying partiality. *Ethical Theory and Moral Practice*, 19(3), 569–590.

Lord, E. (2016b). On the rational power of aesthetic testimony. *British Journal of Aesthetics*, 56(1), 1–13.

Lord, E. (2017a). On the intellectual conditions for responsibility: acting for the right reasons, conceptualization, and credit. *Philosophy and Phenomenological Research*, 95(2), 436–464.

Lord, E. (2017b). What you're rationally required to do and what you ought to do (are the same thing!). *Mind*, 126(504), 1109–1154.

Lord, E. (2018a). Epistemic reasons, evidence, and defeaters. In D. Star (Ed.), *The Oxford Handbook of Reasons and Normativity*. Oxford University Press.

Lord, E. (2018b). The explanatory problem for cognitivism about practical reason. In C. McHugh, J. Way, & D. Whiting (Eds.), *Normativity: epistemic and practical*. Oxford University Press.

Lord, E. (2018c). How to learn about morality and aesthetics through acquaintance and testimony. In R. Shafer-Landau (Ed.), *Oxford Studies in Metaethics*, vol. 13. Oxford University Press.

Lord, E. (MSa). Knowing what it's *like*: how to save the acquaintance principle from photographs, the imagination, and abstracta. Manuscript, University of Pennsylvania.

Lord, E. (MSb). Reasons to withhold and the failure of evidentialism. Manuscript, University of Pennsylvania.

Lord, E. & Maguire, B. (2016). An opinionated guide to the weight of reasons. In E. Lord & B. Maguire (Eds.), *Weighing Reasons*. Oxford University Press.

Lord, E. & Sylvan, K. (FC). Prime time (for the basing relation). In P. Bondy & J. A. Carter (Eds.), *Well-Founded Belief: New Essays on the Basing Relation*. Routledge.

Lord, E. & Sylvan, K. (MS). Reasons: wrong, right, normative, fundamental. Manuscript, University of Pennsylvania and University of Southampton.

Lycan, W. G. (1988). *Judgement and Justification.* Cambridge University Press.

Maguire, B. (FC). There are no reasons for affective attitudes. *Mind.*

Makinson, D. C. (1965). The paradox of the preface. *Analysis,* 25(6), 205–207.

Manne, K. (2014). Internalism about reasons: sad but true? *Philosophical Studies,* 167(1), 89–117.

Mantel, S. (2018). *Determined by Reasons: A Competence Account of Acting for a Normative Reason.* Routledge.

Marcus, E. (2012). *Rational Causation.* Harvard University Press.

Markovits, J. (2010). Acting for the right reasons. *The Philosophical Review,* 119(2), 201–242.

Markovits, J. (2012). Saints, heroes, sages, and villains. *Philosophical Studies,* 158(2), 289–311.

Markovits, J. (2014). *Moral Reason.* Oxford University Press.

Martin, M. (2002). The transparency of experience. *Mind and Language,* 17, 376–425.

McDowell, J. (1994). *Mind and World.* Harvard University Press.

McHugh, C. & Way, J. (2016). What is good reasoning? *Philosophy and Phenomenological Research,* 92(3).

McHugh, C. & Way, J. (FC). Fittingness first. *Ethics.*

McKeever, S. & Ridge, M. (2012). Elusive reasons. In R. Shafer-Landau (Ed.), *Oxford Studies in Metaethics,* vol. 7. Oxford University Press.

McNaughton, D. & Rawling, P. (2011). The making/evidential reason distinction. *Analysis,* 71(1), 100–102.

Mele, A. (2007). Reasonology and false beliefs. *Philosophical Papers,* 36(1), 91–118.

Millar, A. (1991). *Reasons and Experience.* Oxford University Press.

Millar, A. (2004). *Understanding People.* Oxford University Press.

Miller, C. (2008). Motivation in agents. *Noûs,* 42(2), 222–266.

Milligan, D. (1974). Reasons as explanations. *Mind,* 88(330), 180–193.

Miracchi, L. (FC). Competent perspectives and the new evil demon. In F. Dorsch & J. Dutant (Eds.), *The New Evil Demon: New Essays on Knowledge, Justification, and Rationality.* Oxford University Press.

Miracchi, L. (MS). Achievements and exercises: a theory of competence. Manuscript, University of Pennsylvania.

Moore, G. E. (1912). *Ethics.* Oxford University Press.

Neta, R. (2008). What evidence do you have? *British Journal for the Philosophy of Science,* 59(1), 89–119.

Neta, R. & Pritchard, D. (2007). McDowell and the new evil genius. *Philosophy and Phenomenological Research,* 74(2), 381–396.

Newton, I. (1953). *Newton's Philosophy of Nature: Selections From His Writings.* Dover Publications.

Paakkunainen, H. (2014). Vindicating practical norms: metasemantic strategies. In R. Shafer-Landau (Ed.), *Oxford Studies in Metaethics,* vol. 9. Oxford University Press.

Pace, M. (2010). Foundationally justified beliefs and the problem of the speckled hen. *Pacific Philosophical Quarterly,* 91, 401–441.

Parfit, D. (1997). Reasons and Motivation. *Aristotelian Society Supplementary Volume,* 71(1), 99–130.

Parfit, D. (2011). *On What Matters*. Oxford University Press.

Paul, L. (2000). Aspect causation. *The Journal of Philosophy*, 97(4), 235–256.

Pavese, C. (2015). Practical senses. *Philosophers' Imprint*, 15(29).

Peacocke, C. (1993). How are a priori truths possible? *European Journal of Philosophy*, 1(2), 175–199.

Plunkett, D. (2015). Which concepts should we use? Metalinguistic negotiations and the methodology of philosophy. *Inquiry*, 58(7–8), 828–874.

Plunkett, D. & Sundell, T. (2013). Disagreement and the semantics of normative and evaluative terms. *Philosophers' Imprint*, 13(23).

Pollock, J. (1974). *Knowledge and Justification*. Princeton University Press.

Pollock, J. & Cruz, J. (1999). *Contemporary Theories of Knowledge*. Rowman & Littlefield.

Pritchard, D. (2012). *Epistemological Disjunctivism*. Oxford University Press.

Pryor, J. (2000). The skeptic and the dogmatist. *Noûs*, 34(4), 517–549.

Pryor, J. (FC). The merits of incoherence. *Analytic Philosophy*.

Rabinowicz, W. & Rønnow-Rasmussen, T. (2004). The strike of the demon: on fitting proattitudes and value. *Ethics*, 114(3), 391–423.

Railton, P. (1984). Alienation, consequentialism, and the demands of morality. *Philosophy & Public Affairs*, 13(2).

Raz, J. (2005a). Instrumental rationality: a reprise. *Journal of Ethics & Social Philosophy*, 1.

Raz, J. (2005b). The Myth of Instrumental Rationality. *Journal of Ethics & Social Philosophy*, 1.

Regan, D. (1980). *Utilitarianism and Cooperation*. Oxford University Press.

Rosen, G. (2001). Nominalism, naturalism, epistemic relativism. *Noûs*, 35, 69–91.

Rosen, G. (2010). Metaphysical dependence: grounding and reduction. In B. Hale & A. Hoffmann (Eds.), *Modality: Metaphysics, Logic, and Epistemology*. Oxford University Press.

Rosen, G. (2015). Real definition. *Analytic Philosophy*, 56(3), 189–209.

Ross, A. (1944). Imperatives and logic. *Philosophy of Science*, 11(1), 30–46.

Ross, J. (2006). Acceptance and practical reason. PhD thesis, Rutgers University.

Ross, J. (2012). Rationality, normativity, and commitment. In R. Shafer-Landau (Ed.), *Oxford Studies in Metaethics*, vol. 7. Oxford University Press.

Ross, J. & Schroeder, M. (2013). Reversibility or disagreement. *Mind*, 122(485), 43–84.

Scanlon, T. (1998). *What We Owe to Each Other*. Harvard University Press.

Scanlon, T. (2001). Thomson on self-defense. In A. Byrne, R. Stalnaker, & R. Wedgwood (Eds.), *Fact and Value: Essays on Ethics and Metaphysics for Judith Jarvis Thomson*. MIT Press.

Scanlon, T. (2004). Reasons: a puzzling duality? In R. J. Wallace, P. Pettit, S. Scheffler, & M. Smith (Eds.), *Reason and Value: Themes from the Moral Philosophy of Joseph Raz*. Oxford University Press.

Scanlon, T. (2007). Structural irrationality. In G. Brennan, R. Goodin, F. Jackson, & M. Smith (Eds.), *Common Minds: Themes from the Philosophy of Phillip Pettit*. Oxford University Press.

Scanlon, T. (2008). *Moral Dimensions: Permissibility, Meaning, Blame*. Harvard University Press.

Schechter, J. & Enoch, D. (2006). Meaning and justification: the case of modus ponens. *Noûs*, 40(4), 687–715.

Schellenberg, S. (2013). Experience and evidence. *Mind*, 122(487), 699–747.

Schoenfield, M. (FC). An accuracy based approach to higher order evidence. *Philosophy and Phenomenological Research*.

Schossler, M. (2007). Basic deviance reconsidered. *Analysis*, 67(295), 186–194.

Schossler, M. (2012). Taking something as a reason for action. *Philosophical Perspectives*, 41(2), 267–304.

Schroeder, M. (2004). The scope of instrumental reason. *Philosophical Perspectives*, 18, 337–364.

Schroeder, M. (2005a). The hypothetical imperative? *Australasian Journal of Philosophy*, 83(3), 357–372.

Schroeder, M. (2005b). Instrumental mythology. *Journal of Ethics & Social Philosophy*, 1.

Schroeder, M. (2007). *Slaves of the Passions*. Oxford University Press.

Schroeder, M. (2008). Having reasons. *Philosophical Studies*, 139(1), 57–71.

Schroeder, M. (2009a). Buck passers' negative thesis. *Philosophical Explorations*, 12(3), 341–347.

Schroeder, M. (2009b). Means-end coherence, stringency, and subjective reasons. *Philosophical Studies*, 143(2), 223–248.

Schroeder, M. (2010). Value and the right kind of reason. In R. Shafer-Landau (Ed.), *Oxford Studies in Metaethics*, vol. 5. Oxford University Press.

Schroeder, M. (2011a). Holism, weight, and undercutting. *Noûs*, 454(2), 328–344.

Schroeder, M. (2011b). What does it take to 'have' a reason? In A. Reisner & A. Steglich-Petersen (Eds.), *Reasons for Belief*. Cambridge University Press.

Schroeder, M. (2012). Stakes, withholding, and pragmatic encroachment on knowledge. *Philosophical Studies*, 160(2), 165–185.

Schroeder, M. (2015a). Hypothetical imperatives: scope and jurisdiction. In R. Johnson & M. Timmons (Eds.), *Reason, Value, and Respect*. Oxford University Press.

Schroeder, M. (2015b). Is knowledge normative? *Philosophical Issues*, 25(1), 379–395.

Schroeder, M. (2015c). Knowledge is belief for sufficient (objective and subjective) reason. In T. S. Gendler & J. Hawthorne (Eds.), *Oxford Studies in Epistemology*, vol. 5. Oxford University Press.

Schroeder, M. (2015d). What makes reasons sufficient? *American Philosophical Quarterly*, 52(2).

Schwan, B. (FC). What ability can do. *Philosophical Studies*.

Sepielli, A. (2018). Subjective and objective reasons. In D. Star (Ed.), *Oxford Handbook of Reasons and Normativity*. Oxford University Press.

Setiya, K. (2003). Explaining action. *The Philosophical Review*, 112(3), 339–393.

Setiya, K. (2007a). Cognitivism about instrumental reason. *Ethics*, 117(4), 649–673.

Setiya, K. (2007b). *Reasons Without Rationalism*. Princeton University Press.

Silins, N. (2005). Deception and evidence. *Philosophical Perspectives*, 19(1), 375–404.

Smith, M. (1994). *The Moral Problem*. Blackwell Publishing.

Smith, M. (2008). Consequentialism and the nearest-dearest objection. In I. Ravenscroft (Ed.), *Minds, Ethics, and Conditionals: Themes from the Philosophy of Frank Jackson*. Clarendon Press.

Smith, M. N. (2016). One dogma of philosophy of action. *Philosophical Studies* 173(8), 2249–2266.

Smithies, D. (2006). Rationality and the subject's point of view. PhD thesis, NYU.

Snedegar, J. (FC). Reasons for and reasons against. *Philosophical Studies*.

Sosa, E. (2003). Privileged access. In Q. Smith & A. Jokic (Eds.), *Consciousness: New Philosophical Perspectives*. Oxford University Press.

Sosa, E. (2015). *Judgment and Agency*. Oxford University Press.

Soteriou, M. (2014). The disjunctive theory of perception. In E. Zalta (Ed.), *Stanford Encyclopedia of Philosophy* (Fall 2009 edition).

Southwood, N. (2008). Vindicating the normativity of rationality. *Ethics*, 118(1), 9–30.

Spencer, J. (2017). Able to do the impossible. *Mind*, 126(502), 466–497.

Stanley, J. (2011). *Know How*. Oxford University Press.

Stanley, J. & Williamson, T. (2001). Knowing how. *The Journal of Philosophy*, 98(8), 411–444.

Sutton, J. (2007). *Without Justification*. MIT Press.

Swain, M. (1981). *Reasons and Knowledge*. Cornell University Press.

Swain, M. (1988). Alston's internalistic externalism. *Philosophical Perspectives*, 2, 461–473.

Sylvan, K. (2014). *On the normativity of epistemic rationality*. PhD thesis, Rutgers University.

Sylvan, K. (2015). What apparent reasons appear to be. *Philosophical Studies*, 172(3), 587–606.

Sylvan, K. (2016). Epistemic reasons i: normativity. *Philosophy Compass*, 11(7), 364–376.

Sylvan, K. (FC). Knowledge as a non-normative relation. *Philosophy and Phenomenological Research*.

Sylvan, K. (MSa). The achievements of reason. Manuscript, University of Southampton.

Sylvan, K. (MSb). On divorcing the rational and justified in epistemology. Manuscript, University of Southampton.

Thomson, J. J. (1986). Imposing risks. In W. Parent (Ed.), *Rights, Restitution, and Risk: Essays in Moral Theory*. Harvard University Press.

Thomson, J. J. (1990). *The Realm of Rights*. Harvard University Press.

Thomson, J. J. (2008). *Normativity*. Open Court Press.

Titelbaum, M. (2015). Rationality's fixed point (or: In defence of right reason). *Oxford Studies in Epistemology*, 5, 253–294.

Turri, J. (2010). On the relationship between propositional and doxastic justification. *Philosophy and Phenomenological Research*, 80(2), 312–326.

Turri, J. (2011). Believing for a reason. *Erkenntnis*, 74(3), 383–397.

Unger, P. (1975). *Ignorance*. Oxford University Press.

Valaris, M. (2014). Reasoning and regress. *Mind*, 123(489), 101–127.

Valaris, M. (2016). Supposition and blindness. *Mind*, 125(499), 895–901.

Väyrynen, P. (2006). Moral generalism: enjoy in moderation. *Ethics*, 116, 707–741.

Velleman, D. (2000). *The Possibility of Practical Reason*. Oxford University Press.

Vogelstein, E. (2012). Subjective reasons. *Ethical Theory and Moral Practice*, 15, 2239–2257.

Warfield, T. (2005). Knowledge from falsehood. *Philosophical Perspectives*, 19(1), 405–416.

Way, J. (2009). Two accounts of the normativity of rationality. *Journal of Ethics & Social Philosophy*.

Way, J. (2010a). Defending the wide-scope account of instrumental reason. *Philosophical Studies*, 147(2), 213–233.

Way, J. (2010b). The normativity of rationality. *Philosophy Compass*, 5(12), 1057–1068.

Way, J. (2011). The symmetry of rational requirements. *Philosophical Studies*, 155(2).

Way, J. (2012). Explaining the instrumental principle. *Australasian Journal of Philosophy*, 90(3), 487–506.

Way, J. (2013). Intentions, akrasia, and mere permissibility. *Organon F*, 20, 588–611.

Way, J. (2017). Creditworthiness and matching principles. In M. Timmons (Ed.), *Oxford Studies in Normative Ethics*, vol. 7. Oxford University Press.

Way, J. & Whiting, D. (2016). If you justifiably believe you ought to ϕ, you ought to ϕ. *Philosophical Studies*, 173(7), 1873–1895.

Way, J. & Whiting, D. (2017). Perspectivism and the argument from guidance. *Ethical Theory and Moral Practice*, 20(2), 361–374.

Weatherson, B. (2008). Deontology and Descartes' demon. *The Journal of Philosophy*, 105(9), 540–569.

Weatherson, B. (2012). Knowledge, bets, and interests. In J. Brown & M. Gerken (Eds.), *Knowledge Ascriptions*. Oxford University Press.

Wedgwood, R. (2001). Conceptual role semantics for moral terms. *Philosophical Review*, 110(1), 1–30.

Wedgwood, R. (2002). Internalism Explained. *Philosophy and Phenomenological Research*, 65(2), 349–369.

Wedgwood, R. (2006a). The meaning of 'ought.' In R. Shafer-Landau (Ed.), *Oxford Studies in Metaethics*, vol. 1. Clarendon Press.

Wedgwood, R. (2006b). The normative force of reasoning. *Noûs*, 40(4), 660–686.

Wedgwood, R. (2007). *The Nature of Normativity*. Oxford University Press.

Wedgwood, R. (2012). Justified inference. *Synthese*, 189(2), 1–23.

Wedgwood, R. (2013). The right thing to believe. In T. Chan (Ed.), *The Aim of Belief*. Oxford University Press.

Wedgwood, R. (2017). *The Value of Rationality*. Oxford University Press.

White, R. (2005). Epistemic permissiveness. *Philosophical Perspectives*, 19(1), 445–459.

Whiting, D. (2014). Keep things in perspective: reasons, rationality, and the a priori. *Journal of Ethics and Social Philosophy*, 8, 1–22.

Williams, B. (1965). Ethical consistency. *Aristotelian Society Supplementary Volume*, 39(1), 103–138.

Williams, B. (1981). Internal and external reasons. In *Moral Luck*. Oxford University Press.

Williamson, T. (2000). *Knowledge and its Limits*. Oxford University Press.

Williamson, T. (2003). Blind reasoning. *Aristotelian Society Supplementary Volume*, 77(1), 249–293.

Williamson, T. (2009). Replies to critics. In P. Greenough & D. Pritchard (Eds.), *Williamson on Knowledge*. Oxford University Press.

Williamson, T. (FC). Justification, excuses, and sceptical scenarios. In F. Dorsch & J. Dutant (Eds.), *The New Evil Demon: New Essays on Knowledge, Justification, and Rationality*. Oxford University Press.

Worsnip, A. (2015a). Narrow-scoping for wide-scopers. *Synthese*, 192(8), 2617–2646.

Worsnip, A. (2015b). *Rationality's demands on belief*. PhD thesis, Yale University.

Worsnip, A. (2016). Moral reasons, epistemic reasons, and rationality. *Philosophical Quarterly*, 66(263), 341–361.

Worsnip, A. (2018). The conflict of evidence and coherence. *Philosophy and Phenomenological Research*, 96(1), 3–44.

Zimmerman, M. J. (2008). *Living with Uncertainty: The Moral Significance of Ignorance*. Cambridge University Press.

Zimmerman, M. J. (2014). *Ignorance and Moral Obligation*. Oxford University Press.

Index of Cases

Index of Principles & Requirements

General Index